TURNCOAT

TURNCOAT

BENEDICT ARNOLD AND THE
CRISIS OF AMERICAN LIBERTY

STEPHEN BRUMWELL

YALE UNIVERSITY PRESS
NEW HAVEN AND LONDON

Published with assistance from the Annie Burr Lewis Fund.

For information about this and other Yale University Press publications, please contact:
U.S. Office: sales.press@yale.edu   yalebooks.com
Europe Office: sales@yaleup.co.uk   yalebooks.co.uk

Set in Minion Pro by IDSUK (DataConnection) Ltd
Printed in the United States of America.

Library of Congress Control Number: 2018936161

ISBN 978-0-300-21099-6

A catalogue record for this book is available from the British Library.

10 9 8 7 6 5 4 3 2 1

In memory of Bill Speck (1938–2017)

CONTENTS

ILLUSTRATIONS

1. "Colonel Arnold, Who commanded the Provincial troops sent against Quebec, through the wilderness of Canada, and was wounded in storming that city, under General Montgomery," mezzotint, 1776. Yale University Art Gallery.
2. "General Arnold, Drawn from the life at Philadelphia by Du Simitier [*sic*]," engraving after Pierre Eugène Du Simitière, 1778–79. William L. Clements Library, University of Michigan.
3. "The Death of General Montgomery at Quebec," engraving by Christian Wilhelm Ketterlinus, 1808 (after John Trumbull). Yale University Art Gallery.
4. "The attack and defeat of the American fleet under Benedict Arnold . . . upon Lake Champlain, the 11th of October 1776," detail of an engraved map, 1776. William L. Clements Library, University of Michigan.
5. "A Skirmish in America between the King's Troops and General Arnold," engraving, 1780. Keeler Tavern Museum Preservation Society.
6. Margaret "Peggy" Shippen, watercolor by John André, *c.* 1778. Shippen Family Collection of Prints and Portraits (3127), Historical Society of Pennsylvania.
7. West Point in August 1782, detail from "Encampment of the Revolutionary Army on the Hudson River" by Major Pierre Charles L'Enfant, 1782. Library of Congress (LC-USZC4-270).

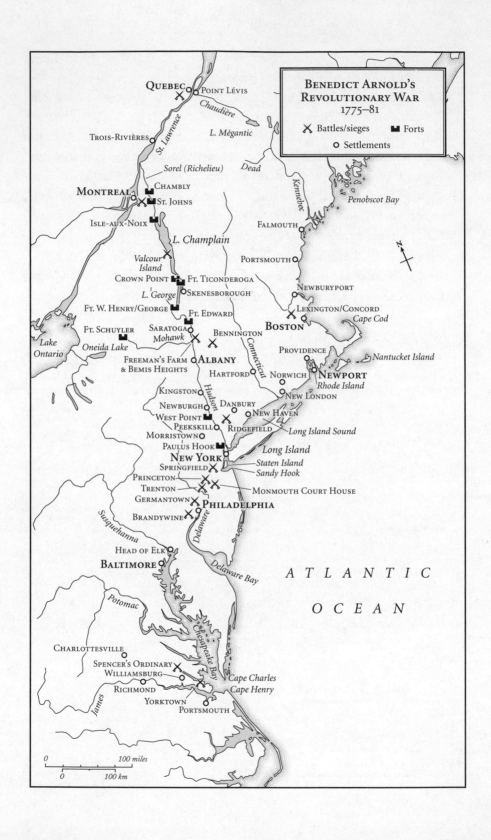

BENEDICT ARNOLD'S
REVOLUTIONARY WAR
1775–81

✗ Battles/sieges   ◼ Forts

○ Settlements

QUEBEC   ○ POINT LÉVIS
Chaudière

TROIS-RIVIÈRES   *L. Mégantic*

St. Lawrence   *Dead*

Sorel (Richelieu)   *Kennebec*

CHAMBLY   *Penobscot Bay*

MONTREAL   ○ ST. JOHNS

ISLE-AUX-NOIX   FALMOUTH

L. Champlain   PORTSMOUTH

Valcour Island   NEWBURYPORT

CROWN POINT   FT. TICONDEROGA
L. George   SKENESBOROUGH   LEXINGTON/CONCORD
Cape Cod

FT. W. HENRY/GEORGE   FT. EDWARD   BOSTON

FT. SCHUYLER   SARATOGA   PROVIDENCE   *Nantucket Island*
Mohawk   BENNINGTON

Lake Ontario   *Oneida Lake*   HARTFORD   NORWICH   NEWPORT
FREEMAN'S FARM
& BEMIS HEIGHTS   ALBANY   *Rhode Island*

KINGSTON   *Hudson*   NEW LONDON

NEWBURGH   DANBURY
WEST POINT   NEW HAVEN
PEEKSKILL   RIDGEFIELD   *Long Island Sound*
MORRISTOWN
PAULUS HOOK   *Long Island*

NEW YORK
SPRINGFIELD   *Staten Island*
PRINCETON   *Sandy Hook*
TRENTON   MONMOUTH COURT HOUSE
GERMANTOWN   PHILADELPHIA
BRANDYWINE   *Delaware*

HEAD OF ELK   A T L A N T I C

BALTIMORE   *Delaware Bay*

Potomac   O C E A N

CHARLOTTESVILLE   *Chesapeake Bay*
SPENCER'S ORDINARY
WILLIAMSBURG   *Cape Charles*
RICHMOND   *Cape Henry*
James
YORKTOWN
PORTSMOUTH

0 ————— 100 miles

0 ————— 100 km

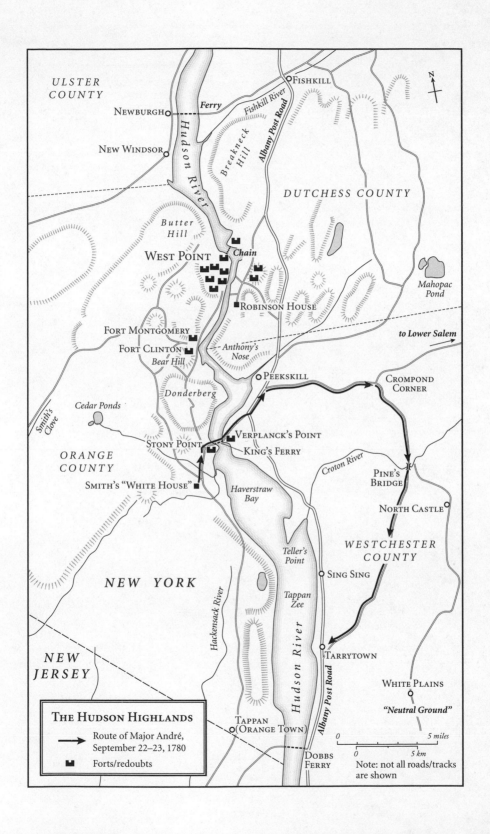

ULSTER
COUNTY

NEWBURGH   *Ferry*

NEW WINDSOR

Hudson River

Breakneck Hill

Fishkill River

FISHKILL

Albany Post Road

DUTCHESS COUNTY

Butter Hill

WEST POINT   *Chain*

Mahopac Pond

ROBINSON HOUSE

FORT MONTGOMERY

FORT CLINTON
Bear Hill   — *Anthony's Nose*

to Lower Salem

Donderberg

PEEKSKILL

CROMPOND CORNER

Cedar Ponds

Smith's Clove

ORANGE
COUNTY

STONY POINT   VERPLANCK'S POINT
KING'S FERRY

Croton River

PINE'S BRIDGE

NORTH CASTLE

SMITH'S "WHITE HOUSE"

Haverstraw Bay

WESTCHESTER
COUNTY

Teller's Point

NEW YORK

SING SING

Hackensack River

Tappan Zee

Hudson River

TARRYTOWN

WHITE PLAINS

NEW
JERSEY

"Neutral Ground"

THE HUDSON HIGHLANDS

→ Route of Major André,
    September 22–23, 1780

▪ Forts/redoubts

TAPPAN
(ORANGE TOWN)

0   5 miles

0   5 km

DOBBS
FERRY

Albany Post Road

Note: not all roads/tracks
are shown

INTRODUCTION

By the summer of 1780 the newly built fortress of West Point was already styled "the American Gibraltar," and with good reason. Like the famed "Rock," its formidable defenses rested on precipitous, craggy terrain and had acquired immense strategic and symbolic significance. Gibraltar safeguarded British sea power and trade throughout the Mediterranean Sea and far beyond, which was why its garrison had recently rebuffed one Spanish assault, and was even now enduring the dangers and privations of a blockade that would be immortalized as the "Great Siege." To American Patriots entering the sixth year of their war for independence from Britain, West Point was no less valuable, and they were equally determined to hold it at all costs.

West Point was so important because its cannon controlled the navigation of the Hudson River, the great waterway that bisected the former colonies now in rebellion against the mother country. If the fortress was lost, the undefended Hudson would open a virtually continuous communication between Britain's main bases in Canada and New York city, so splitting the United States asunder along a north–south axis, and likewise severing the lateral supply line across the river that was vital for the survival of the Patriots' Continental Army. In the estimation of one of America's ablest strategists, Major-General Nathanael Greene, the Hudson, or "North" River, was "the first object upon the Continent" and West Point its "only security."[1]

Since the outbreak of war with Britain in 1775, it had been obvious that the point's dominating bluffs, overlooking a snaking double bend in the Hudson, offered a fine defensive position—the best on the river's 315-mile course. Yet it was only in early 1778, after forts built farther downstream had failed utterly to stop the enemy, that the laborious task of construction on the remote and rocky site began in earnest. Given the high stakes, Congress and its commander-in-chief, General George Washington, now spared no effort to render West Point impregnable.

The evolving defenses were largely designed by the Polish engineer officer Colonel Thaddeus Kosciuszko, a volunteer in the cause of American independence who was recommended by New York's state governor George Clinton as "an ingenious young man . . . disposed to do everything he can in the most agreeable manner." Kosciuszko justified Governor Clinton's confidence. Within two years he had created a sprawling but sophisticated defensive system that was very different from the compact, symmetrical fortresses typical of Europe. Now, both banks of the Hudson were defended by gun batteries which swept the river, backed by an interlocking complex of strongpoints, including substantial forts enclosing barracks, and smaller, self-contained redoubts.[2]

Visitors were unlikely to forget their first sight of the fortress. Approaching on horseback in 1780, one of America's new French allies, Major-General François-Jean, marquis de Chastellux, was awed by its scale and dramatic setting. Craning his neck, the marquis saw "on every side lofty summits, all bristling with redoubts and batteries." Chastellux was obliged to dismount and methodically scan the scene through his telescope, "the only method of acquiring a knowledge of the whole of the fortifications with which this important post is surrounded." While the eastern bank was dominated by two heights, each crowned by a squat, square redoubt, the main defenses clustered on the western side of the Hudson: there, "from the fort of West Point proper which is on the edge of the river, to the very top of the mountain at the foot of which it stands, are six different forts, all in the form of an amphitheater, and protecting each other."[3]

Providing the Continental Army with both a last-ditch rallying point and a secure supply depot, West Point's stone and timber defenses exploited the rugged terrain of the Hudson Highlands. These heavily weathered, yet still daunting, remnants of ancient crystalline mountains rise like a great wall some forty miles above Manhattan, extending northwards in a broad mass twenty-five miles deep. They include peaks looming up to 1,200 feet above the waters of the Hudson. When he first saw the Highlands in 1778, military surgeon James Thacher struggled for words to do justice to their "stupendous magnitude." That task was better suited to "the pen of the poet and the pencil of the painter," he believed—an observation that anticipated by half a century the artists of what became known as the "Hudson River School," who portrayed the region's landscape in a picturesque and romantic light, striving to capture for posterity an idyllic vision of nature in an age of increasing industrialization.

For all their scenic grandeur, during the Revolutionary War the Hudson Highlands posed a major barrier to the movement of armies. In the opinion of Baron Ludwig von Closen, a young Bavarian-born officer in the French army, this "chain of mountains" constituted a zone through which it was "impossible for a man, and even less for troops, to pass"; as late as the 1920s, its valleys still sheltered the isolated cabins of reclusive mountain folk who were only rarely glimpsed by strangers. But as Dr. Thacher emphasized, even this inaccessible terrain of "rocky cliffs and venerable forests" was not impenetrable: the broad Hudson River cut clean through the whole "confused mass" like "a vast canal."[4]

If the Hudson was a canal, then West Point functioned like a lock-gate: a key component in its defensive system was "the great chain" that spanned the river, physically blocking the passage to hostile shipping. Fixed to large blocks on either bank, and covered by gun batteries on both sides, the massive wrought-iron chain was supported on logs and fronted by a floating wooden barrier or "boom." Major-General William Heath, who served two stints as West Point's commander between 1779 and 1781, considered the chain a marvel of engineering. Its effectiveness was enhanced by the peculiar configuration of the Hudson at West Point: the sharp bend there— described by von Closen as "a very considerable elbow, almost turning back on itself"—meant that even a ship sailing upriver with a strong following wind would lose momentum in changing course to round the point. By the time a vessel recovered headway, General Heath noted with approval, she would be up against the chain itself, and all the while "under a heavy shower of shot and shells."[5]

Contemplating West Point's extensive fortifications in September 1780, James Thacher expressed a popular opinion when he concluded that provided they were "properly guarded," they might "bid defiance to an army of twenty thousand men." There was the rub: for all its multiple defenses—the forts, redoubts, batteries, chain, and boom—West Point was worthless without a resolute garrison prepared to fight to the death against all comers.[6]

Ever since West Point's first establishment, George Washington had feared that the crown forces massed in and around New York city might make a sudden lunge up the Hudson against the fortress. It was imperative that command of the Hudson Highlands, of which West Point and its garrison formed the hub, should be entrusted to a worthy officer, a soldier of proven ability who was utterly dependable. In the late summer of 1780, Washington could at least rest easy in the knowledge that responsibility for what Chastellux characterized as the "*Palladium* of American liberty" lay in the safest possible hands. Since Thursday, August 3, as that day's general orders announced, West Point had been entrusted to one of Washington's most celebrated and valued subordinates, Major-General Benedict Arnold.[7]

* * *

In truth, George Washington had never intended that Benedict Arnold should command the Hudson Highlands. This was not because of any misgivings about Arnold's ability to shoulder that heavy burden. On the contrary, Washington was concerned that such a static posting would deny him the services of an outstanding combat officer during what promised to be an active and potentially decisive campaign.

Within months of accepting command of the Continental Army in June 1775, Washington had realized that Arnold was that prized rarity in an army of amateurs: a born soldier and charismatic leader of men. While too many of the senior officers appointed by Congress were overly old and plodding for Washington's taste, the thirty-four-year-old Arnold was a soldier after his own heart, a tenacious fighter who refused to be discouraged by even the most unfavorable circumstances. The restrained Virginian was not a man to bestow praise lightly, but he was unstinting in his approval of the fiery, outspoken Yankee. In December 1775, after Arnold had led a punishing march through the Maine wilderness to Quebec, Washington paraphrased lines from his favorite play, Joseph Addison's *Cato*, to express his undisguised admiration for Arnold's "enterprising and persevering spirit." He wrote: "It is not in the power of any man to command success, but you have done more—you have deserved it." That same day, Washington shared his high opinion of Arnold with Major-General Philip Schuyler, choosing words that, in retrospect, might have caused him to ponder the vagaries of the human psyche. "The merit of this gentleman is certainly great and I heartily wish that Fortune may distinguish him as one of her favorites," he wrote.[8]

It seemed that Fortune did indeed favor the stocky, driven Arnold. On two clear-cut occasions—one a defeat, the other a victory—his determined leadership had made a vital contribution to the struggle for American liberty. In October 1776, as commodore of a ramshackle naval squadron on Lake Champlain, Arnold had fought so stoutly against overwhelming odds that, although beaten, he delayed the projected British invasion of the United States from Canada for a crucial year. When that threat duly materialized in the following summer, and Lieutenant-General John Burgoyne's army advanced south toward Albany, Arnold's role was once again decisive. He was prominent in the intensive fighting that stopped "Gentleman Johnny" in his tracks, and led soon after to his army's capitulation at Saratoga. That stunning outcome was instrumental in convincing the hesitant French to enter into open alliance with the American Patriots, so escalating the Revolutionary War from colonial rebellion to global conflict. Stretching Britain's resources to the limit, the Franco-American pact vastly enhanced the prospects for American independence. With the exception of Washington himself, it could be argued that no individual soldier had made a greater contribution to the "glorious cause" than Major-General Benedict Arnold.

Washington expressed his sincere esteem for Arnold's leadership at Saratoga in a highly personal gesture. In April 1778, while encamped at Valley Forge, near British-occupied Philadelphia, Washington had received a gift from a French admirer, Pierre Penet, consisting of three sets of epaulettes and sword knots. Washington kept one set for himself, but the other two were "to be disposed of to any friends" he should choose. He wrote to Arnold on May 7, 1778: "I take the liberty of presenting them to you and General Lincoln, as a testimony of my sincere regard and approbation of your conduct." As he explained in his letter of thanks to Monsieur Penet, Washington had selected Arnold, and his fellow major-general Benjamin Lincoln, in recognition of the fact that both had been wounded "while rendering very distinguished services, in the last actions, between our Northern army and General Burgoyne's troops."[9]

Soon after, Benedict Arnold's exploits were acknowledged in a very different, but equally telling, fashion. From mid-May 1778, the largest defensive structure at West Point became known as "Fort Arnold." This was a unique distinction. Like other major works at West Point, that fort had originally been named for the officer whose men had toiled to build it. Just as Fort Putnam commemorated Colonel Rufus Putnam, and the Wyllis Redoubt Colonel Samuel Wyllis, so the main strongpoint directly overlooking the Hudson, which Chastellux identified as "West Point proper," was initially named "Fort Clinton," after Brigadier-General James Clinton. Although Clinton was the brother of Governor George Clinton, and had acquitted himself respectably enough against the British, his war record was lackluster in comparison with Arnold's. Indeed, Clinton was best known for failing to hold another fort bearing his name, built six miles downstream from West Point, opposite the mountain known as Anthony's Nose. That Fort Clinton, and its close neighbor, Fort Montgomery, had fallen in October 1777, when a British force under Lieutenant-General Sir Henry Clinton (who was reputedly a distant cousin of the rebel Clinton brothers) pushed upriver from New York in an effort to relieve pressure on Burgoyne's beleaguered army. While spectacularly successful, Sir Henry's strike came too late to influence the outcome of the campaign: on October 7, the day after Clinton's men stormed the twin forts, Burgoyne suffered a bloody rebuff at the battle of Bemis Heights, a decisive reverse that he attributed chiefly to the aggressive tactics of Benedict Arnold.[10]

When Arnold spent several days at West Point in the following May, as guest of the departing commander of the Hudson Highlands, Major-General Alexander McDougall, his heroism at Saratoga was still fresh in the minds of his countrymen. Whatever James Clinton's feelings on the matter, it was scarcely surprising that the most prominent fortification at West Point should be renamed to honor the distinguished visitor, whom newspapers on both sides of the Atlantic had taken to calling "the brave General Arnold."

By the summer of 1780, Washington needed such bold and dedicated fighters more than ever. Five years of warfare had long since taken their toll on the revolutionary movement. The popular fervor, or *rage militaire*, which had sustained the struggle in its opening months, as swarms of rebel militiamen obliged the chastened redcoats to seek refuge behind the defenses of Boston, had long since dissipated. For Washington and his dwindling core of Continental Army veterans, the war-weariness and indifference of their civilian countrymen posed no less a threat than the muskets and bayonets of the British army and its German auxiliaries. It had been hoped that the heavy shock sustained by the loss of Charleston, South Carolina, which surrendered to Sir Henry Clinton on May 12, might finally jolt the jaded Americans to their senses before it was too late, and the patriot war effort succumbed to apathy. But even that disaster had done nothing to revive the old revolutionary spirit.[11]

Lack of enthusiasm for the fight was matched by a chronic dearth of resources to wage it. The rebellion had originated as a rejection of imperial taxation. It was therefore unsurprising, albeit ironic, that Congress lacked the powers to compel the states to raise the revenue required to prosecute the war effectively. Rampant inflation meant that Continental dollars were now virtually worthless: unpaid for months, Washington's rank and file were hungry, grumbling, and mutinous; and each day he reluctantly approved the resignations of experienced officers who, having served their turn while others enjoyed the comforts of civilian life, were impatient to return home and take care of their long-neglected families.

A ray of hope illuminated this gloomy scene in mid-July, with the arrival of a long-expected French fleet, under Commodore, the chevalier de Ternay, which landed an expeditionary force of 5,500 regular troops at Newport, Rhode Island. Their commander, General Jean Baptiste Donatien de Vimeur, comte de Rochambeau, had instructions to act under Washington's orders. In conjunction with this well-trained reinforcement, Washington hoped to launch an attack on the British garrison of New York. It was a blow that Washington had dreamed of landing ever since he had been hustled off Manhattan by Lieutenant-General William Howe back in the fall of 1776, when he was still finding his feet as a commander. Now, if his countrymen rose to the challenge, and the states raised their specified quotas of manpower and supplies, that dream might become reality.

With this tempting scenario unfolding in the summer of 1780, Washington had been puzzled by Arnold's uncharacteristically lukewarm response to the prospect of service in the field with the main army, and his marked preference for a sedentary role as commander of West Point. Six years later, as Washington remembered: "It then appeared somewhat strange to me that a man of Arnold's known activity and enterprise should be desirous of taking so inactive a part." Arnold's reaction to general orders of August 1, which announced his assignment to command the army's left wing, was even more perplexing. Like his friend Major-General Greene, who was to head the right wing, Arnold would exercise command over three entire divisions. It was a prestigious appointment that he might have been expected to jump at, both as undeniable proof of the recognition he had always craved and for the opportunities it could offer to burnish his credentials. But instead of thanking Washington for this conspicuous honor, Arnold remained silent and crestfallen.[12]

Despite Arnold's disappointing reaction, it was hard for Washington to begrudge him his wish. If any of the Continental Army's officers had earned a respite from the rigors of campaign life, it was Arnold. Indeed, his reason for seeking the West Point posting underlined the sacrifices that he had already made for his country. In earlier campaigns, Arnold's left leg had twice been shattered by gunshot. The first wound was sustained at Quebec in December 1775; he suffered the second and more grievous injury less than two years later, at Saratoga. In an era when the surgeon's first response to such grave damage was to reach for his bone saw, Arnold was lucky not to lose the limb. But the scarred leg shrank, obliging him to wear clumsy, built-up footwear to compensate for his lost inches. For the rest of his life, he limped badly and was often racked with pain.

After it was announced that Arnold was to command one wing of the army, he had told Washington's aide, Colonel Tench Tilghman, that his wounded leg "would not permit him to be long on horseback," as such a senior position inevitably required. Washington said nothing at the time, but looking back he recalled how Arnold's behavior had again struck him "as strange and unaccountable." However, when it soon after became clear that the opportunity to attack New York had passed, Washington "determined to comply with Arnold's desire, and accordingly gave him the command of the garrison at West Point." As General Greene later explained, "His Excellency" had agreed to Arnold's proposition both "to gratify an unfortunate officer who had become a cripple in the service of his country" and because he was persuaded "that he would defend the place to the last."[13]

But long before Major-General Benedict Arnold was granted his wish to command the Hudson Highlands, he had conspired to betray his country, comrades, and commander, and had bargained to sell "the Gibraltar of America" to the British.

* * *

On September 26, 1780, the Continental regiments encamped around the little village of Tappan on the west bank of the Hudson, some twenty-five miles below West Point, were paraded to hear their officers read the general orders of the day. For the assembled troops, the opening comments praising the discipline with which they had recently performed their maneuvers were gratifying enough, yet otherwise unremarkable. After months of short rations, and a night disrupted by alarms, many of them were too tired and hungry to care. But the announcement that followed gained the full attention of every man present. It began:

> Treason of the blackest dye was yesterday discovered. General Arnold who commanded at West Point, lost to every sentiment of honor, of private and public obligation, was about to deliver up that important post into the hands of the enemy. Such an event must have given the American cause a deadly wound if not a fatal stab. Happily the treason has been timely discovered to prevent the fatal misfortune. The Providential train of circumstances which led to it affords the most convincing proof that the liberties of America is [sic] the object of divine protection.[14]

Of all the many thousands of general orders proclaimed during the course of the Revolutionary War, these were perhaps the most memorable and widely disseminated. Issued in Washington's absence by his deputy, Major-General Greene, their wording was so concise and effective that they went far to shape the enduring public perception of Arnold's treason. Greene's orders resonated far beyond the ranks of the Continental Army when they were reprinted in newspapers, and in coming weeks their most striking phrases, or variations on them, seeped into many personal letters and diaries. So well did they describe the situation that when seeking to convey his own reaction to Arnold's treason, even such a prolific and thoughtful correspondent as Ensign Benjamin Gilbert of the 5th Massachusetts Regiment simply copied them down, word for word.[15]

Arnold's "hellish plot" failed, but only after it came so close to succeeding that Americans considered their deliverance to be nothing short of miraculous. The conspiracy was exposed at the last moment by pure chance, encouraging many Patriots to echo Greene's belief that a benevolent deity must surely be watching over them. Yet this fortunate outcome did nothing to diminish the widespread shock that, of all men, one of the Revolution's most celebrated and high-ranking soldiers could be capable of such bare-faced and calculating treachery.

In his diary entry for September 26, Colonel Israel Angell of the 2nd Rhode Island Regiment captured the prevailing mood of disbelief: "The most extraordinary affair happened yesterday that ever has taken place since the war [began]," he wrote. "General Benedict Arnold who commanded at West Point went to the enemy." That same day, Dr. Thacher was no less astounded, rating Arnold's treason as "one of the most extraordinary events in modern history."[16]

Arnold's defection unsettled the supporters of American independence more profoundly than anything they had yet experienced. As further details of the plot emerged, revealing the full extent of Arnold's duplicity, their relief and astonishment were subsumed by rage. For example, the newspaper of Arnold's Connecticut birthplace, the *Norwich Packet*, castigated the former local hero, whose "late infernal conduct" had swiftly transformed him into "the truly infamous Arnold." The *Packet*'s correspondent observed: "when we view his conduct from first to last, it represents to the life an American Judas, whose vicissitudes of fortune admit of such peculiar and striking events, as not a parallel perhaps is to be found in the annals of history." Indeed, it was widely assumed that, like Judas, Arnold had acted from that basest of all motives, greed. Writing to a fellow officer from the camp at Tappan on September 30, 1780, Lieutenant Cornelius Russell of the 5th Connecticut Regiment articulated the prevailing mixture of horror and disgust: "it even chills the blood in the circulating veins to think [that] one on whom our dependence was placed should be so lost to virtue, reason and honor and even conscience as to sacrifice the blood of thousands for the sake of gold."[17]

As the tremors from Arnold's treason continued to reverberate outwards from its epicenter in the Hudson Highlands, there were those who wondered whether the unprecedented wave of anger against him could be harnessed to inject fresh momentum into the moribund patriot war effort. Condemning "Arnold's corruption" as "indeed shocking to humanity," the eminent Virginian lawyer and judge Edmund Pendleton now hoped that this narrowly averted disaster would finally rouse the Revolution's supporters "from that apathy from which alone our enemies can hope for success."[18]

Above all else, Arnold's outraged countrymen craved vengeance: they would dearly have loved to see him dangling from the gallows. The Rhode

Islander Nathanael Greene had special cause to be embittered toward his erstwhile colleague. "My pride and feelings are greatly hurt at the infamy of this man's conduct," he confided to his wife, Catherine. "Arnold being an American and a New Englander, and of the rank of major-general are all mortifying circumstances." To another correspondent, Greene made it clear that there could be no mercy for Arnold, "the blackest of all mortals, and the meanest of all creatures." He wrote: "Should he ever fall into our hands he will be a sweet sacrifice."[19]

But thanks to strong nerves and his own generous slice of luck, when the conspiracy was exposed on September 25, Arnold had evaded capture by a slender margin and was soon safe with the British in New York city. There he lost no time in changing the color of his coat from revolutionary blue to royal scarlet, proving himself as keen to fight against the soldiers of Congress as he had once been to lead them into action. Arnold escaped retribution, yet the vilification he suffered in coming months and years was unprecedented in its intensity. Few Americans, before or since, have been execrated with such vehemence. Even after an interlude of nearly two and a half centuries, Benedict Arnold's betrayal of his trust ranks among the most notorious events in US history, and his name remains synonymous with "turncoat" and "traitor."

* * *

When the chevalier de Chastellux visited West Point in November 1780, the fort's central role in the drama that had recently unfolded heightened his excitement as he contemplated its impressive defenses. As the marquis went on his way, his head remained filled with thoughts of how "the fate of the thirteen states has depended in great measure on this important post," and how Arnold—"that extraordinary man, at once the honor and the opprobrium of his country"—had been poised to deliver it to the British.[20]

Six years later, Chastellux shared these observations, and many others, when he published the diary he had kept while traveling through the emerging United States between 1780 and 1782. The marquis wrote in his native tongue, but an English translation soon followed. As Chastellux was already a noted *philosophe* and man of letters, and a close friend of the famed Washington, his *Travels* attracted much attention on both sides of the Atlantic.

The book's eager readers included a distinguished British veteran of the Revolutionary War, Lieutenant-Colonel John Graves Simcoe. Of all the many thousands of soldiers who fought in vain to return the rebellious American subjects of King George III to their former allegiance, few had served more zealously than he. As a twenty-three-year-old lieutenant in the 35th Foot, Simcoe had sailed into Boston harbor on June 19, 1775, just two days after the hard-fought battle of Bunker Hill had made it clear that bringing the rebels to heel would be a long and bloody business. Before the year was out, young Simcoe had bought a captain's commission in the grenadier company of the 40th Foot. Composed of the tallest and most aggressive soldiers in their regiments, and distinguished by bristling fur caps, the army's grenadiers were combined into elite battalions of shock troops that saw much heavy fighting and suffered accordingly. On September 11, 1777, Captain Simcoe was wounded while leading his grenadiers as Sir William Howe trounced George Washington at Brandywine, near Philadelphia.

Just over a month later, Simcoe's impressive leadership record earned him the local rank of major, and command of a battle-hardened "provincial" unit of Loyalists, the Queen's Rangers. Dressed in green (instead of the red of the British regulars), the Rangers were recruited from men enlisted in America: natives or immigrants who had always been faithful to King George, and deserters from Congress's Continental Army who had seen the error of their ways. Raised to the provincial rank of lieutenant-colonel, Simcoe forged this motley band, which was expanded to include both infantry and cavalry, into one of the most efficient and respected formations in Britain's North American army.

In May 1780, Howe's successor as commander-in-chief, Sir Henry Clinton, lauded Simcoe in a dispatch to Lord George Germain, who, as American secretary, was responsible for orchestrating the war's strategy back in London. Clinton wrote that the "history of the corps" under Simcoe's command was of "a series of gallant, skillful, and successful enterprises against the enemy, *without a single reverse*."[21]

But in October 1781, Simcoe's unblemished record came to an end when he and his corps were snared at Gloucester, Virginia, across the James River from Yorktown, where a British army commanded by Lord Charles Cornwallis was obliged to capitulate to a besieging Franco-American force that included Major-General Chastellux. Sent home to England on parole, the exhausted Simcoe savored his first spell of leave in six years. After the

Yorktown debacle, many politicians in Whitehall had little stomach for continuing the fight, although it would be another two years before King George and his hardline ministers grudgingly accepted the inevitable, and conceded American independence.

As the war wound down, Simcoe convalesced in Exeter, the ancient Devonshire city where he had grown up and attended the grammar school, before studying at Oxford. There, he soon discovered that, despite the discouraging outcome at Yorktown, his sterling services across the Atlantic had not gone unnoticed by his countrymen. In January 1782, he was granted the singular honor of the freedom of the city, in recognition of "his very able and spirited conduct in America." That December, Simcoe's fortunes continued to rise when he married a young and exceptionally wealthy heiress, Elizabeth Posthuma Gwillim.[22]

Five years later, the Simcoes were comfortably settled at Wolfson Lodge, an elegant new mansion set amid the gently rolling countryside near the market town of Honiton. While the coveted Simcoe son and heir had not yet made his appearance, there was every prospect that he soon would; the lodge was already lively with the noise of three healthy young daughters. All in all, it was as agreeable a situation as any battle-scarred officer on the British army's half-pay list could hope for.

Even as John Graves Simcoe busied himself with the peacetime pursuits of improving his estate and raising a family, the "late American war" was never far from his thoughts. In early 1787, in his guise as "Lieutenant Colonel Commandant of the late Queen's Rangers," Simcoe was swift to respond to what he deemed to be a grave slur on his own honor and reputation, and on that of the brave and devoted men he had led into battle against the American rebels. As he perused Chastellux's *Travels*, Simcoe was incensed by a lop-sided account of a skirmish involving the Queen's Rangers on June 26, 1781, during the long Virginian campaign that ultimately ended in disaster at Yorktown.[23]

That engagement had been named after a tavern called Spencer's Ordinary, near where the roads to Williamsburg and Jamestown intersected. Simcoe's Queen's Rangers, backed by a detachment of Hessian sharpshooters, or Jäger, under the highly experienced Captain Johann Ewald, had been escorting a convoy of cattle when they encountered advance units pushing forward from the army of Washington's local commander, Major-General Marie-Joseph Gilbert du Motier, marquis de Lafayette. Fought in open woodland, the "smart action" that ensued was a confused, swirling affair of crashing gunfire, flashing bayonets, and clashing sabers, but Simcoe's increasingly outnumbered command held its own until Cornwallis's main force came up in support.[24]

Judging by the speed of his response, Simcoe must have read Chastellux's *Travels* hot off the press. In a riposte befitting an officer who had made his name in a partisan war of lightning raids, Simcoe penned an open letter that was printed in the January 1787 issue of a popular London journal, *The Gentleman's Magazine*. This took Chastellux to task for misrepresenting both the outcome of the action and the casualties sustained. Suddenly transported back from damp, peaceful Devon to sweltering wartime Virginia, Simcoe was able to counter Chastellux so quickly, and in such detail, because he had long been busy compiling an exhaustive *Journal of the Operations of the Queen's Rangers*. A limited edition of Simcoe's book was published privately later that year and distributed to a small circle of acquaintances, with a specially illustrated copy presented to King George III.[25]

While clearly a matter of enduring pride to the touchy Simcoe, for most readers of *The Gentleman's Magazine* the brisk little confrontation at Spencer's Ordinary was just another obscure scrimmage in the long-lost American war. Yet Simcoe, like many other British and loyalist veterans— and the king they had fought for—still found that humiliating defeat hard to accept. He was especially indignant at Chastellux, because Frenchmen like him and Lafayette had interfered in a British domestic dispute, drastically changing its scope and character. Owing to the chevalier and his slippery Gallic countrymen, a war that Simcoe and many other Britons still believed to be winnable well into 1781 was as good as lost before that year was over.

In fact, Simcoe's peppery letter was just the opening shot in a methodical barrage that he subsequently unleashed against the Frenchman's book. Writing anonymously, Simcoe soon after published a chunky pamphlet of *Remarks* that crossed swords with the marquis on a wide range of points, and which allowed him to articulate his simmering resentments at Britain's loss of her prized American colonies.[26]

A particular bone of contention was the dismissive stance adopted by Chastellux and his English translator (who added fuel to the fire by contributing his own rambling and highly opinionated footnotes) toward an event familiar to even the most casual follower of the Revolutionary War—Benedict Arnold's foiled attempt to betray West Point. Aside from its notoriety, this was an episode in which Colonel Simcoe had a strong personal interest. Years later, he remained bitter that the failure of the plan had cost the life of his close friend, the British army's popular young adjutant-general Major John André, who was captured by the rebels while returning from a clandestine meeting with Arnold, and then tried and executed as a spy. In addition, by his own account in his published *Journal*, Simcoe had himself played a significant role in the "important negotiation" that was abruptly terminated by the major's arrest.[27]

In his *Remarks*, Simcoe stayed tantalizingly close-mouthed regarding the specific details of his own participation in the events surrounding Arnold's defection. He nonetheless took the opportunity to make some pointed comments about that episode's broader significance, presenting underlying facts that he was convinced Chastellux had deliberately ignored. Indeed, he insisted, far more had been at stake in September 1780 than the possession of even such a strategically important asset as West Point.

By that stage in the war, Simcoe was certain, the rebellion was teetering on the brink of collapse, with increasing numbers of war-weary Americans disposed toward a negotiated peace settlement with Britain: most significantly, for all the vitriol that Arnold incurred at the hands of his outraged countrymen *after* his plan misfired, the beliefs that led him to turn his coat were actually shared by many of them. Arnold, so Simcoe argued, was not some lone wolf, but rather symptomatic of a far wider discontent. He posed a question: "Could Arnold alone give up West Point?" In Simcoe's opinion, clearly not. Indeed, Arnold's "assertions"—the reasons he gave publicly to explain his conduct in the fall of 1780—"that America in general was satisfied with the offers of the British nation, that it was averse to the French, and [to] the continuation of the war," were, so Simcoe maintained, nothing less than the simple truth.

Had "the active, enterprising American Arnold" and "those who thought [like] him" succeeded in relinquishing West Point and thereby delivering "a severe blow" to Washington's army, the fractured British Empire would have been reunited. In that hypothetical scenario, Arnold would have "enjoyed the blessings" of his contemporaries and been venerated down the years as "the favorite of posterity."[28]

But of course, the plan had unraveled, laid bare by sheer chance when it was on the very cusp of implementation. And, as an intelligent officer like Simcoe must have known, his belated attempts to sway public opinion were entirely futile: far from being hailed as a would-be deliverer of America, Arnold was destined to be reviled as his country's most despicable renegade.

* * *

In his *Remarks*, John Graves Simcoe allowed himself a rather cryptic observation on the Benedict Arnold affair: "Much of this extraordinary event will doubtless ever be concealed: and probably little more than what has already transpired will be known to the present generation." To some extent that prediction still holds true. By definition, conspiracies are covert matters, and as Arnold's unfolded to its tragic conclusion, those involved mostly kept their cards close to their chests. Even after the plot's dramatic denouement, some of them chose to remain silent regarding important aspects of the story, taking key secrets to their graves. Simcoe, it seems, was content to do just that. To the frustration of historians, so was Arnold.[29]

After the revolutionary generation passed on, however, far more evidence was revealed than Simcoe could ever have anticipated. The most significant disclosures involved the secret correspondence between Arnold, Major André, and other collaborators and contacts, preserved among the extensive papers of Sir Henry Clinton that were acquired by the University of Michigan in 1928, and that are now held in its William L. Clements Library. These key documents were printed as an appendix to Carl Van Doren's *Secret History of the American Revolution*, a fine book that has remained essential for students of Arnold's conspiracy ever since its publication in 1941.[30]

Yet the undoubted importance of the selected correspondence reproduced by Van Doren has deflected attention from many other unpublished documents among the Henry Clinton Papers and elsewhere—especially the United Kingdom's National Archives at Kew. In combination with neglected published sources, these not only add fresh details and perspectives that help to explain the broader background to Arnold's conspiracy, but can also be used to challenge prevailing interpretations of his treason's genesis and impact. In particular, such previously unexploited material offers important insights into Arnold's motivation and objectives, making it possible to grapple with the questions at the heart of his story. Why did he betray the cause for which he had previously fought so staunchly? To what extent were Arnold's actions influenced by his mounting resentment at the reluctance of Congress to fully recognize his merits? How significant was his obsession with personal reputation or, as gentlemen of his era preferred to call it, "honor"? And how did he reconcile that strict code with behavior that was widely perceived as utterly *dis*honorable? Finally, when all other factors are taken into consideration, was Arnold ultimately tipped into treason by the alluring jingle of English guineas, as his contemporaries believed and modern writers continue to argue; or were his own expressions of a profound ideological change of heart actually sincere?

To place Arnold's treason in context, it is necessary to test the validity of Simcoe's claim, argued forcefully in his *Remarks*, that for all its unique notoriety, his defection was just a symptom of a far more widespread malaise affecting the patriot cause—a true *crisis* of American liberty. If Simcoe was correct, the American revolutionary movement was perched precariously on an abyss in 1780, and the capture of West Point would surely have nudged it over the edge. Although it is now commonly argued that Arnold's treason achieved exactly what Judge Pendleton hoped it would in October 1780, and inadvertently "saved" the Revolution by finally alerting complacent Patriots to the gravity of their situation, this interpretation of events is difficult to sustain, especially if a broad timeframe is adopted. While Americans were undoubtedly vociferous in condemning Arnold, their palpable anger was not converted into positive action: there was no revival of popular patriotism, no unified national effort to eject the British.

In fact, the supporters of American independence faced their darkest hours *after* the exposure of Arnold's plot. The low-point came in January 1781: unpaid, ill-clad, and hungry, hundreds of exasperated Continentals mutinied and marched on Congress for redress; that same month, Benedict Arnold went on the rampage in Virginia, meeting scarcely any resistance. As a brigadier-general of King George, and with Colonel Simcoe at his side, he was now determined to bring his rebellious countrymen to heel by fire and sword. The crisis continued for a year after Arnold's defection and was only ended by another timely intervention of "Providence," as manifested in the extraordinary combination of circumstances that enabled Washington and his French allies to trap Cornwallis at Yorktown.

Fundamental to any analysis of Arnold's defection, and also to Simcoe's contention that by 1780 many other Americans were equally disillusioned with the struggle for independence from Britain, is the underlying issue of allegiance during the Revolutionary War, and the extent to which loyalties were already fixed, or were capable of shifting as that conflict ground on for year after frustrating year. Recent scholarship on revolutionary America has emphasized how, ironically, the rift between Crown and colonies began to open at a time when their relationship had never been closer. In 1763, Britons on both sides of the Atlantic celebrated victory over their common enemy, France, in the Seven Years' War, a global struggle that included distinct North American campaigns, remembered as "the French and Indian War." They anticipated a bright new future together, under the young King George III, who had succeeded his grandfather, George II, in 1760. Yet the urgent need for colonial revenue to help pay for the long, successful, but costly war, allied to the elimination of the traditional French threat from Canada, generated growing resistance to British taxation, and simultaneously encouraged thoughts of independence from a state whose protection was no longer deemed essential.[31]

Within just twelve years, sporadic protest at British legislation had escalated into armed insurrection. This short time-span helps to explain why, when the fighting erupted, truly committed rebels did not constitute a majority of the population. The most recent estimates—and there is no way of tallying exact numbers—put the Revolution's active supporters at two-fifths of the total. That was perhaps twice the number of firm Loyalists, but equal to the proportion who preferred to remain neutral and play no part in the struggle. In 1775, despite a recent influx of German-speaking settlers, all three groupings still shared overwhelmingly British roots. It has been argued that the emergence of a distinct American "national" identity was a consequence of, rather than a precursor to, the Revolutionary War: the wide-ranging campaigning of the Continental Army throughout the thirteen former colonies, which introduced northern-born soldiers to the South, and vice versa, was vital for the metamorphosis from British Americans to citizens of the United States.[32]

Benedict Arnold's treason unfolded during what was primarily a *civil war* within the British Empire, in which the brunt of the fighting was borne by men of British stock. This interpretation of a conflict that, in retrospect, would be characterized as a war for *American* independence was accepted without question by participants on both sides. For example, responding to reports of the first bloody confrontation between redcoats and militia at Lexington and Concord on April 19, 1775, the Massachusetts lawyer and

Patriot Colonel James Otis had pronounced: "The fearful day has arrived! A civil war has actually commenced in our land." Likewise, a British officer who published a revealing account of the struggle in which he had fought (and while it was still going on) entitled his work *The History of the Civil War in America*.[33]

The short, sharp skirmish at Spencer's Ordinary that Simcoe remembered so clearly reflected the war's underlying fratricidal character in microcosm. That morning, each party to the fighting fielded English speakers born on both sides of the Atlantic. To foreign combatants, even after years of conflict, the distinction between Britons and Americans remained blurred. For example, Jäger Captain Ewald described the Virginian marksmen he faced as the "so-called Wild Irish Riflemen"; although they were now enlisted in the American patriot cause, Ewald identified them primarily in terms of their ethnicity.[34]

In an era of evolving affiliations, the term "American," with all that it now implies, is deceptive. While quickly appropriated by the "Whig" opponents of British rule, and sometimes applied to them by their enemies, the term could be claimed with equal justification by the Loyalists, or "Tories." To avoid the misleading and anachronistic suggestion that the supporters of independence were the only true Americans embroiled in the Revolutionary War, they are here frequently differentiated by more specific terms: "Patriots," "Revolutionaries," or, as the British army typically put it, "rebels."

In open, armed rebellion against their anointed monarch, General George Washington and his comrades were technically guilty of treason, and initially anticipated the hangman's noose if their cause was crushed: the Royal Proclamation of Rebellion, issued in London in August 1775, had called on all crown officers to suppress the insurrection, and "to bring the traitors to justice." But from the very start of the fighting it was clear that the American rebels—who were effectively transplanted Britons, and who enjoyed widespread sympathy among the war's vocal opponents in the mother country—would not face the traditional fate of traitors. That same August, in response to Washington's complaint that his captured officers were being treated as "felons" rather than as their rank deserved, Britain's commander-in-chief in North America, General Thomas Gage, left no doubt that, as rebels customarily "destined to the cord," they had escaped very lightly indeed. Gage knew what he was talking about: as a young officer, he had seen the bloody retribution exacted upon the defeated Jacobites in 1746. Royal veterans of the American Revolutionary War would likewise witness the brutal summary justice meted out to Irish rebels in 1798. But while the British never punished the adherents of American independence as traitors, their opponents took a far harsher view of the Loyalists. As a sobering study of treason in revolutionary Pennsylvania has emphasized, if the patriot cause was to be justified as legitimate, then those who actively supported the Crown must be treated as criminals: ironically, while the British brought no prosecutions for treason against Pennsylvanian rebels, the state's ardent Whigs "proscribed, or prosecuted as traitors, hundreds of citizens who had never deviated from the allegiance in which they were born." What was true of Pennsylvania also applied to other states, notably New York and New Jersey. In a conflict where resistance to a rebellious regime was punished more vigorously than defiance of the established authority, the unrestrained condemnation of its best-known defector becomes easier to comprehend.[35]

The adage that history is written by the winners was never more apt than when applied to Major-General Benedict Arnold. Yet his actions were significant enough to deserve to be judged without the distorting benefit of hindsight. To many of Arnold's shocked contemporaries, his betrayal of a cause for which he had previously fought with conspicuous courage was truly "extraordinary," explicable only as the consequence of insatiable greed and innate evil. Viewed against the backdrop of a stalemated civil war that had reduced much of his country to chaos, however, Arnold's decision to change sides invites other, more nuanced, explanations.

If, as John Graves Simcoe maintained, Benedict Arnold genuinely had his country's well-being at heart, and hoped to resolve a bitter, brutal, and divisive conflict with one devastating blow, then he turned his coat for the very best of reasons. While totally at odds with the prevailing consensus verdict on Arnold and his defining treason, this is an interpretation that merits careful consideration within any balanced re-examination of America's most infamous traitor.

1

BEGINNINGS

Once Major-General Benedict Arnold had undergone his swift and irreversible metamorphosis from revered hero to reviled traitor, it became common to suggest that his infamous behavior was the natural consequence of undistinguished and unsavory origins. Within weeks of his defection in September 1780, a London newspaper had branded him "a man of the most mean and low extraction." In coming decades, as public opinion toward Arnold showed no sign of mellowing, such slurs became embedded in his story. Writing a full century after the treason, the first biographer to take a balanced, objective view of Arnold's career remarked that it had been "quite the fashion" for American historians to "stigmatize" him as the product of "low birth and vulgar habits." But as Isaac Arnold (who was no relation to his subject) went on to emphasize, such accusations were wide of the mark.[1]

In fact, Arnold's ancestors had been prominent in the formative years of New England. In 1636, the first of them to make the perilous transatlantic passage from the old country, William Arnold, built a home on Pawtuxet River, Rhode Island. William's son, the first in a long line of Benedicts, moved to the colony's leading settlement of Newport, where he prospered and served several terms as Rhode Island's elected governor; this was a distinction that his descendant proudly recalled in the summer of 1780, just weeks before he made their shared name notorious. Governor Arnold's son, the next Benedict, also took a seat in the colony's governing assembly, but was dogged by money problems. In consequence, *his* son, the third Benedict Arnold and the father of the future Revolutionary War general, started out as a cooper's apprentice. From humble beginnings, he swiftly set about rebuilding the family's fortunes.[2]

In 1730, along with his brother Oliver, Benedict moved to Norwich, in the neighboring colony of Connecticut. There he exploited the steady demand for his barrels to join the thriving trade network that extended along the seaboard of Britain's mainland North American colonies, and farther south to the West Indies. Benedict's stock continued to rise in November 1733, when he married Hannah King, the widow of a Norwich sea captain and the daughter of one of the town's founders, John Waterman. Bolstered by Hannah's dowry, Benedict expanded his trading ventures. Like other New England merchants, he established links with the sugar islands of the Caribbean, exporting barrel staves, timber, and pork, in exchange for their slave-produced staples of molasses and rum. Prosperity brought respectability and civic responsibilities: Benedict acquired a substantial house and was elected to a succession of local offices. Hannah bore him six children, but the family was cruelly winnowed by disease. Ultimately, just two of the Arnold infants survived the dangerous early years to reach adulthood: Hannah and the brother born a year before her, on January 14, 1741. Inevitably christened Benedict, he would make the hereditary name resonate on both sides of the Atlantic.[3]

Steeped in the stern Old Testament doctrine of New England, Hannah Arnold rationalized the deaths of her children as the will of God. But such spiritual consolation failed to comfort Benedict senior. Coupled with a downturn in trade, the remorseless toll on his young family left him depressed and increasingly inclined to seek solace in the bottle. As he spiraled into alcoholism, his strong-willed and pious wife took the lead in rearing their surviving children. Determined that young Benedict should have a decent start in life, Hannah Arnold arranged his schooling, at first locally and then farther off in the outlying village of Canterbury. From the age of eleven to fourteen, Benedict was taught by the Reverend James Cogswell, a well-respected schoolmaster who gave him a solid grounding in Latin and mathematics; judging by his later correspondence, he learned to express himself forcefully in a clear, bold hand. Dr. Cogswell considered Benedict a capable pupil, although outspoken and overly fond of pranks.[4]

Soon after Arnold's treason, a letter published in the widely read *Boston Gazette* claimed that "in his most early infancy, hell marked him for her own, and infused into him a full proportion of her diabolical malice." Unsurprisingly (given his notoriety), later anecdotes of Arnold's youth likewise cast him in the worst possible light, as a vicious, vindictive lad who delighted in tormenting his playmates and the local wildlife alike. In 1835, Arnold's early biographer, the celebrated historian Jared Sparks, had no qualms about accepting such lurid tales at face value. In Sparks' popular and influential *The Life and Treason of Benedict Arnold*, the villain-in-the-making was characterized by "an innate love of mischief ... an obduracy of conscience, a cruelty of disposition, and irritability of temper, and a reckless indifference to the good or ill opinion of others." But as Sparks conceded, folk memory also emphasized other traits: Arnold was "as fearless as he was wickedly mischievous," the daredevil ring-leader of every dangerous exploit. Given Arnold's undoubted courage and determination—what his admirers would later describe as "intrepidity"—one of the stories passed down to later generations sounds likely enough: to the consternation of onlookers, he would enliven the drudgery of his trips to the grist mill by leaping onto the revolving waterwheel and holding fast as it carried him high into the air, before plunging deep down into the foaming millstream.[5]

As such colorful tales suggest, the dearth of hard evidence for Benedict Arnold's early years, and the lack of anything like a coherent personal memoir, have obliged biographers to supplement the sparse documentary record with less reliable sources. Despite such shortfalls, and after making due allowance for post-treason prejudice, enough credible information survives to identify the formative experiences that shaped Arnold's character, and prepared him to play a conspicuous role when the Revolutionary War erupted in 1775.

A crucial development occurred in 1755, as the family's dwindling finances forced Arnold's mother to cut short his schooling and call him home to Norwich. The resourceful Hannah Arnold turned adversity to advantage: she persuaded her cousins Daniel and Joshua Lathrop, who ran a successful apothecary shop in Norwich, to accept Benedict as an apprentice. Like his father before him, the youngster recognized an opportunity to rebuild the family fortunes and worked hard to convince the Lathrop brothers that they had judged wisely in extending him their patronage.[6]

When the fourteen-year-old Benedict signed his articles of indenture, Britain and her North American colonies were embroiled in the latest round of their long-running power struggle with France. Dating back to 1689, when, as King William III, the Dutch-born William of Orange had harnessed the resources of his new kingdom to oppose the territorial ambitions of Louis XIV, this bitter Anglo-French rivalry endured throughout Arnold's sixty-year lifetime and beyond, only ending in 1815, when Emperor Napoleon Bonaparte was defeated at Waterloo. To fiercely Protestant Britons, especially those inhabiting the frontier provinces of New England and New York, which were vulnerable to hit-and-run raids from the French colony of Canada to the north, the conflict resembled an anti-Catholic crusade. Benedict Arnold matured in an environment in which Frenchmen, whether born in Old or New France, were the hated hereditary enemy.

Ingrained Francophobia intensified during the summer of 1757, when a powerful force of French regular troops, Canadian militia, and Native American "Indian" allies under Louis-Joseph, marquis de Montcalm, thrust south from Montreal to besiege Fort William Henry, at the heel of Lake George. When the outnumbered garrison of British redcoats and locally raised "Provincial" troops surrendered on promise of good treatment, they were attacked by frustrated Indian warriors who had expected to be compensated for their efforts by a rich haul of scalps, prisoners, and loot. Before the French could restore order, several hundred Anglo-Americans, including soldiers' wives and children, were slaughtered or dragged off into captivity. Outraged newspaper coverage transformed this spontaneous mayhem into a cynical war crime that epitomized French cruelty and duplicity. To counter Montcalm's offensive, threatened English colonies mobilized their militias, the part-time amateur defense force that included every able-bodied male aged sixteen to sixty. It is likely that Arnold, who was now old enough to serve, mustered with Connecticut's Norwich company. If so, this first taste of military life was brief and bloodless: when Montcalm withdrew to Canada, the crisis swiftly subsided, and the militia marched back home.[7]

The summer of 1757 marked the high point of France's war effort in North America. Henceforth, Canada was on the defensive, as Britain allocated unprecedented resources to stage a succession of campaigns aimed at eradicating French power on the continent once and for all. The Lathrops profited from lucrative contracts to provide medical supplies for the large armies of regulars and provincials assembled on the New York frontier. As the teenaged Benedict learned his trade, sorting imports and packing consignments for the front lines, he may have hankered to join the fight against the hated French. Stories that Benedict Arnold was indeed lured away from Norwich by the generous enlistment bounties offered by the provincial units recruiting in neighboring New York have a long pedigree, and are still widely credited. These anecdotes have gained acceptance because a Benedict, or "Benidick," Arnold appears on the muster rolls of three different companies raised in New York's Westchester County for the campaigns of 1758, 1759, and 1760. *That* Arnold deserted shortly after his second enlistment: an advertisement published in Weyman's *New York Gazette* on May 21, 1759, offered a forty-shilling reward to whoever apprehended him. The youth in question was described as: "18 years old, [with a] dark complexion, light eyes and dark hair." However, while the age is correct, and the physical details match later descriptions of General Benedict Arnold, the most thorough examination of the evidence suggests that the youngster listed on the New York musters and advertised as a deserter was no more than a namesake, and perhaps a distant relative, of the future turncoat.[8]

If Benedict Arnold really had been advertised as a deserter, the fact would surely have been mentioned in the outcry following his truly infamous defection to the British. An equally compelling argument against the enduring belief that young Arnold flitted in and out of military service between 1758 and 1760 is the fact that the Lathrop brothers not only allowed him to complete his apprenticeship, but increasingly employed him to represent their business interests on trading trips: they would have been unlikely to entrust their hard-earned professional reputation to an irresponsible runaway. By the time Arnold's apprenticeship was up, when he turned twenty-one, both of his parents were dead. His mother, to whom he was devoted, died in 1759; his father in 1761. The long-suffering and devout Hannah Arnold had been widely admired in the close-knit Norwich community, but Benedict senior incurred public scorn and official sanction for his alcoholism: in May 1760, Justice of the Peace Isaac Huntington issued a warrant for his arrest after he was seen reeling around the town, so drunk that "he was disabled in the use of his understanding and reason," which was "against the peace of our Lord the King and the laws of this colony."[9]

When Benedict Arnold came of age, what would later become known as the Seven Years' War was drawing to a close. The Anglo-American capture of Montreal in September 1760 ended hostilities on the mainland, but fighting continued in the Caribbean, where Britain flexed its maritime muscles to seize valuable French sugar islands, and, in 1762, captured the great prize of Havana from France's belated ally, Spain. At the 1763 Peace of Paris, the scale of Britain's triumph over her old enemy became clear. But victory came at a price. French foreign policy would now be dominated by a hunger to avenge such humiliating losses at the first opportunity. That chance came when Britain's efforts to clear huge war debts and to offset the cost of administering expanded territories prompted a program of tax legislation for the American colonies that ultimately goaded their inhabitants into rebellion.

To young Benedict Arnold, and to most of his fellow Britons on both sides of the Atlantic, such a rift would have seemed unthinkable in 1763. British Americans had played their part in dismantling New France, and were loyal subjects of the popular young King George III. They were linked to the old country by strong bonds of kinship, language, religion, and culture, and (in theory at least) by a trading system—embodied in the Navigation Acts of the 1650s—calculated to protect British commerce from foreign competition. But American merchants had a long tradition of flouting the regulations, and had no qualms about trading with Britain's rivals, even during years of open warfare. With the coming of peace, the imperial authorities determined to combat smuggling by overhauling the customs service. It was against this shifting and contentious background that Benedict Arnold embarked on his own business career.

The successful Lathrop brothers clearly found qualities to admire in their former apprentice, and their continued backing was instrumental in establishing Arnold as a shopkeeper and merchant in his own right. According to an account published in 1780, once Arnold's time with them had expired Dr. Daniel Lathrop "was so satisfied with his good conduct" that he gave him the handsome sum of £500, along with equally valuable letters of introduction to his business contacts in London. Armed with both, Arnold sailed to England, took lodgings in the capital's Holborn district, and used credit to buy "apothecary wares and dry goods" worth between £3,000 and £4,000 with which to stock his own store back in Connecticut.[10]

On returning home, Arnold distanced himself from Norwich, instead setting up shop in New Haven. This decision may have been prompted by the lingering stigma of his father's drunkenness, although, with its rapidly expanding population and easy access to coastal trade via Long Island Sound, New Haven was a logical enough location for an ambitious young merchant. The black sign that he hung above his shop still survives, its gilt lettering proudly announcing "B. Arnold, Druggist, Bookseller, &c. From London." Arnold was keen to emphasize his personal connection with the sophisticated capital of Britain's transatlantic empire, a bustling city that most of his countrymen had only read about in their newspapers. The sign's Latin motto *Sibi Totique* ("for himself and for all") advertised the unquestioning self-belief that would become Arnold's trademark, both as a businessman and as a soldier.[11]

Arnold's apothecary business thrived, as his extensive range of goods—everything from medicines and spices to buckles and books—attracted customers whose access to such desirable imports had previously been limited. It also exploited the market offered by the students of Yale College, which had been established in New Haven (as the Collegiate School) in 1716. Arnold's intelligent and strong-willed sister Hannah, with whom he maintained a close relationship throughout his life, moved from Norwich to New Haven to help run the store and handle the accounts. In 1764, Arnold sold the old family home, using the profits to pursue more appealing ventures. "Being of an active disposition, and detesting the languor of still life," Arnold later explained, "he relinquished the business of an apothecary," preferring instead to follow in his father's footsteps and become a sea captain.[12]

By 1766, Arnold controlled a modest flotilla of three small merchantmen: the largest vessel, of forty tons' capacity, was the *Fortune*, followed by the *Charming Sally*, of thirty tons, and the *Three Brothers*, of twenty-eight. That January, he placed an advertisement in his local newspaper, the *Connecticut Gazette*, requesting "large, genteel, fat horses, pork, oats, and hay." Such cargoes, along with timber, were typically shipped to the West Indies in the spring, with a return voyage carrying molasses, rum, and sugar. During the winter, it was reported, Arnold went among the Dutch settlements toward the head of the Hudson River, before moving northward into Canada, where he sold woolen goods such as caps, stockings, and mittens, and cheese. With the proceeds, Arnold bought horses to form part of his next Connecticut cargo to the Caribbean.[13]

In later years, as Arnold wryly acknowledged, he was often described as a "jockey"—at that time an interchangeable term for both a professional rider and a dealer in horses. A plausible account of how Arnold first gained his knowledge of horseflesh (which also sheds light on the periodic problems that he faced in financing his various enterprises) is provided in the *Travels* of that inquisitive French soldier, the marquis de Chastellux. Moving through the state of New York in late 1780, Chastellux encountered the Rhinebeck innkeeper Jacob Thomas, who in the years before the Revolutionary War had "carried on a great trade in horses, which he purchased in Canada and sent to New York, there to be shipped to the West Indies." Thomas assured Chastellux that "within a fortnight he once went to Montreal and brought back with him seventy-five horses which he had bought there." The hardy Canadian horses were easily capable of traveling for eighteen or twenty hours a day, with three or four riders enough to drive a hundred-strong herd before them across the snow and ice-bound wilderness. Thomas maintained that he had "made, or rather repaired the fortune of that rogue of an Arnold" who had mismanaged "the little trade that he carried on at New Haven." He added: "I persuaded him to purchase horses in Canada, and to go himself and sell them in Jamaica. This speculation alone was enough to pay his debts and set him once more afloat."[14]

Still in his mid-twenties, the former apothecary "Dr. Arnold" was ranging far and wide in search of profits, captaining his own vessels on ocean voyages, and familiarizing himself with the inland waterways that together formed a corridor through the rugged region between Albany and Quebec: following the course of the Hudson River, then crossing Lake George and Lake Champlain to reach the Sorel (or Richelieu) River and ultimately the St. Lawrence, this was a route much traveled by armies and raiding parties in previous wars. Arnold had chosen a hard, dangerous life, in which he was his own master, commanding crews and expecting unquestioning obedience. In the process, he became "an expert seaman," and acquired an intimate knowledge of locations that would soon resume their traditional strategic importance.

Whether skippering his own trading vessels in the churning Atlantic, or herding horses across a frozen landscape like some trail boss of the Old West, Benedict Arnold demonstrated his energy and self-reliance, and a readiness to endure extreme danger and hardship in pursuit of profits. Witnesses agree that Arnold was physically well suited to this punishing lifestyle. A younger neighbor in New Haven remembered him as "something below the middle height, well formed, muscular, and capable of great endurance." But there was more to the brawny New Englander than brute force: he was "a finished adept in all athletic exercises," and the most "accomplished and graceful skater" that his neighbor had ever seen. Other contemporaries concur in describing Arnold as of average height, which in eighteenth-century terms would equate to perhaps five feet five or six inches tall. Massachusetts soldier Alpheus Parkhurst, who was at West Point when Arnold defected, remembered him as "a smart-looking man about middling size"; according to the Hessian officer Johann Ewald, who served alongside him in 1781, he was "a man of medium size, well-built, with lively eyes and fine features"; and in the vivid recollection of another old soldier, Saratoga veteran Samuel Downing, Arnold was "dark-skinned, with black hair, and [of] middling height." Downing added, "there wasn't any waste timber on him."[15]

Arnold's proven ambition and determination helped to ensure his acceptance within New Haven's merchant community. This accomplishment was underlined on April 10, 1765, by his admission to the town's Masonic lodge. He was presented for membership by its highly respected Master, Nathan Whiting, who had distinguished himself as a colonel of Connecticut provincial troops during the French and Indian War, achieving the unusual feat of impressing the regular British officers who served alongside him. Freemasonry, like so much else in the maturing Arnold's America, was a British import. From modest beginnings in the 1730s, the movement steadily gained momentum, and by the time Arnold was admitted there were dozens of lodges throughout the colonies. Embodying the reasoning of the Enlightenment, while retaining elements of ritual, Freemasonry offered an alternative to conventional Christianity. Many Masons espoused Deism—a belief in destiny and the presence of a divine, all-seeing Providence. By becoming a Mason, Arnold was entering a select brotherhood whose members already included influential men like Benjamin Franklin and George Washington. Crucially, among the New Haven lodge was his future father-in-law, the town's high sheriff, Samuel Mansfield.[16]

Post-treason accounts claimed that Arnold insinuated himself "into the good graces" of Miss Mansfield as a means of restoring his fortunes after some unspecified "dissipation" led him first astray, and then into the debtors' prison. According to this scurrilous report, when Arnold debauched his daughter and made her pregnant, Sheriff Mansfield ("a very passionate man") initially wanted to shoot him; but a swift marriage ensured that the couple were both "restored to favor." Despite such tales, Arnold's marriage to Margaret "Peggy" Mansfield on February 22, 1767, was no "shotgun wedding": the first of three sons, named Benedict as usual, was conceived *within* wedlock and was born on Valentine's Day 1768; Richard arrived in August 1769, and Henry in September 1772. Instead, Arnold's alliance with a prominent New Haven family testified to the respectability he had achieved since moving to the town just five years before.[17]

With elevated status came an obligation to defend it, at whatever cost. In Europe, "gentlemen" frequently fought duels in response to real, or perceived, slights on their honor, despite growing criticism that such encounters were barbaric. Like Freemasonry, to which it offered a distinctly unfraternal counterpoint, the rise of dueling in North America coincided with Arnold's lifetime. "Affairs of honor" proliferated during the Revolutionary War, when Continental Army officers increasingly regarded themselves as gentlemen required to behave like their touchy British opponents. Dueling likewise gave a lethal edge to political life in the volatile young republic, leaving Alexander Hamilton among its most celebrated victims.[18]

For Arnold, a heightened, even obsessive, concern with personal reputation would become a defining character trait. This lends credence to another early tale, passed down through his mother's family, that he fought a duel while on a trading trip to the Bay of Honduras in Central America. Aggrieved that Arnold had apparently spurned an invitation to socialize aboard his own merchant vessel, a grouchy English captain named Croskie cursed him as a "damned Yankee" who lacked manners. Arnold prickled at this insult and promptly issued a challenge. Croskie accepted, and it was fixed that the "meeting" should take place with pistols next morning on a nearby island, with each duelist accompanied by only his "seconds," there to see fair play, and a surgeon to tend any casualties. But when Croskie's boat approached, he was accompanied by an unauthorized group of locals: Arnold warned him at pistol point to abide by their original agreement, and land without them. In the ensuing encounter, Croskie fired first, but missed. Arnold's answering shot winged his opponent. Once the surgeon had dressed Croskie's flesh wound, Arnold announced his determination to stand another fire; if he survived, he would shoot to kill. At this, the Englishman wisely proffered his apology. Honor satisfied, Arnold accepted.[19]

Arnold's readiness to resort to less formal violence is documented in an incident that highlights the tensions resulting from British efforts to tighten up the regulation of colonial trade after 1763, and the extent to which such policies encouraged his open support for the nascent cause of American liberty. In January 1766, when Arnold's ship the *Fortune* returned to New Haven, one of the crew, Peter Boles, demanded extra pay. It seems likely that his motive was to blackmail Arnold as a smuggler who had flouted the law by trading with foreigners. When Arnold refused his request, Boles went to the customs house to report him. As the collector was away, the sailor decided to withhold his information until that official returned. Learning of his crewman's actions, Arnold tracked him down and meted out what he later described as "a little chastisement." Stubborn or stupid, Boles refused to leave New Haven. The irate Arnold now extracted a written confession that, tempted by the devil, Boles had tried to inform against him. This time Boles swore that he would quit town immediately, never to return. Just hours later, when the exasperated Arnold was notified that Boles had still not budged, he headed a gang of sailors who dragged him from his bolt hole to the town green, stripped and tied him to the whipping post, then gave him forty lashes.

By taking the law into his own hands, Arnold had gone too far for some of New Haven's more conservative leaders. Along with nine others, he was bound over for trial. Yet, given the widespread acceptance of smuggling and the bitter hatred of informers, popular sympathy lay with the accused. The day after grand jury members John Wise and Tilley Blakeslee called for action against Arnold's gang, a mob paraded the two men's effigies through the streets, before hanging and burning them in contempt. Yet Arnold was found guilty and fined fifty shillings. He voiced his anger by writing a letter to the *Connecticut Gazette* sarcastically asking whether it was "good policy . . . to vindicate, caress, and protect an informer—a character particularly at this alarming time so odious to the public." Arnold framed his question within a more general rant against the "oppressive acts" which had provoked fierce opposition and "nearly ruined" the trade on which the colony depended.[20]

As Arnold's uncompromising stance suggests, imperial legislation that sought to control colonial commerce gave businessmen like him a strong financial incentive to champion the rights and liberties of all Americans. The British crackdown on smuggling was behind another episode that stoked Arnold's growing resentments. In January 1767, his "good sloop *Charming Sally*" returned to New Haven after making a long trading voyage to St. Croix in the West Indies, from there across the open Atlantic to Holland, and then back again by the same route to Connecticut. Arnold was not aboard.

According to ship's mate Rutherford Cooke and another crewman, Caleb Comstock, they had arrived in Amsterdam on August 30 to find Arnold waiting for them; when they made sail for St. Croix on October 5, they left him "on shore." In a sworn complaint lodged on February 5, 1767, Cooke testified that on reaching New Haven, he went to His Majesty's Customs House with the ship's register and papers, but was required to leave them with officials while the sloop was searched for contraband. Although nothing illicit was found, and Cooke gave his oath as required by an Act of Parliament, he had since been denied access to the ship and her papers. Evidence for the outcome of the story is missing, but Arnold must have been on hand soon after to deal with the situation in person: he married Margaret Mansfield in New Haven just weeks later.[21]

While Arnold's lengthy absences on far-flung trading expeditions meant that he was often distant from the centers of opposition to British policy, he followed the dispute between Crown and colonies with interest. During the summer of 1770, for example, Arnold was in the West Indies, "in a corner of the world whence you can expect no news of consequence." He nonetheless heard reports of the riot dubbed the "Boston Massacre," which had occurred on March 5, after a menacing mob prompted jittery redcoats to open fire, killing five. Writing to a friend back in Connecticut, Arnold's outraged response placed him among Britain's hardline opponents:

> I was very much shocked the other day, on hearing the accounts of the most cruel, wanton and inhuman murders committed in Boston by the soldiers. Good God, are the Americans all asleep, and tamely giving up their liberties, or are they all turned *philosophers*, that they don't take immediate vengeance on such miscreants.[22]

With growing family commitments, Arnold's prolonged trading trips became increasingly onerous. Writing to his "Dear Peggy" from St. Croix on July 25, 1768, Arnold told how he had sold his freight from St. Kitts, and was busily loading a full cargo for the homeward leg, which would "help make up [for] a bad voyage"—a verdict that Peggy should not repeat. Arnold promised to "make all possible dispatch, as a separation from you is attended with the most cruel anxiety." Back in New Haven, his wife and her friends would struggle to imagine his "impatience to leave this savage island." Indeed, writing home was "the greatest pleasure I have in this disagreeable corner of the earth."[23]

Six years later, little had changed: although the economy had rallied after the post-war slump of the mid-1760s, ready cash to settle outstanding debts was still hard to find; and Arnold, now a father of three, was as anxious and homesick as ever. From an unspecified port in the Caribbean, he forwarded Peggy sixteen "Joannes" (large Portuguese gold coins worth £5 each)—"all I could possibly send you at present"—and hoped that "those people I owe will rest easy until I return," when they could "all depend upon being immediately paid." Money was not the only thing on Arnold's mind. He had just heard of the sudden death of two acquaintances, both "in the prime of life and as likely to live as any of us," which led him to worry for his own far-off family. He mused:

> how uncertain is life, how certain is death ... My dear life pray by no
> means neglect the education of our dear boys, it is of infinite concern,
> what habits and principles they imbibe when young. I hope that this will
> find you all well, and that the Almighty may preserve you in health and
> happiness is the sincere prayers of your loving husband ...[24]

Waiting in a succession of far-flung ports, Arnold fretted whenever New Haven vessels docked without delivering letters from Peggy; he had no idea whether she and the boys were alive or, like his long-dead siblings, had succumbed to an epidemic. Always defensive of his reputation, in 1771 he was concerned to learn that scandalous rumors about him were circulating in New Haven. Propagated by the "master of a Connecticut vessel that traded to the West Indies," these alleged that he "had suffered very materially in an amour at the islands." The gossip maintained that Arnold had consoled himself with a prostitute in the Bay of Honduras, and had contracted venereal disease in consequence. Determined to quash this "evil report," which "occasioned him to be pointed out in the streets," Arnold sent the lawyer Elihu Hall to gather evidence from business contacts prepared to testify to his upright character and conduct. According to one version of the story, when Hall returned and presented the affidavits in court, they were ruled inadmissible, as they had not been sealed in accordance with Connecticut custom. In consequence, Arnold refused to foot Hall's bill, but when the case went to arbitration the ruling fell against him, and he was ordered to pay all expenses, plus legal fees. Whether the stories of an extramarital dalliance were true is unclear; however, given the difficulty of treating syphilis—or as eighteenth-century Britons preferred to call it, "the French disease"—before the availability of penicillin, the symptoms of infection would have been all too obvious to the men asked to refute the rumors. Of course, that does not preclude the possibility that Arnold patronized the prostitutes who clustered at every port to cater for the needs of lonely and frustrated sailors, but escaped infection. The notion is not implausible: as will be seen, there are other hints that Arnold's restless energy was matched by a robust libido.[25]

Whether the stories were true or false, the fact that Arnold became the target of defamatory gossip suggests that his forceful character, combined with a hard-headed approach to business, generated resentment and hostility among his rivals. Arnold's driving ambition ensured his survival in a precarious and competitive environment, but it left seething hostility in its wake. While post-1780 assessments of Arnold's character must always be treated with caution, the recollection of his fellow Connecticut sea captain Jeremiah Wadsworth suggests that a prickly and single-minded tempera-ment was just one factor behind his knack for making enemies. Wadsworth, a successful merchant who later became commissary general of the Continental Army, remembered that "when they were masters of vessels in the West India trade . . . Arnold cheated every man with whom he had any dealings."[26]

Support for this scathing verdict comes from a very different, and far more credible, source. With their economic peaks and troughs, the 1760s and early 1770s were a chancy time for many American traders, especially those—like Arnold—who had run up substantial debts importing goods on credit from British merchants. In 1766, six of Arnold's London creditors, led by the Quaker druggist Thomas Corbyn and including the leading book-seller Thomas Longman, launched an action for the recovery of £1,700 that he owed them. A New York merchant, Bernard Lintot, was hired to bring Arnold to bay. As the harassed Lintot reported to Corbyn in May 1767, it had proved a tough and frustrating assignment. He had spent almost two weeks in New Haven wrangling to bring Arnold "to a more just settlement," not least because the wily Yankee skipper had employed "a most vigorous and designing man"—the local attorney Jared Ingersoll—"to assist him in everything." Concluding that Arnold was determined to do Corbyn and his fellow creditors "all possible injustice," Lintot "arrested his person." But Arnold was released on bail, and it was only when Lintot impounded the *Charming Sally* and her cargo, and after "a good deal of altercation," that it was agreed he should clear half his debt—"ten shillings in the pound on the principal sum and seventy five pounds sterling as interest." The exasperated Lintot gave Corbyn a withering assessment of Arnold's character as a businessman:

> I must now observe that Mr. Arnold has by no means deserved the confidence you placed in him; which confidence induced me to treat with him as one willing to do all the justice in his power to his creditors; whilst he acted on principles directly opposite. Had I not with the greatest dispatch seized the vessel he would have put it out of my power to have secured you anything. It would take up too much of your time to enumerate the many exceptions I have to Mr. Arnold's conduct.

But even that was not the end of the story. Taking advantage of shifting exchange rates between the inflated colonial currency and sterling, Arnold sought to trim the real value of his pay-out. Arnold did not finally honor the settlement made with Lintot until September 1770, and outstanding debts awaited him years later, when he returned to London after his defection to the British. As his "old acquaintance" gleefully noted in 1780: "several merchants in this city remember Mr. Arnold pretty well, for his name still remains in their books."[27]

Benedict Arnold's recalcitrance in clearing his own debts was in marked contrast to the zeal with which he pursued those owing money for goods supplied by him. In 1768, when seeking an overdue sum from the New York merchant John Remsen, he wrote demanding to know why the balance, which he wanted "very much," remained outstanding after three years. Openly contemptuous of Remsen's "threats in regard [to] the contract," Arnold countered by expressing "a consciousness of my uprightness and fairness in regard to our concerns." In coming years, this would be Arnold's consistent response to anyone deemed to have questioned his probity: *he* believed himself to have right on his side, and that was sufficient defense against any criticism. Indeed, he would never allow the opinion of Remsen, "or any other blockhead," to give him "any uneasiness."[28]

While it is clear that Arnold often sailed close to the wind in his commercial affairs, encountering "various loss and gain," he was successful enough to cement his status in the most conspicuous way by constructing a two-story, white-boarded mansion on Water Street, described as "a very fine house, by far the grandest in New Haven." Completed in 1771, the "elegant" property was fronted by a picket fence, and included a coach-house, stables and "a large and fine fruit garden" at the rear. Arnold also owned store-houses and wharves, and in the recollection of Jeremiah Miller, who knew him before the outbreak of the Revolutionary War, was "for several years previous … considered as a merchant of property and did a great deal of business." In early 1780, when the celebrated Major-General Arnold of the Continental Army looked back at his pre-war years, he recalled with justifi-able pride: "I was in easy circumstances, and enjoyed a fair prospect of improving them."[29]

Since the mid-1760s, Arnold had ranked among Connecticut's most strident opponents of British legislation, ready to use violence in defense of American patriot interests, especially when they coincided with his own. By 1774, despite interludes of relative calm, the dispute between Crown and colonies had escalated to a point where civil war looked inevitable. Loyalists were now subject to increasing intimidation from the radical patriot organ-izations known as the Sons of Liberty, which had first appeared a decade earlier to help coordinate resistance to the Stamp Act; clergymen who tried to influence their congregations in favor of king and parliament were espe-cially loathed and at risk of assault. That September, it was alleged, Arnold was the ring-leader of a New Haven mob that gathered to punish a particu-larly outspoken loyalist churchman, Samuel Peters. A native of Hebron, Connecticut, Reverend Peters had attracted the ire of local Patriots by openly condemning the Boston Tea Party of December 1773. For decanting the East India Company's tea into their harbor, the Bostonians incurred punitive measures—the so-called Coercive Acts—that stirred a fresh wave of colonial protest. It was amid this heated atmosphere that the Sons of Liberty ransacked Peters' home in August 1774; a month later, he was beaten up and coerced into signing a confession renouncing his views. Granted refuge at the New Haven home of a fellow clergyman, Peters learned that patriot gangs led by Arnold and the French and Indian War veteran Colonel David Wooster, which had already targeted a Loyalist-leaning religious sect known as the Sandemanians, were approaching. Taking up a musket himself, and handing others to his servant and a "brother clergymen," Peters prepared to stand his ground. Arnold arrived to find the gate barred, and when he demanded that Peters open it, received a defiant response. Having "already been in the power of two mobs," the minister declared, "he would never be in the power of a third while he had life." Urged on by his followers, Arnold grabbed an axe and was poised to swing it when Peters shouted a blunt warning: "Arnold, so sure as you split the gate, I will blow your brains out, and [those of] all that enter this yard to-night!" Convinced that Peters meant what he said, Arnold backed down and his "drunken mob" dispersed. According to Peters, when Wooster's crew arrived soon after, they were likewise warned off at gunpoint.[30]

Although the reliability of Peters' vivid but self-serving version of events has been questioned, there is no doubt that Arnold's patriot townsfolk now looked on him as a natural leader. This was made plain in March 1775, when he was elected captain of a militia unit formed three months earlier, and which was constituted as the "Governor's Second Company of Guards." Command of the sixty-five-strong "Footguards," who were handsomely dressed at their own expense in scarlet coats faced with buff, was a prestigious appointment, affording the thirty-four-year-old Arnold precisely the status and public recognition that he craved. Headstrong, hot-tempered, and sometimes unscrupulous in his business dealings, in the eyes of his peers Benedict Arnold clearly possessed other qualities that outweighed his flaws: he was tough, experienced, worldly wise, and long accustomed to giving orders; and not least, he was a zealous champion of American liberty against British tyranny.[31]

* * *

Captain Benedict Arnold did not have long to wait for an opportunity to display his military leadership. Around midday on Friday, April 21, 1775, news reached New Haven of bloody clashes between British troops and patriot militiamen at Lexington and Concord, in the Massachusetts countryside. Next day, after brow-beating the town's hesitant selectmen into issuing ammunition for his Footguards, Arnold marched them to Cambridge, where an army of New England militia was massing to blockade the redcoats in nearby Boston. Rather than dawdling in the static siege lines, Arnold approached the Massachusetts Committee of Safety with a proposal to lead an expedition to capture the famous, but now dilapidated, fortress of Ticonderoga, at the southern end of Lake Champlain. Begun by the French in 1755, Ticonderoga had fallen to the British during the *annus mirabilis* of 1759—but only after a determined attempt to storm its outlying defenses a year earlier had been repelled with horrendous losses. Arnold reported Ticonderoga to be "in a ruinous condition" and incapable of holding out "an hour against a vigorous onset." It is likely that he had become acquainted with the fort's vulnerability on his trading trips to Canada. As Ticonderoga held artillery that the rebels badly needed to bombard the redcoats in Boston, Arnold's plan won the enthusiastic support of the committee's chairman, the celebrated Patriot Dr. Joseph Warren, and was swiftly approved. On May 3, 1775, Arnold was promoted to colonel in the service of Massachusetts, and appointed "commander-in-chief" of a force, not exceeding 400 men, to be raised in western New England. The committee trusted in his "judgment, fidelity, and valor" to subdue the fort and bring back the crucial cannon.[32]

Unknown to Arnold, another expedition with the same objective was already under way. On April 26, while journeying to Cambridge, Arnold had mentioned Ticonderoga's guns to a fellow Connecticut officer, Colonel Samuel Holden Parsons. Back in Hartford, Parsons convinced other leading citizens to fund a force to fetch the artillery, without awaiting the official approval of Connecticut's Assembly. Ticonderoga, in New York, lay across Lake Champlain from the "Hampshire Grants"; claimed by New York but settled by families from Connecticut, New Hampshire, and Massachusetts, this disputed territory would eventually become the state of Vermont. In 1769, settlers opposed to New York formed a separatist militia, known as the "Green Mountain Boys," led by the charismatic Ethan Allen; the informal Connecticut committee hoped to use this local manpower in an attack on the fort. To complicate the situation even further, when Captain Edward Mott soon after arrived in Hartford seeking recruits to bolster the patriot army at Cambridge, and likewise mentioned the tempting ordnance at Ticonderoga, the local committee decided that he should accompany their expedition, and help to direct it. Heading north, Mott's small Connecticut contingent was reinforced by about forty Massachusetts recruits, and two militia officers who were destined to clash with Arnold: a former tavern-keeper, Colonel James Easton, and an attorney, Major John Brown.[33]

Moving ahead of Arnold, Mott's New Englanders met Allen and his officers at Castleton, and on May 7 discussed the proposed attack at a council of war. As most of the men present had been raised by the popular Allen, and Mott had promised them that they would serve under their own officers, it was decided that the acknowledged leader of the Green Mountain Boys should take command of an operation to surprise the fort from across Lake Champlain during the night of May 9–10. Arnold only learned of Allen's plan at the eleventh hour. Leaving his own recruits to follow on, he rode hard to arrive at Castleton on the evening of May 9, and immediately challenged the council's authority. As Mott reported, they were "shockingly surprised when Colonel Arnold presumed to contend for the command of those forces that we had raised." Mott maintained that Arnold's interference threatened to frustrate the "whole design," as the volunteers would rather shoulder their muskets and march home than serve under any officers save those they had engaged with.[34]

Denied the command that he believed was rightfully his, Arnold galloped after Allen, catching up with him at Hand's Cove, on the eastern shore of Lake Champlain, in the early hours of May 10. Even as the boats were being readied for a crossing under cover of darkness, Arnold flourished his official commission from the Massachusetts Committee of Safety and demanded to lead the attack. Allen was a tall, bulky man who towered over the stocky Arnold, and was no less fiery in temperament; he refused to be intimidated. With time running out before daylight exposed the enterprise, a compromise was reached: Allen proposed that Arnold should march side by side with him at the head of the column, but give no orders. Under the circumstances, Arnold had no option but to accept.

Although the assembled force numbered about 200, the available boats could only accommodate 85 men. By the time the first wave with Allen and Arnold was across the lake, it was 3 a.m. With the skies lightening, they pushed on without waiting for the rest. Allen led them around the fort's eastern wall until they reached a small wicket gate on the south side. The startled sentry presented his musket and pulled the trigger, but the priming powder failed to ignite; as he scampered off to give the alarm, Allen, Arnold, and the whooping Boys poured onto the parade ground. Taken completely off guard, the groggy garrison, which included many invalids, submitted without bloodshed. According to an influential *Narrative* that Allen published in 1779, he confronted the startled commander, Captain William Delaplace, and summoned him to surrender "in the name of the great Jehovah, and the Continental Congress."[35]

Colonel Benedict Arnold had participated in the first offensive mounted by the Patriots, one that would have important strategic consequences.

Yet popular acclaim and credit for an exploit that he had yearned to execute himself went to others. Allen's colorful *Narrative*, which became the accepted version of events, failed to mention that Arnold was even present; the same was true of Allen's report sent to the Massachusetts Congress, although it praised Colonel James Easton, "who behaved with great zeal and fortitude," and "John Brown, Esq., Attorney at Law, who was also an able counsellor, and was personally in the attack." But Delaplace's second-in-command, Lieutenant Jocelyn Feltham, remembered things differently. In his report to Britain's commander-in-chief, General Gage, Feltham made it clear that, as the first officer to confront the intruders, he was informed by both Allen and Arnold that they had a "joint command," with each of them specifying their authority. Feltham also contrasted the "genteel manner" in which "Mr. Arnold" sought to persuade him to surrender the fort with the threats of Allen, who brandished a drawn sword over his head, while his "armed rabble" leveled their guns at him.[36]

No sooner was Ticonderoga in rebel hands than Arnold renewed his demands for sole command, citing his official commission from Massachusetts. But Allen and Mott were unmoved: as Arnold had brought no men, they saw no reason for him to take charge of theirs. In addition, the volunteers who had captured the fort were unwilling to serve under an unfamiliar officer. The situation was resolved when a "Committee of War," chaired by Mott, formally appointed Allen to take command of the fort, pending further directions from Connecticut or the Continental Congress. Recounting events to the Massachusetts Committee, an indignant Arnold warned that the conquerors of Ticonderoga were now "in the greatest confusion and anarchy, destroying and plundering public property, committing every enormity, and paying no attention to public service." It was a precarious situation: as things stood, a hundred redcoats could retake the fortress. In what would become a typical expression of his unswerving self-belief, Arnold continued:

Colonel Allen is a proper man to head his own wild people, but entirely unacquainted with military service; and as I am the only person who has been legally authorized to take possession of this place, I am determined to insist on my right, and I think it my duty to remain here against all opposition, until I have further orders.

Swigging looted rum, the boisterous Green Mountain Boys mocked Arnold's pretensions to command, and even fired their guns at him. Expecting the deference to which he had grown accustomed as captain of the smart and well-disciplined New Haven Footguards, Arnold was so disgusted with this treatment that he preferred the company of the captured British officers.[37]

It was an inauspicious beginning to Arnold's military career. Amid all the acrimony and confusion, Arnold craved a clear-cut opportunity to demonstrate his leadership and win renown. The chance came on May 14, 1775, with the arrival of a schooner confiscated from a wealthy local Loyalist, the British army veteran Major Philip Skene, and christened the *Liberty*. On board were fifty of the recruits enlisted by Arnold's own agents, and one of his select Footguards, the young New Haven distiller Eleazer Oswald. A seasoned sailor, Arnold was now in his element and confident that the *Liberty* could be used to gain control of Lake Champlain. He discussed his idea with Allen, and another council of war appointed him to take command of the schooner and arm her for an expedition to capture a large sloop known to be at the British post of St. Johns, on the Sorel River that linked Lake Champlain with the St. Lawrence. Galvanized by the prospect of action, Arnold swiftly equipped the craft with carriage-mounted ship's cannon and smaller-caliber swivel-guns. Accompanied by a pair of the sturdy rowing boats known as bateaux, *Liberty* sailed north down the lake, and on May 15 arrived at Crown Point. Here, where the lake narrowed, the British had built a sprawling fort in 1759. Damaged by a serious fire in 1773, it was even more run down than Ticonderoga, and had also been captured by Allen's men. Despite encountering strong headwinds, two days later Arnold was within thirty miles of his objective. He crewed the two bateaux with thirty-five men, who rowed through the night; by dawn on May 18 they were close to St. Johns. They waited, Eleazer Oswald reported, "in a small creek, infested with numberless swarms of gnats and mosquitoes" until a scout returned with intelligence that their approach remained undetected. Surprise was complete, and the raiders captured the sloop, "two fine brass field pieces," nine more bateaux, and a sergeant's guard of a dozen men. Warned that British reinforcements were expected, and as the sloop was "just fixed for sailing," Arnold exploited a strong northerly wind to make way to Crown Point with his prizes and prisoners. Taking four of the bateaux, he destroyed the rest, leaving none "for the King's troops, Canadians or Indians, to cross the lake in." Under the original plan, it had been agreed that Ethan Allen should follow Arnold with more men in bateaux to seize and garrison St. Johns. The forces met as Arnold was returning up the lake. By now, Arnold considered such a scheme to be not only "impracticable" but also unnecessary, as they were now "masters of the lake." But Allen and his "mad fellows" would not be dissuaded. They pushed on and encamped across the Sorel from St. Johns—only to be surprised next morning by 200 redcoats and forced to retreat.[38]

Back at Ticonderoga, and buoyed up by his successful raid, Arnold worked with characteristic energy to strengthen his position. The captured sloop, renamed the *Enterprise*, was armed as his flagship, and the schooner *Liberty* was fitted with new guns, while an inventory was made of the cannon and stores seized at Ticonderoga and Crown Point. As Allen's local vigilantes trickled home, and his own officially sanctioned manpower increased, Arnold assumed command of both forts, although he made it clear to the Massachusetts Committee of Safety that he had no desire to stay in such a defensive role. Like Allen, with whom, despite their wrangling, he had much in common, Arnold favored a far more aggressive strategy— nothing less than an invasion of Canada. As a first step, on May 27 they agreed to establish a post at Point-au-Fer, on the west side of the lake and just south of the Canadian border. But it was soon clear that Congress had very different plans. Far from holding onto the captured forts and using them to launch a fresh offensive, the politicians in Philadelphia wanted to abandon both posts and build a new fort farther south, at the base of Lake George. That strongpoint, near the site of the old Fort William Henry, would be defended with Ticonderoga's cannon, although a careful survey should be taken of them, and everything else, so that all could be duly restored to the Crown when the "former harmony" was restored; after just weeks of hostilities, a permanent rupture between Britain and her truculent colonies still seemed unthinkable. Unsurprisingly, Arnold and Allen were outraged. Writing to Congress on May 29, Arnold emphasized that such a withdrawal would expose "a very extensive frontier" to "the ravages of the enemy."[39]

The plan to establish an advanced post far down Lake Champlain was now abandoned as Allen retired to Ticonderoga, and Arnold concentrated on improving the defenses of Crown Point and upgrading his flotilla. But while Arnold was away patrolling the lake, Allen revived the idea of invading

Canada. According to intelligence reports, the British governor, Sir Guy Carleton, was exhorting the Canadians to arm themselves against the American rebels, and on June 9 Allen wrote to Congress, raising the possibility of a pre-emptive strike. Even though Arnold was still absent, Allen called a council of war to discuss the idea. It met on June 10, but had scarcely opened proceedings when news arrived that Arnold's fleet was back. Still regarding himself as undisputed commander, Arnold was livid to learn that the council had been arranged without his knowledge, and he promptly dismissed its members.[40]

The next day, Sunday, June 11, Arnold's pent-up anger erupted in a confrontation with Colonel James Easton at Crown Point. It was Easton whom Mott had sent to the Massachusetts Congress with triumphant tidings of Ticonderoga's capture. He had set off, Arnold noted, "with an announced intention to injure me all in his power." This was an accurate assessment: Easton's verbal report vastly inflated his own role, claiming that he had accepted the surrender of the fort's commander; it barely acknowledged Allen's leadership, and excluded Arnold completely. This vainglorious version of events gained wider currency when it was published in the *Massachusetts Spy, or American Oracle of Liberty* newspaper on May 24. It was against this background of simmering hostility that Easton boorishly interrupted Arnold's conversation with another officer, Major Samuel Elmore. Arnold lost his temper and subjected Easton to a brutal assault that laid bare his capacity for violence. Describing the episode in his journal, Arnold made no attempt to mitigate his behavior: "I took the liberty of breaking his head, and on his refusing to draw like a gentleman, he having a hanger [cutlass] by his side, and case of loaded pistols in his pocket, I kicked him very heartily, and ordered him from the point immediately."[41]

Arnold clearly believed that his actions were justified: perceived as a braggart and a coward who refused to defend his reputation in the approved fashion by fighting a duel, Easton forfeited consideration under the honor code. His public humiliation by Arnold prefigured ugly episodes that would become a fixture of political life in the new republic, where "nose-tweakings" and savage canings were visited on men who ignored challenges or were deemed to be socially inferior to their antagonists. Indeed, Easton's lowly status as a tavern-keeper may have been a factor in his contemptuous treatment by Arnold, who now clearly regarded himself as a "gentleman" of standing.[42]

A postscript to the Easton affair underlined the paramount importance that Arnold placed on his personal reputation. Not content with punishing Easton physically, Arnold now attacked him in the press. Easton's biased account of the capture of Ticonderoga was refuted at length in an article published soon after, in John Holt's *New-York Journal*. Dated June 27, and written from Ticonderoga under the pseudonym "Veritas," this emphasized that Allen and Arnold were the prime movers throughout the attack, while Easton was accused of avoiding danger. "Veritas" concluded by claiming to have "had the pleasure of seeing" Easton "heartily kicked by Colonel *Arnold*, to the great satisfaction of a number of gentlemen present." Given the content and distinctive vocabulary, the letter was likely composed by Arnold himself—or at least under his direction. Easton's claims were also publicly contradicted by the captive Captain Delaplace. In a letter dated Hartford, July 28, 1775, he declared them "totally void of truth."[43]

Like Ethan Allen, Arnold remained drawn to the possibility of invading Canada, and on June 13 proposed his own plan to Congress, based on careful intelligence gathering and personal knowledge of the country. An interpreter sent to the Mohawk mission at Caughnawaga, near Montreal, assured him that the Indians there had no intention of helping the British, while a merchant friend in that city maintained that the French-Canadians were reportedly impatient for the American rebels to invade and support them. Reckoning on an army of 2,000 men, Arnold proposed bypassing the British garrisons at St. Johns and Chambly on the Sorel River to capture Montreal; with their supply lines cut, those forts must inevitably surrender. So would Quebec, unless the British reinforced its garrison before the proposed offensive went ahead. Arnold was sure that a strike against Quebec, which already boasted strong fortifications, would be "more advantageous, and attended with less expense" than laboriously rebuilding Ticonderoga. At this early stage of the conflict, Arnold also remained more concerned with reconciliation than outright independence. Such conquests "would discourage the enemies of *American* liberty, frustrate their cruel and unjust plan of operation, and be the means of restoring that solid peace and harmony between *Great Britain* and her colonies, so essential to the well-being of both," he wrote. If the plan was approved, and no one else came forward to execute it, then Arnold was willing to undertake it himself. In an attached "Memorandum" he gave a detailed breakdown of the necessary equipment and manpower: he envisaged using troops from Connecticut and New York, and his own Massachusetts regiment. Arnold had one proviso: there must be "no *Green Mountain* Boys." It was a competent plan, but Congress laid it aside—for the moment.[44]

In response to Arnold's pessimistic situation reports, the Massachusetts Congress had written expressing its full confidence in his "fidelity, knowledge, courage and good conduct": despite his request to be replaced, he was urged to retain command of the state's troops until the Continental Congress ordered New York or Connecticut to assume responsibility for them. By now, after receiving Arnold's warning that the British were contemplating a strike from St. Johns, Congress had decided to keep hold of Ticonderoga and Crown Point after all. It also resolved that Connecticut should forward the necessary reinforcements and supplies, and that state sent Colonel Benjamin Hinman north with a thousand men. When the colonel arrived at Crown Point on June 17, expecting to assume the command, Arnold flatly refused to hand it over, on the grounds that Hinman was unable to produce a regular order. However, the colonel was soon followed by a committee from Massachusetts sent to inquire into Arnold's execution of its original orders; it also carried instructions that he should now place himself and his men under Hinman. At this, Arnold "seemed greatly disconcerted, and declared he would not be second-in-command to anyone whomsoever." Next day, June 24, "not being able to hold it longer with honor," Arnold resigned his commission and huffily disbanded the two or three hundred men he had recruited, only for many of them to re-enlist under the hated Easton. Bitter and humiliated, Arnold headed south to Albany, where he compiled a report to Congress on the state of the Champlain Valley defenses.[45]

At Albany, Arnold received another, still more terrible blow, with the news that his wife Margaret had died on June 19. She was just thirty years old. In Arnold's absence on Lake Champlain, his sister Hannah had immediately taken care of his three motherless boys, now aged seven, six, and three. Calm and competent, she proceeded to look after his New Haven business affairs, while he headed to Massachusetts to settle his accounts for the summer's campaign. A committee was appointed to investigate Arnold's expenses, and initially agreed to pay less than half of what he claimed; it was only after the intervention of his friend, the Connecticut congressman Silas Deane, that the shortfall of more than £200 was eventually refunded.[46]

For Colonel Benedict Arnold, it was a sorry and inglorious end to his first stint of active military service. From start to finish, his authority had been compromised by provincial rivalries and an ill-defined chain of command. The only exception to the rule of frustration and disappointment was the amphibious raid on St. Johns, a clear-cut success that Arnold had planned and executed himself, and which demonstrated his abilities as a bold and resourceful leader. Arnold resented his treatment, and not without reason: the failure of Massachusetts to back its own legally commissioned commander had left him powerless, exposed to indignities at the hands of men he despised, who used their political contacts to minimize his achievements and denigrate his character.

Yet Arnold's own personality had played its part in his predicament: a less headstrong, arrogant, and sensitive officer would have sought compromise, rather than alienate colleagues by blindly insisting on his right to command; a more restrained one would have controlled his emotions, instead of thrashing a fellow colonel, whatever the provocation. By instilling a conviction that his sincere efforts had gone unrecognized, and sowing a crop of critics only too eager to disparage him, Benedict Arnold's opening campaign established baleful precedents. In time, such friction would temper his enthusiasm for the cause of American liberty, fostering resentments that ultimately contributed to his decision to forsake it.

A DEVILISH FIGHTING FELLOW

In late June of 1775, Congress took the momentous step of authorizing an invasion of Canada. Such an aggressive move, which jarred with the rhetoric of a purely defensive struggle against imperial tyranny, would not only expand American territory, but deny Britain a northern base from which to attack the rebel states. Bolstered by fresh units, the troops already gathered at Ticonderoga were to head north down Lake Champlain to capture St. Johns and Montreal "and any other parts of the country." Such an offensive had recently been proposed by Arnold, and in acting now, Congress was influenced by his warning that Governor Sir Guy Carleton was preparing an offensive of his own, and encouraging the local Indians "to take up the hatchet" against the rebels.[1]

But the politicians in Philadelphia ignored Arnold's offer to lead the Canadian campaign. Instead, command was entrusted to a prominent New York landowner, Philip Schuyler. From an old-established Dutch family, Schuyler had served as a colonel of provincial troops during the French and Indian War; he was appointed by Congress as a major-general with responsibility for what became known as the Northern Department. Upright, courteous, and conscientious, the forty-two-year-old Schuyler was woefully indecisive, and a poor choice to orchestrate an offensive that required quick thinking and unflagging energy to keep it on schedule. Brisk progress was essential, not simply to avoid the hardships of a winter campaign, but also because the enlistments of most of the Connecticut and New York soldiers assigned to the operation were due to expire by the end of the year. Schuyler's shortcomings as a dynamic leader were offset by his second-in-command, the vigorous and capable Brigadier-General Richard Montgomery. Tall and slender, with the heavily pitted complexion common in an era when smallpox was rife, the Irish-born Montgomery was a former British army officer who had previously fought from Canada to the Caribbean. Montgomery's military background had left its mark: as one of his men observed, his "air and manner designated the real soldier."[2]

Montgomery became the driving force behind Schuyler's expedition, which finally began moving down Lake Champlain in bateaux at the end of August, protected by the small flotilla of fighting vessels that Arnold had assembled earlier that summer. By September 4, 2,000 men under Schuyler and Montgomery had landed at the Isle aux Noix, on the Sorel, some twelve miles south of the Americans' first objective, the fort at St. Johns. With less than 1,000 regulars of the 7th and 26th Foot, backed by a few hundred British civilians and the dubious services of a larger contingent of French-Canadian volunteers, Governor Carleton had resolved to make a stand there with more than half of his troops. A smaller force was posted farther north at Chambly, while Carleton established his headquarters at Montreal, from where he could also maintain contact with Quebec. Schuyler soon fell ill with a fever, and was sent back to Ticonderoga; but he played a valuable supporting role throughout the coming campaign, lobbying Congress for supplies and reinforcements. Taking over as the expedition's commander, Brigadier Montgomery pushed the siege of St. Johns as swiftly as the wet fall weather and his sickly, ill-disciplined, and homesick troops allowed.[3]

On September 15, while Montgomery bombarded St. Johns, Arnold's old rival Colonel Ethan Allen was captured by the British, after he rashly attempted to take Montreal with a small force of Canadian volunteers. Bullish as ever, Allen believed that his plan only failed because a cooperating force under Major John Brown—another of Arnold's Ticonderoga antagonists—failed to arrive on time. To discourage support for the American rebels, Allen and the other prisoners of war were paraded before the French-Canadians of Montreal, then "clapped in irons" and consigned to the hold of a warship. Despite this setback, Brown soon helped to strike a bold blow for the Patriots, leading his men alongside a Canadian force commanded by Major James Livingston that captured the post at Chambly without a fight on October 8.[4]

With its supply lines ruptured, and provisions running low, the garrison of St. Johns grew increasingly desperate. Learning that a relief expedition mounted from Montreal by Carleton had been rebuffed, the commandant, Major Charles Preston, surrendered on November 3. The garrison of St. Johns, numbering more than 500, became prisoners of war; they included an officer whose name would become linked with that of Benedict Arnold—twenty-five-year-old Lieutenant John André of the 7th Foot. The Patriots also acquired another sloop, the *Royal Savage*; taking a fancy to this warlike name, they kept it. Carleton had no option but to embark his remaining 150 men aboard eleven small ships at Montreal and head downriver toward the last remaining British outpost, at Quebec. Unopposed, Montgomery's troops marched into Montreal on November 13. Two days later, just above Sorel, Carleton's little fleet was intercepted by an American gunboat, followed by a party showing a flag of truce and proffering a note from Colonel James Easton, the same officer who had been "heartily kicked" by Arnold at Crown Point. Warning of powerful gun batteries downriver, Easton advised the British to surrender. After a futile effort to land, they were persuaded to reconsider Easton's summons, and examine the American batteries for themselves: drawing on his courtroom skills, the canny lawyer Major Brown helped to convince them that the threat was real enough, and the British capitulated on November 19: they surrendered the brig *Gaspee*, with seven sloops and schooners carrying valuable supplies, more than 150 men of the 26th Foot and Royal Artillery, and Brigadier-General Richard Prescott, who had recently fettered the reckless Allen, and now faced the prospect of similar treatment himself.[5]

But the determined Carleton escaped the patriot net. Disguised as a Canadian peasant, he had slipped away in a boat some days earlier, and was eventually picked up by a British brig, which delivered him safely to Quebec on November 19. There, his unexpected arrival gave cause for great celebration. The fortress city stood in dire need of Carleton's calm and competent leadership: just days before, its inhabitants had been disconcerted by the arrival of an army of lean and tattered American rebels, who, wraith-like, seemed to have materialized out of thin air. It was commanded by Colonel Benedict Arnold.[6]

* * *

When Arnold returned from Lake Champlain to Massachusetts that summer, he was mourning the loss of his wife and resentful at the brusqueness with which he had been superseded. But in Cambridge, he was not without sympa-thizers or advocates. They included Congressman Silas Deane, who was convinced that Arnold had been "hardly treated . . . through some mistake or other." As Philip Schuyler had previously written to Deane in Arnold's favor, requesting that he be made adjutant-general of the Northern Department, perhaps something could be done for him now? Deane added: "I think he has deserved much, and received little, or less than nothing"; he would be "very unhappy that any gentleman concerned in the first adventure"—the taking of Ticonderoga—"should be neglected." If Schuyler was heading for Montreal, then Deane hoped that Arnold would be given command of "a body of men, capable of making a powerful diversion in your favor." At any rate, Deane continued, Arnold should be employed *somehow*, not simply to provide for him, "but to take advantage of those abilities, and activities of which I am sure he is possessed."[7]

Arnold was soon granted an opportunity to prove himself. The same plan that Silas Deane envisaged had already occurred to Congress's newly appointed commander-in-chief, George Washington. Now formally adopted as the Continental Army, the patriot forces gathered at Cambridge continued to grow, as the original rump of New Englanders was bolstered by contingents sent from the states to the south. Besides blockading the British in Boston, Washington believed that he could "very well spare" some of this manpower for a diversionary offensive to complement the Northern Army's invasion of Canada. With no time to lose, he acted on his own initi-ative, without formally consulting Congress. Writing to Philip Schuyler on August 20, Washington explained that the plan had "engrossed" his thoughts "for several days." While Schuyler's command fixed Governor Carleton's attention on the traditional warpath to Montreal, another, more easterly, expedition would penetrate the Maine wilderness to surprise Quebec. To reach its objective, this force had to ascend the Kennebec and Dead rivers, cross the rocky and swampy watershed between New England and Canada known as the Height of Land, and then forge down the Chaudière River, which emptied into the St. Lawrence nearly opposite the fortified city.[8]

Such a plan had been proposed to the Massachusetts Provincial Congress that spring by a local man, Colonel Jonathan Brewer. Washington was already aware of its potential when his adjutant-general, Brigadier Horatio Gates, presented him with a similar scheme prepared by Arnold. Like

Richard Montgomery, Gates had served as a redcoat officer during the last American war against the French; fighting alongside Washington, he had survived the carnage of Major-General Edward Braddock's catastrophic defeat on the Monongahela River in 1755. Twenty years later, and by now a zealous defender of the cause of American liberty, his military experience was invaluable in organizing the raw Continental Army. Stooping, gray-haired, and bespectacled, at forty-seven Gates was middle-aged, but looked older; typically mild-mannered and easy-going, he was Arnold's temperamental opposite. Although destined to clash at a pivotal moment of the Revolutionary War, in the summer of 1775 their relationship was amicable. Now, Gates emphasized that Washington was keen to discuss Arnold's plan with him in person. It is clear that Arnold based his own proposal on careful groundwork: he had somehow obtained a manuscript copy of the detailed journal kept by a British army engineer officer, Lieutenant John Montresor, who had traveled and mapped the same route in 1761.[9]

The Kennebec shipbuilder Reuben Colburn was in Cambridge that August, and as a seasoned sea captain and merchant, Arnold was well qualified to confer with him on logistics: the expedition would require 200 sturdy bateaux, each capable of carrying six men and their supplies. When Washington received Schuyler's enthusiastic support for the venture, Colburn was instructed to return "with all expedition" to Gardiner, on the Kennebec, and there start work on the bateaux, engage a maintenance company of twenty artificers, carpenters, and guides, and stockpile pork, flour, and salted beef.[10]

On September 14, 1775, Washington entrusted Arnold with "a command of the utmost consequence to the interest and liberties of America." The Virginian left no doubt of the heavy responsibility that he had given the New Englander: on Arnold's "conduct and courage and that of the officers and soldiers detached on this expedition" would depend not only "the success of the present enterprise and your own honor, but the safety and welfare of the whole Continent." In his detailed instructions, Washington urged Arnold to "use all possible expedition as the winter season is now advancing, and the success of this enterprise (under God) depends wholly upon the spirit with which it is pushed, and the favorable disposition of the Canadians and Indians." Given the late start, Washington allowed Arnold the discretion to return "if unforeseen difficulties should arise or if the weather should become so severe as to render it hazardous to proceed in your own judgment and that of your principal officers."[11]

With the siege of Boston proving uneventful, there was no shortage of volunteers keen to go with Arnold: all had to be "active woodsmen, and well acquainted with bateaux." Totaling about 1,050, his force consisted of ten companies of New Englanders shouldering muskets, and another three of riflemen, one of them from Virginia, and the other two from Pennsylvania. Decked out in typical frontier dress of fringed "hunting shirts," Indian-style leggings and moccasins, and armed with weapons that were accurate over far greater distances than the standard smooth-bore musket, the tough, quarrelsome "rifflers" had already established a formidable reputation among friend and foe alike. They were led by Captain Daniel Morgan, a hulking forty-year-old Virginian backwoodsman renowned as a wrestler and Indian-fighter. Nicknamed "the old wagoner," Morgan had served as a teamster on Braddock's expedition, and "on account of some flagrant misbe-havior," incurred the wrath of its quartermaster-general, Sir John St. Clair: he was sentenced to 500 lashes, "well laid on." Morgan liked to joke that the drummer who wielded the whip had miscounted, and missed one stroke, but he "did not think it worthwhile to tell him of his mistake." He was "a very hardy bold fellow," and his riflemen constituted "a chosen part" of a force already drawn from the "hardiest men of the rebel army."[12]

Now ranking as a colonel on the official Continental Army establish-ment, Arnold marched his command to Newburyport, and on September 19 it sailed eastward, packed aboard eleven sloops and schooners. Avoiding British warships, the force entered the Kennebec two days later and by September 22 had reached Gardiner, where the bateaux were waiting. Arnold was concerned to discover that many of the craft were not only shoddily constructed, but smaller than specified; he ordered another twenty to compensate for the shortfall. With no time to lose, the expedition moved upriver to its starting point at Fort Western. Here the army was split into four divisions. These would move out at intervals to avoid congestion along the route ahead, especially at the "carrying places," where the men had to portage their bateaux around falls or rapids, and across stretches of land between waterways. The advanced guard of Morgan's riflemen left on September 25; the other three groups, led by lieutenant-colonels Christopher Greene and Roger Enos, and Major Return Jonathan Meigs, were all under way by the 29th. Reporting to Washington, Arnold estimated the distance to be covered at "about 180 miles," and from the best available intelligence reckoned to complete the march in twenty days.[13]

Arnold's estimates proved wildly optimistic. The distance was closer to 270 miles, and the march took six punishing weeks. It was characterized by hardships that the survivors never forgot, and which they chronicled in a remarkable number of journals and memoirs. From the outset, it was obvious that the cumbersome bateaux were totally unsuited to the swift-flowing, shallow, and rocky Kennebec River; lighter birch-bark canoes would have been preferable. After some two weeks, the expedition was already badly behind schedule, and still negotiating the long and difficult portage of the "Great Carrying Place," stretching between the Kennebec and Dead rivers. Worried that Washington might consider this pace "tardy," Arnold explained how they had been obliged to haul the bateaux and all their provisions "up against a very rapid stream, where you would have taken the men for amphibious animals, as they were great part of the time under water." Considering "the great fatigue in portage," Arnold hoped that Washington would agree that he had "pushed the men as fast as they could possibly bear." Despite such hardships, Arnold testified that his "officers, volunteers and privates in general" had shown the "greatest spirit and industry." He now hoped that the "greatest difficulty" was "already past"; there remained twenty days' worth of provisions for his 950-strong detachment, and he had "no doubt" of reaching the Chaudière River within another eight or ten days, leaving enough food for the last leg to the St. Lawrence and Quebec.[14]

This assessment reckoned without the worsening weather—"excessive heavy rains," bitter frosts, and the first falls of snow. Another two weeks found Arnold and his advanced troops near Lake Mégantic, which formed the headwaters of the Chaudière River. Most of his command was still strung out far behind. Violent downpours had caused water levels to rise, creating a vast swamp in which it was difficult to identify the way ahead. Sodden and chilled from the start, after weeks of hefting the unwieldy bateaux, the men's shoulders were bruised and raw; to add to their miseries, many of them were suffering from diarrhea caused by drinking dirty flood water. Worst of all, they were hungry: built from green pine, the bateaux promptly leaked, spoiling the dried provisions, and several fully loaded craft were lost in the rapids. Washington had offered the option of turning back if conditions proved too tough, but at a council of war on October 23, Arnold and the officers of his leading divisions determined to press onward with the fittest troops; only the "sick and feeble" were to return. Colonels Greene and Enos, heading the rear divisions, were ordered to bring up as many of their men as they could supply with fifteen days' provisions, and send the rest back. Arnold did not doubt that Enos, who was last of all, would "make all possible expedition" to join him, "as it may be the means of preserving the whole detachment." Meanwhile, he would set out himself with fifteen men to reach the nearest Canadian settlement on the Chaudière, and send back food for his famished men.[15]

Like everything else on the Quebec march, this was easier said than done. The aptly named Chaudière—meaning "cauldron" in French—was "amazing rocky, rapid, and dangerous," hurtling them "about twenty miles in two hours"; in these wild waters, three of the bateaux were staved and lost with all their supplies, although "happily no lives." Arnold observed: "This disaster, though unfortunate at first view, we must think a very happy circumstance on the whole and a kind interposition of Providence; for had we proceeded half a mile farther, we must have gone over a prodigious fall which we were not apprised of, and all inevitably perished." Undeterred, and dividing up the remaining supplies, Arnold pushed on with six others in the two remaining bateaux. They reached the French settlements on the night of October 30, received a friendly reception, and early next morning dispatched the provisions.[16]

Arnold's decisive action saved his men from starvation. Richard Vining of East Windsor, Connecticut, readily acknowledged that debt fifty-eight years later, when he applied for a Revolutionary War pension from Congress. Now aged eighty, Vining swore on oath that Arnold had "pushed on to the French inhabitants as fast as possible," where he "procured a cow and sent [it] back to relieve the army." As Vining recalled, this aid was timely: "Previous to this, our company was obliged to kill a dog and eat it for our breakfast, and in the course of that day I killed an owl, and two of my messmates and myself fared in the repast." Others were even more desperate, and resorted to boiling rawhide intended for making moccasins, surviving on the "liquid that they soaked from it for a considerable time." When Arnold's supplies arrived, captains Simeon Thayer and John Topham both "shed tears of joy" at their "happy delivery from the grasping hand of Death."[17]

Arnold had depended on Colonel Enos to keep advancing, but he turned back with his entire division and its badly needed supplies: convinced that the expedition was doomed, his officers had voted against continuing, and he had failed to over-rule them. This irresolution cost Arnold almost a third of his manpower—some 300 men—and caused much bitterness among those who remained with him. Captain Henry Dearborn of New Hampshire prayed that the deserters "might die by the way, or meet with some disaster, equal to the cowardly, dastardly and unfriendly spirit," they had shown "in returning back without orders." At Cambridge, Enos was court-martialed for dereliction of duty; but with none save his own officers available to give evidence, he was acquitted.[18]

Arnold reached the St. Lawrence on November 8, 1775. Within two days, the remainder of his command, now reduced by sickness and defection to about 650 haggard and ragged men, came safely in. Unstinting in praise of his troops, who had cheerfully borne "an amazing deal of fatigue," surmounting all difficulties with the "greatest fortitude," Arnold made no claims for himself, the officer whose determined leadership and inspirational example had brought them through it all. Yet such modesty deceived no one, least of all Washington; as a youngster, he had endured his own share of hardship, trekking across the Appalachians in the winter of 1753–54, and he appreciated the true significance of Arnold's achievement. Learning of the detachment's arrival before Quebec, he wrote: "My thanks are due, and sincerely offered to you, for your enterprising and persevering spirit."[19]

Arnold's expedition to Quebec was immediately recognized as an exceptional feat, and formed the bedrock for his military reputation. Writing to John Hancock, the president of Congress, Major-General Schuyler declared: "Colonel Arnold's march does him great honor." Indeed, Schuyler was convinced: "some future historian will make it the subject of admiration to his readers." Despite Arnold's subsequent notoriety, this prediction was fulfilled: among many later published accounts, including the vivid recollections of participants, the expedition provided the inspiration for a classic American historical novel, Kenneth Roberts' *Arundel* (1929). It had already captured the imagination of Arnold's contemporaries on both sides of the Atlantic: for example, the London-based *Annual Register* which, in its overview of each year's events provided perhaps the most reliable and balanced contemporaneous account of the ongoing American war, left readers of its 1776 issue in no doubt of Colonel Arnold's exploit, observing that his expedition was "considerably distinguished by its novelty, spirit, enterprise . . . by the difficulties that opposed, and the constancy that succeeded in its execution." Even after Arnold's treason, to have marched with him to Quebec was reckoned a proud distinction among Revolutionary War veterans.[20]

On the same day that Arnold reached the St. Lawrence, he received a dispatch from Montgomery, dated October 29, reporting his own steady progress. Arnold's reply revealed that, as he had suspected, the enemy had now been warned of his coming. On October 13, he had written to a friend in Quebec, entrusting the letter (and another for Schuyler) to an Indian believed to be faithful, but who betrayed him. In consequence, the British destroyed all the boats at Point Lévis, on the southern shore of the St. Lawrence and directly opposite Quebec, to prevent him from ferrying his troops over the mile-wide river. Nothing daunted, with the help of local Indians and sympathetic Canadians, Arnold assembled enough canoes and dugouts for a crossing; once before Quebec, he intended to keep its garrison confined "in close quarters" until Montgomery joined him.[21]

Although the British had two warships—the frigate *Lizard* and the smaller *Hunter* sloop—stationed on the river, Arnold was confident of evading them and their patrolling guard boats. For several days, however, the stiff wind whipping over the St. Lawrence stymied any chance of crossing in the fragile canoes. This unavoidable delay ultimately proved costly. While Arnold waited for the wind to drop, Lieutenant-Colonel Allan Maclean arrived at Quebec with about a hundred recruits for a loyalist battalion, the Royal Highland Emigrants; others had recently arrived by ship from Newfoundland. Maclean had hurried his men onwards from Sorel after intercepting Indians carrying Arnold's reply to Montgomery. Maclean was a bold and experienced fighter. In 1746, as an officer in the Jacobite army of Prince Charles Edward Stuart, he had charged with his clan against the redcoats at Culloden. Maclean survived that bloody day to claim the amnesty offered to erstwhile rebel officers, and in July 1758, in the service of King George II, was badly wounded in the bungled assault on the French entrenchments at Ticonderoga. Now, as a Royal Navy officer noted, the veteran Highlander's "activity and exertions" gave new spirit to Quebec's demoralized inhabitants.[22]

Having come so far, and under such trying circumstances, Arnold remained determined to capture Quebec. In a daring operation, mounted on the night of November 13–14, he succeeded in getting some 500 men across the river. They landed west of the city, at the same cove where British Major-General James Wolfe had come ashore before his famous victory in September 1759. Like Wolfe, Arnold arrayed his army on the Plains of Abraham facing Quebec's walls, hoping that its defenders would emerge to fight him. But they wisely stayed behind their fortifications, and when Arnold sent an officer with a flag of truce to summon the city to surrender, he was answered by cannon fire. Trying again next morning, the envoy encountered the same defiant reception, and narrowly escaped with his life. Such a breach of military etiquette, "contrary to humanity and the laws of nations," incensed Arnold. In a letter to Lieutenant-Governor Hector Cramahé, he remonstrated against "an insult" he would not have expected from a private soldier, let alone a senior officer. As it was offered not only to Arnold, but through him to "the United Colonies," it would be "deeply resented."[23]

Without artillery of his own, Arnold could respond with no more than words. When he first arrived before the city, its inhabitants had feared that his army would "advance and enter the gates without resistance." But while Cramahé was described as "a feeble old man . . . uncertain what measures to pursue," his subordinates were made of sterner stuff. On November 16, following a council of war, Captain John Hamilton and the other Royal Navy officers took decisive action: as Arnold's army had given them the slip and was already over the St. Lawrence, they "endeavoured to animate and encourage the inhabitants to take up arms in their own defence" by laying up their ships, disembarking their crews and cannon to defend the city walls, and building barricades across the streets.[24]

Outnumbered by the garrison he was besieging, with just five rounds of ammunition per man, and warned that Maclean intended to sally out against him, Arnold decided to withdraw from Quebec to await the arrival of Montgomery's army, which was now known to have captured St. Johns and Montreal. On November 19, he moved twenty miles up the St. Lawrence to Pointe-aux-Trembles. As his men marched, they saw a small craft passing downriver; aboard was Governor Carleton, bound for Quebec. With its resolute governor in command, and now defended by 1,200 sailors, Highlanders and civilian militia, the city was a far tougher nut to crack than when Arnold had first paraded his little army before its ramparts less than a week earlier. Despite the lengthening odds, Arnold was impatient for Montgomery's arrival, when he expected to "knock up a dust with the garrison at Quebec."[25]

Transported aboard the shipping captured from the British at Sorel, Montgomery's force arrived on December 3. The brigadier brought the warm clothing and munitions that Arnold's men desperately needed, and an artillery company under the New Yorker Captain John Lamb; but after leaving garrisons to secure the posts he had already captured, and with his men's enlistments expiring, Montgomery could contribute only 300 troops, giving the Americans a combined strength of less than 1,000 men. Montgomery was impressed with Arnold's army: it was "an exceeding fine one, inured to fatigue," he informed Schuyler. As a regular soldier of long standing, he noticed "a style of discipline among them much superior to what I have been used to see this campaign." As for Arnold, Montgomery found him to be "active, intelligent, and enterprising." Such approval is all the more telling because Montgomery had recently complained about his own officers. Writing to Schuyler on November 13, the day he occupied Montreal, Montgomery warned that his troops were grumbling and mutinous, a problem that would be solved by better leadership: "I wish some method could be fallen upon of engaging *gentlemen* to serve," he wrote, "a point of honor and more knowledge of the world to be found in that class of men, would greatly reform discipline and render the troops far more tractable."[26]

Montgomery's favorable assessment of Arnold as an officer and gentleman was reciprocated. Arnold admired "the great, amiable, and brave General Montgomery," and gave him unstinting support from the outset. As Arnold's perceptive biographer Willard Wallace observed, "with truly able leaders"— men like Montgomery and Washington—who understood his personality and recognized his qualities, he worked well enough. "It was generally with the second-raters, officers who were often more interested in their promotions than in their jobs," that Arnold encountered problems. Before the Canadian campaign was over, he would become embroiled in a string of confrontations involving ornery subordinates, with damaging and long-lasting consequences.[27]

The combined armies promptly marched back to Quebec and laid siege to the city. Like Arnold, Montgomery was affronted when the British fired on his flag of truce, "a practice unprecedented, even among savages," he complained to Carleton on December 16. By now the rebels were bombarding Quebec with a six-gun battery, but to very little effect; the enemy, meanwhile, were countering with some "very heavy metal." But in any event, as Montgomery told the expedition's second-in-command back in Montreal, Arnold's New Haven neighbor and brother Mason, Major-General David Wooster, the bombardment was just "a blind": the city must be taken by direct assault. For that task, Montgomery only had about 800 men fit for duty, plus "a few ragamuffin Canadians"; but he believed the enemy must struggle to defend such a large circuit, especially as they would not know from where the attack was coming.[28]

With food supplies running low, and as most of Arnold's New Englanders were entitled under their enlistments to leave for home on New Year's Day 1776, there was no time to lose. To maximize surprise, Montgomery and Arnold agreed to attack under cover of the first stormy night. Each of them would lead assault columns from different directions to converge on the Lower Town, which lay outside the main defenses; once established there, their united force would push on into the Upper Town. It was December 30 before the necessary snowstorm finally howled in. But a deserter had warned Carleton of the plan to attack on the first "wild night," and the garrison was alert. At about 5 a.m. on New Year's Eve, after two small parties began diversions, the main bodies under Montgomery and Arnold trudged forward into the blinding blizzard, all the while struggling to shield the priming powder of their muskets and rifles from the wet.[29]

Moving from Wolfe's Cove along the St. Lawrence shoreline, Montgomery's men passed through two barricades to face a blockhouse equipped with cannon. Boldly pushing onward, Montgomery and several of his officers, including his aide-de-camp Captain John MacPherson, were slain by a blast of grapeshot. The general's corpse was later found frozen with one hand raised, beckoning like Ahab, but for men who would not follow. Amid the confusion, the hesitant Captain Donald Campbell ordered a retreat, which soon became a headlong rout. Volunteer Aaron Burr, future vice-president of the United States and killer of Alexander Hamilton in the era's most notorious duel, tried in vain to rally them.[30]

Quebec's defenders could now concentrate on repelling Arnold's column, which had approached through the northern suburb of St. Roque. To reach the first barrier, his men had to pass down a narrow street, facing cannon fire from the front and musketry from houses on either side. Pressing ahead with the "forlorn hope" of thirty men, Arnold soon fell as a ricocheting musket ball pierced his left leg. Regaining his feet, he limped along between two helpers before being obliged to retire, all the while urging on his troops. Assuming command of Arnold's detachment, the rifleman Daniel Morgan surmounted the stockade, only to be confronted by another. Still hoping for a rendezvous with Montgomery's column, Morgan reluctantly agreed to heed his officers' advice against advancing further. Exploiting this halt, Carleton reinforced the threatened sector: caught in a murderous cross-fire, Morgan's force suffered heavy casualties, including the gunner Captain Lamb, who lost "nearly half his face," scraped away by a round of grapeshot. Cut off from all retreat, Morgan and his men reluctantly surrendered.[31]

The assault had been a desperate gamble, and it ended in unmitigated disaster for the Americans; about 100 of them were killed and wounded, while another 400 became prisoners, including many of those men who "with unparalleled fatigue had penetrated Canada" under Arnold. Fighting from behind cover, the British suffered only twenty casualties. That same day, the shaken Captain Campbell, who was widely blamed for the defeat, sent news of the "unfortunate attempt" to General Wooster. In the "greatest distress of mind" and "with bitterness of soul," he reported how "the gallant and amiable General Montgomery was killed [at] the first fire," while Colonel Arnold suffered "the misfortune of having his leg splintered" and sustained "a considerable loss of blood." Writing to Wooster from his hospital bed, when it still remained unclear whether his own detachment had stormed the Lower Town, been "made prisoners, or cut to pieces," Arnold alerted him to their "critical situation," not doubting that the general would forward "all the assistance" in his power.[32]

Despite the expedition's crippling casualties, and his own pain, Arnold had no intention of lifting the siege. As the survivors of the assault streamed back, it seemed likely that the British would march out to complete their victory. Dr. Isaac Senter, who had just extracted the musket ball from Arnold's leg, was among those who now urged him "for his own safety to be carried back into the country" to escape the enemy. But Arnold refused to budge. The doctor reported in his journal: "He would neither be removed, nor suffer a man from the hospital to retreat. He ordered his pistols loaded, with a sword on his bed . . . adding that he was determined to kill as many as possible if they came into the room."[33]

In the panic and confusion following the failed attack on Quebec, many of the disheartened American troops headed home—whether or not their enlistments were up. With just 700 men, Arnold anxiously awaited rein-forcements from Montreal (which the nervous Wooster was reluctant to send) and hoped to raise a regiment among the Canadians. If Quebec was to be taken—and held—he informed Washington in mid-January, then Congress must authorize a far more formidable army of 5,000 men.[34]

Arnold's determination before Quebec won widespread acclaim. Writing to Congress and to Washington, General Wooster marveled that he had "kept up the blockade . . . with half the number of the enemy," a feat that would "scarcely be credited," but which reflected "great honor" on him. Washington had already concluded that, given the heavy losses on December 31, 1775, the continuing siege was "a most favorable circumstance" that gave "fresh proof of Arnold's ability and perseverance in the midst of difficulties." Such praise soon yielded the formal recognition that Arnold craved: on January 10, 1776, Congress approved a motion that he receive its thanks, as well as promotion to the rank of brigadier-general, "for his extraordinary march" to Quebec and "his other spirited exertions." In reply, Arnold requested John Hancock, the president of Congress, to present his sincere appreciation for "the honorable mark of esteem they have been pleased to confer on me, which I shall study to deserve."[35]

By late February, as he informed Washington, Brigadier-General Benedict Arnold was sufficiently recovered to "hobble about" his room, although his wounded leg was still "contracted and weak." Before long, in the recollection of one of his men, Arnold was fit enough to range farther afield, in search of female company. Josiah Sabin, from Fairfield, Connecticut, was among the reinforcements for Arnold's army. Many years later, when he applied for his Revolutionary War pension, he mentioned an unexpected encounter which testifies to his commander's vigorous constitution. Sabin was on guard duty when "General Arnold, who had been out woman hunting beyond the line of sentinels, late at night attempted to pass this declarant to come into quarters." Private Sabin ordered General Arnold to halt and "give the countersign." But as Arnold had left his quarters before the password was issued, he didn't know it, and "was compelled to remain in this situation until the guard was relieved." Despite these embarrassing circumstances, Sabin recalled, Arnold later complimented him "for his faithful performance of duty."[36]

Arnold's customary consideration for the rank-and-file soldier was not always extended to his officers. While blockading Quebec, he became embroiled in a fresh spat with Major John Brown, who had assumed the rank of colonel, insisting that General Montgomery had promised him that promotion. Unlike Arnold, Montgomery clearly thought highly of Brown, having always found him to be "active and intelligent": the stores captured at Chambly in October 1775 had included the colors of the 7th Foot, and the major was awarded the great honor of presenting these prized trophies to Schuyler.[37]

Although Arnold did not dispute Brown's claim, he wrote a letter to Hancock that framed it in a most unflattering light. Arnold maintained that

Montgomery had told him that both Major Brown and Colonel James Easton (that other old enemy) had been publicly accused of plundering the baggage of British officers captured at Sorel, which was "contrary to the articles of capitulation, and to the great scandal of the American Army." In consequence, Montgomery had hesitated to promote Major Brown until he had been cleared of any misconduct. Adopting a sarcastic tone, Arnold did not doubt that both Brown and Easton had "a sufficient share of modest merit" to apply to Congress for promotion, but as the plundering allegation was still a topic of conversation, he believed it would "give great disgust to the Army in general if those gentlemen were promoted before those matters were cleared up." As an experienced attorney and a man who shared Arnold's fierce pride and ambition, Brown countered with a petition to Congress: this declared that the allegations against him and Easton were unfounded slurs—"false, scandalous and malicious." Brown claimed that Arnold had refused to grant him a court of inquiry; he received the same response when he subsequently applied for redress to Wooster, Schuyler, and to a congressional committee sent to investigate the worsening situation in Canada. Appealing to Congress, Brown did not doubt of receiving "satisfaction," having "been injured in the highest manner and the nicest point of honor." Disappointed in his persistent efforts to obtain a hearing, Brown refused to accept defeat and remained Arnold's implacable enemy.[38]

On April 1, 1776, Major-General Wooster finally arrived at Quebec; but despite his admiration for Arnold's determination, he refused to consult him. Next day, Arnold's wounded leg was badly bruised after his horse slipped and fell. The injury gave an excuse to request leave, but as Arnold explained to Schuyler, he would never have quit camp if Wooster had allowed him to take "an active part." Cantankerous and indecisive, the sixty-five-year-old Wooster lasted only a month before he was replaced by Major-General John Thomas. On May 5, Thomas resolved to raise the siege; the following day, when a long-awaited British fleet carrying the first wave of reinforcements—more than 5,000 redcoats and hired auxiliaries from the German territory of Brunswick—reached Quebec, Carleton sallied out in force, and the American withdrawal soon became a panicked rout toward Montreal.[39]

The Patriots' dismal failure before Quebec was balanced by great triumph at Boston. After a lengthy siege, Washington had obliged the British to evacuate the port in mid-April. General William Howe, who had replaced

Thomas Gage as royal commander-in-chief in North America, was finally dislodged by the formidable "train" of artillery that Arnold had helped to capture at Ticonderoga almost a year before. Arriving at the fort in December 1775, the Boston-born Colonel Henry Knox had orchestrated the transportation of some sixty of its cannon and mortars, ferrying them down Lake George, and then onward by ox-drawn sledges across the snow-covered hills of New England. Threatened by powerful gun batteries, Howe and his garrison sailed north for the British base of Halifax, Nova Scotia, to refit in readiness for another campaign.

At Montreal, as Arnold reported to Horatio Gates, the American army degenerated into "a great rabble"—unpaid, ill-fed, poorly led, and above all, "distressed with the small-pox." That terrible disease, which the British *Annual Register* called the "American plague," had left thousands sick and hundreds dead, including General Thomas; as the *Register* observed, "the dread of infection broke in upon every other consideration, and rendered it difficult, if not impracticable, to sustain discipline or preserve order." Arnold was mortified that they had now "lost in one month all the immortal Montgomery was a whole campaign in gaining"; yet he hoped to have "one bout more for the honor of America," taking a stand at the Isle aux Noix to baffle any British invasion via Lake Champlain that summer.[40]

Given his fighting reputation and local knowledge, Arnold would have been a logical choice to command the demoralized Northern Army. But as a brigadier, he lacked sufficient seniority, and the post went instead to Major-General John Sullivan of New Hampshire. An influential politician and lawyer before the war, Sullivan was to prove himself a brave, patriotic, but singularly unlucky soldier in the revolutionary cause. He faced a well-equipped British army, now increased to some 10,000 men, under the supremely confident Major-General John Burgoyne. When Sullivan's troops promptly suffered a sharp defeat at Trois-Rivières, Arnold accepted that the Canadian venture was finally over. On June 13, he urged Sullivan to abandon Canada and secure America before it was too late. In the face of the enemy's superiority, there would "be more honor in making a safe retreat, than [in] hazarding a battle." Arnold added: "These arguments are not urged by fear for my personal safety. I am content to be the last man who quits this country and fall so that my country rise—but let us not fall all together."[41]

On June 15, as Carleton's fleet approached, Arnold evacuated Montreal. He retreated overland to St. Johns, with the enemy snapping at his heels.

Before leaving Montreal, and acting under directions from the commissioners of Congress, Arnold impounded provisions and other goods from
the city's merchants for the use of the American army, and sent them on to
St. Johns via Chambly; although officially sanctioned, this soon involved
him in a controversy that yielded a fresh harvest of critics and would have
lasting repercussions. At a council of war at St. Johns, it was decided to
withdraw to the Isle aux Noix and then back up Lake Champlain to Crown
Point. By the evening of June 18, almost all of the patriot troops had
embarked, save for Arnold and his nineteen-year-old aide, Captain James
Wilkinson. Born in Maryland, and a medical student in Philadelphia when
the war began, Wilkinson had served with a rifle company at the siege of
Boston, before being sent with reinforcements to the army blockading
Quebec; he arrived just in time to join the headlong retreat back to Montreal.
Wilkinson recounted his long and checkered military career in three
volumes of memoirs, published in 1816. Although his readers remained
oblivious of the fact, he had long been an agent in the pay of Spain, earning
a fortune by selling America's secrets. A traitor himself, in his fluently
written *Memoirs* Wilkinson lost no opportunity to cast the arch-villain
Arnold in the worst possible light. Describing the seizure of goods at
Montreal, for example, he described Arnold's actions as more "mercantile
than military," and contrasted his own disquiet with the general's blasé attitude; by winking at irregularities, "Wilky" implied, his unscrupulous superior was guilty of profiteering.[42]

Wilkinson's account of the final act in the American army's evacuation
was likewise slanted to reflect badly on Arnold. As the advance guard of
British troops under Burgoyne neared St. Johns, Arnold stripped the saddle
and bridle from his horse and placed them in a waiting canoe. Leveling a
pistol, he shot his mount to deny it to the enemy. After reluctantly following
suit, Wilkinson climbed into the canoe and grabbed a paddle. Arnold
shoved them off with his own hands before clambering aboard, thereby, as
Wilkinson sneered, "indulging the vanity of being the last man, who
embarked from the shores of the enemy." Yet the calculated and deliberate
show of defiance was typical of Arnold: abiding by his own personal code
of honor, he had kept his promise to General Sullivan. It had undoubtedly
been a narrow escape. Burgoyne reported to Britain's American secretary,
Lord George Germain, that Arnold had almost been captured by his men,
who had cheerfully made forced marches in the hope of catching him.

Their failure was regretted by Germain, who already considered Arnold to have "shown himself the most enterprising man among the rebels."[43]

* * *

By early July 1776, the sickly and demoralized American army was back at Crown Point; it soon after withdrew farther south to Ticonderoga, where the old French defenses were being strengthened by new redoubts and a star-shaped fort atop a dominating height to the east: this became known as Mount Independence, in recognition of the Patriots' bold declaration of July 4. Having rebuffed the rebels, the British now envisaged an offensive of their own. In line with a strategy devised while the redcoats were still block-aded in Boston, the reinforced British army in Canada was to advance along the Lake Champlain–Hudson River corridor to Albany; there, if all went to plan, the northern force would unite with another, under General Howe, which intended to push up the Hudson after capturing New York city. This double blow would split the rebel states along a vertical axis from north to south, isolating New England, which was considered the hub of disaffec-tion, from the rest.[44]

A prerequisite for the proposed invasion from the north was control of Lake Champlain. With no freshwater fleet capable of challenging even the miniature navy of four vessels that the Americans had acquired since the previous summer, the British had to build one as quickly as possible. To parry any such thrust from Canada, the Patriots needed to augment their own shipping on Lake Champlain. During the summer of 1776, the opposing forces raced each other for naval supremacy.

Even before the American retreat from Canada, General Philip Schuyler, as commander of the Northern Department, had appreciated the importance of strengthening the American fleet; while unsuited to active campaigning, he was nevertheless a diligent and effective administrator, with a flair for logistics. In late May, Schuyler initiated a program to construct several shallow-draft gunboats known as gondolas, or "gundalows": carrying a single mast but also equipped with oars, these craft were armed with one cannon mounted in the bows, and two more positioned amidships on either side of the hull. Building work commenced at Skenesborough, on the narrow southern reaches of Lake Champlain, where there was an iron forge and two saw-mills. It was a remote location, and so Congress offered generous wages to lure skilled shipwrights away from the seaports, where they were usually busy fitting out privateer vessels to prey on British shipping. Some were tempted, along with other skilled craftsmen, such as blacksmiths and sailmakers, but most of the woodworkers recruited were humble house carpenters, not specialists.[45]

Arnold, too, worked to bolster the naval force in the Northern Department. On June 13, before evacuating St. Johns, he had the foresight to order the vessels there to be dismantled and sent to Crown Point; their timbers were "all numbered," enabling them to be "easily put together again." Later that month, he had urged on Washington the "utmost importance" of securing Lake Champlain by building at least twenty or thirty gunboats. From their "industry and strength," Arnold warned that the British would "become masters of the lake, unless every nerve on our part is strained to exceed them in a naval armament." To complete the job, it was "absolutely necessary" to employ at least 300 carpenters, 50 of them from Philadelphia, where the workers were already familiar with building such craft for use on the Delaware River.[46]

The new field commander of Schuyler's Northern Army, Major-General Gates, increasingly relied on Arnold's nautical knowledge. Sent to Skenesborough "to give life and spirit to our dock-yard," his energy and expertise motivated the workforce and increased its productivity. Under Arnold's supervision, the shipwrights not only built the specified number of gondolas, but also several "row galleys"—larger and more heavily armed craft constructed to his own design. Knocked together from green timber, and lacking the elegant lines of traditional warships, by early August they nonetheless formed the basis of a respectable flotilla. One officer at Ticonderoga was confident that in another month "our strength on the Lakes will be very considerable."[47]

But while Arnold's workmen were sawing, hammering, and caulking at Skenesborough, some 150 miles to the north the British had also been active, quite literally assembling a fleet of their own at St. Johns. This was a logistical challenge that required all of the Royal Navy's ingenuity. Faced with extensive rapids on the Sorel River, several vessels that had sailed up the St. Lawrence from Quebec were dismantled, so that their components could be hauled overland from Chambly and then reconstructed at the St. Johns shipyard: they included the schooners *Maria* and *Carleton*, but the most impressive vessel was a three-master carrying eighteen 12-pounders, the

Inflexible. This warship—a "phenomenon" that the rebels "never so much as dreamed of"—sailed from St. Johns just twenty-eight days after her keel was laid down there. The relief convoy from England had also brought the pre-cut components for twelve gunboats, which were now reassembled, while others were built from scratch or dragged over the rapids. Meanwhile, the experienced British artificers worked to construct another formidable vessel, the raft-like "radeau" *Thunderer*. As Lieutenant John Starke of the *Maria* testified, the formation of this "great naval armament" within three months constituted a "very extraordinary and singular piece of service." At Quebec, Britain's local naval commander, Captain Charles Douglas, proudly reported that the creation of a fleet of "above thirty fighting vessels of all shapes and sizes" had involved his crews in "prodigies of labour … far beyond the usual limits of their duty." In addition, more than 200 "prime seamen" from the merchant "transport" ships had volunteered to serve in the armed vessels. With sketchy intelligence from the north, the Patriots had little inkling of the armada that would soon be heading their way to contest the dominion of Lake Champlain.[48]

That summer, as the rival workforces labored to finish their fleets, Arnold was obliged to deal with fall-out from his orders to confiscate the property of the Montreal merchants. Despite the confused, hasty evacuation, and the lack of any expert help from a quartermaster or commissary, Arnold had taken pains to keep the congressional commissioners and his superior officers aware of his actions. For example, on June 10 he wrote to Schuyler that he had "sent to St. Johns a quantity of goods for the use of the Army—some bought and some seized." Three days later, he informed General Sullivan that these goods, which had been sent on via Chambly under the care of a "Major Scott" (actually Captain John Budd Scott), had "been broken open, plundered, and huddled together in the greatest confusion." When Scott arrived at Chambly, he had received Sullivan's orders to go to Sorel, entrusting the goods to Colonel Moses Hazen for storage. But Hazen had refused to receive any of the packages: unguarded, they were opened and pilfered. Amid the resulting mess, Arnold explained, it was impossible to distinguish the goods of individual merchants, or to settle their claims. Arnold had no doubt where the blame lay. "This is not the first or last order Colonel Hazen has disobeyed," he declared. Here, Arnold was apparently recalling an incident in late May, when Hazen had opposed his plan to rescue American soldiers captured by the British and their Indian allies at the Cedars, near Montreal. Eight years older than Arnold, Hazen had served as an officer in Rogers' Rangers during the French and Indian War, and, on the basis of hard-earned experience, believed that the prisoners would be butchered before they could be freed. When other officers backed Hazen, the rescue bid had been abandoned, leaving Arnold "highly irritated."[49]

As Arnold informed General Schuyler, Hazen had *eventually* placed sentries over the merchants' goods, as they lay "heaped in piles on the banks of the river," and forwarded "different parcels" to St. Johns; but by then it was too late. Arnold found them "broken open, plundered, and mixed together in the greatest confusion, and [with a] great part missing." After Hazen saw a copy of Arnold's letter to Sullivan, he demanded a court martial to clear his name. The hearing went ahead at Fort Ticonderoga on July 26, and Arnold called Scott as his principal witness; he was incredulous, and outraged, when the court rejected that officer "as so far interested in the event of Colonel Hazen's trial, as to render his testimony inadmissible." Once other witnesses had testified, Arnold repeated his request that Scott, too, be sworn. On the court's refusal, Arnold solemnly protested against its stance "as unprecedented, and I think unjust." Bristling at this criticism of their authority, the court members refused to minute Arnold's protest, "which appears to them illegal, illiberal, and ungentlemanlike." There was more: its president, Colonel Enoch Poor, was instructed to "demand satisfaction" from Arnold, who had "evidently called in question, not only the honor, but the justice likewise of this court" by his "illiberal protest." Poor continued: "you have drawn upon yourself their just resentment, and … nothing but an open acknowledgement of your error will be conceived as satisfactory."[50]

Given the wording of this rebuke, which reflected the language associated with "affairs of honor," and Arnold's own well-known concern for his reputation, the short note that he wrote in response should have surprised no one. Refusing to apologize, and objecting to the court's unjustified "ungenteel and indecent reflections on a superior officer," he issued what amounted to a group challenge to its members:

> This I can assure you, I shall ever, in public or private, be ready to support
> the character of a man of honor; and as your very nice and delicate
> honor, in your apprehension, is injured, you may depend … I will by no

means withhold from any gentleman of the court the satisfaction his nice honor may require.

Deeming this "extraordinary answer" to add "insult to injury," the court sent its proceedings to Gates with a demand for Arnold's arrest. Throughout the trial, its members maintained, he had shown them "contempt and disrespect."[51]

As the row escalated, Arnold was not without sympathizers; revealingly, they included Captain James Wilkinson, who clearly felt very differently about him in the summer of 1776 than his *Memoirs* of forty years later suggest. In a letter to General Schuyler's secretary, Captain Richard Varick, sent from Ticonderoga soon after the Hazen hearing, he maintained that Arnold had been the victim of unwarranted abuse: "General Arnold's character has been here traduced lately in the most villainous, assassin-like manner," he protested. In the interests of justice, Wilkinson, who had recently witnessed Arnold's "conduct in the hour of danger," testified that he had "always found him the intrepid, generous, friendly, upright, honest man." Fortunately for Arnold, his supporters also included Major-General Gates. After perusing the proceedings, Gates forwarded them to Congress and dissolved the court martial—without arresting Arnold. Gates had acted "dictatorially," as he explained to John Hancock, but for a very good reason: "The United States must not be deprived of that excellent officer's service at this important moment."[52]

Impressed by Arnold's zeal in forwarding the construction and manning of the fleet for Lake Champlain, Gates had recently given him a daunting responsibility. Without consulting either Schuyler or Washington, he relayed his decision to Hancock:

General Arnold (who is most perfectly skilled in naval affairs), has most nobly undertaken to command our fleet upon the Lake. With infinite satisfaction, I have commanded the whole of that department to his care, convinced he will add to that brilliant reputation he has so deservedly acquired.

Unaware of Gates's action, Washington had already endorsed it. Command of the fleet would require both courage and activity, he reminded Gates. Then he added: "If assigned to General Arnold, none will doubt of his exertions." On his part, Schuyler was "extremely happy" at Arnold's appointment, even though he superseded his own earlier choice to command the original Lake Champlain flotilla, Captain Jacobus Wynkoop.[53]

Aboard the *Royal Savage*, and still innocent of the new arrangement, the Dutchman countermanded Arnold's orders for the *Liberty* and *Enterprise*, prompting an angry response. It was Wynkoop's duty to obey him, Arnold wrote, adding with mounting exasperation, "you surely must be out of your senses to say that no orders shall be obeyed but yours." If the stubborn Wynkoop refused to comply with his directives, Arnold warned him, "I shall be under the disagreeable necessity of convincing you of your error by immediately arresting you." When Wynkoop protested to Gates, the general responded by ordering Arnold to arrest his predecessor and send him to Ticonderoga. Having established his authority as commodore, Arnold had no interest in persecuting the pompous but patriotic Wynkoop, and interceded with Gates to ensure that he was not dismissed in disgrace.[54]

On August 24, 1776, as the British worked to complete their fleet at St. Johns, Benedict Arnold headed north from Crown Point with ten sloops, schooners, gondolas, and supporting bateaux. Gates had ordered him to wage a defensive war, using his fleet to block an invasion if possible, but avoiding a risky fight against the odds; if heavily outmatched, he should retire to Ticonderoga. After nearly a month of patrolling, Arnold announced his plan to fall back from his advanced position at Isle la Motte to Valcour Island, close to the lake's western shore; the narrow bay there was "a good harbor" that offered both a sheltered anchorage and a strong defensive position: as he explained to Gates, "we shall have the advantage over the enemy." The position could only be approached by a few vessels at once, and they would be exposed to the fire of Arnold's entire fleet. If the enemy proved too strong, retreat was possible. Not doubting that the British aimed to advance soon, Arnold urgently requested a reinforcement of "at least one hundred good seamen." As things stood, he had only a "wretched, motley crew": the marines were "the refuse of every regiment," while few of the seamen "were ever wet with salt water." Despite these deficiencies, Arnold now made it clear that he not only intended to stand and fight, but envisaged an *aggressive* action: he wanted to mount a 6- or 8-inch howitzer in each of his row-galleys; capable of lobbing explosive shells, they would be "of infinitely more service than guns, especially to attack a large vessel." Two weeks later, at Valcour Island, he remained in dire need of ammunition, requesting "doubled-headed" and "chain-shot" to destroy enemy masts and rigging, along with "all the useless old iron that will do for langridge [a crude but murderous close-range projectile]." Last, but not least, Arnold repeated his desperate plea for seasoned crewmen, with "no land lubbers."[55]

Although Arnold was signaling his intention to fight at Valcour, Gates issued no orders for the fleet to shift. Ignorant of naval affairs, he was content to trust to his commodore's experience. On the morning of October 11, Arnold's judgment was tested, as the formidable British fleet rounded Cumberland Head and, with a strong northerly wind filling its sails, headed up the lake. It passed beyond Valcour Island before spotting Arnold's fleet of fifteen vessels, arrayed behind in a line across the bay. The advantage of Arnold's chosen position now became clear: aboard the *Maria*, Governor Carleton was exasperated to discover that the hitherto "favorable" wind had become a hindrance, and "entirely prevented us being able to bring our whole force to engage them." Sailing into the wind, the five British warships struggled to make headway: only the score of oar-powered gunboats, each with a single heavy cannon in its bows, could readily approach the American line; after great efforts, the schooner *Carleton* joined them. But most of the formidable vessels that the British had laboriously built at St. Johns could not even be brought into action: despite his marked inferiority in ships, armament, and manpower, Arnold had succeeded in leveling the odds against him. As the British struggled in vain to deploy their superior firepower, the *Royal Savage* and the row-galleys probed forward to the attack.[56]

Just before noon, Arnold reported, "the engagement became general and very warm." The enemy "beat and rowed up within musket shot of us," continuing "a very hot fire, with round and grape shot, until five o'clock, when they thought proper to retire to about six or seven hundred yards distance, and continued to fire until dark." Early in the fight, the *Royal Savage* drew concentrated British fire; badly damaged, she was run aground and abandoned. The American gondola *Philadelphia* "was hulled in so many places" that she sank soon after the firing ceased, while Arnold's own flagship, the row-galley *Congress*, was riddled by more than twenty shot. The *Washington* galley likewise suffered a pounding. The fight had been all the more desperate because, for all Arnold's pleas, the Patriots still lacked skilled seamen and gunners. In consequence, he added: "I was obliged myself to point most of the guns on board the *Congress*, which I believe did good execution." In fact, Arnold's crews performed well enough to earn the respect of their opponents. By 1 p.m., reported Captain George Pausch of the Hessian artillery, who commanded one of the British gunboats, this "naval battle began to get very serious." As a professional gunner, Pausch conceded that the "cannon of the rebels were well served." Their effectiveness was later clear from the state of the British ships, which had to be "pretty well mended and patched up with boards and stoppers." Owing to the damage inflicted on the British line by this "very unequal cannonade," and because "the rest of the fleet could not be brought up to sustain them," as Carleton reported, they had been ordered to "fall back." At the cost of the *Royal Savage*, which now blazed fiercely, one gunboat sunk outright, and about sixty of his men killed and wounded, Commodore Benedict Arnold had repelled the first attack of the British fleet.[57]

Yet when the firing finally ceased, the battered and bloodied American flotilla remained penned within Valcour Bay: as the British still held their line across it, there seemed precious little prospect of any escape up the lake to Crown Point. Come daylight, the Royal Navy would surely redeem its fighting reputation, and finish the job. Writing to Captain Douglas on October 12, General Burgoyne was confident that the rebels must already have surrendered, or "given us battle upon our terms"; and as Britain's Iroquois allies were lining the lakeside, there could be no escape by land. With a dramatic flourish worthy of an established playwright, Burgoyne added: "You may therefore expect my dear sir, in a day after this news, the important decision of the Lakes." Not for the last time, Gentleman Johnny had underestimated his enemy. Carleton soon set him straight: "to our great mortification," he wrote, "we perceived at day break, that they had found means to escape us unobserved by any of our guard boats or cruisers." For all his frustration, the general acknowledged the "great diligence used by the enemy in getting away from us."[58]

On the evening of the battle, Arnold had consulted his subordinates. As almost three-quarters of their ammunition had been expended, and the enemy was "greatly superior" in ships and men, "it was thought prudent to retire" and make for Crown Point. That night, under cover of a heavy fog and with muffled oars, Arnold's battered craft followed each other in single file close to the western shore, slipping past the British squadron. It was, as Arnold wrote to Gates from Schuyler Island at 8 a.m. on October 12, "a very fortunate escape." The respite was temporary. That day, strong southerly winds hampered both fleets and forced the exhausted Americans to strain at their oars in an effort to gain headway. But as Carleton reported, the following day "the wind sprung up fair" from the north; after a "long chase," the faster-sailing British vessels were able to "get up with the rebels." They swiftly closed in, and near Split Rock Mountain commenced a second pell-mell engagement that lasted for two and a half hours, as both fleets ran south before the wind. By now, in Arnold's words, the *Washington* was in "such a shattered condition," with so many killed and wounded, that she struck her colors after receiving "a few broadsides." His own *Congress* was engaged by three ships—the *Inflexible*, *Maria*, and *Carleton*—carrying a total of forty-four cannon against his eight. Their "incessant fire" was briskly returned, and the uneven combat continued until the "sails, rigging, and hull of the *Congress*" were shredded and splintered. Conscious that he could not prevail against such heavy odds, Arnold ordered his flagship and four gondolas run aground in a bay on the eastern shore, then burned to deny them to the enemy; six other American craft, which had been farther south when the fight commenced, managed to get away. In another act of calculated defiance, Arnold refused to quit the *Congress* until she was well ablaze, leaving her American flag—thirteen stripes, with the Union Jack still in the upper-left canton—flying bravely in the breeze.[59]

Traveling through the woods, and only narrowly avoiding an Indian ambush, that evening Arnold and his crewmen reached Crown Point. Early next morning, Arnold came into Ticonderoga, "exceedingly fatigued and unwell having been without sleep or refreshment for near three days." Greatly relieved, Gates informed Schuyler: "It has pleased Providence to preserve General Arnold. Few men ever met with so many hairbreadth escapes in so short a space of time." At Albany, Captain Varick, too, gave thanks for Arnold's deliverance, trusting that "he will still humble the pride and arrogance of haughty *Britons*, and convince them that one defeat does not dispirit *Americans*." Although Arnold had veered away from the cautious, defensive strategy that he had recommended, Gates did not blame him for the loss of most of the flotilla: indeed, he wrote, "it would be happy for the *United States* had the gallant behavior and steady good conduct of that excellent officer been supported by a fleet in any degree equal to the enemy's."[60]

Inevitably, Arnold had his detractors. They included Brigadier-General William Maxwell of New Jersey. "Scotch Willie" characterized Arnold as "our evil genius to the north," who, "with a good deal of industry, got us clear of all our fine fleet." He accused Arnold of "a pretty piece of admiralship," first allowing himself to be trapped between Valcour Island and the mainland, and then, by ordering a retreat, leaving his fleet "an easy prey." Such assessments reached Congress in Philadelphia, and influenced opinion there: Virginian representative Richard Henry Lee informed Thomas Jefferson that the "fiery, hot, and impetuous" Arnold had sacrificed his fleet by failing to retire in the face of a superior force.[61]

Arnold's British opponents admired his skill and courage. In a letter to Lord George Germain, which was highly critical of Carleton's leadership, Lieutenant-Colonel Gabriel Christie reflected common opinion when he described Arnold as "a spirited fellow . . . by no means ignorant of the naval department." Ungrudging British testimonies were reflected in a thoughtful assessment in the popular *Annual Register*. This maintained that Arnold's conduct had "raised his character still higher than it was before with his countrymen." Here was an unusually versatile warrior: he had "not only acted the part of a brave soldier," but "amply filled that of an able naval commander." Those hard years as a merchant sea captain had not been wasted. Indeed, the *Register* believed that even "the most experienced seaman could not have found a greater variety of resources, by the dexterity of maneuver, evolution, and the most advantageous choice of situation, to compensate for the want of force, than he did." There was high praise, too, for Arnold's "resolution" in fighting on until "his vessels were torn almost to pieces." Above all, his fellow Patriots "chiefly gloried in the dangerous attention he paid to a nice point of honor, in keeping his flag flying, and not quitting his galley till she was in flames, lest the enemy should have boarded and struck it."[62]

But Arnold had salvaged far more than a symbolic victory from defeat. Harping on the destruction of the American fleet, his critics failed to appreciate the full significance of the stubborn engagements on Lake Champlain, and the frantic arms race that had preceded them. True, Arnold's naval command had been virtually eliminated; but its very existence, and willingness to fight, had bought the Patriots crucial time. While the British, through herculean efforts, were assembling their powerful armament at St. Johns, Ticonderoga was being upgraded from a run-down frontier fort to a far more formidable defensive complex. The old French works were repaired and new redoubts built to defend the Ticonderoga peninsula's shoreline. When he arrived there, dog-tired, on October 15, Arnold found about 9,000 men working to complete the fortifications: properly supported, he did not doubt that they would stop the "career" of the enemy; by the end of the month, the extensive new fortifications at Mount Independence were linked to the original site by a substantial pontoon bridge, itself protected by gun batteries. If the British came, they would be met by a reinforced army ensconced behind substantial defenses.[63]

By late October, the prospects for a further British offensive were dwindling. On October 14, the same day that Arnold burned his boats, Guy Carleton conceded as much in a dispatch to Germain. After reporting his face-saving victory over "the rebel fleet upon Lake Champlain," Sir Guy concluded on a less triumphant note: "The season is so far advanced, that I cannot yet pretend to inform your Lordship whether anything further can be done this year." British troops were landed at Crown Point, but it was not until October 28 that the wind permitted Carleton's gunboats to probe south, toward Ticonderoga. A disembarkation was made nearby, but no attack was authorized. The defenders were now numerous and defiant, and as one of them wrote to his friend in Boston, confident of giving "Mr. Carleton a severe drubbing." By then, Sir Guy had already concluded that, with winter fast approaching, it was too late to besiege Ticonderoga, or even refurbish and garrison the ruined fort at Crown Point as an advance post for future operations. By November 3, he had withdrawn all his forces back down Lake Champlain to Canada.[64]

For the outcome of the Revolutionary War, the significance of Carleton's failure to penetrate to the Hudson is hard to exaggerate. By early December 1776, General Howe's southern army had not only ejected Washington's forces from Manhattan, but pursued them through New Jersey, only halting once they had been pushed across the Delaware River. If Carleton's Northern Army had advanced to Albany as intended, taking a position to menace the rear of Washington's depleted and demoralized command, in all probability the rebellion would have been crushed. But the opportunity was lost. After Howe ended his own victorious campaign and went into winter quarters, the resilient Washington riposted with deadly effect: between December 25, 1776 and January 3, 1777, he staged a stunning offensive from Pennsylvania, capturing the Hessian garrison of Trenton, and mauling a British brigade at Princeton. Taken together, those victories revived patriot morale when it had reached its nadir.

Among historians, even Arnold's bitterest critics have been obliged to acknowledge his crucial role in helping to preserve the cause of American liberty at its darkest hour. Such verdicts are all the more telling because they are uttered through gritted teeth. For example, in his *Naval History of the American Revolution*, published in 1913, Gardner W. Allen observed: "It thus came about through a singular instance of the irony of fate, not altogether pleasant to contemplate, that we owe the salvation of our country at a critical juncture to one of the blackest traitors in history."[65]

* * *

Basking in the public acclaim for his gallant exploits at Valcour Island, Brigadier-General Benedict Arnold headed across his home state of Connecticut to reach Providence, Rhode Island, on January 12, 1777. His new task was to help orchestrate a campaign to liberate Newport, which had been captured a month earlier by British and Hessian troops from New York under General Sir Henry Clinton.

In early February, the available manpower at Providence consisted of "about five thousand raw militia"—an inadequate force to pitch against 4,000 enemy regulars. Arnold was nonetheless keen to try as soon as he had strengthened his forces. He informed his friend General Schuyler: "We are exceeding busy in collecting and building boats, and making other necessary preparations, to pass over to Newport, which we shall certainly attempt if we can muster a sufficient number of men." Arnold rode north to Boston, seeking the services of five battalions of Massachusetts Continentals to bolster his army. But Massachusetts had no men to spare for operations on Rhode Island, as Washington had ordered them to Ticonderoga instead. Meanwhile, as Connecticut's troops were slated to undergo mass inoculation against smallpox, Arnold had no choice but to "act on the defensive only."[66]

Back in Providence, on March 10, Arnold's mood of frustration was exacerbated when he unsealed a letter from his mentor, General Washington. As the apologetic commander-in-chief ruefully explained, Congress had decided to promote five brigadiers to the rank of major-general. Despite his seniority in the Continental Army, and his conspicuous combat record at Quebec and on Lake Champlain, Arnold's name was missing from the list. Washington, who had not been consulted about the appointments, assumed that there had been some mistake, and begged Arnold to avoid taking "any hasty steps" before he had been given a chance to investigate and adjust matters. As a long-standing admirer of Arnold, Washington feared that the slight—whether unintentional or deliberate—might provoke his resignation.

When Washington discovered that Arnold had been passed over because Connecticut already had its full quota of two major-generals, he lost no time in writing to him again, offering the consolation that while Congress had followed "a strange mode of reasoning," it had not implied "any want of merit in you." Washington was not alone in his disquiet at Arnold's treatment. Writing to his wife Lucy, the army's chief of artillery, Brigadier-General Henry Knox, was incredulous that, in announcing its "promotion of general officers," Congress should have "skipped over General Arnold who was the eldest [most senior] brigadier." This was, Knox continued, a move that "most infallibly pushes him out of the service."[67]

Unsurprisingly given his touchy temperament, Arnold viewed the announcement in the most negative light, as "a very civil way of requesting my resignation, as unqualified for the office I hold." For Arnold, reputation mattered. He made this plain in his reply to Washington: "The person who, void of the nice feelings of honor, will tamely condescend to give up his rights, and hold a commission at the expense of his reputation, I hold as a disgrace to the army and unworthy of the glorious cause in which we are engaged." In justice to his "own character," and for the "satisfaction" of his friends, Arnold promptly requested a court of inquiry into his conduct. While stung by the "ingratitude" of Congress, Arnold assured Washington that he would avoid any rash action that might harm the patriot cause. Indeed, he added, "every personal injury shall be buried in my zeal for the safety and happiness of my country, in whose cause I have repeatedly fought and bled and am ready at all times to resign my life."[68]

Meanwhile, Arnold's professional disappointments were matched by personal ones. While in Boston, he had begun courting "the heavenly" Miss Elizabeth Deblois. He was hopeful that Lucy Knox, who was asked to pass on Arnold's love letter, supplemented by a whole trunkful of dresses, would soon have it in her power to forward "some favorable intelligence." Until then, he would remain "under the most anxious suspense," all the while undergoing the alternate sensation of "glowing hopes and chilling fears." But Arnold's cause found no favor with the picky Miss Deblois. Lucy soon reported how she had "positively refused to listen to the general"—a "further mortification" that would hit him all too hard.[69]

Whatever her untasted charms, Miss Deblois could not compete with the call of patriotic duty. Arnold was soon given a chance to prove that his promises to bleed and, if need be, die for American liberty were not just empty words. In late April, while Arnold was visiting New Haven, General Howe sent an expedition into Connecticut to destroy the crucial rebel supply depot at Danbury. William Tryon, who had been ousted and then reinstated as royal governor of New York, was commissioned major-general of loyalist troops, and given command of a strike force of nearly 2,000 for a mission that appealed to his hardline instincts and hoarded resentments. About 300 of his men were locally raised provincials; the rest were regulars, detached from six seasoned regiments. They were accompanied by six light field-pieces and a dozen mounted dragoons.[70]

The war's first fighting had flared up in April 1775 after a similar search-and-destroy column was dispatched from Boston into the Massachusetts countryside. On that occasion, the redcoats' homeward march became a murderous gauntlet, after thousands of Yankee militiamen turned out to harry them, sniping from behind the cover of field walls and houses. Yet it seemed that much had changed during two bitter and grueling years of imperial–colonial conflict. The fiery patriotism that had inflamed the Massachusetts militia throughout the war's first summer now burned low. Landing near Norwalk, Connecticut, on the evening of April 25, Tryon's men marched inland virtually unopposed, and swiftly covered the twenty-three miles to Danbury. At his headquarters at Morristown, New Jersey, Washington was depressed by incoming reports that an enemy force could brazenly march through an easily defendable "strong and rough country" without encountering the slightest resistance. He had no doubt that the raiders would achieve their objective.[71]

Next day, April 26, Tryon's troops torched much of Danbury and its labo-riously stockpiled stores, including rum, meat, biscuit, and badly needed tents. The destruction was extensive and depressing: visiting Danbury soon after the conflagration, Connecticut soldier Joseph Plumb Martin found the town "in ashes," its streets greasy with melted fat from burned barrels of salted pork. Congressman John Adams blamed the loss of this "fine maga-zine" on the "stupid, cowardly, Toryfied country people" who had tamely let the enemy "pass without opposition."[72]

Adams, like Washington, underestimated the New Englanders' fighting spirit. Even as Tryon's men set blazes and stove barrels, bands of militia were mustering and plodding doggedly through heavy rains to confront them. First in the field was brigadier-general of militia Gold Selleck Silliman, who was soon reinforced by Continental Major-General David Wooster.

Together, they gathered about 600 men—militia stiffened by a handful of Continentals—at Redding, some eight miles south-east of Danbury. There they were joined by Arnold, who spurred up from New Haven as soon as he heard of the crisis. All three generals pushed on to the village of Bethel, just four miles from Danbury. Mid-morning on April 27, they learned that Tryon had already begun withdrawing to the coast. Wary of the fate of their comrades on the march back from Concord, the British wisely chose a different route to the one they had come by.

With Wooster and 200 men following close behind the British, Arnold and Silliman pushed ahead across country with the majority of their troops, to block the redcoats' path at Ridgefield, ranging their inexperienced and heavily outnumbered militia behind makeshift barricades. General Wooster had been widely castigated for his lackluster performance during the previous year's botched Canadian campaign, but he now made amends, encouraging his nervous militiamen to stand firm against the regulars. He soon fell, mortally wounded by a shot through the groin. Wooster's son refused to leave him. As a British officer conceded, the son "behaved remarkably well, refusing quarter and died by the bayonet." This grievous double loss to one family gave a hint of the true price of liberty for those still prepared to face the enemy. It was also, as the same officer noted, just one of "several instances of astonishing temerity" demonstrated by the rebels, as they maintained a galling fusillade from behind houses, walls, and fences.[73]

Tryon's disciplined troops swiftly surmounted the sketchy defenses at Ridgefield, but not before Arnold had given a striking demonstration of his own courage and conduct. As the British broke through and the defenders fell back, a whole platoon leveled their muskets at Arnold and fired a volley. In a vivid report that gained wide circulation, *The Connecticut Courant* recounted his miraculous deliverance: "the General had his horse shot under him, when the enemy were within ten yards of him, but luckily received no hurt, and recovering himself he drew his pistols, and shot the soldier who was advancing [on him] with his fixed bayonet." It was another opportunity for Arnold to demonstrate "the coolness of his temper." After "disengaging himself from the dead animal, he cut the girth, and throwing the saddle over his back, retreated with so much deliberation, that his enemies, in whose sight this transaction happened, bore testimony to his merit as a soldier." Without doubt, Arnold was lucky to escape unscathed. Locals who salvaged the hide of his slain mount found it perforated by no fewer than nine bullets.[74]

Following the brisk skirmish at Ridgefield, Tryon's increasingly weary troops formed a defensive oblong and rested until daybreak on April 28, before marching on south toward their rendezvous with the shipping waiting in Long Island Sound to ferry them back to New York. Despite his "very close rub" at Ridgefield, Arnold had no intention of letting them go on their way unmolested. Back in the saddle, he rallied the scattered militia and force-marched them to intercept Tryon's column. Arnold was now reinforced by four 6-pounder cannon under his old comrade Eleazer Oswald, who had accompanied him on the expedition to Quebec as his secretary and been captured during the disastrous assault of December 31. Exchanged by the British, Oswald was now lieutenant-colonel of a regiment of artillery commanded by another Quebec veteran, John Lamb. Arnold had a strong personal interest in Lamb's unit: his dead wife's brother, Samuel Mansfield, was among the captains, and also, as Congress was tardy in forwarding enlistment funds, he had loaned Lamb £1,000 to help raise recruits. Bolstered by Oswald's guns, Arnold now took up a strong position commanding the bridge across the Saugatuck River. Rather than fight their way over, the regulars broke into a trot and bypassed the 500-strong blocking force to reach an unguarded upriver ford. With another turn of speed, they headed back down toward the coast, running past the bridge before Arnold could shift his troops across to oppose them.[75]

But even now, Arnold was not content to let the raiders go, and maintained a dogged pursuit. As one well-informed British commentator conceded, given all their exertions, Tryon's men were now "almost exhausted of strength, as well as of ammunition." The prospect of re-embarking from a rocky shore with a persistent enemy snapping at their heels was daunting, and General Tryon, better than anyone, knew the hazards involved. Back in 1758, as a young captain in the 1st Foot Guards, he had been obliged to wade up to his armpits in the sea and cling onto the stern of a boat full of survivors, after another British raiding expedition was overwhelmed and forced to evacuate under fire from St. Cast on the coast of Brittany.[76]

At Compo Hill, within sight of the British shipping, Tryon finally found a strong position where he could turn at bay and make a stand against the persistent rebels. With their cartridge boxes empty, the redcoats were obliged to resort to cold steel. Spearheaded by a dozen-strong squad of volunteers, about 400 of the fittest troops under Brigadier-General Sir William Erskine executed a bayonet charge that utterly scattered their opponents, despite Arnold's best efforts to rally them. Once again, he was in the thick of the fighting, with musketry and grapeshot rattling all around him; once again, he miraculously escaped unscathed, although his replacement mount was not so lucky, taking a shot in the neck. Colonel Lamb, who had arrived at Compo Hill in time to lead an assault on the British artillery, was knocked down as a round of grape tore through his torso. Content with dispersing their pursuers, Tryon's raiders were evacuated without further incident, under cover of their warships' guns.[77]

Although the official British reports heralded the raid as a masterly coup, the reality had been very different. On their return march from Danbury, Tryon's column had been roughly handled, "harassed . . . exceedingly almost the whole way from Ridgefield to near the water-side," and was lucky to get off so lightly. Although the rebels had failed to prevent the crown forces from achieving their objective and re-embarking, they had inflicted nearly 200 casualties on them while suffering far fewer themselves. To Henry Knox, this gave "pleasing proof that the yeomanry of America have not lost the Lexington spirit [and] that an inferior number dare attack a vastly superior number of what are called *British veterans*."[78]

In his own post-combat report, written soon after the British re-embarkation, Arnold paid tribute to the dying Wooster, and conceded that "many of the officers and men behaved well." Vexed that the British had escaped, and writing under "extreme hurry and fatigue," he was less charitable toward the unreliable militia, wishing "never to see another of them in action"—a judgment deemed too harsh by Congress, which chose to suppress it. While Arnold played down his own contribution to the day's fighting, his determined leadership in hounding the raiders was widely acknowledged by other participants. One of his subordinates at Saugatuck, Colonel Hugh Hughes of the quartermaster's department, was deeply impressed by what he witnessed, writing: "General Arnold behaves with the greatest intrepidity and coolness." This was a rare—and formidable—combination in a commander: Hughes added that Arnold kept notably calm, "even to the best language, under the most aggravating circumstances."[79]

Arnold's latest battlefield performance consolidated his reputation on *both* sides of the Atlantic. It is significant that while the British and American newspaper accounts of the affair inevitably put a partisan slant on events, minimizing their own losses and inflating the enemy's, they were unanimous in praising Arnold's bravery. That consensus was echoed by the influential *Annual Register*. Throughout the "sharp" fighting at Ridgefield, it reported, Arnold "displayed his usual intrepidity."[80]

Writing in the wake of the raid, one of Washington's most trusted subordinates, the Rhode Islander Major-General Nathanael Greene, proudly told John Adams: "The enemy gives General Arnold the character of a devilish fighting fellow." Indeed, the feisty Arnold now emerged as a role model that Adams believed other Patriots would do well to emulate. Replying to Greene, the Boston lawyer felt that Arnold's exploits in Connecticut—which had been equaled "by few such scenes in the world"—would make an ideal subject for the first in a projected series of commemorative medals. The design Adams contemplated was a detailed visual record of Arnold's admirable sangfroid. One side would depict "a platoon firing at General Arnold, on horseback, his horse falling dead under him and he deliberately disentangling his feet from the stirrups and taking his pistols out of his holsters before his retreat." In a further test of the engraver's skill, the reverse should show Arnold at Compo Hill, mounted on a fresh horse receiving a wound in its neck from another blast of musketry. Justifying the "utility of medals," Adams believed that they satisfied a universal craving for recognition: "Pride, ambition, and indeed what a philosopher would call vanity, is the strongest passion in human nature, and next to religion, the most operative motive to great actions," he wrote. This was a general observation, but it applied to no one better than Benedict Arnold.[81]

Arnold's medal was never authorized, but his inspired leadership could no longer be ignored: on May 2, 1777, Congress finally raised him to the rank of major-general. As John Adams reported to his wife Abigail, Arnold's promotion recognized his "vigilance, activity, and bravery in the late affair at Connecticut." Congress's action gave Washington "much pleasure," as Arnold had "certainly discovered in every instance where he has had an opportunity, much bravery, activity, and enterprise." However, as the date of Arnold's new commission still left him junior to the five men promoted over his head in February, the old grievance festered, and Washington was worried that "he will not act most probably under those he commanded but a few weeks ago."[82]

While dragging its heels over the issue of Arnold's seniority, Congress did at least go some way to publicly recognize his bravery, when it took the step, on May 20, of voting him a horse as a replacement for the mount recently killed beneath him. It was to be handsomely harnessed—"properly caparisoned . . . as a token of their approbation of his gallant conduct." This was a curiously archaic gesture for such a revolutionary body, better suited to the age of chivalry than the age of reason. At best it was a sop.[83]

3

SARATOGA

It was Benedict Arnold's fate to make enemies who tore at him with the tenacity of mastiffs baiting a bull. None of them was more determined than his old antagonist from the ill-fated Canadian campaign, John Brown. On May 20, 1777, the very day that Congress honored Arnold's bravery in Connecticut by voting him a fine horse, he was obliged to parry Brown's latest thrust in their long-running duel. Although Congress had eventually approved Brown's promotion to lieutenant-colonel, he had failed in his efforts to secure a court of inquiry to clear him of the accusation of pillaging British officers' baggage at Sorel in November 1775, and to prove that, if anyone was guilty of misconduct, it was Arnold. In August 1776, Congress had resolved that Brown's request for an inquiry, made jointly with Arnold's other old enemy, Colonel James Easton, was "reasonable." But when Brown promptly petitioned Major-General Horatio Gates for a hearing, he was brushed off like the outraged members of Moses Hazen's court martial, and for the same reason: that summer, with a British fleet preparing to move up Lake Champlain, Commodore Arnold was indispensable.[1]

Yet Colonel Brown was persistent. In early December, he resumed his offensive against Arnold with another letter to Gates. Having "been led an expensive dance from Generals to Congress, and from Congress to Generals," before finally being referred to the Board of War, Brown now called for Arnold's arrest on no fewer than *thirteen* charges: the allegations ranged from disparaging Brown's character, to plundering the merchants of

Montreal, "suffering small-pox to spread" through the camp at Quebec, and "great misconduct" leading to the loss of the American fleet. There was even an accusation of treachery: back in the summer of 1775, Brown alleged, Arnold had tried to defect to the enemy at St. Johns. Impatient for a response, next day Brown dashed off two more letters to Gates. The general was obviously irritated by Brown's hectoring tone: but since he was "so importunate for an answer in writing," responded that same day, agreeing to lay the petition before Congress. Despite Gates's assurance, Brown forwarded his own copies of their correspondence to Congress, again requesting a "peremptory rule ... for my own as well as General Arnold's trial." Brown's letter, and its enclosures, were duly noted, but no further action was taken.[2]

Frustrated at his continuing inability to vindicate himself and to prove Arnold's villainy, Brown resigned his Continental Army commission in February 1777. But even as a civilian, he continued his vendetta. Changing his strategy, Brown launched a public attack on Arnold, disparaging him in a handbill printed in his hometown of Pittsfield, Massachusetts, on April 12, 1777. This broadside, which repeated the long list of far-fetched allegations sent to Gates, reportedly accused Arnold of resorting to "every possible art to prevent a trial, as if his character was not worth a sixpence." The handbill closed with a sentence that would inevitably acquire a prophetic ring: "Money is this man's god, and to get enough of it he would sacrifice his country."[3]

Brown's extraordinary attack obliged Arnold to defend himself. On May 20, he wrote to the president of Congress, John Hancock, enclosing a copy of the handbill and requesting an inquiry to clear up the matter once and for all. Arnold was "exceeding unhappy to find that after having made every sacrifice of fortune, ease, and domestic happiness to serve my country, I am publicly impeached ... of a catalogue of crimes ... which if true, ought to subject me to disgrace, infamy, and the just resentment of my country." Choosing words that he would resort to again, Arnold continued:

> Conscious of the rectitude of my intentions (however I may have erred in judgment), I must request the favor of Congress to point out some mode by which my conduct, and that of my accusers, particularly Lieutenant-Colonel John Brown's, may be inquired into, and justice done the innocent and injured.

To show that he had nothing to hide, Arnold also requested a committee to examine his accounts, which were "ready for their immediate inspection."[4]

Arnold's plea was referred to the Board of War amid a groundswell of support from delegates. That same day, Virginia's Richard Henry Lee viewed Brown's handbill as part of a deliberate campaign by the Patriots' enemies "to assassinate the characters of the friends of America in every place, and by every means." He added: "At this moment, they are now reading in Congress an audacious attempt of this kind against the brave General Arnold." John Adams, who had spent the evening of May 21 with Arnold at the War Office, assured his wife Abigail that the general, whom the British credited with fighting "like Julius Caesar," had "been basely slandered and libeled." The board was swift to reach a decision. Its members had conferred with Arnold, who laid before them "a variety of original letters, orders, and other papers." Crucially, Arnold's own account was corroborated by board member Charles Carroll, who had been one of the congressional commissioners sent to Canada in 1776. Taken together, the evidence and testimony had given the board "entire satisfaction ... concerning the general's character and conduct, so cruelly and groundlessly aspersed in the publication."[5]

Arnold could not have wished for a more handsome exoneration, yet even now John Brown remained unrepentant, convinced that his arch-enemy was guilty as charged; despite congressional approval of the board's unequivocal finding, his allegations would continue to fester before finally erupting again. In addition, the committee appointed to scrutinize Arnold's accounts failed to reach a clear-cut decision. Some members remained curious to know exactly what *had* happened to $55,000 of the $67,000 Congress had advanced Arnold to cover his expenses for the Canadian campaign. This was certainly a large discrepancy, but while it was all too easy for Arnold's enemies to suggest that he had craftily pocketed government funds, the criticism of civilians failed to recognize harsh military realities. Throughout the period under investigation, from September 1775 to October 1776, Arnold been under intense physical and mental strain, facing a chain of challenges that left scant time for poring over routine accounts. Even at his busiest, Arnold had not shirked essential paperwork: besides leading his men against the enemy and playing an important role in organizing logistics, he had conscientiously reported developments in regular detailed and cogent dispatches to his superiors. While seeking to focus on his primary role as a field officer, required to implement orders under the most trying conditions, Arnold was hampered by the lack of support from an efficient commissary department, capable of undertaking the chore of day-to-day administration. He had made repeated appeals for experienced paymasters and quartermasters, and had even borrowed cash to ensure that soldiers with pockets full of worthless paper currency could buy food. Under all the circumstances, especially the utter chaos of the retreat from Canada, it is little wonder that Arnold's accounts did not add up.[6]

More pressing concerns were now shunting such matters into the background, for the moment at least. That spring, Sir William Howe engaged in a bout of strategic fencing with Washington in New Jersey, attempting to lure him from his strong defensive position at Middlebrook into a major battlefield confrontation. Meanwhile Philadelphia—the political heart of the Revolution—remained an obvious British objective. On June 14, the battle-hardened Arnold was sent off to command militia concentrating on the Delaware River to oppose any attack on that front. Despite his recent criticism of the militia's performance in Connecticut, Arnold called for Pennsylvania's levies to join those of New Jersey, so that Howe could be attacked, as Congressman Francis Lightfoot Lee put it, "while the spirit of the people is so high." Arnold's aggressive leadership helped to assuage fears for Philadelphia. On June 18, John Adams assured his beloved Abigail: "We are under no more apprehensions here than if the British Army was in the Crimea." Adams was confident that America's "Fabius" (as Washington was nicknamed, after the republican Roman general whose evasive strategy had baffled Hannibal of Carthage) would be "slow, but sure," while Arnold "you see, will have at them if he can." Taken together, Washington and Arnold made a formidable team.[7]

Amid all the speculation about where, and when, Howe would strike, Arnold continued to nurse his personal grievances. Following a fresh round of wrangling with Congress, which failed to win any adjustment to his ranking in the list of major-generals, he formally tendered his resignation. Justifying this decision despite the growing seriousness of the military situation, Arnold once again left no doubt that nothing mattered more to him than his personal reputation: "Honor is a sacrifice no man ought to make; as I received [it], so I wish to transmit it inviolate to posterity," he declared.[8]

That same day, July 11, Congress received an urgent request from Washington that Arnold be detached to the Northern Department, to help rally the militia defending the frontiers of New York against a fresh British invasion from Canada. Washington praised Arnold as "active, judicious, and brave"—an officer capable of stiffening the resolve of part-time soldiers. With a 9,000-strong British force under the command of the supremely confident Lieutenant-General John Burgoyne rolling south along the Champlain–Hudson corridor, such charismatic leadership was badly needed to shore up that front. Sniffing the prospect of action, Arnold requested that his resignation be suspended, then immediately headed north.[9]

By July 21, when Arnold joined General Schuyler's army at Fort Edward on the Hudson some forty-five miles north of Albany, Burgoyne had made steady and alarming progress. Fort Ticonderoga, a strongpoint of immense strategic and symbolic significance, was once again under British colors. On July 6, both the old stone fort and the new defenses on Mount Independence were abandoned after Burgoyne's capable chief of artillery, Major-General William Phillips, defied all expectations and established a gun battery on the craggy and undefended summit of Sugar Loaf Hill, thereby dominating the American position. When Ticonderoga's commander, Major-General Arthur St. Clair, summoned a council of war, its members recommended immediate retreat. Most of St. Clair's 2,300-strong garrison reached Fort Edward, after fighting a brisk rear-guard action at Hubbardton on July 7. Leaving behind a strong garrison to hold Ticonderoga, Burgoyne halted at Skenesborough, twenty-odd miles north of Schuyler's troops.[10]

Gentleman Johnny's campaign had begun with a spectacular success; but it soon encountered serious setbacks. While Burgoyne rested his army, Schuyler sent out gangs of axmen to fell trees across the forest track between them: when the crown forces finally resumed their lumbering advance, it took them twenty days to cover as many miles. Even when he reached Fort Edward, on July 29, Burgoyne was obliged to wait for his supplies, which had to be laboriously forwarded from Fort George, at the southern end of Lake George. With only about 4,500 men fit for duty, many of them poorly armed militia, Schuyler retreated five miles to Moses Creek; but Arnold's division, consisting of two brigades of Continental troops, and another of militia, was advanced at Snook Kill, midway between the two armies. With Burgoyne's Iroquois allies prowling the woods, this was a hazardous post: each day, as Arnold reported to Washington, his detachments were "insulted by the Indians," who exacted a rising toll in killed and scalped. But it was not just soldiers who fell under the knife: "a young lady of family" had been abducted near Fort Edward, and was "shot, scalped, stripped, and butchered in the most shocking manner." Arnold was referring to one of the most notorious episodes of Burgoyne's campaign, the murder of Jane McCrea. Although she was betrothed to a Loyalist, the brutal killing of a helpless young woman presented a propaganda gift to the Patriots: faced with the prospect of Burgoyne's "savages" running amok, militiamen who feared for their families now had a personal incentive to turn out and fight him.[11]

Arnold's zeal in confronting Burgoyne failed to impress Congressmen, who remained suspicious that the personal ambitions of army officers did not reflect true republican principles, and that—whatever the color of their coats—swaggering, bullying soldiers posed a real threat to civilian liberties. Such attitudes exploited a distrust of permanent, or "standing," armies, and the use to which such forces might be put by an unscrupulous monarch or military dictator, that was enshrined in "radical Whig" ideology on both sides of the Atlantic. Although the first patriot army had been composed of volunteers enlisted for a year or less, the prospect of a protracted war led to the introduction of longer terms of service in 1776, coupled with cash bounties for recruits: the more closely the Continental Army resembled its professional British and German opponents, the more it was perceived as a potential enemy to American liberties. On August 8, a motion that Arnold's commission as major-general be backdated, as he wished, was defeated by an overwhelming margin of sixteen votes to six. Those voting against now included John Adams. The man who had deemed Arnold worthy of a medal for his distinguished services at Ridgefield and Compo Hill, and undeserving of John Brown's abuse, had become thoroughly disillusioned with Continental officers who increasingly seemed more concerned with their own prestige than with the greater good of the revolutionary cause, selfishly "scrambling for rank and pay like apes for nuts," as he had previously remarked. This lop-sided vote has been identified as a significant turning point for Arnold, who was now already convinced that he and the politicians in Congress held wildly divergent views on the fundamental nature of honor and virtue.[12]

* * *

Had they foreseen the decisive role that Benedict Arnold was about to play in the campaign to thwart Burgoyne's invasion of New York state, and its far-reaching consequences for the cause of American independence, the politicians in far-off Philadelphia might have viewed his case more sympathetically.

Burgoyne had opened his campaign in the firm belief that he would be acting in conjunction with the British army to the south, under Howe's personal command. With no clear instructions from London, instead of cooperating with Burgoyne by moving up the Hudson River from New York, Sir William decided to strike at Philadelphia, calculating that Washington would risk battle to defend the city. Rather than fight his way across rebel-held New Jersey, Howe opted to approach his objective by a long and convoluted sea voyage to Pennsylvania via Chesapeake Bay. Finally embarking from New York in late July, he left behind his second-in-command, Sir Henry Clinton, with no more than a vague permission to assist Burgoyne if he could make a diversion in his favor without imperiling Manhattan's defenses.[13]

As Schuyler's army slowly retreated south before him, crossing to the west bank of the Hudson at Saratoga, falling back first to Stillwater, and then to the Mohawk River just nine miles above Albany, Burgoyne suffered two serious setbacks. Experiencing supply problems, he was tempted by intelligence that stores of food, ammunition, and livestock were at Bennington, in what would soon become Vermont. On August 11, a force of 500 men—a mixture of redcoats, Loyalists, Indians, and horseless Brunswick dragoons—was sent out under a German officer, Lieutenant-Colonel Friedrich Baum. His adviser was the local Loyalist Major Philip Skene, founder of Skenesborough, and owner of the schooner that Arnold had used to raid St. Johns two years before. As he advanced, Baum was harassed by growing numbers of militia, riled up by the murder of Jane McCrea. When Baum requested reinforcements, Burgoyne dispatched Colonel Heinrich Breymann, with 600 men and two field guns. On August 16, before reaching his objective, Baum's force was attacked by New Hampshire militia under Brigadier-General John Stark, another Patriot who had served his military apprenticeship in the hard finishing school of Rogers' Rangers. Deserted by the Indians and Loyalists, Baum's regulars fought on until their ammunition was gone, and then tried to break out with cold steel. But they were overwhelmed by numbers; when Breymann finally arrived, he was rebuffed by the victorious Stark, who had been reinforced by another 400 men under Colonel Seth Warner. At a total cost of 70 casualties, Stark killed, wounded, and captured about 600 of the enemy.[14]

Bennington was a heavy blow to Burgoyne, and it was soon followed by another. While his army continued its sluggish advance, hobbled by an

extensive "train" of artillery and a dragging tail of camp followers, a comple-
mentary supporting force under Lieutenant-Colonel Barry St. Leger
launched a flanking attack from Lake Ontario, intended to reach the Hudson
via the valley of the Mohawk River. By early August, St. Leger's command of
1,700 regulars, Loyalists, and allied Iroquois warriors was besieging the
bastioned strongpoint of Fort Schuyler, and had already fended off a relief
force at the hard-fought battle of Oriskany on August 6. Discouraged by
that bloody encounter, most of General Schuyler's subordinates opposed
detaching any more men from the main army facing Burgoyne. Despite this
prevailing mood of pessimism, Arnold convinced Schuyler to let him head
a fresh attempt to lift the siege, and set out on August 15 with a brigade of
1,200 men. As Arnold advanced, he exuded confidence, issuing a patriotic
proclamation castigating the misdeeds of St. Leger's "banditti," while promising amnesty for all Loyalists who promptly acknowledged the error of
their ways, laid down their arms, and swore allegiance to the United States.
This "most audacious proclamation" by the "rebel General Arnold" clearly
intrigued London newspaper editors, who later presented it to their readers
as a "literary curiosity."[15]

Intelligence suggested that the British force besieging Fort Schuyler was
too formidable to attack. A council of war at German Flats on August 21
urged caution, and Arnold reluctantly abided by its verdict, meanwhile
requesting 1,000 reinforcements: this appeal went to Major-General Gates,
who had now been directed by Congress to replace Schuyler as commander-
in-chief of the Northern Department; Schuyler had been discredited by the
loss of Ticonderoga, while Gates enjoyed far more popularity among the
vocal New England faction in Congress and with the Yankees who formed
the majority of the Northern Army. Learning that the British trenches were
now within just 200 yards of Fort Schuyler's walls, Arnold "determined, at
all events, to hazard a battle" rather than see the garrison sacrificed. On
August 23, as he force-marched his men along the wooded Mohawk Valley,
Arnold encountered a courier bearing tidings from the fort's commandant,
Colonel Peter Gansevoort: on the previous afternoon, the Dutchman wrote,
"several deserters came in, who informed me that General St. Leger, with
his army, was retreating with the utmost precipitation." St. Leger had
decamped after receiving information that "General Burgoyne's army had
been entirely defeated, and that General Arnold was near at hand with a
reinforcement for the garrison of three thousand men with ten pieces of

cannon." This alarming intelligence was transmitted to St. Leger by a "deserter," variously identified as "John Jost Cuyler," "Hanjort Schuyler" or "Hon Jost Schuyler": whoever he was, his ruse raised the siege of Fort Schuyler without further bloodshed.[16]

Although Arnold did not mention it in his correspondence, contemporary evidence suggests that he authorized this subterfuge, and deserves credit for its spectacular success. According to an account published just weeks later, "Jost Cuyler" was among a band of Loyalists led by Lieutenant Walter Butler, sent to "terrify and seduce the inhabitants of the Mohawk Valley." Captured and brought into Arnold's camp, he expected to be executed, but "was released on his parole, to be pardoned on condition of bringing good intelligence from the enemy." Cuyler's brother was kept hostage, to ensure his return. Back at Albany, Dr. James Thacher heard that the idea of sending Cuyler as a "deceptive messenger" was first proposed by his captor, Lieutenant-Colonel John Brooks of Massachusetts, and approved by Arnold. As a finishing touch to his cover story of escaping from Arnold's clutches, Cuyler's coat was shot through with bullets. True to his word, the "impostor" reached the camp of St. Leger's Indians, "where he was well known," and spread his alarming tidings that a strong force of rebels was fast approaching, headed by that fearsome warrior, General Arnold. Mohawk Valley folklore maintains that Cuyler was a "half-wit"; as the Indians believed that such "madmen" enjoyed the gift of prophecy, and as they were already disheartened by their heavy casualties at Oriskany and the tedium of a siege, his news was decisive. They resolved to leave, and advised St. Leger to do likewise. With his force halved, he had no choice but to lift the siege of Fort Schuyler and fall back toward Oswego. A key component of Burgoyne's strategy had been thwarted by Arnold's determination to save the garrison, and his readiness to use deception and call his opponent's bluff.[17]

When Arnold rejoined the Northern Army above Albany, he came under the command of Gates, an officer with whom he had previously worked well, and who had consistently praised his courage and resourcefulness, even saving him from arrest and disgrace. As late as August 24, 1777, when he wrote to inform Gates that St. Leger really was gone from Fort Schuyler, he signed off cordially: "I am, dear General, Your affectionate B. Arnold." In coming weeks, however, their relationship grew strained: Arnold's primary loyalty was to Schuyler, and in a recent letter to Washington, he had regretted "to hear his character has been so unjustly aspersed and calumniated." It's also possible that, as the climactic clash with Burgoyne loomed closer, Arnold was irritated by the knowledge that Congress had refused to settle the question of his seniority, and this undermined his standing within the Northern Army. Arnold's friction with Gates was likely exacerbated by their clashing temperaments. Gates was naturally cautious and defensive-minded; as a former British army officer, he doubted whether the Continentals and militia he now commanded had the spirit and discipline to face Burgoyne's professionals on the open battlefield. The younger, more fiery Arnold, whose gut instinct was to attack whenever opportunity offered, had no such misgivings. Both men would stay true to their characters during the major confrontation that was now looming.[18]

Intent upon pushing on for Albany, sited on the west side of the Hudson River, on September 13 Burgoyne built a pontoon bridge of boats and began shifting his army across from the east bank. Deducting his losses at Bennington, and the garrison left to hold Ticonderoga, he now commanded some 7,000 men. Gates's army was swollen by incoming militia to roughly the same number. It lay entrenched in a strong position just over a mile to the south, on Bemis Heights near Stillwater; here, the broad Hudson protected its right flank, and the more vulnerable left was anchored on dominating high ground. Maintaining his defensive mentality, Gates resolved to await attack behind his fortifications.

Burgoyne obliged him on the chill and foggy morning of September 19, sending forward three columns, incorporating most of his manpower. But as these contingents were operating in broken, wooded terrain, and had no effective means of communication, they presented Gates with an opportunity to overwhelm them individually, before they could unite in support of each other. The wary Gates intended to stay within his earthworks: it was Arnold who persuaded him to send out troops from his left wing, to monitor and harass the advancing enemy. These units were commanded by his old Quebec comrades Daniel Morgan, now the colonel of a battalion of riflemen, and Henry Dearborn, appointed major of a select formation of light infantry. They confronted the redcoats of Burgoyne's central column at the scrubby clearing around the scatter of shacks known as Freeman's Farm. That afternoon, as the engagement escalated, Arnold pushed forward seven more regiments to support them.[19]

Any attempt to reconstruct the "Battle of Freeman's Farm" is complicated by the scrappy, sprawling character of the fighting and the rumpled, forested landscape. When the chevalier de Chastellux toured the battlefield in 1780, he was obliged to confess himself utterly unable to reconcile the ground with elaborate published plans. Yet, as the chevalier discovered, evidence for the sheer intensity of the combat was clear enough on the trunks of trees gashed and pocked by cannon shot and musketry.[20]

Participants on both sides testified to the fight's ferocity. A week later, Colonel Alexander Scammell of the 3rd New Hampshire Regiment wrote that "the battle was as hot, of as long duration and steady as ever happened in America." Scammell had been in "close engagement" for three and a quarter hours, most of that time within musket range of five field pieces "which constantly played upon us with grape and canister shot." He was lucky to escape with one ball through the breech of his light musket, or "fuzee," and another that ripped his tight-fighting overalls.[21]

Among the pine stumps and stubble around Freeman's Farm, three understrength redcoat regiments squared off against relays of Continentals and militia. While the Americans fielded more than twice as many men, this advantage was offset by the professional pride of the British. That ingrained *esprit de corps* fueled the firefight all afternoon, long after it should have fizzled out. Before it ended, the Yankees and New Yorkers had shot the redcoat line to tatters: more than half of the British engaged in that sector were killed or wounded; the 62nd Foot, at the center of the line, sustained a casualty rate of 80 percent without breaking: callow, teenaged ensigns and tough, seasoned rankers alike fell where they stood.

Casualties were especially high among the British officers, and the men of the Royal Artillery, who stuck to their guns with dedication. Both groups offered tempting marks for Morgan's riflemen. As Burgoyne reported, the Virginian and Pennsylvanian sharpshooters "hovered on the flanks" and clambered up into trees behind their own lines, exploiting every momentary gap in the dense clouds of gun-smoke to identify targets and drop them with a single shot. Indeed, that day's fighting was one of few in the Revolutionary War to reflect the enduring popular stereotype of eagle-eyed riflemen sniping hapless redcoats.[22]

Burgoyne maintained his position and so was technically the victor. But his losses told a different story: with more than 600 men killed and wounded, they were double those of his opponents. Gentleman Johnny paid tribute to the valor of his regiments, "in continual and close fire for four hours." Their bravery should not be diminished because "their opponents were irregulars and militia"; in fact, Burgoyne conceded, the rebels too had displayed "a very respectable share" of that same quality. While it is often stated that it was not until the battle of Monmouth Courthouse in June 1778 that American Continentals "came of age" as disciplined troops capable of facing enemy regulars on equal terms, it is clear that they had already passed that test on September 19, 1777. Major Dearborn, whose hand-picked light infantry were involved in the fighting from the start, saw the stubborn engagement as proof of his countrymen's resolve: "I trust we have convinced the British butchers, that the cowardly Yankees can, and where there is a cause for it, will fight," he declared.[23]

The impartial British *Annual Register* likewise highlighted the redcoats' surprise at the unexpected boldness of their opponents "who seemed as eager for action, as careless of danger, and as indifferent with respect to the ground or cover as themselves." That same journal maintained that Arnold led the rebel attack. Indeed, he "sought danger with an eagerness and intrepidity, which though much in his character was at no time more eminently distinguished."[24]

The evidence for Arnold's role at Freeman's Farm is less clear-cut than this account suggests. Two days after the battle, in a letter to Brigadier-General St. Clair, James Wilkinson, who was now a lieutenant-colonel and Gates's deputy-adjutant, stated categorically that "General Arnold was not out of camp during the whole action." The fickle "Wilky" was no longer among Arnold's admirers; in the same letter, he mocked him as a "certain pompous little fellow." Although clearly prejudiced, Wilkinson's blunt statement of Arnold's whereabouts, which was repeated decades later in his *Memoirs*, has been widely credited.[25]

Set against Wilkinson, although also far from unbiased, is the testimony of Arnold's "supernumerary" aide-de-camp, General Schuyler's former secretary, Lieutenant-Colonel Richard Varick. In a letter to Schuyler written on the evening of the action, of which Varick had "remained a spectator to the close," and which was penned while the wounded were still groaning all around him, he emphasized the pivotal role of the troops under Arnold's command. After the opening skirmish involving Morgan's and Dearborn's men, he wrote, "the General [Arnold] had intelligence that the enemy were coming down through the woods in two divisions." As successive battalions were ordered out to counter this move, Varick explained, "almost the whole of Arnold's division . . . were engaged."[26]

While Arnold was instrumental in feeding units into action, Varick said nothing of his actual presence alongside them. Evidence for Arnold's front-line leadership comes from a British participant, volunteer Joshua Pell of the 24th Foot, who noted his appearance on the battlefield toward the end of the afternoon's fighting, when Brigadier-General Simon Fraser came to Burgoyne's aid. "At half past 5 o'clock General Arnold with a detachment of 1,500 men, advanced on our right," Pell noted in his diary, adding that this move was rebuffed by the British grenadier battalion. Whether Pell actually saw Arnold across the smoke-wreathed battlefield or merely repeated hearsay is debatable. Yet the fact that Pell believed that Arnold *was* present is itself significant, and suggestive of the way in which his broader contribution and established reputation influenced British accounts of the fighting.[27]

Arguing over Arnold's precise whereabouts overlooks an underlying truth: as an acting divisional commander, even if he did not lead his men in person, he clearly exercised a key role in promptly sending them where they were most needed. Here, the recollection of Major William Hull of the 8th Massachusetts Regiment is especially revealing. On September 19, Hull commanded an advance party on the left flank. When Morgan was pushed back by Burgoyne, Hull remembered, his corps "was soon reinforced by a number of regiments from the left wing of the army, commanded by General Arnold." Once "the action had recommenced," Arnold rode up to Hull's position, assembled the officers, and called for 300 volunteers to bolster the troops already engaged with the British. Major Hull secured Arnold's permission to leave his post and lead forward the reinforcements. They came under the direction of Brigadier-General Poor of New Hampshire, whose firing line was holding steady in the center and left, but buckling on the right, where "a body of militia were hard-pressed." As Colonel Thaddeus Cook's Connecticut militia began falling back, Hull's volunteers—who had been organized and forwarded on Arnold's initiative—plugged a dangerous gap in the American line, fighting with "signal ardor."[28]

According to Varick, Arnold instigated a far more aggressive engagement than the defensive-minded Gates had envisaged. Three days later, when he again wrote to Schuyler, he had no doubt about the respective contributions of the two generals: "This I am certain of, that Arnold has all the credit for the action on the 19th, for he was ordering out troops to it," while Gates, so Varick maintained, was far away from the fighting, in the hut of the army's surgeon-general, Dr. Jonathan Potts, "back-biting his neighbors." Indeed, if

Gates had complied with Arnold's "repeated desires" for reinforcements, he would have gained a decisive victory. Varick added: "But it is evident to me, he never intended to fight Burgoyne, till Arnold, urged, begged, and entreated him to do it."[29]

As his men were too worn down to renew their assault next day, September 20, Burgoyne instead consolidated his hard-won position at Freeman's Farm with fortifications of his own: they included two extensive fieldworks screening his right flank, constructed from logs laid horizontally on each other; one redoubt was later named after a British officer, Major Alexander Lindsay, earl of Balcarres, the other for a German, Colonel Breymann. Meanwhile, other men toiled to dig makeshift graves for the slain. These pits were too shallow to discourage the wolves that came down from the hills at night to gnaw on the bodies. They were not the only interlopers to flit across the darkened battlefield; Morgan's riflemen crept close to the British lines, taking pot shots at weary sentries.

Once he had strengthened his own position, Burgoyne contemplated renewing his attack on the rebel lines. But on September 21 he received heartening news from Lieutenant-General Clinton, commanding the British garrison of New York city. Clinton's letter was written to guard against the danger of interception. Its true meaning was only revealed if it was covered, or "masked," by another sheet of paper with an hourglass-shaped cut-out: the message was contained in the words within the hourglass. Burgoyne had "lost the old cypher," or mask, but understanding the principle, was able to make out the message. Writing on September 11, Clinton had offered to detach 2,000 men to attack the rebel-held Fort Montgomery in the Hudson Highlands. Such a move might be expected to force Gates to weaken his army by syphoning off manpower to counter the threat to his rear. Sir Henry stated that he *hoped* to launch his offensive in about ten days—the same day, in fact, on which Burgoyne read his encouraging dispatch. But while Clinton mentioned that he was expecting reinforcements, he failed to emphasize that his projected schedule of operations would depend on their timely arrival.[30]

* * *

Clinton's objective lay about forty miles above Manhattan, sited on the east bank of the Hudson River, opposite the jutting mountain known as

Anthony's Nose. In fact, Fort Montgomery was just one half of a larger defensive system: it was separated from another strongpoint, Fort Clinton, by a narrow creek. More compact than its neighbor, Fort Clinton occupied slightly higher ground: any attacking force must therefore subdue both bastions. Commenced in June 1776, the forts lay five miles upriver from King's Ferry, the Continental Army's lowest and most convenient crossing point on the Hudson, and therefore a crucial route for supplies. Despite its obvious strategic importance for the Americans, King's Ferry—like West Point—was still unfortified: in the fall of 1777, forts Montgomery and Clinton were the only significant patriot defenses on the Hudson. If they were eliminated, there would be little to stop a British force from pushing upriver to Albany and beyond.

In the timetable outlined to Burgoyne, Sir Henry Clinton had anticipated starting his offensive on September 21. But the reinforcements he had been awaiting only reached New York on the 24th. When the 1,700 British and German recruits finally began to disembark, Clinton activated his plan. At the first favorable tide, on October 3, he began moving up the Hudson with a force of 3,000 men—a third larger than he had originally intended. They were a mixture of regular troops—both British and German—and regimented loyalist provincials. Clinton relied on the cooperation of his experienced naval colleague, Commodore Sir William Hotham, and the availability of shipping able to carry, land, and protect his force. A list of nineteen merchant vessels, or "transports," had already been compiled in September. Ranging from the 229-ton *Ocean* to the 338-ton *Two Sisters*, they had the combined capacity to shift 4,000 men. All were capable of carrying the "flat-bottomed boats" needed to get the troops ashore. These purpose-built landing craft could each accommodate sixty soldiers seated on benches, besides the sailors who manned the oars. While designed to handle a heavy swell, and well adapted for freshwater operations, they were also light enough to be stacked aboard the transports during longer sea voyages, and then hoisted out quickly when required.[31]

Supporting firepower was provided by a small but potent force of warships. With two decks carrying a total of fifty guns, Hotham's flagship HMS *Preston* made an impressive sight under canvas on the Hudson. In addition, there were two versatile single-decked frigates, the *Tartar* and *Mercury*, respectively carrying twenty-eight and twenty guns, a smaller brig, HMS *Diligent*, and three "row-galleys"—the *Dependence*, *Spitfire*, and

Crane, similar to the gunboats used at Valcour Island. Relying primarily on a single heavy cannon in their bows, the oar-powered galleys could move independently of the wind, while their shallow draft enabled them to operate close inshore. They were ideal for predatory raiding.[32]

While assembling the troops and shipping, great care had been taken to keep the expedition's objective secret. Even within the royal army, it was widely believed to be bound for Long Island Sound, and Clinton had deliberately "given the enemy jealousy for every object but the true one." In planning his campaign, Sir Henry also benefited from the local knowledge of Colonel Beverly Robinson, a prominent Loyalist who had a strong personal stake in its success. Robinson's background underscores the extent to which the American Revolutionary War was also a civil conflict, in which former friends who followed their consciences became enemies. Born in Virginia in 1722, Robinson had moved to New York in his twenties. In 1748, the young merchant pulled off the spectacular feat of marrying Susannah Philipse, heiress to a 60,000-acre share of the vast Philipseburg Manor adjoining the Hudson River. Beverly's older brother John was widely respected as Virginia's treasurer, and the speaker of its elected House of Burgesses. In that role, John Robinson had tendered the burgesses' official thanks to Colonel George Washington and his brother officers in the Virginia Regiment for their stubborn but futile stand against the French and Indians at Fort Necessity in July 1754, an early episode in the vicious colonial bickering that prefaced the official outbreak of war between Britain and France two years later.[33]

Although Beverly Robinson was Washington's senior by ten years, like his brother John he maintained an amicable relationship with the younger man, signing off his letters as "Your affectionate friend and humble servant." In early 1756, when Washington passed through New York city on his way to and from Boston, where he had gone to lobby for his regiment to be upgraded from colonial American to regular British status, Washington was the Robinsons' guest. The lanky, ambitious, and impulsive young colonel tried to emulate his fellow Virginian by securing the hand and fortune of Susannah's sister, Mary Eliza, known as "Polly." Washington's romantic advances, like his bid to secure a prestigious commission as a red-coated officer of the king, were brusquely rejected.[34]

In 1758, Beverly Robinson built a handsome two-story house on the eastern bank of the Hudson, across and just downriver from the conspicuous promontory of West Point. With a brick interior clad in white boarding, surrounded by farmland and lush orchards and served by its own riverfront landing place, the mansion was named "Beverly." It would become better known as "The Robinson House." During what the *Gentleman's Magazine* later characterized as the "unhappy contest between the parent country and her colonies," Robinson refused to renounce his allegiance to King George III. When his sprawling estates and comfortable home were confiscated by the New York state legislature, he joined the British on Manhattan. There he recruited the King's Loyal American Regiment from among his former tenants, with several of his relatives serving under him as officers.[35]

Robinson and his green-coated Loyal Americans were aboard the imposing flotilla that appeared off Verplanck's Point—the eastern terminus of King's Ferry—early on the morning of Sunday, October 5, 1777. Thanks to Clinton's campaign of misinformation, surprise was complete and the heavily outnumbered defenders decamped without firing a shot. Some of Clinton's troops had come upriver in the flat-bottomed boats; others who had been carried aboard the transports now clambered down to take their places in the landing craft, and were swiftly rowed ashore.

The practiced efficiency of these landings reflected an expertise in amphibious warfare that Britain's armed forces had first acquired during the Seven Years' War, and perfected since. Hard lessons learned from blundering raids on the French coast in 1757–58 led directly to the development of the flat boats, and the evolution of drills intended to disembark troops on a hostile shore, and in good enough order to tackle whatever awaited them. The results were impressive: the new proficiency in combined operations permitted the daring nighttime descent of the St. Lawrence River to attack Quebec in 1759, and the large-scale landings that prefaced the conquests of Martinique and Havana in 1762. During 1776, the same techniques had allowed the Royal Navy to deposit powerful British forces on Long Island, Manhattan, and Rhode Island without loss or confusion.[36]

But the landing at Verplanck's Point was just a diversion, intended to deflect attention from the raid's true objectives. Major-General Israel Putnam, who headed about 2,000 American troops at Peekskill, several miles farther up the Hudson's east bank, was duped into assuming that he was the target. The brave, burly Putnam was something of a folk hero for his exploits as a ranger in the savage backwoods warfare waged against the French and their Indian allies during the 1750s. But he was more of a fighter than a thinker, and at fifty-nine was growing old for an active field command.

Before falling back, "Old Put" weakened the garrisons of forts Montgomery and Clinton to reinforce his own command. That left just 600 men—some of them Continentals, but mostly raw militia—to hold both posts.

That same day, October 5, Sir Henry received two messages from Burgoyne that together emphasized the growing seriousness of his situation. The first, dated September 23, was a short and direct response to Clinton's dispatch of September 11. Burgoyne emphasized that "an attack or even the menace of one upon Fort Montgomery would be of great use to him." He added that Clinton's advance would "draw away" a part of Gates's army, and he promised to "follow them close." Burgoyne ended by exhorting his "dear friend" Clinton to act "directly." The second message, written on September 28, was brought in by Captain Colin Campbell of the Loyal Highland Emigrants, who delivered a detailed verbal report of Burgoyne's plight. In the five days since the previous messenger had left camp, this had grown still more desperate. After combat casualties, Burgoyne now fielded fewer than 5,000 men to set against an opposition reckoned to number 12,000 or even 14,000, plus another "considerable body" to his rear. With provisions only expected to last until October 20, Burgoyne now sought Clinton's direct orders either to attack Gates or retreat north to lakes George and Champlain. Burgoyne pointed out that he would never have given up his communication with Fort Ticonderoga if he had not expected to find "a co-operating army at Albany." If he heard nothing by October 12, he would fall back.[37]

Clinton postponed responding until he knew the outcome of his own impending operations. At daybreak on October 6, most of his troops were ferried across to the west bank of the Hudson, landing at Stony Point. An advance guard of 900 men, led by Lieutenant-Colonel Mungo Campbell of the 52nd Foot, commenced a strenuous march over five miles of punishing terrain, skirting the dominating Dunderberg ("Thunder Hill") to secure a pass known as the "Timp"; this approach route was reckoned inaccessible, and had been left undefended. There they were joined by the main body, consisting of another 1,200 men under Brigadier-General John Vaughan. The attackers now forked in two directions: Campbell's men swung out on a seven-mile trek around Bear Mountain to take up a position to the rear of Fort Montgomery, while Vaughan approached Fort Clinton by a shorter and easier route. He was supported by units of the rearguard, brought up by provincial Major-General Tryon, the royal governor of New York, who had recently been chivvied out of Connecticut by Arnold.

After a hard scramble, it was 5 p.m. when Campbell's panting column reached its designated ground. By then, Vaughan's contingent, which was accompanied by Sir Henry Clinton, was already in place and had captured an outlying stone breastwork. Vaughan waited for Campbell's attack on Fort Montgomery before beginning his own on Fort Clinton. As it was impossible to transport field artillery across such difficult terrain, the coordinated assaults were made with "small-arms"—muskets and bayonets—alone; but they were backed by naval gunfire and encouraged by the sight of "the galleys pressing forward with their oars and the frigates crowding every sail to support them." Colonel Campbell was soon killed, but his place was immediately taken, with equal spirit, by his second-in-command, Colonel Robinson. His men, like the other Loyalists of the New York Volunteers and Lieutenant-Colonel Andreas Emmerick's Corps of Chasseurs, advanced under heavy fire with no less determination than the regulars, testimony to their discipline and motivation.

Both forts were stormed, although not before their outnumbered garrisons had inflicted nearly 200 casualties, including 40 killed. According to a New York newspaper, Sir Henry only narrowly escaped a blast of grapeshot. The defenders also lost heavily, with almost two-thirds of them killed, wounded, or captured. The remaining 200 or so escaped under cover of darkness, impulsively torching two precious Continental frigates, the *Montgomery* and the *Congress*, along with some galleys and other vessels lying up the river. Next morning, October 7, Clinton sent a boat north with a flag of truce to summons the surrender of Fort Constitution, a feeble defense established on the low-lying island opposite West Point. For answer, its garrison opened fire on the boat, despite its white flag; like Arnold and Montgomery before Quebec, Clinton was angered by such a blatant breach of military etiquette. On October 8, after the chain and floating boom below Fort Montgomery had been broken, Clinton and Commodore Hotham moved up the Hudson at the head of a strong force to avenge that "insult," only to find Fort Constitution already burned and abandoned. There, another, less formidable chain was sundered by Hotham's artificers, so opening the passage upriver toward Albany.[38]

With the Highlands forts subdued, Clinton replied to Burgoyne's anxious messages with two of his own. His guarded responses, which scarcely suggested a fixed determination to pry open the jaws of the trap that had closed around Gentleman Johnny's beleaguered force, offer a useful insight into the personality of the man who would soon assume command of Britain's army in North America. In 1777, Sir Henry Clinton was thirty-nine years old, middle-aged by eighteenth-century standards, but still young for a lieutenant-general: Howe was forty-eight. The son of Admiral George Clinton, who had become royal governor of New York in 1743, Henry Clinton had spent his boyhood in the colony before returning to England and entering the British army. Aided by aristocratic family connections, Clinton's bravery and intelligence during the Seven Years' War earned him a reputation as a rising young officer. In that conflict's German theater, he served as aide-de-camp to Prince Charles of Brunswick, and reached the rank of colonel. Sent to America as a major-general in 1775, Clinton had shown cool courage and clear-headed leadership amid the shocking carnage of Bunker Hill. Next year he had met with a stinging reverse at Charleston, South Carolina, but he more than made amends that August by devising the bold flanking move that rolled up Washington's troops on Long Island: that action gained him his knighthood and further promotion. Yet Clinton's strengths as an unusually professional soldier were offset by his moody and unpredictable character: he alternated between aggression and timidity, arrogance and self-doubt, brisk action and indecisive dithering. In addition, Sir Henry was a diffident man (or, as he phrased it, "a shy bitch"), who often struggled to strike up friendships with his fellow officers: at times he could be a truculent subordinate, a prickly, uncooperative colleague, and an over-bearing and suspicious commander.[39]

Replying now to Burgoyne, Sir Henry made it clear that, despite achieving what he had offered to do in his letter of September 11, which he modestly hoped would prove "serviceable" to him, it was unrealistic to suppose that he could penetrate to Albany with the small force at his disposal. Carefully noting down his conversation with Burgoyne's messenger, Captain Campbell, Clinton elaborated on his reasoning: "That not having received any instructions from the commander-in-chief [Sir William Howe] relative to the northern army, and unacquainted even of his intentions concerning the operations of that army, excepting his wishes they should get to Albany," he could not presume to give any orders to Burgoyne. The foot-sore Captain Campbell set off on the morning of Tuesday, October 7, to deliver Clinton's pessimistic answer.

As a back-up, much the same message was sent the following evening by another courier, Daniel Taylor, who had already undertaken the hazardous trek through hostile territory to Burgoyne and back again. It is likely that he was the same man mentioned in intelligence forwarded by Israel Putnam, who reported how "one Taylor of middling stature, dark complexion, short brown hair ... is constantly employed as an express from New York to G. Burgoyne." This seasoned messenger was now entrusted with a tiny note—concealed in a hollow silver sphere about the size of a pistol ball—on which Clinton had written his hope that his "little success" would facilitate Burgoyne's operations, and emphasized that only Gates now lay between them. Beyond that, however, he offered nothing more substantial than his hearty wishes for Burgoyne's success.[40]

Taylor had barely started his hazardous hike before he was intercepted by rebel troops. He was misled by the red coats worn by Colonel Samuel Webb's Additional Regiment, and was collared before he realized his error. The Continental Army was often woefully clad, and Webb's men wore captured British uniforms from necessity. Yet even the punctilious George Washington was not above using them as decoys to deliberately deceive the enemy. Under the established Laws of War, which sought to regulate and restrain the conduct of armies, if captured under such circumstances Webb's men could themselves have been regarded as spies and executed.

Daniel Taylor now faced that grim prospect. Taken before Governor George Clinton, he had promptly swallowed the silver ball. To retrieve it, a local physician was summoned and administered "a very strong emetic, calculated to operate either way." As Governor Clinton reported to the New York Council of Safety, this dose had "the desired effect." But Taylor was nothing if not game. Having disgorged the ball, he deftly snatched it back and gulped it down again. Clinton, who had been ejected from Fort Montgomery at bayonet point just days before, was rapidly losing patience: he now threatened to string Taylor up and find the ball by cutting him open, a ploy that "brought it forth" once more. In his subsequent "confession," Taylor revealed that Sir Henry Clinton had instructed him to assure Burgoyne "that they had now the key of America," meaning "the passes through the Highlands of Hudson's River." Despite this bold claim, from the laconic contents of the intercepted note Governor Clinton concluded that Sir Henry was in "no way confident of their being able to form a junction of their armies, though there are nothing but bars [the spiked *chevaux de frise* sunk in the Hudson near New Windsor] between them."[41]

For all the damning evidence against him, Taylor did not face summary justice. He was brought before an official general court martial at New

Windsor on October 13, charged with "lurking about the camp as a spy."
Taylor denied that count, citing his specific instructions to steer well clear
of the enemy's encampments, although he readily admitted to being a
courier. Facing the hangman's halter, Taylor now claimed that he was a first-
lieutenant in Captain Stewart's company of the 9th Foot, a British regiment
serving with Burgoyne. Yet there is no record of a Lieutenant Taylor, or a
Captain Stewart, in the 9th at that time. Seeking to save his neck, Taylor may
have reasoned that while the rebels would have no qualms about hanging a
Loyalist, they might think twice before executing a British officer. If so, he
was mistaken. The court found him guilty as charged and sentenced him to
death. George Clinton approved, and ordered the execution to take place on
the morning of October 17, "when the troops are paraded and before they
march." But Taylor's execution was postponed for a day, by which time the
soldiers had gone: instead of making his exit before hundreds of spectators,
he died more prosaically, "hanged from the limb of an apple tree," watched
by a handful of bystanders.[42]

It was with good reason that Burgoyne had requested all Clinton's
messages to him be sent in "triplicate," to increase the chances that one at
least of the couriers would get through. Not long before Taylor was caught,
a loyalist officer had been arrested under "suspicious circumstances" in
General Putnam's camp at Peekskill. When General Tryon demanded his
return, and threatened dire vengeance if he was harmed, "Old Put" sent a
characteristically blunt response:

> Sir,
>
> Nathan Palmer, a lieutenant in your king's service, was taken in my
> camp as a *spy*, he was tried as a *spy*, he was condemned as a *spy*, and you
> may rest assured, sir, that he will be hanged as a *spy*.
> I have the honor to be . . .,
> P.S. *Afternoon*—He is hanged.

The common fate of Taylor and Palmer illustrates the high risks run by
what Dr. James Thacher described as "messengers or persons in the character of spies," a phrase suggesting that little, if any, distinction was drawn
between them.[43]

Sir Henry Clinton had made better progress than he had expected, but was
wary of over-reaching himself by forging ahead to Albany. He had to secure

the ground that he had taken, and safeguard his own rear lines of communication with New York, especially as he remained unsure of the whereabouts of
Washington's army. Although Clinton now knew that Washington had been
beaten by Howe at Brandywine Creek, near Philadelphia, on September 11, he
had not been crushed: it was still possible that the wily Virginian would send
a detachment eastward to Stony Point, so threatening Clinton's route of withdrawal. To guard against that, Sir Henry dismantled Fort Montgomery and
strengthened the dominating Fort Clinton, enabling his foothold in the
Highlands to be maintained by relatively few men.

During Clinton's absence up the Hudson, his deputy in New York,
Brigadier-General James Robertson, had fallen ill, placing the city's security
in the hands of a Hessian officer known to be overly fond of the bottle. Sir
Henry now headed back downriver to assume personal command. There,
he was alerted to the possibility of doing something more to help Burgoyne,
when Major-General Robert Pigot at Rhode Island offered to spare him
1,000 men from his garrison. Those additional troops allowed Clinton to
make another detachment to the Highlands, and to arrange for six months'
provisions for 5,000 men "to be directly put on board vessels of proper draft
for running up the river to Albany." General Vaughan was detached with
2,000 men, under escort of Captain Sir James Wallace and the versatile,
shallow-draft row-galleys, with "orders to feel his way to General Burgoyne
and do his utmost to assist his operations, or even join him if required."[44]

* * *

While Burgoyne dug in and waited for news of Clinton's progress, the
American army was racked by an unseemly and potentially damaging
dispute between Arnold and Gates. In Colonel Varick's opinion, the underlying cause was Gates's resentment that Arnold's division had acquired "the
honor of beating the enemy on the 19th." In fact, relations between Gates
and his subordinate had been under strain for weeks. On September 10,
Arnold's action in assigning the New York militia to a brigade within his
own division had been countermanded—without any prior notification—in
the next day's general orders. While this breach of protocol was the work of
the officious adjutant-general Colonel Wilkinson, Gates had assured Arnold
that the mistake was his own, and would soon be rectified. Yet nothing was
done. In consequence, as Arnold later complained, he considered himself

"in the ridiculous light of presuming to give orders I had no right to do, and having them publicly contradicted."[45]

The row escalated on September 22, fueled by two separate documents. Reporting the satisfactory outcome of the recent battle to Congress, Gates neglected to mention Arnold, or even allude to the vital contribution made by his division. Instead, Gates phrased his post-action dispatch to imply that he, and not Arnold, had been instrumental in forwarding the successive "detachments" that had backed Morgan's and Dearborn's men, and blocked Burgoyne's offensive.[46]

Arnold's swift and angry response—which Gates never disputed—also offers the clearest contemporaneous evidence for his own crucial role in the fighting of September 19:

> when advice was received that the enemy were approaching, I took the liberty to give it as my opinion that we ought to march out and attack them. You desired me to send Colonel Morgan and the light infantry and support them. I obeyed your orders, and before the action was over, I found it necessary to send out the whole of my division to support the attack. No other troops were engaged that day except Colonel Marshall's regiment of General Pattison's brigade.[47]

Arnold's mood was not improved by a general order issued that same day which arbitrarily removed Morgan's riflemen and Dearborn's light infantry— the "elite" of the army—from his division. Considering himself slighted by this double blow, that same evening Arnold stormed into the modest log hut that served as Gates's headquarters and promptly became embroiled in an ugly slanging match with his commanding officer. In the recollection of James Wilkinson (whose meddling had exacerbated the quarrel), both men resorted to "high words and gross language." Incensed, Arnold now demanded that the role of his division on September 19 be publicly acknowledged, besides that of "particular regiments or persons."[48]

Gates countered by querying whether Arnold still held his major-general's commission: after all, he had recently sent Congress his resignation. Arnold, who had withdrawn his resignation before joining the Northern Army, raged out of the meeting, but only after requesting a pass to Philadelphia for himself and his staff: there, he would join General Washington and hopefully render useful service to his country. But when Gates responded next day, rather than directing that Arnold report to Washington, he gave permission for him to attend Congress, where so many of his own partisans were clustered. When Arnold rejected that solution, Gates issued a "common pass" for him to go wherever he liked: it was immaterial where his troublesome subordinate went, so long as it was far away from the Northern Army.[49]

But Gates had overplayed his hand. Arnold was, according to another of his aides, Colonel Henry Brockholst Livingston, "the life and soul of the troops," who would, to a man "follow him to conquest or death." When word spread that he aimed to quit camp, most of his fellow generals drafted a statement urging him to stay on at such a "critical moment." Arnold eventually agreed to do so, although he remained at loggerheads with Gates. General Schuyler was among those relieved to learn that his "gallant friend General Arnold" would serve until the campaign was decided. He wrote: "Everybody I have spoken to on the subject of the dispute between Gates and him thinks that Arnold has been extremely ill-treated." Schuyler was puzzled by Gates's attitude toward Arnold, predicting that he would "probably be indebted to him for the glory he may acquire by a victory." Or perhaps, Schuyler conjectured, that was the point: Gates was now so confident of beating Burgoyne that he had no intention of sharing the credit.[50]

As Congress alone was empowered to appoint or dismiss senior officers, Gates could not strip Arnold of his rank; in his letters, he continued to address him as "Major-General Arnold." However, by reorganizing his army's command structure, he could deprive him of his division, and thereby his position as second-in-command. Both responsibilities had in fact been temporary, as Arnold was outranked in seniority by Major-General Benjamin Lincoln of Massachusetts, who had been operating away from the main army, in Burgoyne's rear. Lincoln's troops included John Brown, now a colonel of Massachusetts militia. On September 18, Brown led 500 men in a surprise attack on crown forces guarding the portage between Lake George and Ticonderoga; although the old French fort and Mount Independence held out, Brown's men overran the outlying posts, captured about 300 redcoats and Canadians, and released 100 American prisoners. The haul included 200 bateaux, several gunboats, and a sloop: boldly executed and with minimum losses, it was a coup of which Arnold would have been proud.[51]

Lincoln rejoined the army on September 22. Three days later, Gates assigned Lincoln the army's right wing and personally assumed command of the left, so leaving Arnold with nothing. Suspended from command, blanked by Gates, and denied access to headquarters, Arnold stayed on with the army as no more than a volunteer, yet one who still held the prestigious title of "general" and who remained determined to play his part in the impending confrontation with Burgoyne. Despite his "repeated ill treatment" by Gates, which he bluntly blamed on "a spirit of jealousy," Arnold assured him: "I am determined to sacrifice my feelings, present peace and quiet, to the public good, and continue in the army at this critical juncture, when my country needs every support."[52]

* * *

The campaign's crisis was not long in coming. Unknown to Sir Henry Clinton, on October 7—the day after he had stormed the Highland forts—the fate of Burgoyne's army was decided during another bloody encounter at Freeman's Farm, misnamed the "Battle of Bemis Heights" to distinguish it from the earlier fight. Days before, a British council of war had considered the possibility of falling back across the Hudson and re-establishing links with Canada, all the while awaiting the outcome of Clinton's offensive. But the headstrong Burgoyne opposed any suggestion of retreat, and as a compromise solution it was agreed to stage a reconnaissance in force. This move would hopefully gather badly needed forage for the army's draft horses, while testing the strength of the rebel defenses. Just before 11 a.m. that Tuesday, a detachment of more than 2,000 men—mostly British and German regulars, but including clusters of Loyalists, Canadians, and Indians—moved forward from Freeman's Farm.[53]

Since September 25, Arnold had lacked any official command in Gates's army, though at the same time he made clear his determination to stay with his comrades and continue fighting. Although the details are obscure, it seems that by October 7 the dispute between Arnold and Gates had lost much of its heat, not least because two of the men who had previously fanned the flames—Arnold's outspoken champions, Richard Varick and Henry Livingston—had decamped for Albany more than a week before.

The likelihood of a rapprochement between Gates and Arnold gains strong support from a recently discovered letter. It was written just two days after the battle by Lieutenant Nathaniel Bacheller, the adjutant of the New Hampshire militia, whose regiment was ordered to join Arnold's former brigades on the uplands around his headquarters. Bacheller informed his wife that on October 7 Arnold and an aide had ridden out to reconnoiter the reported enemy advance. He wrote: "General Gates soon arrived to our lines and inquired for General Arnold and was told he was out of the lines to view the enemy." Gates then ordered forward one of the units of Arnold's erstwhile division, with a warning to him not to fire on it by mistake. Not long after, Arnold returned from his reconnaissance and reported to Gates that "the enemy design was to take possession of a hill about a quarter of a mile to the west of our lines." Bacheller, who apparently overheard the conversation, added: "General Arnold says to General Gates it is late in the day but let me have men and we will have some fun with them before sun set."[54]

Lieutenant Bacheller's account of Gates and Arnold calmly conferring about how best to counter Burgoyne's advance is certainly credible, especially given the convincing language attributed to Arnold. Yet it runs counter to the widely accepted—and far more dramatic—version of events presented in Wilkinson's *Memoirs*: this maintains that Arnold's intervention was hottempered, rash, and unauthorized. "It was remarked," wrote Wilkinson, that when the fighting began he rode about the camp "betraying great agitation and wrath"; and "it was said"—once again, a resort to rumor—that Arnold "was observed to drink freely." Finally erupting onto the battlefield and "exercising command," Arnold "exposed himself with great folly and temerity," flourishing his sword so wildly that he allegedly wounded an American officer in the head. Wilkinson's portrait of a rampaging, rum-crazed madman proved so striking that it remains the dominant interpretation of Arnold's behavior that afternoon. But it is based on nothing more than gossip, carefully marshaled to prove Wilkinson's case that Arnold "neither rendered service, nor deserved credit on that day."[55]

"Wilky" was not alone in claiming that Arnold acted without Gates's authorization on October 7; but he was unique in stating that his intervention made no difference to the outcome. As will be seen, others were adamant that, by defying Gates, Arnold won him the battle. Contrary to Wilkinson, there is compelling evidence that Arnold provided bold leadership where it was most needed. After the first clash involving Colonel Morgan's light troops on the left, fierce fighting soon erupted on both flanks; increasingly outnumbered, Burgoyne ordered a withdrawal. But the general's messenger was shot before he could deliver his instructions, and the action shifted to the center of the British line, held by Balcarres' red-coated light infantry and Major-General Friedrich Riedesel's blue-clad Brunswickers. The Germans had just rebuffed an assault by Ebenezer Learned's brigade when Benedict Arnold appeared on the scene.

Riding "a small brown horse" loaned by his Wethersfield friend Leonard Chester, and wearing his blue and buff Continental general's uniform, Arnold galloped up and down the American firing line, arraying the troops for a fresh attack. He rode over to the left, where Morgan's marksmen were now trading fire with Balcarres' light infantry. The redcoats there were being steadied by an officer on an iron-gray horse, Brigadier-General Fraser. A Scottish Highlander, Fraser was among the most experienced officers in the British army, with more than thirty years of service in Europe and America, including the celebrated siege of Quebec in 1759. According to Connecticut militiaman Samuel Woodruff, Fraser "was greatly distinguishing himself by his activity" when he was brought down by "one of Colonel Morgan's sharpshooters." Like Fraser, Arnold knew the value of inspirational frontline leadership and accepted the hazards involved. Woodruff maintained that it was Arnold who had ordered Morgan to direct his riflemen to target the gallant Scotsman. As Woodruff recalled, the British "now began reluctantly to give ground, and their line, within a few minutes, appeared broken," although they still "kept up a respectable fire, both of artillery and musketry."[56]

Pursued by Enoch Poor's brigade, the redcoats fell back to the Balcarres Redoubt, which now formed the linchpin of Burgoyne's crooked line. Far from behaving like some Viking berserker, Arnold was thinking coolly: according to Colonel Philip Van Cortlandt of the 2nd New York Regiment, he ordered Brigadier Poor to bring his disorganized men into "better order" before they attacked. But the strongpoint was defended with determination, and Poor's men were rebuffed. Seeing Learned's brigade still off to the left, Arnold galloped between the opposing firing lines to reach it, a daring move that Wilkinson dismissed as a "mad prank." Arriving unscathed, he directed Learned's men to advance and displace the enemy from two log huts that filled the gap between the Balcarres and Breymann redoubts. As more rebel regiments came up, the German-held fieldwork looked increasingly vulnerable: its capture would enable the Americans to roll up Burgoyne's line from right to left. While Morgan's corps attacked the fortification from the front, Arnold targeted the broad rear exit, or "sally port." Despite Breymann's frenzied efforts to steady his men, they buckled before the double-sided onslaught. As Arnold rode into the confused, milling mass, a squad of

Brunswickers fired a last, defiant volley. One musket ball smashed his left leg, the same limb wounded at Quebec, and killed his horse; the falling animal crashed down on top of him, its dead weight adding to his injuries.[57]

The drama of that moment was captured by Oliver Boardman of Colonel Cook's regiment of Connecticut militia. In his journal, he reported how a headlong assault "drove the enemy from their artillery" and continued "upon the full go to the Hessian [sic] camp, where our general little thought of danger, forced his way through and spared none till a ball broke his leg and killed his horse." Boardman's account highlights Arnold's bold leadership, and the proprietorial pride of the men who served under him in what had until recently been his division. With his example, Boardman continued, they were unstoppable: "but his brave men not discouraged with their misfortune drove them from their camp and took it, with their tents standing and pots boiling."[58]

Even as his exultant troops chased after the fleeing Germans, and while he lay pinned down by the body of his horse, Arnold continued to bark out orders and encouragement, shouting "rush on, my brave boys." When Major Dearborn asked him if he was seriously wounded, Arnold mastered his pain for long enough to growl out that he "wished the ball had passed his heart." Had Major-General Benedict Arnold died leading the assault that decided the fate of Burgoyne's invasion, his name would undoubtedly have headed the list of valiant Patriots who had made the ultimate sacrifice for the cause of American liberty. His last moments would have offered the perfect subject for an artist like John Trumbull, whose dramatic brushwork immortalized the deaths of Arnold's friend Dr. Joseph Warren at Bunker Hill, and of his old comrade Richard Montgomery before Quebec.[59]

But Arnold survived. Militiaman Woodruff remembered how one or two others helped him to haul the stricken general from under his fallen horse, place him on a litter, and send him back to Gates's headquarters. Arnold had been wounded at sunset, and darkness soon halted the day's fighting. During the second battle of Freeman's Farm, by the close of which his position had become untenable, Burgoyne's heavily outnumbered troops had again suffered more than 600 casualties in killed, wounded, or captured. His opponents sustained far fewer—perhaps 130 in all. Concentrated within a small area, the carnage was shocking. Massachusetts' Continental Ezra Tilden, who had prayed fervently that his life might be spared, was on picket duty about half a mile behind the fighting, but heard it clearly, "a continual and incessant cracking of small arms and the roaring of cannon, the like I never heard before." Such a din was awful enough, but as Ezra recorded in his diary, actually witnessing "the horrors of war" was "much worse." Next day, as his unit marched toward Saratoga, he not only saw the carcass of Arnold's horse "that was before shot under him," but the naked corpses of combatants strewn all about. He added: "a good many of our men, and the enemy, lie dead at General Gates's head-quarters, others, very badly wounded, just a dying and everything looked sadly with regard to the most wounded creatures."[60]

Reduced to fewer than 4,000 men capable of shouldering a musket, on the evening of October 8 Burgoyne's battered and demoralized little army began a painful retreat northward through the dripping woods, now ablaze with rich fall colors. This dispiriting withdrawal upriver to the village of Saratoga, shadowed by ever-growing swarms of emboldened militiamen, led inevitably to negotiations for a capitulation. Agreement was imminent when, on October 16, Burgoyne threatened to break off talks, alleging that Gates had breached the "cessation of arms" by exaggerating the size of his army. As Colonel Wilkinson explained, the night before "a spy" had reached Burgoyne's camp with news of Clinton's capture of Fort Montgomery, an event that belatedly revived hopes of fighting through to Albany.[61]

The same intelligence, combined with alarming reports that the shallow-draft British "mosquito fleet" had easily negotiated the submerged *chevaux de frise* off New Windsor and then reached Esopus Creek on October 15, raised concern among the rebels. Next day Brigadier Vaughan's troops marched upriver and torched the New York state capital of Kingston: in a "very short time," the *New-York Packet* reported, "that very pleasant and wealthy town was reduced to ashes." At Albany, Dr. Thacher noted the "prevalent opinion" that "by taking advantage of wind and tide," the British could be conveyed there within five or six hours, after which a march of twenty miles would take them to Stillwater, so causing Gates "inexpressible embarrassment and difficulty, by placing him between two armies, and thereby extricating Burgoyne from his perilous situation."[62]

Governor Clinton was no longer so sure that there would be no union between Sir Henry's men and Burgoyne's; on October 16, as the British neared Kingston, he warned Horatio Gates to "take such steps as may appear to you necessary to render the acquisition of this town of as little importance as possible." He added: "It is possible the enemy may push on to

Albany." But this "menacing prospect," as Dr. Thacher called it, never materialized. The limit of Vaughan's progress was Livingston's Manor, still forty-
five miles short of Albany; beyond that, the pilots of his transports refused
to go. Unable to make contact with Burgoyne, and with substantial rebel
forces now gathering on both banks of the narrowing Hudson, Vaughan
dropped back downriver to Fort Clinton.[63]

As the last hope of help from the south faded, Burgoyne's army formally
surrendered near Saratoga on Friday, October 17, 1777. It was a moment
that witnesses never forgot. In his journal, Oliver Boardman noted: "The
hand of Providence worked wonderfully in favor of America this day."
That afternoon he watched as Burgoyne's men "marched through our army
that was paraded on the right and left," before a guard escorted them to
Boston. In a later note, he wrote: "It was a glorious sight to see the haughty
Britons march out and surrender their arms to an army which but a little
before, they despised and called poltroons."[64]

Burgoyne had capitulated, but the final terms of the "Convention" were
far more lenient than he had expected—strong evidence that Gates was
unsettled and pressurized by the belated, but determined, British push for
Albany. One royal officer maintained that the rebels were so apprehensive
about Vaughan's move up the Hudson that, even when they received certain
intelligence of his withdrawal, it "scarce gained credit," and such concerns
influenced the negotiations. That was certainly how events were interpreted
both by Colonel Samuel Webb (who considered that Gates had granted
Burgoyne "much easier terms than he need have done," causing "much
uneasiness") and by Congress, which eventually overruled them. Instead of
being shipped home, where they could assume the duties of troops sent to
replace them in America, Congress decided that the officers and men of the
"Convention Army" should be impounded as prisoners of war at Cambridge,
just outside Boston.[65]

Even if he could not save Burgoyne, Sir Henry Clinton was determined
at least to keep what he had won—to "retain the footing we were now
possessed of in the Highlands." Yet even that hope was dashed when Howe,
as commander-in-chief, ordered Clinton to send him a sizeable reinforcement from his army, including several units operating under Vaughan. On
October 22, Clinton reluctantly ordered Vaughan to return from the
Highlands without delay. As if this was not galling enough, Clinton soon
received a further order from Howe to dismantle Fort Clinton. As Sir Henry

bitterly recalled: "I was under the mortifying necessity of relinquishing the Highlands and all the other passes over the Hudson, to be reoccupied by the rebels whenever they saw proper." Many years later, Clinton still struggled to contain his anger that the surprisingly effective lunge up the Hudson had proved so contrary to Howe's wishes:

> I had … flattered myself with hopes that, as soon as he found I had opened the important door to the Hudson, he would have strained every nerve to keep it so and prevent the rebels from ever shutting it again— even though he had been obliged to place the back of his whole army against it. And I hope I shall be pardoned if I presume to suggest that, had this been done, it would most probably have finished the war.

Against that major strategic gain, Sir Henry maintained, even the loss of Burgoyne's army might have been seen as "a necessary sacrifice."[66]

For all its deeply disappointing outcome, Clinton's well-planned and briskly executed Highlands campaign suggested the viability of further blows against the same objective. That October, British regulars and regimented American Loyalists had both demonstrated their ability to operate far upriver in conjunction with the Royal Navy, surmounting punishing, mountainous terrain, and then swiftly storming their objectives without resorting to a formal siege demanding cumbersome artillery. Already tried and tested, such a venture might work again: back in New York city, reopening the "door to the Hudson" would become Sir Henry's enduring objective. But the ease with which he had taken forts Montgomery and Clinton had alerted George Washington and Congress to their weaknesses, and that underlay the decision to lose no more time in siting the Hudson's fortifications where they always should have been: West Point.

* * *

Major-General Benedict Arnold was denied the satisfaction of witnessing Burgoyne's surrender, the outcome for which he had fought so hard and so effectively. Following his wounding, he was carted back to the busy base hospital at Albany, a complex established by the British during the French and Indian War. Now it was "crowded with officers and soldiers from the field of battle"—British, Germans, and Americans, all under the same roof, but tended by their own surgeons. With more than a thousand wounded and sick in the city, it had been necessary to accommodate patients in the Dutch church and private homes. Dr. Thacher was among the thirty surgeons and their mates who were constantly employed in "amputating limbs, trepanning fractured skulls, and dressing the most formidable wounds."[67]

Arnold's new wound was clearly more serious and complicated than the injury he had sustained at Quebec. The bone was splintered and refused to knit. Bed-bound, racked with pain, and facing the grim prospect of amputation should his leg turn gangrenous, Arnold grew increasingly depressed and irritable. Far from demonstrating the stoicism he had shown at Quebec, he vented his frustration on the medical men who were trying to cure him. Dr. Thacher, who tended Arnold on the night of October 11, noted that his famous patient, "whose leg was badly fractured by a musket ball," was "very peevish, and impatient under his misfortunes." Months later, on Christmas Eve, the Northern Department's surgeon-general James Browne had the same unfavorable impression of the "gallant general Arnold," contrasting his ill-tempered outbursts with the calm, gentlemanly resolution of another high-ranking casualty, General Lincoln. And while Arnold's wound was initially less dangerous than Lincoln's, it was taking longer to heal. Arnold blamed his doctors: "He abuses us for a set of ignorant pretenders and empirics," Browne grumbled. But perhaps the damage to Arnold was not merely physical: although the condition was not recognized in 1777, it is possible that he was also suffering from post-traumatic stress disorder. Given what he had endured during more than two years of active service, culminating in the condensed horror of the Albany hospital, with all its disturbing sights, sounds, and smells, such a diagnosis is not implausible.[68]

Arnold's temper was not improved by a deepening sense of injustice, and a feeling that his services were being marginalized. While he lay helpless and hospitalized, other men were reaping the recognition and rewards that should by rights have been his. Now at least, Arnold's contribution, and the seriousness of his wound, had been too conspicuous for Gates to ignore him completely. In his report to Congress on October 12, he could not refrain from mentioning "the gallant General Arnold." On November 4, Congress officially passed a vote thanking Gates, Lincoln, *and* Arnold "for their brave and successful efforts in support of the independence of their country." But Congress still did nothing to address the niggling question of Arnold's seniority within his rank as major-general. This failure was all the more galling because James Wilkinson, a junior lieutenant-colonel, had been elevated to brigadier-general simply because the euphoric Gates had lauded him as a "gallant officer, and a promising military genius," and picked him for the plum job of delivering his victory dispatches.[69]

Horatio Gates's command of the army that eliminated Burgoyne brought immense prestige, not least among those members of Congress who saw him as their biddable tool. It earned him a gold medal—the very honor that had been contemplated for Arnold in acknowledgment of his sterling services in Connecticut. Among the veterans of the Continental Army, there was more skepticism, grounded on a belief that the real credit for Burgoyne's surrender lay elsewhere. Nathanael Greene later dismissed Gates as lucky—"a mere child of fortune"—who had reaped the rewards of other men's labors. Indeed, Greene believed, "the foundation of all the Northern successes" was laid by Schuyler long before Gates replaced him, while "Arnold and Lincoln were the principal instruments in completing the work." Although influenced by Gates's growing rivalry with George Washington for command of the Continental Army, Greene's comment nonetheless underlined the truth that—whatever Congress might think—Burgoyne had been defeated by a long-term team effort; Gates had played his part but so, too, had others.[70]

Had Arnold known of it, he might have taken some consolation from British reaction to Burgoyne's downfall. When news of Saratoga reached London in early December, newspaper coverage reflected the accounts of veterans who virtually ignored Gates and instead highlighted Arnold's dynamic presence. Initial reports of the fighting on October 7 even referred to "Arnold's army" and claimed that he "was certainly killed," owing to "a wound in his thigh, which turned to an almost instantaneous mortification." Soon after, readers learned how the "brave General Arnold" was in fact still alive, although his leg was "terribly shattered."[71]

Ironically, the greatest plaudits for Arnold came from the general he had helped to humble. In seeking to explain his disastrous defeat to his professional colleagues and countrymen at large, Gentleman Johnny emphasized Arnold's role. On arriving at Albany, but as a captive not a conqueror, Burgoyne wrote to Sir Henry Clinton, unfairly attributing his defeat on October 7 to the lackluster performance of his German regiments: had they "fought like the British, Mr. Arnold (for it was his doing) would have paid dear for coming out of his lines," he wrote. In a detailed explanation to Parliament in 1779, Burgoyne was more specific:

I have reason to believe my disappointment on that day proceeded from an uncommon circumstance in the conduct of the enemy. Mr. Gates, as I have been informed, had determined to receive the attack in his lines; Mr. Arnold, who commanded on the left, foreseeing the danger of being turned, advanced without consultation with his general, and gave, instead of receiving battle.

With hindsight—and a good measure of wishful thinking—Burgoyne believed that if Gates's defensive stance had been followed, his own troops "should in a few hours have gained a position that, in spite of the enemy's numbers, would have put them in my power." Burgoyne's deputy quartermaster-general, Captain John Money, also testified that rebel officers had confirmed to him that "General Arnold had marched out on the 7 October, without orders from General Gates." During the winter of 1777–78, much the same story was circulating in George Washington's encampment at Valley Forge, near Philadelphia: one of the general's aides, Colonel Tench Tilghman, reported how, on October 7, Arnold had "sent Morgan to begin the engagement and pawned his honor to support him." When Arnold advanced to help his old comrade, and Gates sent him "word to halt, he returned for answer, that he had promised Morgan to support him and support him he would by God." Tilghman continued: "Victory crowned the work, and the surrender was the consequence of it."[72]

Whether or not such talk was actually true, Burgoyne eagerly seized on it to mitigate his own defeat: to be beaten by Horatio Gates, of whom few Britons had even heard, was inexcusable; but to be worsted by the proverbially intrepid Benedict Arnold, whose name was already familiar to every follower of American affairs—well, that was quite a different matter.

When Burgoyne testified before Parliament, the American War of Independence had already been transformed by the most significant consequence of his defeat. Itching for an opportunity to avenge France's humiliating losses during the Seven Years' War, Louis XVI and his ministers had watched the worsening quarrel between Britain and her American colonists with close interest. Once fighting erupted, they had covertly sent cash and munitions crucial to sustaining the patriot war effort: thousands of the muskets carried by American troops at Brandywine and Freeman's Farm were manufactured in French workshops. Yet Britain's old enemy hung back from open intervention on the side of the rebels until the startling news of

Saratoga, which reached Paris on December 3, 1777, removed any last hesitation. French and American diplomats signed treaties of "Commerce and
Alliance" on February 6, 1778, but the military implications were already
clear enough. Henceforth, the British Empire would face a global conflict
that stretched its resources to the limit: quelling the American insurrection
became secondary to other priorities—defending the prized sugar islands
of the West Indies, and even Britain itself.[73]

If, as scholars agree, the Saratoga campaign marked a truly pivotal
moment in America's struggle for independence, it was no less significant
for Benedict Arnold. The man who had done as much as anyone to defeat
Burgoyne believed himself denied the recognition he deserved. Others
concurred. While he could never "attempt to justify" Arnold's treason, one
early historian of Burgoyne's campaign, Charles Neilson, felt it only fair to
inform his readers: "it has been the common belief, especially in this
[northern] part of the Union, that one cause of his turning a traitor as he
did, was in consequence of his not having received due credit for his
management and gallantry in and during the truly 'memorable battles' on
Bemis's Heights."[74]

The long months that Arnold spent recuperating only compounded a
growing mood of grievance. His bitterness was exacerbated by the gravity of
his injuries. The ricocheting gunshot suffered before Quebec had bequeathed
little more than a slight limp; but this latest wound was of a different magnitude. While Arnold was lucky not to lose his leg, as the torn muscles withered
it shrank by two inches, obliging him to resort to awkward, built-up footwear. Arnold's "old acquaintance" observed: "since his wound in the leg, he
appears rather shorter, and wears the heel of one shoe much higher than the
other." The man who had once been renowned for his athleticism would
never again strap on his skates to glide gracefully across New England's
ponds. Each day, as he stumped about like a cripple, Major-General Benedict
Arnold was reminded of the high personal price that he had paid for
American liberty, and of the grating ingratitude of his civilian countrymen.[75]

4

PHILADELPHIA

On November 29, 1777, while Benedict Arnold lay bed-bound in Albany, the new president of Congress, Henry Laurens, sent him news that he had long awaited. Following the recommendation of a board of officers "for settling rank and precedence," a resolution had been passed to restore Arnold to his seniority among the Continental Army's major-generals. Forwarding this formal ruling, Laurens added a personal message: "Permit me to assure you, Sir, that I respect your character as a citizen and soldier of the United States of America, that I rejoice at your recovery from the dangerous wounds which you lately received in the defense of your country, that I wish you perfect health and a continued succession of honor, that I am with very great respect and esteem …" Arnold had previously pursued this outcome with a persistence that bordered on obsession, arguing that his prized honor and reputation depended on it. Yet now that the promotion was finally approved, Arnold seemed indifferent: when he eventually replied to Laurens, early in the new year, he did not even mention it; after three months immobilized by his injuries, the real question was when, if ever, he would be capable of exercising his rank and commanding a division in the field.[1]

George Washington did not forward Arnold's new commission until January 20, 1778; he had been unable to do so earlier, owing to pressure of business and a lack of printed forms. Signed by Laurens, the commission was backdated to February 17, 1777. In consequence, Washington told him, "you will find that you are restored to the rank you claim in the army." Of course, this meant that Arnold now outranked those generals previously promoted over his head. One of them was Benjamin Lincoln of Massachusetts. That same day Washington wrote to him, explaining the belated adjustment: "General Arnold is restored to a violated right; and the restitution, I hope, will be considered by every gentleman concerned, as I am sure it will be by you, as an act of necessary justice." With the issue of Arnold's rank resolved, Washington was anxious to learn when he would once more be up on his feet: "as soon as your situation will permit, I request that you will repair to this army, it being my earnest wish to have your services the ensuing campaign."[2]

When he replied to Laurens in early January, Arnold had hoped that a few more weeks would find him capable of hobbling about "with the help of a crutch." But his wounds stubbornly refused to heal. Writing to Washington on March 12, he reported: "they have been closed and broke out again, occasioned by some loose splinters of bone remaining in the leg, which will not be serviceable, until they are extracted." Arnold's surgeon was uncertain how long his recovery would take: he reckoned on two months at the least, but possibly as long as six. As soon as he was fit enough to ride, Arnold assured Washington, he would join him at headquarters: it was his "most ardent wish to render every assistance in my power, that your excellency may be enabled to finish the arduous task, you have with so much honor to yourself and advantage to your country, been so long engaged in, and have the pleasure of seeing peace and happiness restored to your country on the most permanent basis."[3]

Arnold wrote from Middletown, Connecticut, where he was the guest of another former merchant, militia general Comfort Sage. While recuperating there, he took the opportunity to renew his advances to Betsy Deblois of Boston. He was rebuffed as before, but kept copies of his love letters; before long they would once again come in useful. On May 4, Arnold arrived back at New Haven to a hero's welcome. The Footguards paraded in his honor, and he was given a thirteen-gun salute. Among the thronging dignitaries and townsfolk were the proud and eager faces of Arnold's sister Hannah and his three boys.[4]

This was the zenith of Arnold's fame. Popular acclaim for the general who had been crippled fighting for American liberty was matched by symbolic recognition of his real contributions to the cause: that same month,

Washington expressed sincere admiration through his highly personal gift of a sword-knot and epaulettes; and when Arnold stayed at the Robinson House, on his way to headquarters at Valley Forge, Pennsylvania, the most prominent of the newly built fortifications on nearby West Point was renamed in his honor. Arnold arrived at Valley Forge on May 21, 1778, "to the great joy of the army," as his old comrade Henry Dearborn noted. On May 30, he took the oath of allegiance to the United States of America that was required of all Continental Army officers in camp. Before his friend— the tall, portly, and genial Brigadier-General Henry Knox—Arnold swore to do his utmost to "support, maintain, and defend" them against "King George the Third, his heirs and successors, and his or their abettors, assistants, and adherents." When Arnold gave his oath, there was nothing to suggest that he would not keep it. Yet within a year he was prepared to break that solemn pledge and return his allegiance to the monarch he had renounced.[5]

* * *

Throughout spring 1778, George Washington left Benedict Arnold in no doubt of his ambition to employ him in the next campaign against the British: indeed, he could have used his abilities in the last. Acutely conscious of his own reputation, Washington was vexed that while Horatio Gates's Northern Army had won a stunning victory over Burgoyne, the "Grand American Army" under his personal command had experienced only frustration and defeat in Pennsylvania. When news of Burgoyne's heavy losses at Bemis Heights reached Washington's army on October 15, 1777, he had congratulated his own men on such a "signal victory," while hoping that it would stimulate them to win laurels of their own. He appealed: "What shame and dishonor will attend us, if we suffer ourselves in every instance to be outdone?" Washington found it difficult to hide his bitterness that Gates had enjoyed the vigorous support of the New York and New England militias, leaving him to do his best with the manpower of Pennsylvania, a state with an unusually high proportion of Loyalists and neutrals, including many pacifist Quakers. As he explained to his old friend Landon Carter: "the disaffection of a great part of the inhabitants of this state, the languor of others, and internal distraction of the whole, have been among the great and insuperable difficulties I have met with, and have contributed not a little to my embarrassments this campaign."[6]

Despite his best efforts, and a hard-fought engagement at Brandywine Creek on September 11, 1777, Washington had been unable to prevent Sir William Howe from achieving his objective and capturing Philadelphia— or, as Nathanael Greene styled it, "the Rome of America"; as the British approached, Congress was obliged to decamp to the shabby little township of York. On Friday, September 26, Howe's army took possession of the city, led by the British and Hessian grenadiers and two squadrons of light dragoons, whose drawn sabers glittered in the sunshine. The victors received an enthusiastic reception, although some of them doubted its sincerity: Captain John Peebles of the Black Watch noted that the streets were "crowded with inhabitants who seem to rejoice on the occasion, though by all accounts many of them were publicly on the other side before our arrival."[7]

The entourage of staff officers who accompanied Sir William as he savored his imperial triumph included Captain John André of the 26th Foot. Described as "well-made, rather slender, about five feet nine inches high, and remarkably active," with a dark complexion and good, if "somewhat serious" countenance, he had a gift for charming males and females alike. Born in London in 1750 to a Swiss father and French mother, André was schooled at Hackney, before spending several years in Geneva; thanks to this expansive education, he "excelled in many elegant accomplishments, such as drawing, painting, and dancing; and possessed the modern languages, particularly French, Italian, and German, to an uncommon degree of perfection." André also wrote poetry, an interest encouraged by his friendship with the older, and widely celebrated, Anna Seward; he regularly traveled up from London to join her circle of devotees in Lichfield, Staffordshire. There was talk of a romance between André and Miss Seward's ward, seventeen-year-old Honora Sneyd; but if it was ever anything more than a contrived arrangement to gratify poetic expectations, it came to nothing. André's father was "a very considerable merchant in the Levant trade," and the young man spent some years wielding a quill in his "compting house." But the family business held no attractions for him. On November 1, 1769, he wrote: "An impertinent consciousness whispers in my ear, that I am not of the right stuff for a merchant." Instead, André joined the peacetime British army, purchasing his first commission in early 1771.[8]

For much of 1772 and 1773, Lieutenant André toured Germany, visiting the principal courts of the territorial princes, and polishing his education at Hanover's University of Göttingen. In the estimation of Christoph

Lichtenberg, the eminent philosopher and professor of physics, he possessed "an excellent mind." Writing in 1780, Lichtenberg believed that André and Sir Francis Clerke (who died of wounds sustained at Bemis Heights) were the "most distinguished Englishmen" to have studied at Göttingen "during the last sixteen years"; and of the two, André was the more "sympathetic and engaging."[9]

By the time André returned to Britain, his regiment, the 7th Foot, or "Royal English Fusiliers," was deployed to Canada. He sailed to join it in 1774, arriving in Philadelphia that September, as the First Continental Congress convened. After stopping at Boston, he journeyed overland to Quebec. During the final months of peace between Britain and her American colonies, André enjoyed a carefree existence among the English and French inhabitants, dancing and sleighing, and sketching the Canadians and Indians in their native costumes. In March 1775, while the landscape remained buried under five feet of snow, he composed a letter to his sister Mary in Southampton that reveals something of his zest for life: "We are to see nature wear the twelfth-cake-like appearance a couple of months longer," he wrote. "I own I am not tired of it. The spirit of society which reigns here during this season and the dress we wear banish the idea of cold, and the brightness of the weather cheers one's spirits."[10]

Captured when St. Johns surrendered to Montgomery's army in November 1775, André was sent on parole to towns in the interior of Pennsylvania—first Lancaster, and later Carlisle. Traveling down the Hudson Valley en route to his banishment, André chanced to meet Colonel Henry Knox, who was on his mission to retrieve the captured guns of Fort Ticonderoga and transport them to Boston; despite their conflicting loyalties, they enjoyed a convivial evening, and following the custom in cramped frontier inns, shared a bed. Farther south at Albany, André enjoyed the more refined hospitality of the courteous Philip Schuyler, befriending his wife and three teenaged daughters.[11]

In December 1776, after William Howe captured Manhattan and chased Washington out of New Jersey, André gained his freedom in an exchange of prisoners, and was soon promoted to a captaincy in the 26th Foot—the "Cameronians." At New York, André wrote a report drawing on his recent experiences in America, "so exceedingly able and intelligent" that he won Sir William's patronage. For an officer without connections or "interest," such influential backing was invaluable. That summer, when Major-General

Charles Grey joined the army without an aide-de-camp, Howe "begged to recommend to him a young officer of great abilities, who for some time he had wished to provide for."[12]

Grey was a highly experienced and ruthlessly effective officer: as his aide during the ensuing campaign, André witnessed some of the war's bloodiest fighting. In contrast to his light-hearted family letters, the captain's personal journal leaves no doubt that his artistic and poetic tendencies were matched by a tough, unsentimental professionalism. Ten days after participating in Howe's victory at Brandywine, André was present when Grey led a force, including light infantry and Scottish Highlanders, in a nighttime attack on a brigade of Pennsylvanians commanded by Anthony Wayne. His description of what the Patriots dubbed "the Paoli Massacre" is unflinchingly direct: "No firelock was loaded and express orders were given to rely solely on the bayonet," he reported. "We ferreted out their pickets and advanced guards, surprised and put most of them to death, and coming in upon the camp rushed on them as they were collecting together and pursued them with a prodigious slaughter." About 200 killed or badly wounded Americans remained on the field; of those who got away, "a very great number were stabbed with bayonets or cut with broadswords"; at a cost of about seven or eight British casualties, Wayne's "harassing corps" had been "almost annihilated."[13]

Not long after the British entered Philadelphia as conquerors, and then encamped in the outlying village of Germantown, Washington's troops exacted a measure of revenge. Just before daybreak on October 4, 1777, having force-marched through the night, the Patriots burst out of the fog to surprise the outlying British pickets, tumbling them back on Howe's main force and instigating a confused firefight. As a mounted staff officer, Captain André was with the regiments that rallied and counter-attacked, "rushing up the street and scrambling through the gardens under a pretty heavy fire and not without some loss." As the redcoats advanced, they relieved several companies of the 40th Foot, "who with great presence of mind and equal gallantry had maintained themselves in a house, strewing the yard, garden, avenue, etc. with a prodigious number of rebel dead." Washington's attack was eventually rebuffed, but it had been a close shave. André's horse was nicked by four or five buckshot, which thankfully "hurt him so little" that the captain wished he had received them himself "to make people stare with the story of five wounds in one day."[14]

Chastened by Germantown, Howe withdrew his army behind a chain of redoubts screening Philadelphia, and focused on clearing the Delaware River of rebel obstructions, so that British ships could get through with supplies. At the end of November, André reported these developments to his sister Louisa, reverting to his playful, self-deprecating mode: "The whole of our business has been reducing about a dozen acres of mud which had very impertinently started up in the River Delaware and proudly assumed the name of an island," he wrote. "On this the Rebels had a fort [Fort Mifflin] that presented very uncivil batteries toward the channel through which ships were obliged to pass to come to Philadelphia." After several weeks of bombardment, the garrison quit the island and burned their shipping, leaving the British masters of the river. André had enjoyed the cannonade all the more for being at a safe distance: "I used every morning to attend and take peculiar delight in the clatter, nothing being so pleasant to behold as battles where one is an unconcerned spectator." With Washington now ensconced some fourteen miles off, fighting had dwindled to skirmishes between patrols. In consequence:

> The only hardships I endure are being obliged to sleep in my bed, to sit down to a very good dinner every day, to take a gentle ride for appetite's sake, to exercise my horses or to gossip in Philadelphia or to consider of something fashionable to make me irresistible this Winter. Le pauvre homme! You see what we poor soldiers go through.

André's professional progress had been remarkable, and looked set to continue on its upward trajectory: "I have every day more reason to be pleased with my situation," he assured Louisa. "General Grey shows me continually the greatest marks of friendship and will, I am persuaded, take the first opportunity of favoring my advancement."[15]

* * *

That December, the rump of Washington's army encamped at Valley Forge, nearly twenty miles from Philadelphia. There, the rigors of winter were exacerbated by a chronic shortage of food and clothing. These deficiencies, which threatened the Continental Army's very existence, largely resulted from the lack of an organized transportation system to shift supplies from the depots and storehouses where they were stockpiled—and the reluctance of the inhabitants to trade their produce for depreciating paper Continental dollars, rather than hard British cash. The supply crisis, like Washington's understrength battalions, underlined the fatal weakness inherent in the Patriots' elected central government: Congress lacked the power to tax the states and fund a national war effort, or even to enforce its requests for supplies and manpower.

While Washington's Continentals shivered and went hungry in their crude and drafty huts, Howe's redcoats occupied snug winter quarters in Philadelphia. The presence of so many British officers in the city encouraged a lively social scene. On February 26, 1778, Miss Rebecca Franks wrote a gossipy letter to her friend Mrs. Anne Paca, whose husband William was a congressional delegate from Maryland, currently exiled with his colleagues in dreary York. "You can have no idea of the life of continued amusement I live in," she gushed. "I know you are as fond of a gay life as myself—you'd have an opportunity of raking as much as you choose, either at plays, balls, concerts or assemblies." Earlier that week, Miss Franks had attended a dance and concert at Howe's headquarters at the John Penn mansion. Ever the gallant, Sir William readily approved her request to send a handkerchief to Mrs. Paca, in order "to show the fashions," even though she was "a delegate's lady." For the naive and unwary, all this heady gaiety came at a price. On March 15, Sarah Logan Fisher noted in her diary: "Very bad accounts of the licentiousness of the English officers in deluding young girls."[16]

Of the British officers who oversaw Philadelphia's giddy round of entertainments, none was more ubiquitous than the debonair and affable Captain André. Thanks to General Grey's friendship and consideration, his staff duties were scarcely onerous, leaving ample scope for acting, directing, and painting scenery at the popular Old Southwark Theater, and for paying social calls. André soon struck up a close friendship with Peggy Chew of Germantown, the daughter of an interned Loyalist, Pennsylvania's former chief justice, Benjamin Chew. It was Justice Chew's sturdy stone-built home, "Cliveden," that had been turned into a makeshift British strongpoint during the recent battle, and it remained scarred by cannon shot and musketry. Now, in the ornamental gardens that he had lately seen littered with dead and dying rebels, Captain André presented Miss Chew with mildly flirtatious verses.[17]

That winter, André also became acquainted with another Peggy, Miss Chew's friend Margaret Shippen. Born in June 1760, Peggy was the youngest of four daughters of Edward Shippen. Like Benjamin Chew, he was a lawyer; but his carefully neutral stance had allowed him to maintain his position under the Patriots and British alike. In addition, his uncle, William Shippen, served as a member of Congress in 1778–79, and his cousin, William Shippen junior, was, for four years, the Continental Army's director-general of hospitals. During Howe's occupation, Edward Shippen's elegant home on Fourth Street was a magnet for young British officers, including John André. Although there is no hard evidence of any romantic liaison between them, he and Peggy Shippen were clearly on friendly terms; a letter he later composed for Peggy Chew recalled "the pleasure of frequenting yours and the Shippen family." Tellingly, André also sketched Peggy Shippen's likeness. He drew her dressed for a ball, resplendent in a ruffled gown, and smiling coyly from beneath her fashionably towering head-dress.[18]

Of all the many entertainments staged in British-occupied Philadelphia, none was more extravagant than the so-called Mischianza (from the Italian for "medley"). It was held on May 18, 1778 in tribute to Sir William Howe; after many frustrations, he had resigned as commander-in-chief in North America. Captain André was heavily involved in the preparations for this pageant, painting furnishings and designing costumes, and he wrote a detailed account of proceedings that appeared in the *Gentleman's Magazine*: this listed Peggy Shippen and two of her sisters among the damsels, who, as he explained in another report, were picked from the "foremost in youth, beauty, and fashion." According to family lore, however, even though their Turkish-themed dresses were finished, and their names included on the official program, at the very last moment a delegation of stern, disapproving Quakers persuaded Edward Shippen to withhold permission for his daughters to attend in such shameless costumes: forbidden to go to the ball, the sisters went into "a dancing fury." Their tantrums were justified: witnesses agree that they missed a magical occasion. After a regatta on the Delaware, the 400 guests disembarked to watch a spectacular tournament fought between two teams of officers (the "Knights of the Blended Rose" and the "Knights of the Burning Mountain") dressed in striking silk costumes inspired by the sixteenth-century fashions current during the reign of King Henry IV of France. André, whose shield bore the device of two fighting cocks, championed the honor of Miss Peggy Chew, who *was* allowed to attend. Superbly mounted on gaily caparisoned horses, the "knights" jousted with lances, fired pistols, and clashed sabers for the esteem of their ladies and the entertainment of all and sundry. Then there was dancing in a candlelit ballroom, in which "a great number of looking glasses multiplied every object." After supper in another "magnificent saloon," the night sky was illuminated by spectacular fireworks: "twenty different exhibitions" were executed with "the happiest success, and in the highest style of beauty." The display was planned and directed by the army's versatile chief engineer, Captain John Montresor, who had recently overseen the methodical subjugation of Fort Mifflin on Mud Island, and whose Kennebec River journal and map had been consulted by Arnold during his celebrated march to Quebec in 1775. The guests danced on until 4 a.m., when, exhausted but exhilarated, they finally retired. All in all, André believed, it was "the most splendid entertainment . . . ever given by an army to their general."[19]

* * *

Few would have disputed André's proud boast, but there was widespread tutting at such extravagance when Britain's fortunes in America gave precious little cause for celebration. With France expected to enter the war in the wake of Burgoyne's defeat, Howe's successor, Sir Henry Clinton, had already received orders from London to evacuate Philadelphia and shift his army to New York. Once there, he was to send hefty contingents to the Caribbean, where the French island of St. Lucia invited attack, and to Florida, which was thought to be a likely target for Britain's other old enemy, Spain; although never allied with the American rebels, in 1779 Spain joined the war against Britain in compact with France, so expanding the conflict still further.[20]

   In London, tidings of Saratoga prompted a frantic diplomatic initiative to settle the Anglo-American conflict before the French could intervene. The prime minister, Lord Frederick North, rushed two "conciliatory" bills through Parliament. The first offered the Americans virtually everything they had demanded in 1775, revoking the tax legislation that had provoked waves of protest since 1765; but critically, it fell short of recognizing an independent United States. The second created a commission to negotiate on the basis of the proposed concessions. The commissioners were headed by Frederick Howard, earl of Carlisle, joined by a gifted and ambitious young lawyer and MP, William Eden, and the older George Johnstone, a naval officer and former governor of West Florida. Once in America, they would co-opt William Howe and his brother, Admiral Richard Howe, and the incoming commander-in-chief, Sir Henry Clinton.[21]

The draft bills, which had yet to be passed by Parliament, left for America aboard the *Andromeda* on February 20; simultaneously, the *Sensible* was plying across the Atlantic with copies of the Franco-American treaties of alliance. Although *Sensible* won the race, arriving on April 13, British naval patrols obliged her to dock far to the north, at Falmouth in Maine. Carried overland by Silas Deane's brother Simeon, her vital documents only reached Congress at York on May 2. *Andromeda* made New York on April 14, and General Tryon lost no time in printing and distributing the bills: Washington received a copy at Valley Forge on April 17, and transmitted it to Congress next day. Intended to tempt war-weary Americans into accepting Britain's generous peace terms, Tryon's action backfired by allowing Congress to pre-empt and undermine the proposals long before Carlisle and his colleagues even arrived to negotiate them.[22]

Still unaware of the French alliance, on April 22 Congress unanimously voted to reject the British offer; that same day, North's commissioners finally set sail for America. On May 4, after news of the alliance arrived, it was ratified by Congress; two days later, Washington's troops at Valley Forge marked the pact with an elaborate *feu de joie*. When the "Carlisle Commission" eventually reached Philadelphia on June 6, 1778, it was too late and already redundant. Not only was a firm congressional opposition already in place, but the commissioners' credibility was fatally undermined by London's orders to Clinton: convinced that their negotiations could only succeed if backed by credible military strength, they were exasperated by the decision to evacuate Philadelphia, a move of which they had not even been informed when they left England. Howe had already begun the embarkation of thousands of pro-British "Tories," and advised the remaining inhabitants to secure themselves and their property by pledging allegiance to Congress—moves scarcely calculated to inspire confidence in a royal resurgence. Meanwhile, British officers and Loyalists alike were shocked at how much London was willing to concede: hearing that Parliament would "not impose any tax or assessment on America," and that the commissioners were appointed "to make up matters with the Americans and put them on the footing they were in 1763," Captain Peebles considered the terms "very humbling to Great Britain." Subsequently learning that "everything but independence" was up for negotiation, he lamented: "Alas Britain, how art thou fallen." When Sarah Logan Fisher's husband Tommy met Johnstone, and was shown the treaty articles, he found them to be "humiliating indeed." Sarah noted: "If independence is but given up in name, everything is granted they could desire or ask." As the commissioners were effectively powerless from the outset, and American independence was non-negotiable, Congress decided simply to ignore them.[23]

Britain's weakness was underscored when Clinton withdrew the last of his troops from Philadelphia on June 18, 1778. The Americans marched in next day, headed by the city's military commandant, Major-General Benedict Arnold. When he announced Arnold's new assignment on May 28, Washington intended to recognize and reward the merit of a deserving officer who remained unfit for active service in the field; made in all good faith, the appointment would prove to be one his worst misjudgments. In the aftermath of British occupation, Philadelphia belied its claim to brotherly love: it was a divided city, its social fabric fissured by raw, angry wounds. Although more than 3,000 diehard Loyalists had left with the departing British, many of the remaining inhabitants were suspected by returning Patriots of collaboration; staunch republicans were scarcely better disposed toward the numerous "neutrals" uncommitted to either side in the struggle. In addition, Philadelphia's political scene was complicated, because it was not only the seat of Congress, but also the capital of Pennsylvania, a state with an unusually radical constitution, whose elected representatives prickled at any show of federal authority.

Arnold's arrival added another volatile ingredient to an already unstable mix. He symbolized the military authority that some civilians increasingly feared—anxieties which his arrogant self-righteousness did nothing to alleviate. And while Arnold was a bona fide war hero in New York and New England, where he had demonstrated his courage on the battlefield at the head of locally recruited troops, Pennsylvanians had little direct experience of his dynamic leadership. With its tainted atmosphere, Philadelphia was the worst possible posting for a soldier of Arnold's headstrong temperament, and his negative experiences there affected him profoundly.

Arnold's first task was to stave off disorder during the tricky transition from British to American control. Washington instructed him: "You will take every prudent step in your power to preserve tranquility and order in the city, and give security to individuals of every class and description; restraining as far as possible, till the restoration of civil government, every species of persecution, insult or abuse, either from the soldiery to the inhabitants, or among each other." Appointing Arnold to command, Washington forwarded him a copy of Congress's resolution "to prevent the removal, transfer, or sale of any goods, wares, or merchandise in the possession of the inhabitants" until a joint committee appointed by the Supreme Executive Council of Pennsylvania had established what property, if any, belonged to King George III and his supporters. On June 19, Arnold issued a proclamation placing the city under martial law. For a week, all shops and stores would be closed so that the quartermaster, commissary, and clothier generals might "contract for such goods as are wanted by the army." This deeply unpopular measure was issued under the guidance of leading local politicians; but it became associated primarily with Arnold, and unfairly stoked resentment against him.[24]

In his new post, Arnold missed the last major battle of the Revolutionary War's northern theater. Sir Henry Clinton had been instructed to ferry his troops to New York by way of the Delaware River and Bay, and then the open Atlantic. But as a powerful French fleet was known to be heading for America, and might arrive in time to intercept his vulnerable convoy at sea, he opted to march the bulk of his forces overland, across New Jersey. As his army retreated, making laborious progress in the intense summer heat, Clinton was trailed by Washington. His Continentals had not only survived their punishing sojourn at Valley Forge, but, thanks to an intensive training regime overseen by a former Prussian officer, Baron Friedrich Wilhelm von Steuben, were now far better drilled and disciplined. On June 28, near Monmouth Court House, leading American units under Major-General Charles Lee caught up with Clinton's rearguard: this rounded on its pursuers, pushing them back toward Washington's main army. A series of strong defensive positions, defended by stubborn infantry and well-handled artillery, defied determined British attacks; with mounting combat casualties, and scores more felled by the baking temperature, the engagement ended inconclusively, although Washington and his officers considered that they had won a victory, and thereby expunged the lingering shame of the British occupation of Philadelphia. Brigadier-General Wayne, who had been caught off guard at Paoli, reveled in the losses inflicted on the British officer corps, which included "numbers of the richest blood of England." He urged the secretary to the Board of War, Richard Peters, to tell "the Philadelphia ladies that the heavenly, sweet, pretty redcoats, the accomplished gentlemen of the Guards and grenadiers, have humbled themselves on the plains of Monmouth." Betraying his resentment against those Philadelphian belles who had consorted with the enemy and patronized the Mischianza, Wayne added: "The 'Knights of the Blended Rose' and 'Burning Mount' have resigned their laurels to *Rebel* officers, who will lay them at the feet of those virtuous daughters of America who cheerfully gave up ease and affluence in a city for Liberty and peace of mind in a cottage." The surviving "Knights," including Captain André, accompanied Clinton as he continued his march to Sandy Hook on the Jersey shore, from where his weary army was ferried safely to New York in Admiral Howe's transports.[25]

Transferred to New York, Britain's peace commissioners were in a weaker position than ever, especially since the expected French fleet under Vice-Admiral Charles Hector, comte d'Estaing appeared off the port on July 11; with sixteen formidable ships of the line, it heavily outgunned Lord Howe, who kept his own fleet tucked safely inside New York harbor. Despite such discouraging circumstances, the commissioners attempted to salvage at least something from their compromised mission. Shortly before quitting Philadelphia, George Johnstone tried to exploit his parliamentary reputation as "a friend of America" to open unofficial negotiations. Through Mrs. Elizabeth Ferguson of Philadelphia, the wife of the loyalist commissary of prisoners, Hugh Henry Ferguson, he approached the prominent Philadelphia lawyer and politician Joseph Reed, who was both a congressman and a member of Pennsylvania's Supreme Executive Council.

Born in New Jersey in 1742, Reed was educated at the college that would become Princeton University, and completed his legal training in London. A leading lawyer at the outbreak of the Revolutionary War, Reed became a lieutenant-colonel of Pennsylvania militia, and was soon appointed military secretary to George Washington. In June 1776, he replaced Horatio Gates as adjutant-general of the Continental Army, and served throughout the disastrous New York campaign. Following the fall of Fort Washington in mid-November, he wrote a flattering letter to General Charles Lee that was also critical of Washington's "indecisive mind." When Washington inadvertently opened Lee's reply and was confronted with Reed's disloyalty, their previously close relationship became strained. Full of remorse, Reed intended to resign, but stayed on to play a role in Washington's crucial offensive of Christmas 1776, urging the surprise attack on Trenton that heralded the patriot revival. In May 1777, he was promoted to brigadier-general; but he declined command of the army's cavalry and became increasingly involved in Pennsylvanian politics, as a radical member of Congress.[26]

According to Mrs. Ferguson's testimony, Johnstone was especially keen to secure Reed's involvement in the proposed peace negotiations, and was ready to reward his services in very handsome fashion: if he could, "after well considering the nature of the dispute . . . conformable to his conscience and view of things, exert his influence to settle the contest, he may command ten thousand guineas and the best post in the government." Soon after Mrs. Ferguson communicated this offer to Reed, he revealed it to Congress. On August 11, its members condemned such a brazen attempt to bribe and corrupt them: in future, they would hold no "manner of correspondence or intercourse with the said George Johnstone, especially to negotiate with him upon affairs in which the cause of liberty is interested."[27]

Johnstone's ill-advised gambit was a propaganda gift to the Patriots. Writing in the *Massachusetts Spy*, "Bob Centinel" cautioned his countrymen against the treacherous Britons: "Take care that their *gold* be not more fatal to you than their *lead*," he warned. "The last has slain its thousands, the first may purchase chains for millions." Unabashed, Johnstone denied the count of bribery, and from New York, published a manifesto on August 26 maintaining his object of promoting "a reconciliation between Great Britain and her Colonies." Johnstone claimed to care nothing for the good opinion of Congress, a body that was "deaf to the cries" of "fellow-subjects who are suffering by the miseries of this war." Seeking to exploit traditional anti-French prejudice, Johnstone accused Congress of acting from "motives of private ambition" and sullying "the principles upon which their first resistance was made" by siding with "the ancient enemy of both our countries, from whose hostile designs Great Britain has so often rescued the inhabitants of North America."[28]

Indeed, the old enmities soon resurfaced, when the first experiment in Franco-American military cooperation ended in abject failure. In early August, Major-General John Sullivan assembled a force of 8,000 Continentals and militia to attack the 3,000-strong British garrison of Newport, Rhode Island, in conjunction with d'Estaing's fleet. Prospects for a combined assault by land and sea looked promising—until the determined "Black Dick" Howe appeared off Newport with a strengthened armament. After an impending sea battle was stymied by a storm, d'Estaing retired to Boston to repair his battered ships, leaving Sullivan to beat a retreat before the redcoats were reinforced from New York. Unlucky as ever, Sullivan was disgusted by this "betrayal," and his intemperate comments almost wrecked the alliance when it had barely begun. Writing to the tactful Nathanael Greene, who had joined the expedition in the hope of seeing his birthplace liberated, Washington urged him to spare no pains to ease tensions, stifling "all illiberal expressions and reflections" from American officers already disillusioned with their new Gallic comrades.[29]

The "unnatural" French alliance also loomed large in the commissioner's last-ditch attempt to make stubborn Americans see reason. On October 3, they issued a final "Manifesto and Proclamation," once again urging Congress, the states, and individual citizens to accept their benevolent peace offers. If they persisted in spurning them, they must now accept the consequences: Britain would no longer act with restraint against the misguided colonies, but instead use "every means in her power [to] destroy or render useless a connection contrived for her ruin and for the aggrandizement of France."[30]

But Britain had already unleashed the dogs of war. Just days earlier, in an ill-timed reprise of the "Paoli Massacre," light infantry commanded by Major-General Grey had fallen on more than a hundred men of Colonel George Baylor's elite regiment of Continental light dragoons in their billets near Old Tappan, New Jersey. To ensure surprise, the redcoats once again relied on their bayonets and musket butts. Captain André recorded the bloody consequences: "The whole corps within six or eight men were killed or taken prisoners." Grisly reports of this latest "massacre" were distributed by Congress to help foster anti-British sentiment: the commissioners' threats, like their offers, were to no avail. They returned to England that fall with nothing to show for their efforts.[31]

* * *

As commandant of Philadelphia, it did not take long for Benedict Arnold to realize that he had been handed a poisoned chalice. Within a month, he was already exploring options that would take him far away from its hostile atmosphere. In mid-July he wrote to Washington, sounding him out about the possibility of a naval command. Given his long experience as a merchant captain, and his impressive performance as commodore on Lake Champlain, this seemed like a logical change of tack. It would also exploit Arnold's fighting skills at a time when his wound still ruled out a command on land. As he assured Washington, that injury would be no such handicap aboard ship. But while Washington hoped to see Arnold "in a situation where you can be of the greatest advantage, and where abilities like yours may not be lost to the public," he confessed himself ignorant of "marine matters . . . so far out of my line." Yet the idea clearly held strong appeal for Arnold. In early September, he presented Congress with a scheme for a "secret expedition." The newly arrived French envoy, Conrad Alexandre Gérard, heard that the objective was Britain's vulnerable West Indian islands, which Arnold knew well from his trading days. But although the proposal was referred to a congressional committee of five members, who conferred with him, it was never adopted. And while Gérard reported that Arnold had obtained a naval command, this intelligence was faulty. It is possible that such a roving, independent commission would have offered Arnold an alternative to the path he ultimately chose, giving ample opportunities for glory and prize money. Without doubt, it would have removed him from a role for which he was woefully unsuited, and from a situation that soon left him angry, disillusioned, and increasingly desperate.[32]

Animosity toward Arnold, particularly among the radicals who drew strong support from the city's humbler workers, the artisans and "mechanics," was only compounded by his conspicuously lavish lifestyle. Arnold enjoyed entertaining. He had long since aspired to the status of a gentleman, hankering after the fine things that went with it. Now, after more than three years of active service in which he had been twice wounded, he perhaps felt that he had earned some comforts. He lost little time in moving into the handsome John Penn house on Market Street, which had recently served as Sir William Howe's headquarters, and furnished it "in an elegant and expensive manner." During the British occupation it had hosted balls and dinners, and Arnold saw no reason to break with precedent. When Gérard arrived in July 1778, Arnold gladly extended his hospitality to the diplomat and his entire "suite," providing them with "apartments, and bed and board" for several weeks, until Congress arranged accommodation. Arnold's habit of traveling about the city in a horse-drawn coach, with servants liveried like London flunkeys, was another instance of ostentation that stuck in the craw of austere Patriots.[33]

In addition, Arnold's fondness for luxuries, and his patronage of entertainments like the theater, ran counter to both popular and official reaction against such "unpatriotic" indulgences. On July 4, for example, after a suitably modest banquet had been held at the City Tavern to celebrate the second anniversary of the Declaration of Independence, "the mob" staged a procession mocking the extravagant hairstyles first adopted by fashion-conscious Philadelphian women during the British occupation, and still worn by some of them, even though the redcoats were gone. A "woman of the town," also described as a "strumpet" or "old negro wench," was decked out in the "most extravagant high head-dress that could be got," as popularized by the "mistresses and whores of the British officers"—and sported by Peggy Shippen in André's sketch. "Continella," whose head-dress was "about three feet high, of proportionate width, and with a profusion of curls," was paraded through the city's crowded streets to the din of beating drums. This public display of disapproval was clearly effective: within days, female wigs were lower. That fall, Congress recommended that the states take action to close down theaters and suppress other popular "diversions," such as horse-racing and gambling, that were "productive of idleness, dissipation, and a general depravity of principles and manners." When the Old Southwark ignored this puritanical edict and defiantly staged another performance, Congress reacted with a resolution that embraced Arnold, decreeing that "any person holding an office under the United States who shall act, promote, encourage, or attend such plays shall be deemed unworthy to hold such office and shall be accordingly dismissed."[34]

Without doubt Arnold appreciated money and what it could buy. But he was no miser, and did not hesitate to share his wealth when he had it. Just as he had readily advanced his Quebec comrade John Lamb cash to recruit a regiment of artillery in the spring of 1777, so he now intervened to help the distressed family of another old friend, Joseph Warren. Among the first of the Revolution's martyrs, Warren had been killed in the desperate fighting at Bunker Hill in June 1775, just weeks after he had helped to secure Arnold his first military command for the expedition against Fort Ticonderoga. More than three years later, Arnold had not forgotten Warren's support. In the spring of 1778, he was surprised to learn that Warren's orphans were "entirely neglected by the State," and in dire need of assistance. Warren had died leaving his affairs unsettled, but it was clear that once his debts were paid, there would be little left for his children's education. In fact, in January 1777, at the instigation of Samuel Adams, Congress had resolved that Warren's oldest son, Joseph, should be schooled at public expense. But there had been no provision for his siblings, two girls and a boy. Keen to offer practical help, on July 15, 1778 Arnold wrote to Warren's bereaved fiancée, Miss Mercy Scollay:

My intention is to use my interest with Congress to provide for the family. If they decline it, I make no doubt of a handsome collection by private subscription. At all events, I will provide for them in a manner suitable to their birth, and the grateful sentiments I shall ever feel for the memory of my friend.

As a first measure, Arnold sent $500 to Miss Scollay via John Hancock, emphasizing that she should not hesitate to call on him to cover any further expense. Learning of this generosity, Sam Adams called on Arnold in Philadelphia and "thanked him for his kindness." When Congress failed to offer any further help, Arnold forwarded another $500 and continued to lobby for action. Ironically, the strongest opposition within Congress came from Warren's own state, Massachusetts: its delegates felt that they alone should shoulder responsibility for the dependents of their local hero. But Arnold refused to give up. After two years, and largely owing to his persistence, Congress finally passed a resolution to provide for the younger children, defraying the cost from the major-general's half-pay that would have been due to Warren had he lived, backdated to his death, and continuing until the youngest child came of age. Arnold had no ulterior motive for helping Warren's children; even such a harsh critic as the historian Jared Sparks felt obliged to "heartily approve" of his "generous sentiments."[35]

* * *

By the summer of 1778, Joseph Reed was becoming worried about what he believed to be an increasing toleration of "disaffection to the interests of America, and even assistance to the British interest." In Reed's eyes, Benedict Arnold was part of a "settled fixed system to subvert the Whig interest," by openly favoring the Revolution's enemies—the Loyalists or Tories. Writing to Nathanael Greene on November 5, the day he was elected president of the Executive Council, Reed observed: "Will you not think it extraordinary that General Arnold made a public entertainment the night before last of which not only numerous Tory ladies and the wives and daughters of persons prescribed by the State and now with the enemy at New York, formed a very considerable number?" If that trend continued, Reed added, every Continental Army officer heading for Philadelphia would be well advised to shed his uniform before he arrived, and "procure a scarlet coat as the only mode of insuring respect and notice."[36]

With the benefit of hindsight, Reed's complaint is, of course, uncannily prescient. Yet there is no evidence that Arnold was contemplating turning his own coat that winter. In addition, Joseph Reed nursed a personal grievance against Philadelphia's commandant. The timing of Arnold's party was viewed as a calculated insult to Pennsylvania's Council. It was held on the eve of the execution of two Quakers, Abraham Carlisle and John Roberts, who had been convicted of treason against the state for collaborating with the British: in a controversial trial, Reed had been their prosecutor. Despite widespread clamor for clemency, the pair were hanged on November 4 as a warning to others. By staging an "entertainment" on the night before Carlisle and Roberts swung, Arnold seemed to be flaunting his sympathy for the condemned traitors, and disdain for their judges.[37]

Not everyone shared Reed's concerns. Likewise writing to Greene, General John Cadwalader maintained that Arnold had behaved appropriately, and that allegations of his favoritism toward the Revolution's enemies were "too absurd to deserve a serious answer." Indeed, Arnold's conduct was highly approved by "every man who has a liberal way of thinking." Cadwalader reported that the general had been "civil to every gentleman" who had taken the oath of allegiance to Congress, but "intimate with none." As for the ladies, both the "good approved Whigs" and those who had taken what wags styled "an active part" during the British occupation were "visited and treated with the greatest civilities." To Cadwalader, the charges leveled against Arnold might "serve the purposes of party or faction, but can never injure the character of a man to whom his country is so much indebted."[38]

The households that enjoyed General Arnold's "civilities" included the Shippens of Fourth Street. Although his second courtship of Betsy Deblois had proved no more successful than the first, Philadelphians were soon gossiping that Arnold had set his sights on their own much-admired Peggy Shippen. That summer, Peggy had just turned eighteen; Arnold was thirty-seven. Despite being twice her age, still limping badly from his wound, and responsible for three sons from his previous marriage, Arnold presented himself as a serious and determined suitor. His first surviving letter to Peggy, written on September 25, 1778, quarried several of the phrases with which he had tried to woo Miss Deblois back in April: "Twenty times have I taken up my pen to write to you, and as often has my trembling hand refused to obey the dictates of my heart," he copied. As his happiness depended on Peggy alone, how could she doom him to "languish in despair"? He added: "shall I expect no return to the most sincere, ardent, and disinterested passion?" Explaining his feelings, Arnold now used words that he had not previously written to Betsy:

> My passion is not founded on personal charms only; that sweetness of disposition and goodness of heart, that sentiment and sensibility which so strongly mark the character of the lovely Miss P. Shippen, renders her amiable beyond expression and will ever retain the heart she has once captivated.

Emboldened by the depth of his emotions, Arnold had presumed to write to Peggy's "Papa," requesting formal permission to make his addresses.[39]

At first, Arnold's progress was frustratingly slow. In October, Sarah Bache gave an insight into his impatience, when she wrote telling her father, Benjamin Franklin, about her baby daughter Betty: "You can't think how fond of kissing she is, and she gives such old-fashioned smacks that General Arnold says he would give a good deal to have her for a school mistress to teach the young ladies how to kiss." The evidence suggests that Arnold was genuinely smitten: that November, Mrs. Mary Morris informed her husband Robert "that Cupid has given our little General a more mortal wound, than all the host of Britons could . . . Miss Peggy Shippen is the fair one." As 1778 drew to a close, Arnold's persistence was yielding results. The charismatic war hero, who mixed freely with the cream of Philadelphian society, was not without attractions of his own: even his disabling wound, acquired honorably in the cause of American liberty, marked him as a man of experience who had lived dangerously. Having recently seen his daughter Betsy married to Edward Burd, a major in the Continental Army, on December 21 Edward Shippen informed his father: "My youngest daughter is much solicited by a certain General, on the same subject; whether this will take place or not depends upon circumstances. If it should, I think it will not be till spring." And on 3 January, 1779, Major Burd assured his brother-in-law, Jasper Yeates, that the sole "obstacle" to the match was a "lame leg." He added: "But a lady who makes that the only objection, and is firmly persuaded it will soon be well, can never retract, however expressly conditional an engagement may have been made." From his "slight knowledge" of Arnold,

Major Burd believed him to be "a well-dispositioned man, and one that will use his best endeavors to make Peggy happy, and I doubt not will succeed."[40]

* * *

It was obvious that Arnold's spending in Philadelphia outpaced his pay as a major-general, which was both unequal to his expenses and in arrears. His business interests in New Haven, now neglected for nearly four years, contributed little more. Under the circumstances, it is scarcely surprising that a hard-nosed trader like Arnold should be tempted to exploit his new position to pursue money-making ventures. Arnold embarked on his first speculation within days of assuming command of Philadelphia, while its shops were still closed by his own orders. On June 23, he secretly entered into an agreement with the army's clothier-general, James Mease, and his deputy, William West, by which public credit was used to buy not only "goods and necessaries" for the army, but also "sundry articles not wanted for that purpose": these surplus items could then be bought at the subscribers' risk and sold for "their joint equal benefit." Such profiteering was illegal, although, as the involvement of Mease and West demonstrates, scarcely unusual among supply officers given an opportunity for graft; as quartermaster-general from March 1778, Nathanael Greene collected large commissions on official purchases.[41]

Arnold's scam was only fully uncovered after his defection to the British; but his critics soon found other charges to level against him. The general's first clash with the powerful Pennsylvania Council was not sparked by any financial malpractice, but arose from the perpetual tussle between civilian and military authority. Underlying tensions were exposed by a trivial incident in October 1778 that swiftly escalated into something far more serious. Ironically, the episode did not even involve Arnold directly, but originated with one of his young aides, Major David Solebury Franks. The major, who was something of a dandy, sent a servant girl to the orderly sergeant of militia, with instructions to go and fetch his barber. Sergeant William Matlack complied, but the barber was not home. When Franks ordered him to try again, the sergeant bristled at being treated like an errand boy. Next morning, he complained in person to Arnold. In Matlack's recollection, the general had reacted with restraint: "he informed me it was customary for sergeants to do such duty; and gave me to understand, not in an abrupt manner, that if I did not like such duty, I should not have come there." Arnold had also told Matlack that "if Major Franks had insulted me at the time he gave me the order, it was wrong, and he did not approve of that."[42]

The affair would in all likelihood have ended there, had Sergeant Matlack not mentioned it to his father, Timothy, who just happened to be secretary of the Supreme Executive Council. The forty-two-year-old Matlack, who now took his place alongside Arnold's most inveterate enemies, was another formidable foe. Noted as a brewer of "mild ale and porter," and a promoter of cock-fights, Matlack proved as belligerent as one of his own spurred birds. Elected colonel of Philadelphia militia, he led his battalion at Princeton on January 3, 1777. As Nathanael Greene conceded, on that morning these part-time soldiers fought as stoutly as Continentals, facing a hail of grape-shot "with a spirit that would do honor to veterans." Matlack was also noted for his remarkably elegant penmanship, which earned him many commissions to "engross" official documents; most notably, his copperplate hand-writing inscribed the vellum of the original Declaration of Independence.[43]

When Matlack picked up his quill to write a stiff letter of protest to Arnold, he met with a firm response that left no doubt of the general's views on the relationship between soldiers and civilians: "No man," he wrote, "has a higher sense of the rights of a citizen and freeman than myself. They are dear to me, as I have fought and bled for them, and it is my highest ambition and most ardent wish to resume the character of a free citizen whenever the service of my country will permit." However, Arnold continued, "whenever necessity obliges the citizen to assume the character of a soldier, the former is entirely lost in the latter, and the respect due to the citizen is by no means to be paid to the soldier any further than his rank entitles him to it." Military discipline depended on obedience; if a citizen's feelings were hurt in consequence, surely that was a small price to pay for his country's safety? But Arnold's letter did nothing to pacify the implacable Matlack senior. When he threatened to withdraw his son's services and to publish his reasons, Arnold refused to be intimidated. If Franks had issued his orders in a high-handed way, then he was at fault; but it was a dispute between the major and the sergeant, and not a quarrel in which Arnold intended to become embroiled.[44]

But that was not the last of the matter. On November 14, the *Pennsylvania Packet* printed an article from "A Militia Man," who reported the barber episode and expressed resentment at being "ordered on the most menial services" upon the mere "whim and caprice" of a member of Arnold's "suite." In any event, asked the anonymous author (who was ostensibly William

Matlack, but probably Timothy), what need had General Arnold for a militia guard? "From Tories, if such there be among us, he has nothing to fear, for they are all remarkably fond of him," he observed, in a sally at Arnold's willingness to socialize with suspected Loyalists. As for the patriotic Whigs, they were all "sensible of his great merit and former services and would risk their lives in his defense." The sting lay in the word "former."[45]

This row overlapped with another, involving a British sloop, the *Active*, which was seized by four captive American crewmen while on passage from Jamaica to New York. As their bold leader, Gideon Olmstead, was steering *Active* for the port of Egg Harbor, New Jersey, the sloop encountered the Pennsylvania state brig *Convention*, which escorted her instead to Philadelphia. *Convention*'s crew claimed that they had helped to capture *Active*; despite Olmstead's blunt denials, a local Court of Admiralty awarded him just one-quarter of the prize money. Arnold took an interest in the case, backing an appeal against the decision to Congress, and entering into secret agreement with Olmstead, who was from Hartford, Connecticut—for half of the proceeds of any final settlement. Arnold's involvement was noted in another anonymous comment in the *Pennsylvania Packet* of November 12, 1778, the latest contribution from the dogged Timothy Matlack. He wrote: "It is whispered, that some Gentlemen of high rank, now in this city, have introduced a new species of champerty, by interesting themselves in the claim of the sloop *Active*." Although not actually named, Arnold quickly responded in the *Packet* of November 17: as he despised "anonymous calumny," he didn't care whether the insinuation was leveled at him or not. However, if his reputation was called into doubt, that could harm the cause of the *Active*'s worthy captors. Arnold explained his intervention on their behalf: "some of my countrymen and neighbors were here in distress, they had bravely risked their lives in taking a vessel from the common enemy, and were in a fair way of being deprived of the fruits of their spirited conduct." As he had given their appeal his "countenance and protection," it was likely that any slander directed at him would hurt *them* too. Arnold failed to mention his own financial interest in the outcome of the case. In December, the congressional committee upheld Olmstead's appeal, awarding the value of the *Active* and her cargo to him and the three others who had helped take the sloop. But any hope of a rich haul for Arnold was short-lived: the committee's decision was challenged by the Pennsylvania court, which seized the proceeds from the sale of the cargo. Unwilling to antagonize such an important state, Congress backed down. The *Active* case dragged on for years, and was only settled in Olmstead's favor in 1809—long after Arnold's death.[46]

But it was Arnold's involvement with another ship that precipitated a full-blown conflict with Reed and his council. Back in May, after his appointment as commandant of Philadelphia, but while he was still at Valley Forge, Arnold had independently granted permission for the *Charming Nancy*, which was owned by residents of that city, to unload her cargo at any port of the United States. In consequence, the vessel docked at Egg Harbor, some sixty miles away. In early October, the British raided that notorious nest of privateers, burning houses and ships. Arnold, who had acquired a share of the *Charming Nancy*'s cargo, requested John Mitchell, the deputy quartermaster-general, to send wagons to collect his goods and prevent them from falling into enemy hands. On October 22, twelve wagons trundled off under Jesse Jordan. When the council eventually heard about the episode, it began an immediate investigation. On January 18, 1779, Mitchell was ordered to explain himself. He replied that he had agreed to Arnold's request because teams were available, and the general intended to reimburse the public for the costs of shifting his private property.

Reed immediately forwarded Mitchell's statement to Arnold for comment. His response of January 25, 1779 made clear his contempt for the president and his council. He concluded: "I shall only say, that I am at all times ready to answer my public conduct to Congress or to General Washington, to whom alone I am accountable." That same day, Reed wrote to John Jay, the newly appointed president of Congress, leaving no doubt of the real issue at stake:

The indignity offered to us on this occasion, as well as a due regard for the violated rights of the freemen of this state, calls upon us to resent such treatment, and in their names we shall call upon the delegates of the United States for justice, and reparation of our authority, thus wounded by one of their officers.

Next day, January 26, Reed requested that Congress examine Arnold's alleged misuse of the state's wagons; a committee of five was appointed to investigate. In the meantime, Reed urged, Arnold must be prevented from leaving Philadelphia, or exercising any command there.[47]

* * *

Arnold's tribulations in Philadelphia encouraged him to explore the possibility of a fresh start amid more congenial surroundings. When his longstanding supporter General Philip Schuyler wrote to inform him that New York was keen to recognize his services, he began to consider the possibility of securing a large landed estate within its territory, either on the unsettled frontier or on confiscated loyalist property. Such a tract might be settled with officers and soldiers who had served under Arnold's command; he would be like some medieval warlord, defending a well-earned border fiefdom with the help of his trusty retainers and henchmen. One area which Arnold already knew from his campaigns on Lake Champlain had belonged to Major Philip Skene. Believed to sprawl across 40,000 acres, it included established sawmills and ironworks; but then again, Skenesborough was said to be unhealthy in the fall, its marshy surroundings breeding fevers and ague. Another possibility with which Arnold was also familiar from his recent military service was the grant formally made to Britain's superintendent of the northern Indians, Sir William Johnson; "Kingsland," which bordered the Mohawk River between German Flats and Fort Schuyler, was rumored to run to 130,00 acres.[48]

New York's governor, George Clinton, received enthusiastic endorsements for Arnold's plan from the state's congressmen. Gouverneur Morris wrote that he had discussed the scheme with Arnold, who would be presenting it to Clinton and his legislature in person. Morris explained: "his design appears to me well calculated for the purpose of serving in some degree our western frontier and consequently enriching the intermediate country." It would encourage the settlement of "good industrious subjects," hardy folk worth two of any other. To Morris, Arnold's military exploits spoke for themselves: "I have only to say that the honorable stars he gained at Bemis Heights will be a better recommendation than I can give." Congress's president, John Jay, was himself a New Yorker, and favored the idea. He had the backing of all the state's delegates, and they lobbied Clinton for his legislature's blessing: "To you, Sir, or to our state, General Arnold can require no recommendation," they wrote. "A series of distinguished services entitle him to respect and favor." For Jay especially, a battle-hardened Patriot like Arnold was an asset. He, too, hoped that New York would remember Arnold's services "and the value of such a citizen to any state that may gain him." On February 3, 1779, Arnold set out for Poughkeepsie, New York, to meet Governor Clinton and to seek the counsel of Schuyler.[49]

*　*　*

A country estate, which Arnold could have ruled as his own domain, respected by his tenants and neighbors, was an attractive proposition that would likely have satisfied his cravings for status and recognition. But like the phantom naval command, it came to nothing. The scheme was promptly blocked by Arnold's enemies in Philadelphia. The same day that he departed for New York against Reed's wishes, Pennsylvania's Supreme Executive Council published a handbill with a long list of accusations against him. To maximize publicity, copies were distributed to Congress, and then further disseminated in local newspapers.

Reed and his council wanted to see Arnold prosecuted for "such illegal and oppressive conduct as is cognizable in the courts of law." Having "maturely considered the general tenor and course" of Arnold's military command in Philadelphia, a board of councilors resolved unanimously that Arnold had been "in many respects oppressive to the faithful subjects of this State, unworthy of his rank and station, highly discouraging to those who have manifested their attachment to the liberties and interests of America, and disrespectful to the supreme executive authority of this State." Acknowledging that Arnold had "formerly distinguished himself in public service," the board had only acted with reluctance: indeed, its members had been restrained from taking "proper notice of General Arnold," ever "hoping that every unworthy transaction would be the last." But alas, "finding that tenderness has only led to insult and further oppression," they had been obliged to act in the interests of the state and "the good people thereof, who must be affected by all abuses of power."

The board considered Arnold culpable on no fewer than eight counts. The first, which related to the *Charming Nancy*, maintained that while Philadelphia remained under British occupation, Arnold gave permission for a ship belonging to "persons then voluntarily residing in this city with the enemy, and of a disaffected character," to enter a port of the United States without authority from the state of Pennsylvania or General Washington; second, despite having shut Philadelphia's shops when he entered the city, "he privately made considerable purchases for his own benefit"; third—in reference to William Matlack—he had imposed "menial duties" on the sons of Pennsylvania's freemen; fourth, when a prize (the *Active*) was brought into Philadelphia by the state brig *Convention* and a dispute arose about the capture, Arnold prevented an amicable settlement "by an illegal and unworthy purchase of the suit"—an intervention which led to regrettable delays and the likelihood of disputes between Pennsylvania and Congress; fifth, he had used state wagons for the transportation of private property (the seventh count was of refusing to explain this when asked to do so); sixth, although the state had the exclusive right to "recommend persons desirous of going within the enemy's lines," Arnold had nonetheless applied to the council for such a permit—and for a person "deemed utterly improper to be indulged with such permission"; the eighth and final charge concerned Arnold's "discouragement and neglect . . . to civil, military, and other characters, who have adhered to the cause of their country," while displaying "an entire different conduct towards those of a different character."[50]

These charges reached Arnold the following day, February 4; but instead of returning immediately to Philadelphia to confront his accusers, he continued onward to Washington's headquarters at Middlebrook, New Jersey. After consulting with the commander-in-chief, Arnold wrote to Congress, formally requesting an inquiry into his conduct. Under the circumstances, and owing to the poor state of the winter roads, he postponed his meeting with George Clinton and the New York state legislature, and headed back to face his detractors in Philadelphia.

Returning at least offered the consolation of a reunion with Peggy, who was now widely viewed as Arnold's bride-to-be. Predictably enough, given Arnold's martial credentials, commentators could not resist comparing his courtship to a siege, in which he methodically battered Peggy's defenses until she finally capitulated. On January 29, 1779, Elizabeth Tilghman wrote to her cousin, Betsy Shippen, asking after "the gentle Arnold . . . and when is he like to convert our little Peggy?" Mrs. Tilghman had heard that Peggy intended to "surrender soon." She added: "I thought that the fort would not hold out long; well, after all, there is nothing like perseverance, and a regular attack." By early February, capitulation was imminent. The artilleryman Henry Knox, who knew all about bombardments, reported to his brother: "Our friend Arnold is going to be married to a beautiful and accomplished young lady, a Miss Shippen, of one of the best families in this place."[51]

Writing to Peggy from headquarters on February 8, 1779, Arnold left her in no doubt of his feelings:

Never did I so ardently long to see or hear from you as at this instant. I
am all impatience and anxiety to know how you do; six days absence,
without hearing from my dear Peggy, is intolerable. Heavens! What must
I have suffered had I continued my journey—the loss of happiness for a
few dirty acres. I can almost bless the villainous roads, and more
villainous men, who oblige me to return.

Arnold begged Peggy not to allow the "rude attacks" on him to give her any
"uneasiness." He returned, braced by the support of Washington and his
officers, who had treated him with the "greatest politeness" and who, he
claimed, "bitterly execrate Mr. Reed and the Council for their villainous
attempts to injure me." There are hints that the charges *did* cause concern
among Peggy's relatives: Edward Shippen of Lancaster had seen "a number
of things laid to the charge of General Arnold" and wanted further details.[52]

On February 9, Arnold responded to the council's charges with a letter
"to the Public," expressing his outrage at such accusations. He was especially
aggrieved that printed copies of the allegations had been distributed
"through the several States, for the purpose of prejudicing the minds of the
public against me," an action all the more "cruel and malicious" at a time
when it was well known that he would be away from Philadelphia. Arnold
had therefore appealed to Congress for a court martial to examine his
conduct. Meanwhile, he hoped his countrymen would suspend their judgment until he had had a fair hearing. He concluded with a defiant counter-
allegation of his own:

I hope the issue will show that, instead of my being guilty of the abuses
of power with which I am accused, the present attack upon me is as gross
a prostitution of power as ever disgraced a weak and wicked administration; and manifests a spirit of persecution against a man (who has endea-
vored to deserve well of this country) which would discredit the private
resentments of an individual, and which ought to render any public body
who could be influenced by it, contemptible.[53]

Arnold was not without sympathizers. To Elizabeth Tilghman, the accusations seemed outrageous, symptomatic of a world that was "running mad."
Writing to her cousin Betsy Burd, she wondered: "What demon has possessed
the people with respect to General Arnold?" He was "certainly much abused"

by "ungrateful monsters"—hard treatment indeed for "a character that has been looked up to, in more instances than one, since this war commenced." After reading the state's charges in the newspapers, Brigadier-General Knox believed he would be "exceedingly mistaken if one of them can be proven," and hoped his friend Arnold would "vindicate himself from the aspersions of his enemies." Always keen to exploit dissension in the patriot ranks, the British, too, noted the persistent hounding of one of their most formidable opponents. On February 17, 1779, New York's *Royal Gazette* commented: "General Arnold heretofore has been styled another Hannibal, but losing a leg in the service of Congress, the latter considering him unfit for any future exercise of his military talents, permit him thus to fall into the unmerciful fangs of the executive council of Pennsylvania." Published to foment discord, this scarcely exaggerated Arnold's predicament.[54]

Inevitably, the widespread publication of the charges against Arnold alerted his old enemy, John Brown of Pittsfield, Massachusetts. Sniffing blood, on March 7 Brown wrote to Joseph Reed, enclosing a copy of "an impeachment" against Arnold, who had previously "found means in a very extraordinary manner, and by the help of some extraordinary minds, to evade a trial." In a postscript, Brown explained that he had since received a letter from Timothy Matlack, enclosing charges against Arnold. Brown could not conceal his delight: "I am extremely happy to hear, that so great a villain is at last detected, or the old proverb verified 'give a thief length of rope, and he will hang himself.'" Eager to learn the outcome, Brown hoped to be in Philadelphia soon. There he would talk with Reed, "particularly on the subject of General Arnold," his enduring obsession. Matlack replied on March 29 that he had already made use of a "publication" signed by Brown; this was the damning broadsheet published at Pittsfield nearly two years earlier. Indeed, Matlack had raked up Brown's old charges against Arnold in the *Pennsylvania Packet* of February 27, 1779. The exasperated Arnold replied on March 4, wearily pointing out that Congress had already dismissed them as groundless. Two days later, the relentless Matlack countered that, while Brown's list of allegations might well be over-long, whenever *he* encountered Arnold's carriage in the streets, and considered the splendor of his lifestyle, he wondered how he could fund it—unless his "riches" derived from Montreal's plunder. Matlack assured Brown: "Every day turns up something new relating to the course of this phenomenon"; he would send on the further proceedings as soon as the case was closed, "as it is probable they will produce important consequences one way or another."[55]

But Arnold's prosecution did not proceed as smoothly as the Supreme Executive Council anticipated. The committee appointed by Congress to investigate the original allegation concerning the wagons had just finished its enquiries when Reed and his colleagues published their extended list of charges. These went before the same five committee members, although their chairman, William Paca, was clearly irritated by this "new exhibition" and by the council's marked reluctance to share its evidence against Arnold. In a curt letter of March 4 to councilor George Bryan, he observed: "We cannot see the propriety of the Congress founding charges upon allegations the evidence of which is known to you and not to them." Although Paca's committee had requested the documentation two weeks since, it was still waiting. He added: "We mean to close our enquiries tomorrow evening: we have directed General Arnold to attend us and we doubt not your zeal for public justice will induce you to furnish us by that time with all the evidence you are possessed of."

This drew an angry response from the council, to which the unrepentant Paca retorted with heavy sarcasm: "We are fully apprised of the delicacy of your feelings, and perfectly knew what exalted ideas you had, of rank, dignity, and power. Whatever therefore may be the expressions of our letter, we could not possibly mean to address you in the style of authority." Paca also resented accusations that his committee members had held "private interviews" with Arnold; if the council had proof, it should present it at the earliest opportunity.[56]

Delivered on March 17, 1779, the committee's report was extremely favorable to Arnold. Of the eight charges, it ruled, the first, second, third, and fifth could only be tried by a court martial; the fourth was of a civil nature, and so solely triable in a common law court; the sixth, seventh, and eighth charges were not triable anywhere, "or subject to any other punishment than the displeasure of Congress." Further, the Supreme Executive Council had only furnished evidence in relation to the fifth and seventh charges; it had provided nothing to sustain the others, "despite fruitless applications" over three weeks. During that time letters had been exchanged in which the council had threatened the committee, and accused it of partiality. The committee considered that the first, second, sixth, seventh, and eighth counts were either unproven or insufficiently serious even to justify a trial. It recommended that only *two* of the eight charges—the third (imposing menial duties) and the fifth (using state wagons)—should be "transmitted to the commander-in-chief."[57]

That same day, Arnold wrote to John Jay, hoping that he would "recommend to Congress to examine and decide" on the committee's findings as soon as possible. He increasingly viewed himself as the victim of a vendetta: "I am sensible of the multiplicity of business before Congress, yet I flatter myself that they will consider the cruel situation in which I am placed by the persecution of my enemies and relieve me by a speedy decision." Arnold was confident that the committee's report would acquit him of the charges "to the entire satisfaction of the honorable Congress." Back in January, when Washington visited Philadelphia to confer with Congress, he had given Arnold permission to resign his command and retire from the service until his wounds healed. However, as Arnold explained to him, "the villainous attacks made on my character, by the President and Council of this State in their publications, made it necessary for me to continue in the command until their charges were cleared up, or resign under the idea of compulsion or disgrace." Now that the committee had reported in his favor, Arnold was willing to resign and hand over his command to Brigadier-General James Hogan. Directly his wounds permitted, Arnold would be happy to "take a command in the line of the army ... at all times rendering my country every service in my power." He expected that Congress would "determine in a day or two, on the report of the committee." When it did, he would transmit the proceedings to Washington.[58]

Arnold's optimism was misplaced. He reckoned without the persistence of Joseph Reed, and the influence of his council. Colonel Charles Pettit reported that "discontent between certain parts of Congress and the Council of this State is grown to a disagreeable height." The committee appointed to investigate "General Arnold's affair" had "taken a good deal of pains in the inquiry, but the Council disliked their mode of proceeding, and some altercation happened by letters in the course of it." Pettit heard that the committee had recommended an acquittal, at which the council seemed "much dissatisfied." The dispute was now about more than the reputation of Benedict Arnold: it had morphed into a contest between federal and state authority, a confrontation which threatened to destabilize the patriot cause at a critical point in the war with Britain. Anxious to avoid a rift with Pennsylvania at all costs, Congress decided that its own committee should confer with a joint committee of the state's assembly and executive council.[59]

As the new inquiry dragged on, Arnold struggled to conceal his impatience. On March 27, he appealed to John Jay: six weeks had elapsed since the first committee was appointed, and he was still "held up to the public as a most notorious criminal." He implored: "If I am guilty, public justice requires a speedy and exemplary punishment. If I am innocent, justice is equally due to an injured character." A week later, on April 3, the committee of Congress announced its resolutions, which amended those made in March. Washington was now directed to appoint a court martial to try all *four* of the charges (the first, second, third, and fifth) deemed cognizable under military law. Other resolutions tabled that day left no doubt that the revisions were a pragmatic response to the overriding need for unity. Indeed, "that unanimity and harmony between the representatives of the United States in Congress assembled and each state individually, has been, under God, the happy means of our past success, and the only sure foundation whereon to rest our future hopes of terminating the contest with Great Britain with honor and advantage." For the greater good, Congress was ready to humble itself before Reed and his colleagues. Being "highly sensible of the importance and services of the State of Pennsylvania in the present contest," it must "regard with sincere concern and regret every event which may tend to lessen the mutual confidence and affection which has hitherto subsisted." Turning to the old anxieties about over-mighty military men, the resolutions made it clear that civil power was paramount, and "any disrespectful and indecent behavior of any officers of any rank, under the appointment of Congress, to the civil authority of any State in the union, will be discountenanced and discouraged." There must be no deviation from this line: when Thomas Burke ventured his opinion that the Supreme Executive Council of Pennsylvania "had acted in a waspish, peevish and childish manner," he was swiftly "called to order."[60]

In a letter to Jay, Arnold evinced surprise that a court martial should be ordered to try him for offences including "some of which the committee of Congress in their report say 'There appears no evidence to prove the same.'" But he was under no illusion about the real reason behind the revised resolution—that he had been abandoned to appease Pennsylvania: "If Congress have been induced to take this measure for the public good and to avoid a breach with this state, however hard my case may be, and however I am injured as an individual, I will suffer with pleasure," he wrote. Arnold was sure that when the court martial sat, it would acquit him of those charges "a second time."[61]

* * *

By now, Arnold's marriage to Peggy was imminent. On March 22, 1779, he took out a mortgage on Mount Pleasant, a fine mansion set in almost a hundred acres of grounds on the eastern bank of the Schuylkill. It had previously belonged to the father of Captain John MacPherson, the aide who had been killed alongside General Montgomery at Quebec in the early hours of December 31, 1775, on the night when Arnold had suffered his first wound. Although the estate was settled on Arnold and his future wife for life, he rented it out while staying on at the Penn house.[62]

On April 8, 1779, Arnold and Peggy Shippen were married at Judge Shippen's mansion. It was eighteen months since Arnold had been wounded while storming Breymann's Redoubt, but he remained unable even to stand unaided for long: during the wedding ceremony, he had to be "supported by a soldier, and when seated his disabled limb was propped up on a camp stool." According to gossip, Arnold's injuries did not prevent him from consummating his marriage with enthusiasm. Post-treason rumor picked up in Philadelphia by George Grieve, the English translator of General Chastellux's *Travels*, maintained that Arnold was so delighted with his wedding night that he left his brother officers in no doubt of its pleasures. Grieve (who lost no opportunity to insert bawdy anecdotes within his lengthy footnotes to the chevalier's text) tutted: "With what delicacy could be beloved a woman by that miscreant, who made the mysteries of the nuptial bed the subject of his coarse ribaldry to his companions, the day after his marriage!"[63]

Despite his domestic happiness, Arnold was becoming increasingly frustrated by the charges that still hung over his head. On about April 18, he wrote to Washington requesting that a court martial be summoned to sit as soon as possible. This was now his only means of vindication: "though Congress, to avoid a breach with this state, have declined deciding on the report of their committee, I have no doubt of obtaining justice from a court martial, as every officer in the army must feel himself injured by the cruel and unprecedented treatment I have met with from a set of scoundrels in office."[64]

In obedience to Congress's resolution, on April 20, 1779, Washington informed Arnold that he had ordered a court martial to sit at headquarters, Middlebrook, on May 1, to try him on the four charges transmitted by Congress. The hearing was soon postponed for at least a month, because the prosecution needed time to assemble witnesses now serving in the South.

Washington explained to Arnold that while the delay "must be irksome," it was justified, allowing "the necessity of a free and full investigation both for the sake of public justice and for your own honor." The hearing was finally fixed for June 1, "unless something very extraordinary" intervened. It did: the trial was deferred again on June 2, "the exigency of public service not permitting to sit at this time." It was not until December 23, 1779, that proceedings finally opened.[65]

When Arnold heard that the court martial was to be put off until June or even July, he wrote Washington a letter that left no doubt of his agitation, and which hints at some inner turmoil. Arnold believed that the Pennsylvania Council was deliberately evading a trial, the result of which would show them "in their true colors as a set of unprincipled, malicious scoundrels, who have prostituted their honor, and truth, for the purpose of gratifying their private resentment against an innocent person." As Arnold went on, he adopted an almost hysterical tone, out of all proportion to the charges against him; it suggests genuine desperation:

If Your Excellency thinks me criminal, for Heaven's sake let me be immediately tried and, if found guilty, executed; I want no favor, I ask only for justice. If it is denied me from Your Excellency I have nowhere to seek it but of the candid public before whom I shall be under the necessity of laying the whole matter. Let me beg of you, Sir, to consider that a set of artful, unprincipled men in office may misinterpret the most innocent actions, and by raising the public clamor against Your Excellency, place you in the same disagreeable situation I am in. Having made every sacrifice of blood and fortune, and become a cripple in the service of my country, I little expected to meet the ungrateful returns I have received of my countrymen, but as Congress have stamped ingratitude as a current coin, I must take it.

Arnold continued in the same wild vein: "I have nothing left but the little reputation I have gained in the army. Delay in the present case is worse than death." He maintained that the matter ought to have been settled long since; Reed and his council were only prevaricating, so that the trial would be delayed until the campaigning season opened, "concluding undoubtedly that the service will then prevent the court from sitting, the trial postponed to the end of the campaign, and their cruel and villainous purposes answered."[66]

But what were those unspecified "purposes"? Was Arnold suggesting that Reed and his followers were deliberately pushing him toward some momentous decision? As events would show, by hounding the increasingly beleaguered Arnold to answer a raft of mostly minor charges, they influenced his decision to commit a far graver crime than even they could have imagined.

On May 15, Washington responded to Arnold's extraordinary, unrestrained letter with his customary moderation. He had read it "with no small concern." While assuring Arnold that he had no unfavorable sentiments toward him, he must nonetheless be seen to be impartial while a "full and fair trial" went ahead. Washington considered his own situation to be "truly delicate and embarrassing." Arnold's "anxiety" was "very natural in such circumstances"; and "the convenience of the army" was another reason to push for "a speedy conclusion." On the other hand, Washington reasoned, "the pointed representations of the state on the subject of witnesses, and the impropriety of precipitating a trial so important in itself" left him no choice.[67]

Two weeks later, Arnold's close friend Silas Deane wrote from Philadelphia to General Greene. The letter would be delivered by Arnold himself, "who though deprived of the use of either leg, and in constant pain, feels so much more severely the wounds his character has received from base and envious men." Deane added:

> Great God! Is it possible that after the bold and perilous enterprises which this man has undertaken, for the service and defense of his country, the loss of his fortune and the cruel, and lingering pains he has suffered from the wounds received fighting these battles, there can be found among us men so abandoned to the hard and infernal passions of envy and malice as to persecute him with the most unrelenting fury and to wish to destroy what alone he has the prospect of saving out of the dreadful wreck of health, fortune, and life, his character?[68]

But by then, Benedict Arnold had already embarked on the treason that would cost him even that.

5

EMBARKING UPON TREASON

For Captain John André, Monday, May 10, 1779 began like most other days at Sir Henry Clinton's headquarters at Number 1 Wall Street, near the tip of Manhattan Island. André's hard-fighting mentor Major-General Grey had returned to England at the close of the previous campaign, but such was the captain's "conspicuous merit and amiable manners" that Sir Henry promptly accepted him into his own military "family" as an aide-de-camp. André's winter quarters in New York had proved as convivial as his last in Philadelphia. Once again, he had taken to the stage and written witty compositions that were published by the loyalist press. Despite such diversions, André had not neglected his profession, and was reckoned the most promising and capable of Clinton's young aides. As a versatile staff officer, André "soon became the chief person about the General," while his "affability, his candor, and his politeness, gained him universal esteem." If this sounds suspiciously like a panegyric, other testimony confirms that André was an unusually popular officer. The strongest proof of his winning personality was the warm friendship that he developed with Clinton, a socially awkward man who struggled to form meaningful relationships.[1]

André's diligence and discretion had recently earned him the responsibility of sifting through the intelligence reports brought into headquarters by Sir Henry's own agents, deserters from the enemy, and civilians inclined to sell useful information; this was vital work that Clinton had previously overseen himself. That May morning, the captain was entrusted with an assignment of unusual importance: Joseph Stansbury, a Londoner who now ran a glass and china shop on Philadelphia's Front Street, had come to New York seeking an urgent interview. Among the Patriots, Stansbury was well known for his loyalist leanings. He was an opponent of independence, who had cooperated with the British when they occupied the city; but like others, he was permitted to stay on after Clinton's withdrawal when he took the oath of allegiance to Congress. Now Stansbury had crucial intelligence to divulge. His information was of such a momentous and sensitive nature that he had undertaken a risky journey across rebel-held New Jersey to communicate it in person. At first, Stansbury's words were difficult for André to credit, leaving him in a "kind of confusion." His consternation was understandable: Major-General Benedict Arnold, the celebrated paladin of American liberty, wanted to enlist in the service of His Britannic Majesty, King George III.[2]

According to a declaration made by Stansbury nearly five years later, Arnold first contacted him "about the month of June 1779." In fact, as the known date of Stansbury's interview with André reveals, they met several weeks before, in early May. Stansbury recalled that Arnold had sent for him, and "after some general conversation, opened his political sentiments respecting the war carrying on between Great Britain and America, declaring his abhorrence of a separation of the latter from the former as a measure that would be ruinous to both." Under a "solemn obligation of secrecy," Arnold mentioned "his intention of offering his services to the Commander-in-Chief of the British forces, in any way that would most effectually restore the former government and destroy the then usurped authority of Congress, either by immediately joining the British army, or cooperating on some concerted plan with Sir Henry Clinton." Given the clear importance of Arnold's offer, Stansbury had lost no time in traveling "secretly to New York with a tender of his services" to the general.[3]

Directly Stansbury had delivered his startling intelligence, André informed Sir Henry. Pondering over the full significance of Arnold's over-tures, the captain then wrote a detailed and reasoned response for Stansbury to communicate to him; a draft of this document was kept at headquarters for reference. While André was sure that he had expressed his views fully and clearly during their conversation, he was leaving nothing to chance: the subject was "of too much importance not to take further pains that all may be perfectly well comprehended." Although there is no surviving record of Stansbury's verbal report of Arnold's opening offer, André's written reply makes it possible to reconstruct its key proposals and demands. The captain's letter also provides a useful basis for addressing the central enigma of Benedict Arnold's extraordinary life: why was he prepared to turn his back on the cause for which he had fought with such conspicuous courage, and defect to the British?[4]

Before considering the evidence in detail, it should be emphasized that any analysis of Arnold's motivation is skewed by the fact that almost all of his own surviving testimony dates from *after* the exposure of the treason on September 25, 1780. However, the reasons he subsequently gave to justify his conduct—in a letter to Washington written just hours after escaping to the British, in an address "To the Inhabitants of America" published in New York that October, and in repeated attempts to secure compensation and patronage from the British government—are remarkably consistent. This unwavering position could be interpreted as a self-serving mantra, and just another example of Arnold's stubborn, single-minded faith in his own "rectitude"; but its core arguments reflect those recalled by Stansbury, and are corroborated by the independent evidence of others, notably the most senior British officer to be involved in his treason from the outset, Sir Henry Clinton. Crucially, some of this testimony dates from *before* Arnold's arrival in New York, and the onset of his efforts to vindicate himself.

* * *

Once Major-General Benedict Arnold of the Continental Army had turned his coat, it was widely believed that he had been artfully "seduced" by the British; approached by Sir Henry's agents, it was reported, he was "brought over" to the royal cause. Lieutenant Christopher Hele of the Royal Navy and Colonel Beverly Robinson of the Loyal American Regiment were both cred-ited with this achievement, but in neither case is the evidence convincing. According to the English translator of Chastellux's *Travels*, George Grieve, Hele "was undoubtedly a very active and industrious spy in Philadelphia in the winter of 1778," being sent there under a bogus flag of truce. Hele was arrested by Congress after he sailed up the Delaware River in command of the tender *Hotham* in October 1778, carrying the last-ditch "Manifesto and Proclamation" of Lord Carlisle's peace commissioners; in December, he was released on giving his parole to stay within Philadelphia, and it is possible that he spoke with Arnold then. Yet nothing has been found to support

Grieve's confident claim that there was "every reason to suppose that Arnold's treachery took its date" from their "connection" at that time.[5]

Unlike Hele, Colonel Robinson was an established player in Sir Henry Clinton's intelligence-gathering operations. His personal knowledge of the Hudson Highlands, combined with detailed reports from his agents, contributed to the success of Clinton's strike against the rebel forts there in October 1777. Robinson's responsibility for recruiting his own network of spies emerges from a letter that André wrote to him on Clinton's behalf two years later, and which offers a glimpse into the workings of the British espionage system—and the proliferation of double-agents:

> The commander-in-chief has received your letter and desires you would employ the man you speak of on the service proposed. He will give the required reward for any dispatches of importance and a proportion where there shall have been evident enterprise and risk. He only leaves you the care of not suffering ourselves to be imposed upon.

Robinson's informant is unidentified; but given the dating, he was clearly not Arnold, who had offered his services five months earlier. In his *Biographical Sketches* of American Loyalists, published in 1847, Lorenzo Sabine noted Robinson's conspicuous role in "cases of defection from the Whig cause." Concerning Robinson's involvement with Arnold, he added: "it is supposed he was acquainted with the traitor's purpose before it was known to Sir Henry Clinton, or any other person." But "supposed" does not withstand close examination of the sources first revealed by Carl Van Doren nearly a century later: while Robinson certainly played an important role in the final stages of Arnold's conspiracy, there is no reliable evidence that he initiated a British effort to "turn" him.[6]

As André's interview with Stansbury makes clear, and as George Washington's astute and well-informed aide, Lieutenant-Colonel Alexander Hamilton, swiftly deduced, the "project . . . originated with Arnold himself." Given Arnold's well-known need for funds to sustain his costly lifestyle, his outraged countrymen quickly attributed his actions to simple greed: former comrades voiced this consensus view when they declared that the traitor was "corrupted by the influence of British gold," a commodity for which he had an "inordinate thirst." While later historians have acknowledged that Arnold was influenced by a variety of factors, in weighing up their relative importance they have typically echoed the verdict of 1780. In 1954, for example, Willard Wallace observed: "More certain than any of Arnold's reasons for selling himself to the British was his desire for money"; sixty years later, Nathaniel Philbrick likewise concluded that when all else was considered, Arnold "was doing this first and foremost for the money."[7]

Despite the lurid stories that his contemporaries accepted so readily, Arnold was not tempted into treason by a British bribe like that recently proffered to Joseph Reed by the rogue peace commissioner George Johnstone. Yet the question of payment for services rendered and compensation for losses sustained certainly figured in his negotiations from the outset, and would become an enduring theme. As befitted a former merchant accustomed to driving a hard bargain, Arnold saw no reason why he should not receive adequate recompense for the risks run, the costs incurred, and the property that he stood to forfeit if it transpired that he had picked the wrong side. For helping to end a bloody war and restore crown rule, he expected commensurate dividends. On that score, Captain André was quick to reassure him: in his response of May 10, he promised "that in the very first instance of receiving the tidings or good offices we receive from him, our liberality will be evinced." Something more substantial—"any partial but important blow"—based on accurate intelligence and ready cooperation, would result in "rewards equal at least to what such service can be estimated at." But if Arnold's "abilities and zeal" should lead to the defeat of a "numerous body" of enemy troops, or the capture of an "obnoxious band of men" (such as Congress), "then would the generosity of the nation exceed even his own most sanguine hopes." If all Arnold's efforts failed, and he was obliged to flee to the British, André pledged that "the cause in which he suffers will hold itself bound to indemnify him for losses and receive him with the honor his conduct deserves."

Other evidence suggests that money was not Arnold's primary motivation, although it was clearly an important consideration. Indeed, it can be argued, the issue of payment only arose in consequence of a decision that he had *already* reached on different grounds, both personal and ideological. While the point is often overlooked, chiefly because Arnold's treason is inevitably associated with his attempt to deliver up West Point in September 1780, he was ready and willing to join the British army seventeen months before he actually did so; he only refrained because Sir Henry Clinton insisted that he could "render more essential services by continuing in the

American army, and corresponding and cooperating" with him. The fact
that Arnold was prepared to defect in May 1779, but desisted in deference to
Clinton's wishes, is important when assessing the financial incentive against
other motivations: it undermines the common assertion that he embarked
on his treason with the intention of deliberately prolonging negotiations
until he had secured the best possible price for his services.[8]

The timing of Arnold's first move is itself suggestive of motivations other
than money. Arnold made his opening approach to Sir Henry just days after
the emotional letter of May 5, 1779, in which he had appealed for George
Washington to expedite his court martial on the charges urged so persistently
by Pennsylvania's Supreme Executive Council. Unless Arnold's decision to
defect was virtually spontaneous, triggered by continuing uncertainty over
the date of his impending trial, he must have been thinking over his options
for some time before he contacted Joseph Stansbury. A range of evidence
supports the latter interpretation: Arnold's decision stemmed from the steady
accumulation of grievances spanning years, eventually brought to a head by
the coalescence of several different issues within a shorter timeframe.

A theme that emerges clearly from Arnold's efforts to vindicate himself
is his gradual disillusionment with the Patriots' political leadership, matched
by a growing disenchantment at the changing nature and scope of the
Revolutionary War. Friction with politicians can be traced back to Arnold's
first military campaign in 1775, when he struggled to secure repayment of
his legitimate expenses from Massachusetts; he subsequently became
embroiled in a more protracted tussle with Congress to achieve rank and
recognition that was only resolved in December 1777, as he was recuperating from his crippling Saratoga wound; worst of all was his bitter feud
with Pennsylvania's radical Patriots. In both his 1780 address to the "inhabitants of America," and four years later, when seeking compensation from
the British commissioners appointed to assess loyalist claims, Arnold made
no secret of the fact that he had entered the conflict as an ardent supporter
of American liberties in the face of oppressive crown taxation: "When I
quitted domestic happiness for the perils of the field, I conceived the rights
of my country in danger, and that duty and honor called me to her defense,"
he declared. Believing Great Britain's claims on America "to be unjust he
took up arms and joined his countrymen in opposition." Back in 1775, he
maintained, his sole object had been a "redress of grievances, of which in
his opinion the Americans justly complained." Arnold had "not a wish or

idea of promoting a separation of that country from Great Britain, or throwing off the Government of the latter, and forming an independent Government there." He considered the Declaration of Independence to be "precipitate," but had nonetheless "acquiesced"; busy fighting in the field, he had served on with the "negligent confidence of a soldier." That was true enough: in the summer of 1776, Arnold had been preoccupied with the task of preparing a flotilla to contest a British invasion from Canada via Lake Champlain.[9]

Writing to George Johnstone in 1784, Arnold claimed that his "sentiments respecting the war" were constant and unchanging throughout its course; they were well known to the Loyalist Major Philip Skene and "several other British officers, to whom I declared that my only object was to obtain a redress of grievances, and at the same time I disclaimed any idea of independence or a separation from Great Britain." Neither Skene nor the other unnamed officers left any confirmation of Arnold's avowed "sentiments." Nor is the "time" at which he expressed his views to them specified, although one possibility is his traumatic stay in the sprawling military hospital at Albany during the fall of 1777; both British and American casualties were treated there, and when Burgoyne's captured army passed through the town on its way to Boston, there would have been a further opportunity to fraternize with redcoat officers curious to meet the intrepid patriot general who was widely credited with engineering their defeat. Arnold's dispiriting months in Albany, when the physical pain of his dangerous wound was compounded by a mounting resentment against Congress, may have nurtured seeds of disaffection that soon after sprouted into full-blown treason.[10]

The arrival of Johnstone and his fellow peace commissioners in America in the spring of 1778 marked a definite turning point for Arnold, or so he later claimed: "conceiving the overtures and proposals made by Great Britain to America ... for peace and reunion of the two countries to be just and equitable, [I] used [my] endeavors and influence to have them accepted," he testified in 1784. There is no surviving evidence that Arnold actively lobbied Congress, or any other body, to that end, although it is certainly possible that he discussed the proposals for reconciliation informally, not least among the pro-Tory circles in which he moved in Philadelphia, arousing the scorn and suspicion of radical Patriots like Joseph Reed. In his 1780 address, Arnold maintained that, as the "whole world saw, and all America confessed," the offers of the 1778 commission "exceeded our wishes and expectations." Some months earlier, before finally going over to the British, Arnold had apparently expressed similar sentiments to Joshua Hett Smith, who would become an unwitting accessory to the treason's culmination. While Smith's published *Authentic Narrative* is frequently unreliable regarding his own involvement in events, it contains other incidental information, not bearing on his actions, that deserves careful consideration. Smith recalled that Arnold was adamant that the "overtures made on the part of Great Britain by her commissioners . . . were founded in *all sincerity* and *good faith*, [and] that they fully met the *ultimatum* that the generality of Americans desired."[11]

The blunt rejection of Carlisle and his colleagues coincided with another development that Arnold drew on to justify his defection. To Joshua Smith he "expressed his detestation of the French alliance." As a staunchly Protestant native of New England, where a hatred of the long-standing Catholic enemy in Canada had been transmitted intact across the generations, Arnold had strong traditional grounds for his animosity. But Smith recalled that Arnold had objected to the French because of the "perfidiousness of their national character" and had "ridiculed the solecism and inconsistency of an absolute monarch being the ally of a people contending for freedom, who kept his own subjects in the most desperate and absolute slavery." In addition, Arnold "thought it was an unnatural union, of no duration, and that it was not made by France until she saw the Americans were able to defend themselves, which would be more to their own national honor and glory."[12]

Sir Henry Clinton highlighted the importance of the French alliance in changing Arnold's allegiance: in a draft letter to Germain, written in October 1780, he noted that Arnold's first "secret correspondence" had "expressed a displeasure at the alliance between America and France," while in an undated memorandum written sometime after the end of the Revolutionary War, he observed: "G. Arnold supported the rebellion as long as he thought the Americans right; but when he thought them wrong, particularly by connecting themselves with France, he told them so [and] opened a correspondence with me, offering his services in a manner I would accept them." In his memoir of the American war, Sir Henry also recalled that when Arnold initially approached him, he was "dissatisfied with many late proceedings of the American Congress, particularly their alliance with France." If Smith and (especially) Clinton are to be believed, Arnold's dissatisfaction at Franco-American cooperation was not simply cited retrospectively, as an additional post-treason justification for his treacherous behavior, but had riled him from the very outset.[13]

* * *

Arnold's exasperation at the failure of Congress to treat with the Carlisle Commissioners, and instead form an alliance with the old enemy of Britons on both sides of the Atlantic, was only exacerbated by the succession of problems he soon after faced as military commandant of Philadelphia. When Arnold opened up to Joshua Smith during the tense late summer of 1780, he had "complained of being ill used by Congress and the Executive Council of Pennsylvania, which *had treated him with injustice*, in not *sufficiently estimating his services*." After coming to New York, he had told much the same story to Lieutenant-General James Robertson, a veteran Scot who admired Arnold's fighting record and welcomed him into his household. Reporting back to the British army's commander-in-chief in London, Lord Jeffery Amherst, Robertson explained that Arnold had "squabbled with a General Reid [sic], the Congress sided with the last, and Arnold thought himself ill-used, and found means eighteenth [sic] months ago to offer his service to the King." In the immediate wake of the treason, Alexander Hamilton believed that Arnold had turned to the British because "the ingratitude he had experienced from his countrymen, concurring with other causes, had entirely changed his principles." Hamilton's incisive mind cut to the heart of Arnold's treason: mounting resentment at his treatment by politicians who had impugned his honor and reputation had eventually caused a profound ideological conversion.[14]

The converging grievances that alienated Arnold from the Patriots underpinned his most striking justification for turning his coat, one that allowed him to reconcile his prized honor with conduct that would be condemned as utterly dishonorable. He explained his reasoning to an appalled George Washington, just hours after his treason was finally exposed: aware of taking "a step, which the world may censure as wrong," Arnold claimed that he had "ever acted from a principle of love for my country, since the commencement of the present unhappy contest between Great Britain and the Colonies." That same principle "actuates my present conduct," he wrote, "however it may appear inconsistent to the world, who very seldom judge right of any man's actions." From British-held New York city, he declared publicly that his defection was in the best interests of his countrymen, and calculated to staunch an "effusion of blood."[15]

Arnold's perception of himself as a healer of the gaping fratricidal wound between Crown and colonies supports Stansbury's recollection of his "abhorrence" of a "ruinous" conflict. A letter that Arnold wrote to Washington in mid-May 1779, just days after he had sent Stansbury to New York with his offer to turn traitor, uses language that is highly suggestive of his thinking at that time. Happy to learn that his court martial had finally been fixed for June 1, Arnold explained that while he had been "ungratefully treated" by "a set of men who, void of principle, are governed entirely by private interest," he did not blame his "countrymen in general" for his predicament. He added: "The interest I have in the welfare and happiness of my country, which I have ever evinced when in my power, will I hope always overcome my personal resentment for any injury I can possibly receive from individuals." Of course, timed as it was, this letter could be cited as an instance of Arnold's bare-faced hypocrisy; yet the possibility remains that its wording reflects beliefs that provided him with a powerful incentive to resolve what seemed like an increasingly misguided and futile war—in any way he could. This was certainly Arnold's stated goal from the outset: in June 1779, barely a month after his first approach, Sir Henry Clinton reminded him "that you proposed your assistance for the delivery of your country."[16]

In 1784, when seeking compensation for his wartime losses, Arnold was still adamant that he had defected in the hope of ending the "civil war in America." Eight years later, he continued to emphasize that his objective had been to "bring about a reunion of Great Britain and her colonies." Appealing for Sir Henry Clinton's patronage, Arnold made it clear that he remained proud of both his American birth and his broader British identity: "I beg leave to observe that neither money or any other consideration but the cause I was embarked in could have induced me to run the hazards which I did, and from the whole tenor of my conduct, I am convinced that you are sensible that I have not been governed by interest, but by principles of Loyalty, and by attachment to both countries," he wrote. In response, Clinton reiterated his own belief in Arnold's sincerity. If he had not been convinced that his negotiation "arose solely from principle and a conviction of your error" he would never have "paid that regard to it I did," as "being ultimately deceived . . . would have been the probable consequence of my entering into so important a treaty with a person manifestly actuated by interest."[17]

When considering whether Arnold's dedication to a rapprochement between Crown and colonies really was a deeply held conviction or whether it was concocted retrospectively to bolster his own persistent claims on the British government, the timing of his opening gambit to Sir Henry Clinton is once again significant. In May 1779, the British were demoralized and despondent: following upon the humiliating evacuation of Philadelphia and the abject failure of the Carlisle Commission, Clinton's veteran army had been severely weakened by the hefty detachments sent to the Caribbean and elsewhere in response to French military intervention on the side of the American rebels. Clinton was so pessimistic about British prospects that, like William Howe before him, he wanted to resign his command. If Arnold was simply hoping to switch from a losing to a winning cause, and share the spoils of an overwhelming imperial victory, then he had picked an inauspicious moment to do so. Arnold's readiness to defect when the war's outcome was uncertain supports a contention that the reasons he gave to Stansbury in Philadelphia were made in all sincerity: thoroughly disillusioned by his shabby treatment at the hands of Congress, he now wished to see that body overthrown, and the fractured British Empire reunified and reinstated for his country's good.

Arnold's commitment to a restoration of the old regime was made clear during Stansbury's interview with André. He wanted a guarantee that Britain was determined to maintain its efforts to crush the rebellion, and would not relinquish the struggle by conceding American independence. And as a native-born American, like the professed Loyalists Arnold had a far more personal stake in the outcome of the contest than British or German officers whose families and properties were safe on the far side of the Atlantic; he had no intention of joining an army that was ready to give up the fight. Here, André was once again quick to offer "the strongest assurances of our sincerity, that no thought is entertained of abandoning the point we have in view." On the contrary, he continued, "powerful means are expected for accomplishing our end."

The role that Arnold envisaged for himself in helping to overthrow the "usurping Congress" and "restore the former government" was encapsulated in his chosen codename, by which André referred to him in his reply: "Monk." To anyone familiar with British history, as educated Anglo-Americans were, there was no mistaking its significance. During the last English civil war of the mid-seventeenth century, Major-General George Monck had served in the Parliamentarian forces against the Royalists of Charles I. After the king's execution in 1649 and the establishment of the Commonwealth under Lord

Protector Oliver Cromwell, Monck had commanded in Scotland. But in 1660, Monck deserted the republican cause and, by marching his troops south in support of the exiled Charles II, became a key player in restoring the Stuart monarchy: "Monk" was therefore an apt moniker for a rebel general prepared to switch allegiance to the royal regime against which he had previously fought.

The parallel resonated with Clinton and with other British officers who served in the American war. In his memoir of the conflict, Sir Henry recalled that an "overture" from "an officer of Mr. Arnold's ability and fame, could not but attract my attention; and I thought it possible, that like another General Monk [sic], he might have repented of the part he had taken and wish to make atonement for injuries he had done his country by rendering her some signal and adequate benefit." Some years later Colonel John Graves Simcoe, who came to know Arnold well, confirmed that Sir Henry had always considered him "as desirous of playing the role of Monk [sic]."[18]

For his decisive intervention, George Monck had earned handsome rewards from his grateful monarch: honors, wealth, and the hereditary title of duke of Albemarle. He was also awarded tracts of land across the Atlantic, in what would become the colony of North Carolina, chartered by Charles II in honor of his martyred father. If Arnold matched Monck's success, he could expect no less from George III, who was more determined than any of his subjects to restore the rebellious American colonies to the British Empire. Arnold would secure the acclaim and social standing that he had always craved. The prize was dazzling; but it does not detract from the possibility that Arnold, as Simcoe would argue in 1787, had come to see himself as the savior of his distressed and distracted countrymen, intent on delivering them from the horrors of another bloody civil war.

* * *

In assessing the motivations behind Benedict Arnold's treason, a final factor must be considered. How far did his young wife influence his actions? Once again, the timing is highly suggestive: Arnold was married on April 8, 1779; within a month he had contacted Joseph Stansbury to offer his services to Sir Henry Clinton. Under the circumstances, it's tempting to see Peggy Arnold as a catalyst, encouraging her besotted and conflicted husband to turn to the British, or even, as some writers have argued, originating the treason herself.

Peggy Arnold was never openly accused of complicity in the plot during her own lifetime; but her friendship with British officers like John André, and the loyalist sympathies of her father, Edward Shippen, gave grounds for speculation and gossip as soon as the conspiracy was exposed. When he visited Philadelphia in December 1780, that keen observer of American life, the chevalier de Chastellux, was invited to drink tea at the house of Colonel Bland. He recorded that the "scene was graced by several married and unmarried ladies." Among those claiming "particular distinction" was Miss Nancy Shippen, the daughter of Dr. William Shippen—and the cousin of Mrs. Peggy Arnold. Chastellux observed:

> Thus we see in America the crimes of individuals do not reflect upon their family; not only had Dr. Shippen's brother [actually his cousin, Edward] given his daughter to the traitor Arnold a short time before his desertion, but it is generally believed that being himself a Tory, he had inspired his daughter with the same sentiments, and that the charms of this handsome woman contributed not a little to hasten to criminality a mind corrupted by avarice, before it felt the power of love.[19]

Congressman Charles Thomson had already wondered about Peggy Arnold's hold over a man who was "brave but avaricious, fond of parade, and not very scrupulous about the means of acquiring money to defray the expenses of it." While unconvinced of Peggy's involvement in the plot itself, Thomson's suspicions were aroused by her "Tory" connections. After all, he wrote, she was a "young woman who had been distinguished by General Howe's Mischianza knights, and her father was not remarkable for attachment to the American cause." As reported in the *Pennsylvania Packet*, Peggy had received correspondence from John André *after* the British departed Philadelphia for New York; whether there was a more sinister purpose to the letter, written "under pretense of supplying her with millinery," Thomson could not say, and its true significance was not revealed at that time.[20]

For a century and a half after Arnold's defection, historians were virtually unanimous in absolving his wife of any *deliberate* part in his despicable crime, while also recognizing that her sympathies and social network played some role in turning him toward the British. For example, Jared Sparks considered that Arnold's marriage "probably had a large share among the original causes" of his defection. Besides his wife's "biases" toward such British officers as

Captain André, the "alliance" brought Arnold into "perpetual contact with persons who had no sympathy with the friends of liberty . . . but who, on the contrary, condemned their acts, and secretly hoped that the power of the British King would crush all opposition and again predominate." But for all that, Sparks stopped short of actually accusing Peggy herself, believing that, despite her influence on her husband, she remained oblivious of his treasonable correspondence.[21]

For Peggy's contemporaries, the prevailing belief that she was entirely innocent of treason was largely a consequence of her youthful beauty and engaging personality, which played on both the lustful and the chivalrous instincts of susceptible males of all ages. But it also reflected ingrained patriarchal attitudes toward women of Peggy Shippen's refined background, who were assumed to be morally and mentally incapable of such brazen duplicity. These well-meaning but patronizing views also influenced the opinions of many nineteenth- and early twentieth-century historians. In 1865, one scholarly editor observed of Peggy: "she was, probably, unconscious of the true facts of the case, and of too light and frivolous a character, to be trusted with a plan in which silence and mystery were essential elements of success." Clearing Peggy of any involvement in the plot, Winthrop Sargent's 1861 biography of André lauded her "purity and elevation of character." Writing in 1907, Albert Bushnell Hart, a professor of history at Harvard, acquitted her of any wrong-doing on the extraordinary grounds that "To be Mrs. Benedict Arnold was in itself a heavy fate, and there is no need to add the guilt of treason."[22]

While there is no *conclusive* proof that Peggy Arnold persuaded her husband to change sides, still less that she originated his treason, it is now clear that she not only knew of his designs, but was involved in the conspiracy from its inception. Her participation was first uncovered in 1941, when Carl Van Doren published papers from the headquarters of Sir Henry Clinton, including André's careful record of his interview with Stansbury. In response to a query raised during their conversation, the captain commented: "The lady might write to me at the same time with one of her intimates." He added: "she will guess who I mean." André would himself write to the friend, "to give occasion for a reply." A letter that André composed soon after was addressed to Miss Peggy Chew, who had accompanied him to the Mischianza a year earlier: this leaves no doubt that "the lady" in question was Mrs. Peggy Arnold.[23]

After apologizing to Miss Chew for failing to forward drawings of the head-dresses fashionable in New York, André casually inserted the crucial sentence:

> I trust I am yet in the memory of the little society of Third and Fourth Street, and even of the *other Peggy* now Mrs. Arnold who will, I am sure, accept of my best respects and with the rest of the sisterhoods of both streets peruse not disdainfully this page meant as an assurance of my unabated esteem for them.

It is clear that André expected Peggy Chew to show his letter to Peggy Arnold. As the recipient of the captain's letters, Peggy Chew would give her replies to Mrs. Arnold, so that they could be formally sent to André in British-occupied New York city under a flag of truce, or by an officer crossing the lines in an exchange of prisoners. Using an espionage technique known as "interlining," André explained to Stansbury, Peggy Arnold could transform her friend's innocent letters into valuable communications. This method involved adding phrases in invisible ink between the lines already written by Peggy Chew; once received by André, the secret message would be "discovered" by a reactivating process, involving either flame or acid. Whether André actually sent his letter to Peggy Chew remains unclear; but as Arnold's treason unfolded, "the lady" would play a part that the British were ready to acknowledge and reward.

* * *

When he met with Joseph Stansbury at headquarters, Captain André's priority was to provide the assurances that Benedict Arnold required, before acting on his decision to dedicate himself to the service of King George. Once he had addressed those overriding concerns, André turned to the question of how "Monk" could best aid the royal cause. Naturally enough, Arnold's "own judgment" would indicate his most useful services, but André took the opportunity to offer some "hints."

The captain's wish list was comprehensive, ranging from the gathering of routine intelligence to more ambitious ploys. He was interested in the proceedings of councils of war, and the contents of dispatches from the rebels' foreign allies; if they could be intercepted and forwarded to headquarters, so much the better. Also welcome were details of troop strengths and disposi-tions, including the origin, timing, and destination of reinforcements; like-wise the location of any new magazines or stores. In addition, Arnold could consider ways of delivering some decisive "blow of importance." André's "hints" included suggestions that provide an insight into the British high command's growing belief that the American rebellion could be broken from within, by exploiting widespread dissatisfaction with Congress: to that end, Arnold might exert his influence to sway other high-ranking officers who shared his "favorable disposition" toward the Crown, and to foment "any party which when risen to a height might perhaps easily be drawn into a desire of accommodation rather than submit to an odious yoke." Finally, Arnold could work to achieve "an exchange of prisoners for the *honor* of America." This was a reference to the "Convention Army" surrendered at Saratoga in October 1777, but still impounded by Congress, in breach of the overly lenient terms that the flustered Horatio Gates had granted to Burgoyne.

Before closing his letter for Stansbury, André turned to the technical details of *how* the secret correspondence with Arnold would be carried on between them. When sending coded messages, both were to use a copy of an identical "long book"; in the initial exchanges, this was the hefty *Bailey's Dictionary*, which ran to more than 900 pages; soon, *Blackstone's Commentaries* were also employed. When referring to the book in question, three sets of numbers would create a code to identify each word in the message: the first denoted the page, the second the line, and the third the word itself. As a further level of security, when conveying "general information, as to the complexion of affairs," the true meaning could be disguised by reference to "an old woman's health." If invisible ink was used, as in the "interlining" recommended for Peggy Arnold, or for an entire "blank" page, the letter "F" would indicate messages to be revealed by fire, and "A" by acid. Using this system, Arnold's correspondence would be encoded by Stansbury, and then forwarded by him to André. The captain would either decipher the message himself or entrust that task to Jonathan Odell, a loyalist clergyman in New York, who had probably helped to arrange the meeting with Stansbury.[24]

The forty-two-year-old Odell, who later claimed to have "rendered confi-dential services of essential importance to the British Government," was chaplain to a loyalist regiment and, like Stansbury and André, dabbled in poetry. Born in New Jersey, he had been a missionary with the Society for the Propagation of the Gospel in Foreign Parts before settling into a "moderate" but "decent" living at Burlington in 1767. However, his "open and decided character as a Loyalist" and his attempts to sway his congregation against "such measures as tended to throw the country into confusion and draw the people into acts of rebellion" led to his arrest in October 1775 by order of the Provincial Congress of New Jersey. By treating him as an "enemy to his country," Odell believed, that body had tried "to make him the victim of popular resentment"; but the peaceably disposed folk of Burlington refused to turn against him. After the Declaration of Independence, however, "when the usurpation of all the powers of Government was completed," Odell was arrested again, and confined within the bounds of his parish. On December 12, 1776, a party of men "with fixed bayonets" landed from a galley and "made a diligent search from house-to-house, avowing their determination to secure him dead or alive." After a narrow escape, "and finding it no longer in the power of his parishioners to screen him even by concealment from the vindictive malice of his enemies," Odell was obliged to take refuge within the British lines at New York. Exiled from his wife and four children, his subsequent work for the Crown had been met with "flattering marks of approbation." During the British occupation of Philadelphia, Sir William Howe had appointed him to superintend the printing offices at a salary of £50 a year; while there, and later at New York, he wrote and published in the newspapers "sundry occasional essays, with a view to serve the interests of truth and loyalty in that misguided country."[25]

Captain André's long day dealing with Stansbury and his revelations left him feeling unwell and in need of some restorative country air. But he was consoled by the belief that his exertions had been worthwhile. André hoped that Sir Henry would agree that, as far as General Arnold was concerned, "a sufficient foundation" had been laid, and everything done which time permitted: Stansbury could not afford to linger on Manhattan for any longer than absolutely necessary, and had to return to Philadelphia before he was missed and suspected by the Patriots. André arranged for him to be taken off that same night by sloop and whaleboat to Prince's Bay, on Staten Island, and then put ashore in New Jersey for his nerve-jangling homeward journey: if stopped and searched by a rebel patrol, and found to be in possession of a suspicious document, he would face the customary fate of couriers and spies—death by hanging.[26]

As a known loyalist sympathizer, Stansbury was acutely aware that his own role in "conveying" Arnold's correspondence was highly dangerous.

Increasing use was therefore made of less conspicuous couriers, most notably John Rattoon, a vestryman of St. Peter's church in South Amboy, New Jersey. Stansbury characterized him as "the best conveyancer I am acquainted with." Odell agreed, assuring André that he was "more fully assured" of Rattoon's "fidelity" than of "almost any other." Their "slender friend" was given the codename "Mercury," after the Roman god of messengers. In the correspondence that Rattoon regularly carried between Philadelphia and New York city, Arnold initially identified himself by the initials "A.G.," or by "a name beginning with A." He subsequently adopted the aliases "Gustavus" and "Moore," with Peggy Arnold becoming "Mrs. Moore." As for André, although Stansbury and Odell sometimes called him "Joseph Andrews" or "Lothario," the captain himself soon fixed upon the alias "John Anderson."

For all André's care and precautions, it rapidly became clear that his methods were far from foolproof. Before he received Arnold's reply, there was a frustrating false start. On May 31, 1779, Jonathan Odell was obliged to write to the captain in some embarrassment. He had opened a letter from Stansbury that included a page for André written in invisible ink. In his excitement, Odell had "flown to the fire" to reveal the message by applying heat to the paper, but was "mortified to death" to discover that it had somehow "got damp on the way." To his "inexpressible vexation," the invisible solution had spread, transforming the hidden message into "one indistinguishable blot, out of which not the half of any one line can be made legible." There was some consolation in the fact that Arnold ("our friend") had not been "negligent or tardy in beginning his expected correspondence." And as the "unfortunate letter" was dated May 21—before Stansbury could have received Odell's own most recent message—he was "in hourly expectation" of another.[27]

Despite the reverend's optimism, the impatient André had to wait for more than a week before he received a further, undamaged, letter from Arnold. Dated May 23, it was keyed to the twenty-first edition of *Bailey's Dictionary*; this time the captain decoded it himself. As Arnold considered "the interest of America and Great Britain inseparable," Sir Henry could depend on his "exertions and intelligence." To demonstrate his good faith, Arnold forwarded some general information, although none of it was so sensational that it could not have been learned through existing channels. Arnold would offer his further assistance whenever the opportunity arose; although unable to "promise success," he would strive to "deserve it." In return, "as life and everything is at stake," Arnold expected "some certainty": he wanted security for his property, and "a revenue equivalent to the risk and service done." Arnold believed it would be impossible for him to cooperate effectively without a "mutual confidence," and he was keen to assure the British general that *his* would not be misplaced. On that vital issue of trust, Arnold's message included a request that may have caused André to pause in his laborious deciphering, and wonder whether the famous rebel general really was determined to betray the cause for which he had fought with such distinction, or was playing some deeper game of double-bluff: if he was entrusted with a knowledge of Sir Henry's own plans, Arnold pledged, "he should never be at a loss for intelligence" from him. In closing his letter to André, Arnold added a postscript: "Madam Arnold presents you her particular compliments." This could be interpreted as polite pleasantry—or as a sign that Peggy was happy to play her part in the evolving conspiracy.[28]

* * *

It was some weeks before Captain André had an opportunity to compose a considered response to Arnold's message of May 23. In the meantime, he had been called away from Manhattan on active service. Reinforced by the timely return of troops and shipping sent on a successful foray to Virginia's Chesapeake Bay, on May 30 Sir Henry Clinton launched another strike against his perennial objective, the Hudson Highlands. He targeted the crucial crossing-point at King's Ferry, where the Hudson narrowed to little more than half a mile. By now the Patriots had sought to secure the passage by building a fort on Verplanck's Point, on the river's east bank; another, on the opposite shore at Stony Point, was still unfinished. Besides defending each terminus of the ferry, the two posts were intended to function as outlying southern bastions for the far stronger fortifications sixteen miles upriver at West Point, which the British had taken to calling "Fort Defiance."[29]

Thanks to a fair wind and the "zealous assistance" of the naval commander Sir George Collier, who provided "frigates, galleys, and gunboats," by June 1 Sir Henry had captured both positions. He gave his favorite aide Captain André the honor of formally receiving the surrender of the outpost on Verplanck's Point; this was named Fort Lafayette, after the young French volunteer Marie Joseph, marquis de Lafayette, who had won Washington's esteem and affection since joining the American rebels in 1777 and been given the rank of

major-general by Congress. In performing this duty, André could not resist a
theatrical flourish. He announced the surrender terms "on the glacis of Fort
Fayette," a formal phrase which suggested that the conquest involved some
mighty citadel, fortified along the scientific principles of Europe, rather than
a humble redoubt enclosing a blockhouse, with a battery of just four guns and
garrisoned by a paltry seventy men. A correspondent to the *New Jersey
Gazette*, who was probably the state's governor, William Livingston, could not
resist mocking such unwarranted "pomp" and "vainglorious solemnity." He
wondered what Sir Henry could intend by such a "farce," and asked: "What
excuse will a person of Mr. André's reputed sense find for this parade?"[30]

Although West Point blocked any further British advance up the Hudson
River, Clinton's swift strike dealt a hefty blow to Washington. As Captain
John Peebles commented, King's Ferry was "the principal communication
the rebels make use of to pass their troops and stores across the North River."
Now, Colonel Charles Stuart observed, their east–west supply route would be
lengthened by a "considerable detour through a mountain country and by
bad roads." Sir Henry estimated that this alternative "circuit" to the north
would oblige Washington's convoys to lengthen their journeys by "at least
sixty miles." In coming weeks, the British worked to consolidate their hold on
King's Ferry by establishing strong forts on both the points. Clinton was
delighted by his coup, and judged correctly that Washington must be no less
mortified. But Sir Henry's expectation that his opponent would risk a battle
to restore his lateral communications was misplaced. Washington moved
from Middlebrook, New Jersey, to bolster West Point, but showed no inclina-
tion to leave that formidable position. Clinton, who was impatiently awaiting
another belated consignment of reinforcements from Britain, was still too
weak to attack him there.[31]

* * *

When André finally replied to Arnold's message in mid-June, he opened by
making it clear that Sir Henry could not "reveal his intentions as to the present
campaign, nor can he find the necessity of such a discovery, or that a want of
a proper degree of confidence is to be inferred from his not making it." Once
he had addressed that point, André hammered home others already touched
on during his interview with Stansbury: Clinton was insistent that the war
"would be prosecuted with vigor and that no thought is entertained of giving

up the dependency of America"; and valuable services would meet with rewards beyond Arnold's "warmest expectations." Through André, Sir Henry reminded Arnold that he had offered himself to secure his country's deliverance. Clinton was already considering how Arnold's inside knowledge and influence could be exploited to inflict a devastating knock-out blow on the rebels. "You must know where the present power is vulnerable," André wrote, "and the conspicuous commands with which you might be vested may enable us at one shining stroke, from which both riches and honors would be derived, to accelerate the ruin to which the usurped authority is verging, and to put a speedy end to the miseries of our fellow creatures." In his current position, "centrically stationed 50 miles up the North River," Sir Henry was well placed to move either against the coast or farther into the country, and to cooperate in "almost any plan" that Arnold might propose. Here again, André had some helpful suggestions: "Join the army, accept a command, be surprised, be cut off—these things may happen in the course of maneuver," without being "censured or suspected." Such a plan would be settled by André meeting Arnold under cover of a flag of truce, or by some alternative method, as soon as they came within reach of one another. Now, for the first time, André put a price-tag on treason: a "complete service," resulting in the elimination of an entire corps of 5,000 to 6,000 men, "would be rewarded with twice as many thousand guineas." Sir Henry was confident that Arnold's "abilities and firmness" justified his hopes for the success of such a stratagem; meanwhile, in another reminder, perhaps Arnold could work to secure the exchange of the "Convention Army"? After all, given his role in Gentleman Johnny's defeat, no one could urge such an "act of justice" with "more propriety" than he. It would crown "the shining revolution" that Arnold might soon be "instrumental in effecting."[32]

Before sending his letter to Arnold, Captain André had begun another that was never dispatched, but which reveals more about how Sir Henry Clinton hoped to exploit his new asset to break the continuing deadlock with Washington and yield a decisive British victory. One approach was to reveal the deliberations of Congress, so that its plans could be countered in good time. Gathering such intelligence was a necessary business, but inevitably slow. Clinton and André were both far more excited by the prospect of inflicting a heavy defeat on the king's enemies—"the most brilliant and effectual blow finally to complete the overthrow of the present abominable power." That objective could be achieved either by a "grand stroke or by successive partial but severe blows." In André's estimation, a "partial blow" would involve capturing a major seaport and defeating the local rebel forces, allowing the British to drive off the "disaffected"; by displaying both "prowess and lenity," this would encourage the "suffering people" to return to their former allegiance. If Arnold could obtain the command of North and South Carolina, such a plan could be implemented there. Alternatively, Arnold could suggest an objective for the British to menace—a supply depot or a port on Long Island Sound, for example—as a means of luring a "considerable body" into an ambush. As for a more ambitious "general project" against the main American army under Washington, any suggestions that Arnold might have would be gladly received. Meanwhile, André wondered whether a British lunge into New England would tempt Washington into crossing from the west bank of the Hudson to fend off the attack. If Arnold could secure command of Washington's advance guard, like Major-General Charles Lee at Monmouth Court House, "it might be concerted where and when it should be surprised, defeated, or obliged to capitulate." Then, with accurate intelligence, the supply line of Washington's main body could be ruptured. Facing multiple difficulties and with strained resources, the American commander would be forced to fight at a disadvantage, or to disperse his starving troops. Such a moment, when the most "boisterous spirits" among the rebels were off serving with the army, would also provide a fine opportunity to seize Congress and so "decide the business." The Royal Navy would play its part in this happy scenario, staging diversionary coastal raids, and whisking away the kidnapped Congressmen.[33]

Of course, all such schemes depended on Major-General Arnold returning to active service, with responsibilities that reflected his rank and reputation. Although Arnold had long since resigned as military commandant of Philadelphia, he had not yet rejoined the American army or been allocated a new command. While Arnold had assured Washington that he wanted to return to duty directly his wounds permitted, until he was acquitted of the charges that still hung over him he was "effectually" prevented from doing so. In an ironic twist, Sir Henry's sudden thrust up the Hudson was responsible for prolonging Arnold's absence from Washington's side. On May 29, it had been confirmed that his court martial, on the four charges referred by Congress, would open, as anticipated, on June 1. Arnold traveled to Middlebrook with the object of finally clearing his name. Before the court was sworn in, he objected to three of its members: Brigadier-

General William Irvine, Colonel Richard Butler, and Lieutenant-Colonel Josiah Harmar. His intervention was upheld, but caused an adjournment until next morning. Proceedings were about to open when they were over-taken by events. As Washington moved north to counter Clinton's worrying offensive, the court was dissolved and its members ordered to rejoin their commands. On June 2, general orders announced that "the meeting of the court for the trial of Major-General Arnold is deferred until further orders, the exigency of the public service not permitting it to sit at this time."[34]

In mid-July, after most of Clinton's troops had withdrawn from King's Ferry, leaving garrisons at Stony Point and Verplanck's Point, Arnold again appealed to Washington for a swift decision on a new trial date. At long last, Arnold believed his return to active service was imminent: "my wounds are so far recovered that I can walk with ease, and expect soon to be able to ride on horseback," he wrote. If the court was unable to meet promptly, Arnold would ask Congress for a few months' leave to attend to his private affairs. In fact, the court martial would not be reconvened until December.[35]

With his fate unresolved, the frustrated Arnold returned to Philadelphia. There, if gossip could be credited, it was not only his old enemies in Congress and on Pennsylvania's Supreme Executive Council who resented his luxurious lifestyle and apparent indifference to republican values. Soon after the King's Ferry raid, André questioned an escaped British prisoner of war, Duncan Drummond of the 82nd Foot. He had come into New York via "the Jerseys." Before slipping away from Philadelphia, the Scot had spent "six weeks keeping the bar of the Coffee House" there, and heard talk that General Arnold was "in no repute." Ironically, given the accusations they leveled at Arnold, Philadelphians were themselves notorious for their greed. Samuel Tenny, the surgeon to the 2nd Rhode Island Regiment, who later spent a winter in the city, considered them "a set of avaricious, inhospitable fellows." Dr. Tenny observed: "Gold is their god, and they attend to a man only in proportion as they suppose they can fleece him of it."[36]

Philadelphia's hostile atmosphere may go some way to explain Arnold's distinctly jaded response to André's latest approach. As Stansbury informed Odell, the captain's letter had arrived on the evening of July 7, and he had imme-diately delivered it to "Mrs. Moore." Stansbury had expected a memorandum from Arnold to encode and send off to New York; but all he received was a note that expressed disappointment at "the little attention paid to his request" and André's apparent indifference "respecting the matter" of guaranteed payment.

In consequence, Stansbury had a long conversation with Arnold. As André's letter had been written in Odell's hand, the general was also worried that his true identity was now known to him, too. To calm Arnold's fears, Stansbury had lied that "Mr. Osborn (Odell) only knew that a Mr. Moore was concerned in the business."

Arnold's concerns were communicated to André on July 11. Now calling himself "John Stevens," Stansbury informed the captain: "I delivered Gustavus your letter. It is not equal to his expectations." Arnold wanted certainty on the issue of compensation: "He expects to have your promise that he shall be indemnified for any loss he may sustain in case of detection, and, whether this contest is finished by sword or treaty, that £10,000 shall be engaged to him for his services, which shall be faithfully devoted to your interest." This was close to the figure that André had mentioned as an appropriate reward for delivering up an entire corps of rebels; but Arnold wanted the sum to be underwritten regardless of the results. To sweeten the pill, he included another selection of intelligence regarding patriot military operations and troop dispositions. While acceptable enough, none of this information provided a basis for the kind of decisive blow that Clinton was contemplating.[37]

* * *

As long as Arnold remained in Philadelphia, distant from Washington's headquarters, there were limitations on the quality of the military intelligence that he could forward to the British. This shortcoming was underlined by his failure to warn Clinton of a patriot counter-attack that left him shocked and depressed. In his continuing efforts to tempt Washington to battle, in early July Sir Henry had sent Vice-Admiral Collier and Major-General Tryon to raid the Connecticut coast. The vigorous Collier relished an opportunity to punish the rebel privateers who proliferated in Long Island Sound, "destroying their whaleboats and other piratical craft to prevent a continuance of their depredations." As a fervent advocate of a hardline "fire and sword" approach to the American rebels, Tryon likewise reveled in his task, and fulfilled it with a zeal that exceeded Clinton's wishes. At New Haven, stores and shipping were torched, but at Fairfield and Norwalk, where the raiders came under persistent fire from concealed snipers, the burning was indiscriminate, with homes and even churches consumed.[38]

Despite this provocation, Washington refused to take Clinton's bait and march his main army into New England. Instead, he struck back with a devastating blow of his own, surprising the British garrison of Stony Point. The mission was entrusted to the ambitious and aggressive Brigadier-General Anthony Wayne. Like the redcoats who had inflicted such a bloody defeat on his Pennsylvanians at Paoli in September 1777, by Washington's specific order Wayne was to attack "with fixed bayonets and muskets unloaded." His command consisted of 1,200 "chosen men" drawn from the light infantry companies that each Continental regiment had been ordered to form in May 1778; following British army practice, on campaign these elite units were temporarily brigaded together. Washington knew that the success of any such attack hinged on tight security. He advised Wayne: "As it is in the power of a single deserter to betray the design, defeat the project, and involve the party in difficulties and danger, too much caution cannot be used to conceal the intended enterprise, from all but the principal officers of your corps, and from the men till the moment of execution." Washington urged Wayne to establish patrols to ensure that no deserters could reach the enemy and reveal the plan.[39]

Despite such precautions, the British received warnings that an attack on Stony Point was highly likely. Since May 26, in line with his new duties as Clinton's intelligence officer, Captain André had kept a hardbound ledger in which incoming reports were consolidated. Under the date July 13, a dozen American deserters were listed in his "Intelligence Book," six of them from Wayne's light infantry. Their testimonies left little doubt that plans were afoot for a strike at Stony Point, although none of them knew exactly *when* the expected blow would fall. André recorded the deserters' information, but apparently failed to evaluate its importance or forward it to his superiors. Intelligence was just one of André's staff duties, and the pressure of other paperwork may have prevented him from acting more promptly. Whatever the reason, it was a costly lapse.[40]

Two days later, just after midnight on July 15, the garrison of Stony Point was overpowered in a bold and well-planned assault. While a detachment of two companies staged a feint frontal attack to distract the defenders and draw their fire, stronger columns advanced through the swamps on either side of the peninsula on which the fort was built. Under what Wayne described as a "most tremendous, and incessant fire of musketry and cannon loaded with grapeshot," his men "forced their way at point of bayonet through every obstacle" to storm the defenses and overwhelm the garrison. At a cost of 15 killed and 85 wounded, including Wayne himself, the Americans slew 63 redcoats, wounded another 70, and took 442 prisoners. An elated Wayne reported that his light infantry had "behaved like men who are determined to be free."[41]

Captain André was soon given a vivid first-hand account of the attack by one of Wayne's victorious soldiers. John Wilmot of the 6th Pennsylvania Regiment, who clearly had his own idea of freedom, deserted from the site of the old Fort Montgomery on July 22, and was interrogated at headquarters two days later. Wilmot confirmed Wayne's determination to maintain operational secrecy. He and his comrades "were not informed on what service they were going till within a mile of the place." At that point, "half a pint of rum was served to each man and the whole warned that any man that flinched would be run right through." Wilmot told André that the simultaneous attacks had caught much of the garrison off guard, with some of them "partly dressed and the rest in their shirts." Many redcoats "were put to death in the huts and tents," although "there were orders to spare every man who would take quarter."[42]

In deliberate contrast to the ruthlessness shown by the British in their own nighttime bayonet attacks at Paoli and Old Tappan, as Wilmot claimed, at Stony Point the Americans had spared all who sought to surrender. British officers were impressed by their enemy's courage and humanity. Sir George Collier conceded that the rebels attacked "with a bravery they never before exhibited" and showed "a generosity and clemency which during the course of the rebellion has no parallel." Congress was so delighted at Wayne's coup that it voted to award him a gold commemorative medal; Lieutenant-Colonel François Louis de Fleury and Major John Stewart, who had commanded the advanced guards of the flanking columns, received silver versions. It was also resolved that the considerable military stores captured at Stony Point should be valued, and the proceeds divided among the "gallant troops."[43]

Although Stony Point fell to Wayne's determined men, a half-hearted attempt on Verplanck's Point was easily rebuffed by the British. Four days later, Washington contented himself with demolishing the fortifications at Stony Point, before falling back to his old position near West Point. Enjoying naval control of the lower Hudson, the British soon returned and reoccupied both of the King's Ferry forts. In strategic terms, therefore, Washington's

1. "Colonel Arnold, Who commanded the Provincial troops sent against Quebec, through the wilderness of Canada, and was wounded in storming that city, under General Montgomery." There is no suggestion that this mezzotint, published by Thomas Hart of London in March 1776, provides a genuine likeness of Arnold. Nonetheless, it demonstrates how his reputation as a determined fighter for American liberty was swiftly spread among Britons.

2. "General Arnold, Drawn from the life at Philadelphia by Du Simitier [*sic*]." Taken by the Swiss artist and collector Pierre Eugène Du Simitière in 1778–79 during Arnold's residence in the city, this is the only authentic likeness of the celebrated soldier before his defection to the British. Published in London in March 1783, this engraved version reflects the continuing interest in Arnold even as the Revolutionary War ended.

3. "The Death of General Montgomery at Quebec," an engraving made in 1808 by Christian Wilhelm Ketterlinus from the 1786 painting by John Trumbull. This was one of a series of iconic images by which Trumbull commemorated pivotal moments in the Revolutionary War, dramatizing the sacrifices and victories of the Patriots. Had he not turned traitor, it's likely that Arnold's exploits would have featured among them.

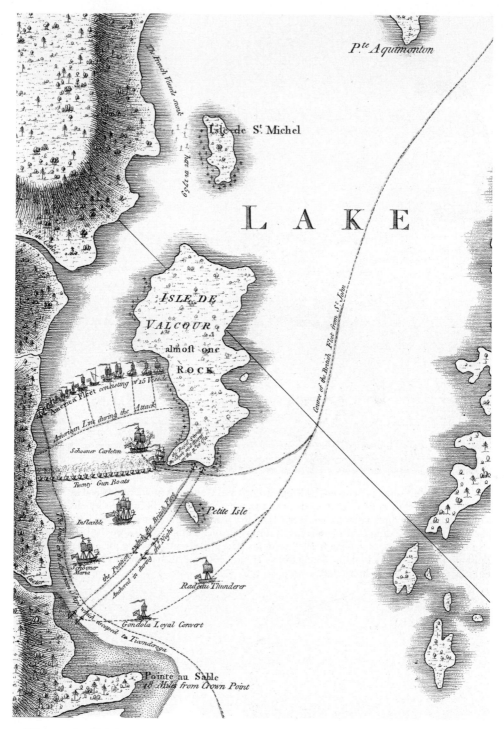

4. "The attack and defeat of the American fleet under Benedict Arnold ... upon Lake Champlain, the 11th of October 1776." Based on a participant's sketch, this engraved map of the battle of Valcour Island was published in London by William Faden within two months, on December 3, 1776. This detail shows how Arnold exploited the congested location to restrict the superior British fleet.

5. "A Skirmish in America between the King's Troops and General Arnold." Published by James Sharpe of London in April 1780, this rare print commemorates Arnold's "intrepidity" at Ridgefield, Connecticut, some three years earlier. While Danbury blazes in the distance, Arnold prepares to pistol a bayonet-wielding British grenadier. A unique image, dating from before the revelation of Arnold's treason, it draws upon published accounts. The print is on display at the Keeler Tavern Museum in Ridgefield, a building dating from 1713 in which a British cannonball fired during the fighting of 1777 remains embedded.

6. Margaret "Peggy" Shippen depicted in a watercolor by John André, worked up from a pencil sketch he made before June 1778. The teenaged Peggy is dressed for a formal ball and sports the exaggerated style of headdress that outraged Philadelphia's radical Patriots once the British army had evacuated the city. Soon after, she attracted the attentions of her future husband, Major-General Benedict Arnold.

7. West Point in August 1782, shown in a detail from a panorama of the "Encampment of the Revolutionary Army on the Hudson River," by Major Pierre Charles L'Enfant. A French volunteer and engineer in the Continental Army, L'Enfant was wounded during the siege of Savannah in 1779 and captured at Charleston in 1780. Although West Point's fortifications are indistinct, his watercolor gives a strong sense of their dramatic setting.

8. "General Washington," a mezzotint by Valentine Green, published in London in 1799, and based on John Trumbull's painting of 1780. Trumbull, who had served as an aide to Washington early in the Revolutionary War, portrayed him at the time of Arnold's treason as a lean and active forty-eight-year-old. Shadowed by his slave Billy Lee, Washington is posed against a rugged landscape resembling the Hudson Highlands.

9. A self-portrait by Major John André, made on the morning of October 1, 1780, when he was confined at the Mabie Tavern, Tappan, and expected to be executed within hours. André worked without a mirror and presented the pen and ink drawing as a keepsake to one of his guards, Ensign Jabez Tomlinson of Samuel Webb's Additional Continental Regiment. He was hanged at noon the next day, October 2.

10. "Major John André, Adjutant-General to His Majesty's forces in North America under the command of Sir Henry Clinton." André was a prolific artist, and this engraving by John Keyse is based upon an earlier self-portrait. Published in London in 1784, it testifies to the enduring public interest in his fate; this was heightened in 1782 when a monument to his memory was erected in Westminster Abbey.

11. "A Representation of the Figures Exhibited and Paraded through the streets of Philadelphia." Issued as a broadsheet, this crude print gives a vivid impression of the procession staged on September 30, 1780 to vilify Arnold for his treachery. It illustrates the realistic effigies of Arnold and Beelzebub that were specially created for the event by local artist Charles Willson Peale. In the background, Arnold escapes to HMS *Vulture*.

12. Another, far rarer, image of the same Philadelphia procession, made for an almanac catering to Pennsylvania's German-speaking immigrants. Testifying to the unusually widespread interest in Arnold's treason, this lively woodcut imagines West Point as a medieval castle, and shows both Major André and Joshua Hett Smith hanging from a gallows; although tried for complicity in Arnold's treason, Smith was acquitted through lack of evidence.

offensive had little impact. But it gave a timely boost to patriot morale, and badly dented Clinton's fragile self-confidence. Sir Henry's despair was clear when he "opened his mind" to Colonel Stuart. Writing to his father, the former prime minister Lord Bute, Stuart reported how Clinton "told me with tears in his eyes that he was quite an altered man—that business oppressed him, that he felt himself incapable of his station." Seeing a grenadier passing his door, Clinton admitted to Stuart that he would happily swap places with that humble soldier, adding: "let me advise you never to take command of an army."[44]

* * *

For all his frustrations, Sir Henry hoped that the intrigue with Benedict Arnold might yet yield a dramatic solution to his conundrum. But as the summer dragged on, the correspondence between Arnold in Philadelphia and John André in New York gave him little cause for encouragement. Always sporadic, it had now become even more sluggish, and seemed destined to come to an inconclusive end. It had taken over a week for Arnold's latest lukewarm response to reach Jonathan Odell. The reverend informed André that their regular courier, John Rattoon, had been "detained by some embarrassments" along the way: unlike his mythical namesake, "Mercury" did not have winged sandals to speed him out of trouble. Although Odell was pained that Arnold had apparently misunderstood André's letter, and had no doubt disappointed the captain's expectations, he took the liberty of recommending persistence: "I could wish you to write once more at least—as it cannot do any harm, and *may* possibly be still worthwhile." As for Arnold's concerns that Odell knew of his involvement, which might have contributed to his "unreasonable reserve," perhaps when André next wrote he could reassure him that his suspicions were groundless—even though they were not.

Odell was more concerned that the "late unfortunate event"—Wayne's surprise attack on Stony Point—would deflect the captain from continuing with such a "*seemingly* fruitless correspondence." He hoped that André would be able to give him his reply as soon as possible. "Mercury" was already suspected by the Patriots of having traveled to New York, and was anxious to "return without delay." In his letter to Odell, Stansbury had included a shopping list of "Articles for Mrs. Moore," consisting of fabrics and other domestic items. Written in Arnold's own hand, this may have been a method of emphasizing that Peggy at least remained on cordial terms with André, and willing to cooperate with him.[45]

André responded to Arnold's latest approach in late July; if he was starting to feel exasperation at the general's intransigence, he did not betray it. He regretted the continuing "hesitation," and made it clear that rewards of the kind Arnold expected would require "real advantage," or at least clear evidence that a "generous effort" had been made. There were indications that André was becoming frustrated by their indirect written correspondence: he believed that the "only method" of establishing mutual confidence and "making arrangement for important operations" was a personal meeting. If Arnold was to take up a field command and arrange a rendezvous with André, the captain was confident that a "few minutes" of conversation would satisfy all parties. In the meantime, while grateful for the intelligence that Arnold had already supplied, and hopeful that he would send more as often as possible, André now had a specific suggestion for him: "Permit me to prescribe a little exertion," he wrote. "It is the procuring of an accurate plan of West Point." This was the first mention of that increasingly important post.[46]

This time, Arnold made no direct reply to André's letter, and the captain only learned of its reception from Stansbury. Arnold had sent for the shopkeeper, shown him the letter, and remarked that it contained no response to his requested terms. While not doubting André's honor, he was anxious that there was still no guarantee that his property "should be indemnified from any loss that might attend unfortunate discovery." For Arnold, such clear risks outweighed the vague rewards. His commitment to ending the war had to be set against the future of his wife and sons. He had told Stansbury that "however sincerely he wished to serve his country in accelerating the settlement of this unhappy contest, yet he should hold himself unjust to his family to hazard his all on the occasion and part with a certainty . . . for an uncertainty." In his last letter, André had suggested that Sir Henry Clinton's close friend General William Phillips, who had been captured with Burgoyne and was expected to come to New York on parole, might serve as a useful go-between—provided Arnold was willing for him to be made privy to the negotiations. Here at least, Arnold was prepared to cooperate: if Phillips passed through Philadelphia, he would make a point of seeing him, and perhaps "open himself to that gentleman." Regarding the requested plan of West Point, Arnold had been unable to obtain one, as the "draught" remained with Washington and the engineers who had drawn it up. However, when he visited the stronghold, which had now been strengthened with many new works, he would be able to make a plan himself easily enough. On the crucial question of a meeting with André, as Arnold hoped to rejoin the army in about three weeks he would try to "contrive an interview" then.[47]

In fact, Arnold did not rejoin the army that summer, and Captain André would have to wait longer than a year for his interview. From that point forward, until the following spring, the negotiations stalled; the correspondence between Philadelphia and New York dwindled, with no more than an occasional letter forwarded by Stansbury enclosing Arnold's routine intelligence. But for Benedict Arnold, there could now be no realistic prospect of turning back. Should he retract, the British had enough evidence for his countrymen to hang him as a traitor; at the very least, they could use the threat of exposure to blackmail him into doing their bidding. Yet both Clinton and André knew that such pressure was unlikely to be necessary: by offering to join the British when he first approached them in May, Arnold had left no doubt that he had already reached his decision. After Sir Henry decided that Arnold would be more useful where he was, matters had become increasingly complicated, and immediate defection had been replaced by cautious negotiation. But despite all his concern to secure a cast-iron guarantee of indemnification, Arnold never hinted that he had regretted his decision to change his allegiance, or that he no longer saw himself as another General Monck, well qualified to end the civil war between the mother country and her stubborn, misguided offspring.

Even though the correspondence with Arnold, which had seemingly promised so much, tailed off late that summer, Captain André apparently believed it was still worth pursuing Peggy as a contact in her own right. On August 16, 1779, he wrote to her, by way of the paroled American major Aquila Giles, seeking her "remembrance," and passing on his respects to her and the "fair circle" of their mutual friends in Philadelphia. As the Mischianza had made him "a complete milliner," he would be happy to help out in that department, and "enter into the whole detail of cap-wire, needles, gauze, &c." from which "trifles" he hoped she would "infer a zeal to be further employed" by her. It was this apparently harmless letter that was found among Arnold's papers in Philadelphia after the treason's discovery, and which aroused the suspicion of commentators like Congressman Thomson. Peggy Arnold finally replied on October 13. She passed on her "best respects" to Captain André, and was much obliged for his "very polite and friendly offer." Major Giles had himself promised to secure such "trifles" as Peggy needed, but she assured André that her "friendship and esteem for him" were "not impaired by time or accident." While not straying from her husband's noncommittal stance, this left open another potential conduit for treasonable correspondence.[48]

* * *

Before the summer was over, the American rebels deepened Clinton's depression with another daring hit-and-run raid that once again demonstrated the Continental Army's growing élan. On August 19, they attacked the vulnerable post of Paulus Hook, on the New Jersey shore, within cannon shot of New York city. The well-planned and daring operation was conducted by the Virginian Major Henry Lee—father of the Confederate General Robert E. Lee—and although the garrison held out, 150 of them were taken prisoner. As Washington appreciated, while "small on the great scale," such exploits increased his army's confidence and disgraced the enemy. Colonel Stuart observed that this latest "affair, treading upon the heels of the former" attack on Stony Point, "served to inspirit the Rebels and gave a degree of venom" to General Clinton's critics. In the wake of the "two unlucky blows," Sir Henry once again tendered his resignation. As before, Lord George Germain refused to accept it.[49]

The reinforcements that Clinton had awaited so anxiously finally arrived on August 25, under convoy of his new naval colleague, Vice-Admiral Marriot Arbuthnot. To Sir Henry's acute disappointment, the fleet brought barely half of the 6,600 troops that he had been promised. After their long, cramped Atlantic crossing, most of them were sick with "jail fever," or typhus; on disembarking, they promptly infected the army at New York. Soon, thousands of men were hospitalized, and further military operations were impossible until they had recovered. Epidemic illness was bad enough, but for Clinton the fleet brought something even worse: Admiral Arbuthnot. The formidable challenges of the American theater required that Britain's naval commander should possess both energy and resourcefulness. But Arbuthnot had neither: he was now almost seventy, although observers believed him even older. While the mercurial Clinton could prove a difficult man to work with, he had collaborated well enough with competent naval officers like Richard Howe and George Collier. Yet, as Clinton's biographer William B. Willcox emphasized, Arbuthnot was the worst possible partner that the Admiralty could have foisted on him: he was "a pompous weather-cock," and the "only constants in his character were slowness to take respon-sibility and quickness to take alarm." Willcox added: "Even in a war replete with official blunders, the appointment of Arbuthnot was notable." Before long, any hope of efficient inter-service cooperation was wrecked, with results that would prove disastrous for Britain's attempt to subdue America.[50]

Ever since his outnumbered and inexperienced army had been beaten from Manhattan by William Howe's disciplined redcoats and Hessians in the fall of 1776, George Washington had longed to expunge the shame of that ignominious defeat, and recover New York city. During the summer of 1779, it seemed that the enduring dream might finally become a reality: news that the French Admiral d'Estaing was once again expected off the North American coast excited Washington to the possibility of a Franco-American assault on the British garrisons of both New York and Rhode Island—an ambitious plan that, if successful, would surely secure American independence. But instead of cooperating with Washington, d'Estaing kept far off to the south, joining his warships and troops with American forces under Major-General Lincoln to besiege the British-held city of Savannah, in Georgia. This latest allied effort proved no more successful than the last, against Newport, Rhode Island. When a bold frontal assault on October 9 was repulsed with heavy casualties, d'Estaing promptly returned his bloodied command to the West Indies, where possession of rich sugar islands like St. Vincent, Martinique, and St. Lucia remained a priority for the French and British alike.

Washington's high hopes of reconquering New York were swiftly dashed, yet even the threat of an offensive against that port was enough to exert a profound influence on British dispositions, as Clinton reacted by concen-trating his dispersed forces there to face the expected assault. In October, he relinquished the forts at Verplanck's Point and Stony Point. Much of the indecisive summer campaign of 1779 had been spent in a to-and-fro tussle for them and the supply route they controlled. After so much effort, Clinton's decision to deliberately abandon both posts now baffled his officers, espe-cially, as Captain Peebles grumbled, "the taking and making of which, and the losing and taking and making again," had cost "7 or 800 men and seems to have been the whole business or object of the campaign."[51]

More significant in the long term was Sir Henry's decision to accept the advice of Admiral Arbuthnot and withdraw the garrison of Newport, Rhode Island, which had been held by crown forces ever since he had first seized it back in December 1776. In several respects, Newport was a far superior anchorage to New York. Unlike the convoluted waterways around Manhattan Island, where navigation was further complicated by treacherous sandbars, Newport's harbor was broad and deep. In the opinion of one of Britain's most effective naval officers, Sir George Brydges Rodney, relinquishing Rhode Island was "the most fatal measure that could possibly have been taken." Writing to Lord George Germain, the admiral lamented that the evacuation "gave up the best and only harbor of consequence in America during this unhappy war." Not only was Newport capable of "holding the whole fleet of Britain," but it was a base from which squadrons could have been sent to blockade Boston, Philadelphia, and New York within forty-eight hours. Crucially, unlike those three ports it was not liable to freeze in the winter, making it a "harbor at all seasons of the year."[52]

Despite the deeply discouraging outcome of French military intervention in both 1778 and 1779, George Washington never doubted that his Bourbon allies would return yet again, and that their sea power would provide the vital ingredient needed to inflict a decisive defeat on the British. Now, with Newport left vacant by the enemy, any future French expeditionary force that managed to slip past the overworked warships of the Royal Navy would enjoy the immense advantage of an easily defensible naval base from which to stage operations against objectives up and down the coast.

That fall, Sir Henry Clinton's tribulations did nothing to halt the remarkable rise of his trusted aide and confidant, John André. In early September 1779, his friend Lieutenant-Colonel Lord Francis Rawdon, who had quarreled with Clinton, resigned as adjutant-general. Rawdon's deputy, Lieutenant-Colonel Stephen Kemble had naturally hoped to step into his shoes; but when Clinton refused to discuss his promotion, Kemble also resigned. On October 23, Clinton appointed André in Kemble's place, with the rank of major in the 54th Foot; both promotions were "local" to North America, and subject to official approval from London. Strictly speaking, André was only *deputy* adjutant-general; but as the senior post remained vacant, he gradually assumed those duties, too.[53]

By the age of twenty-nine, John André had already gone far: not only had he secured a staff appointment of immense influence, but he was the indispensable adviser of Britain's commander-in-chief in North America. In the coming year, as Sir Henry's crucial contact with the renegade General Benedict Arnold, Major André achieved a celebrity far beyond even his wildest dreams of military glory. But it would be acquired at a heavy price.

6

CRISIS OF LIBERTY

In January 1780, North America's eastern seaboard was enduring the grimmest winter in living memory. As far south as Virginia, the Rappahannock River had been frozen solid for weeks, and ships anchored in the upper reaches of Chesapeake Bay were blockaded by ice. In the James River, "vast quantities of floating ice" prevented the crews of two boats from reaching either bank. A ship's barge sent to assist the men was unable to penetrate through the floes. Nothing had been seen of them since, and it was feared that they had perished from exposure. In the same waterway, the privateer brig *Jefferson*, "a fine new vessel" about to embark on her maiden voyage, was crushed by the remorseless ice and foundered off Jamestown. To the superstitious, the dismal fate of a ship named in honor of Thomas Jefferson, Virginia's governor and the driving force behind America's Declaration of Independence in July 1776, might have been seen as symbolic of the sorry state to which his country's cause had now sunk.[1]

Farther north, at New York, conditions were even worse. There, the "very remarkable and long-continued severity of the weather" was attributed to the "incessant intenseness of the cold, the great depth and quantity of the snows, following in quick succession one on the back of another, attended with violent tempests of wind." This sustained meteorological onslaught had left the roads impassable, stopping up "all the avenues of intelligence and social intercourse" and putting an end to every kind of business.[2]

The bitter weather only exacerbated the miseries of George Washington's troops as they hunkered down in their winter quarters at Jockey Hollow, near Morristown, New Jersey. Conditions were bad enough for threadbare, shivering soldiers obliged to shelter under canvas until they had felled trees to build themselves huts; but the unrelenting snowstorms meant that men long accustomed to going hungry now faced the prospect of outright starvation. The deep snowdrifts that clogged the region's roads barred them to supply wagons: once local depots had been depleted, there could be no prospect of relief from further afield for many weeks to come.

Even before the barrage of blizzards, Washington's "Grand Army" had suffered from a chronic lack of supplies. On December 16, 1779, just days after encamping at Morristown, Washington sent out an uncharacteristically blunt circular letter to the states. The army's supply situation was "beyond description alarming," he wrote. All its magazines were bare, and the commissaries lacked the cash or credit to replenish them. By now, Washington's Continentals had been on half rations for five or six weeks; there was scarcely enough bread for another three days; and once that was gone, they must glean the countryside around Morristown. On previous occasions there had been temporary glitches caused by what Washington tactfully described as "accidental delays in forwarding supplies," but this latest crisis was unprecedented: "We have never experienced a like extremity at any period of the war," he warned. Without "extraordinary exertions" by the states from which the army drew its supplies, it must "infallibly disband in a fortnight."[3]

The desperate plight of Washington's army reflected the wretched state of the American economy. With confidence in Congress at low ebb, and inflation running out of control, local farmers were more reluctant than ever to exchange their surplus produce for drastically depreciated Continental dollars. By the onset of 1780, Washington's ravenous veterans had resorted to plundering local farmsteads of whatever they could find. Washington understood the dire consequences of such pilfering for his army's discipline and for its precarious base of civilian support; but seeing the genuine distress of his men, he hesitated to punish them. To prevent more marauding, Washington appealed to the neighboring county magistrates of New Jersey to impose requisitions of cattle and grain. He had no doubt that the specified quotas would be delivered voluntarily: if not, they must be taken by force. Faced with this stark ultimatum, the civil leaders responded with uncommon zeal: the supplies were delivered and starvation averted—for the moment at least.[4]

Besides an outbreak of pillaging, the bleak conditions at Morristown led inevitably to an increase in desertion. The perennial bane of all eighteenth-century armies, desertion was especially prevalent among the royal and rebel soldiers who had faced each other on the lower Hudson for the past year. Most of them not only spoke the same language, but they occupied static positions, within just a day's march of each other: it was all too easy for a man to turn his coat—if he still had one. That month, worn-out clothing and empty bellies at Jockey Hollow ensured that the deserter traffic was overwhelmingly one-way. Washington took harsh measures in a bid to halt this worrying drain of manpower. On January 3, general orders announced courts-martial verdicts on a long list of seventeen convicted deserters. Three of the most notorious were sentenced to death; another ten were to endure floggings of a hundred lashes on their bare backs; by way of variation, each of the remaining four was to "run the gauntlope through the brigade to which he belongs." This punishment obliged the culprit to pass between two lines of his comrades, each of whom was to strike him with a ramrod or switch. To ensure that the sufferer did not actually "run," and so pass through the "gauntlet" too quickly, an officer or sergeant walked slowly backward before him, with a drawn sword or fixed bayonet leveled at his breast. As these unfortunates were to receive blows from every man in their respective brigades, each composed of three regiments, it was lucky for them that those formations were now woefully undermanned, with the numbers actually present and fit for duty far less than those marked down on the pay rolls.[5]

* * *

Among the many courts martial held at Morristown that winter, one attracted unusual interest. On December 23, 1779, the long-delayed trial of Major-General Benedict Arnold finally reconvened. The prosecution case was presented by the Continental Army's senior lawyer, Judge Advocate General John Laurance; Arnold conducted his own defense. Including recesses, the hearing lasted for more than a month. Although the court was only concerned with the four charges referred by Congress (independently issuing permission for the *Charming Nancy* to enter a United States port; making purchases in Philadelphia for his own benefit; imposing "menial duties" on citizens; and using state-owned wagons to shift his private property), Arnold's defense encompassed all *eight* of the counts originally put forward by Pennsylvania's Supreme Executive Council in February. For the embattled Arnold, the hearing was a long-awaited opportunity to vindicate his tarnished reputation—and to exact a measure of vengeance on the hated men who had brought the charges against him.[6]

The court president was South Carolina's Brigadier-General Robert Howe. This time, Arnold had no objection to him or to any of his judges. Witnesses included both Matlacks, Deputy Quartermaster-General John Mitchell, and Arnold's foppish aide, Major David Franks. On January 21, 1780, once the evidence against him had been heard, Arnold took the stand. He began by reminding the court of his illustrious past services to America—not, he hastened to add, from "an ostentatious turn of mind," but rather "honest indignation" at his situation. Arnold declared: "I was one of the first that appeared in the field, and from that time to the present hour, have not abandoned her service." In support, Arnold read glowing testimonials from Washington and Congress that highlighted his exploits as a defender of American liberty, especially in 1777 at Ridgefield, Connecticut, and at Freeman's Farm. He then asked the court whether it was "possible that having acquired some little reputation . . . I should all at once sink into a course of conduct equally unworthy of the Patriot and soldier?" Of course, Arnold was only addressing the relatively trivial charges actually before the court, not the far more heinous crime of which its members were utterly unaware.[7]

Throughout, Arnold assumed the role of the steadfast soldier, unfairly traduced by malicious enemies. Not without some reason he claimed: "Uncommon assiduity has been employed in propagating suspicions, invectives, and slanders to the prejudice of my character." He continued: "The presses of Philadelphia have groaned under libels against me . . . indeed, every effort that men ingeniously wicked could invent, has been practiced to blast and destroy my character." Arnold addressed each of the eight charges brought against him by the Pennsylvania Council, maintaining his innocence of them all; on one count, the charge of profiting from the closure of Philadelphia's stores, he was guiltier than his judges knew. Even though Congress had already dismissed the final allegation—that as commandant of Philadelphia, he had favored Loyalists at the expense of Patriots—Arnold gave it his special attention: "I am not sensible, Mr. President, of having neglected any gentleman, either in civil or military line, who have adhered to the cause of their country, and who have put it into my power to take notice of them," he told the court. As for "those of an opposite character," his conduct toward them "was justified on the principles of common humanity and politeness." He now relished the chance to publicly lambast his most inveterate critics, the "president and council of Pennsylvania." Arnold hoped "they will pardon me, if I cannot divest myself of humanity, merely out of complaisance to them." He added: "It is enough for me, Mr. President, to contend with men in the field; I have not yet learned to carry on warfare against women, or to consider every man as disaffected to our glorious cause, who from an opposition in sentiment to those in power in the state of Pennsylvania, may, by the clamor of party, be styled a tory."[8]

Arnold saved his harshest words for his arch-enemy, Joseph Reed, using the hearing to turn the tables and make a grave accusation against him:

> Conscious of my own innocence, and the unworthy methods to injure me, I can with boldness say to my prosecutors in general, and to the chief of them in particular, that in the hour of danger, when the affairs of America wore gloomy aspect, when our illustrious general was retreating through New Jersey, with a handful of men, I did not propose to my associates, basely to quit the general, and sacrifice the cause of my country to my personal safety, by going over to the enemy, and making my peace. I can say that I never basked in the sunshine of my general's favor, and courted him to his face, when I was at the same time treating him with the greatest disrespect, and vilifying his character when absent. This is more than a ruling member of the council of the state of Pennsylvania can say, "as it is alleged and believed."[9]

Arnold was raking up gossip that, in the dismal final weeks of 1776, Reed had been guilty of more than merely comparing George Washington unfavorably with Charles Lee. The precise allegation was revealed in a bitter dispute that erupted in 1782, after Major-General John Cadwalader attacked Reed in a Philadelphia newspaper, the *Independent Gazetteer*, run by Arnold's old comrade, Eleazer Oswald. Writing under the pseudonym "Brutus," Cadwalader eagerly knifed Reed's reputation. Just days before the momentous raid on Trenton, at Christmas 1776, he claimed, Reed had told Washington that "our affairs looked very desperate, and that we were only making a sacrifice of ourselves." In the ensuing pamphlet war, Cadwalader printed a letter from Alexander Hamilton, recalling a conversation they had had at headquarters during the Pennsylvanian campaign of 1777. As Hamilton remembered,

> ...you mentioned to me, and some other gentlemen of General Washington's family, in a confidential way, that at some period in seventy-six, I think after the American army crossed the Delaware in its retreat, Mr. Reed had spoken to you in terms of great despondency reflecting the American affairs, and had intimated that he thought it a time for gentlemen to take care of themselves, and that it was unwise to follow the fortunes of a ruined cause, or something of a similar import.

Reed strenuously denied the accusation, instead maintaining that his advice to Washington had encouraged the bold strategy that soon after delivered the pivotal Trenton victory.[10]

Cadwalader's reminder that "charges of the same nature" were leveled by Arnold in the course of his court martial had met with Reed's heavy sarcasm; allowing "full weight to so respectable a connection and testimony," he had simply ignored it. But Cadwalader retorted that in January 1780, *before* his treason was disclosed, Arnold's "rank and character" still merited Reed's notice. When Arnold commanded in Philadelphia, Cadwalader had treated him with courtesy and respect. He told Reed: "To my civilities at that time, I thought him entitled, from the signal services he had rendered his country—services infinitely superior to those you so much boast of." Of course, Arnold's subsequent "treacherous conduct exceeded" even Reed's "idea of his baseness."[11]

Leaving aside his own guilt of far more than the charges before him, Arnold's lengthy defense of his conduct and his stinging attack on Reed remain remarkable for their arrogance and self-righteousness. If it is remembered that he spoke out at a time when he had already spent more than six months engaged in a treasonable correspondence with the British, then his hypocrisy is breath-taking. In fact, Arnold's arguments were so unabashed, and his belief in his "rectitude" so strong, that it is tempting to speculate that, by his own measure at least, he really did believe himself innocent of any wrong-doing: Arnold had made his decision to defect on grounds that he considered to be justifiable. By such reckoning, he was in the right, and those who thought differently to him were wrong.

However cynical it might appear in hindsight, Arnold's "very spirited" defense won him considerable sympathy within the Continental Army, where his disgust with civilian politicians was widely shared. As his trial neared its end, Lieutenant-Colonel Ebenezer Huntington of Connecticut reported the expectation that he "would be acquitted with honor." But when they delivered their verdicts on January 26, Arnold's judges found that he had acted improperly in issuing the permit for the *Charming Nancy* and in making use of the wagons. He was sentenced to receive a reprimand from Washington. Congress approved the verdict on February 12, but was so slow in notifying Washington that he only complied with the court's instructions on April 6. The commander-in-chief worded his rebuke in the mildest terms. Washington

> ... would have been much happier in an occasion of bestowing commendations on an officer who has rendered such distinguished services to his country as Major-General Arnold; but in the present case a sense of duty and a regard to candor oblige him to declare, that he considers his conduct in the instance of the permit as peculiarly reprehensible, both in a civil and military view, and in the affair of the wagons as "imprudent and improper."[12]

After the verdict, the body responsible for Arnold's trial, Pennsylvania's Supreme Executive Council, wrote Congress a letter that was strangely at odds with its previous attitude toward him. It could not "affect ignorance of what is the subject of public conversation"—the sentence "tending to impose a mark of reprehension on General Arnold." The council added: "We find his sufferings for, and services to, his country so deeply impressed upon our minds as to obliterate every opposing sentiment." It begged that Congress would dispense with any "public censure" likely to "most affect the feelings of a brave and gallant officer." Joseph Reed's belated contrition was recalled by Cadwalader during their later spat; at Arnold's trial, "with a half shamed face," Reed had "seemed to apologize for being his prosecutor, and became his fulsome panegyrist."[13]

Such expressions of regret came too late to appease Arnold. Unaware of his earlier dealings with Sir Henry Clinton, contemporary commentators like the Loyalist soldier and historian Charles Stedman assumed that Arnold's treason was a natural consequence of his "mortification" at the court-martial verdict and Washington's reprimand. But Arnold had long since made his decision; and for all their tardy repentance, Reed and his colleagues had played their part in his defection. As even some of Arnold's harshest critics have conceded, their attitude amounted to little short of persecution. If Arnold now felt no remorse at betraying the cause in which he had first taken up arms, then a large share of the blame lies with Pennsylvania's radicals.[14]

* * *

Prominent among the qualities that had made the forty-seven-year-old Washington indispensable to the patriot war effort was his unwavering determination to maintain the struggle for independence under even the most discouraging circumstances. In January 1780, while striving to resolve the supply crisis at Morristown, he remained alert for any chance to land a blow on the enemy. Despite his enduring reputation as a cautious "Fabian" general, by instinct Washington was an aggressive commander, keen to take the offensive whenever opportunity beckoned. For all the misery they inflicted, after the frustrations and disappointments of 1779 the frigid blasts that heralded the New Year revived Washington's hopes for an attack on the British in and around New York city. The complex of waterways surrounding Manhattan Island was now frozen thick enough to support the weight not only of men, but of horses, sleighs, and even artillery. This temporary transformation of the landscape offered opportunities for the Americans and British alike; but for Washington, the scenario was especially tempting. Instead of enjoying the protection of wide moats, dominated by the roving firepower of the Royal Navy, the British garrisons on both Manhattan and Staten Island were now accessible directly from the New Jersey shoreline, and were within striking distance of the American army at Morristown.

That month, the British garrison at New York looked especially vulnerable, because it had just undergone a substantial cut in strength. Even before he withdrew his outlying troops from Rhode Island and the King's Ferry posts, and concentrated them behind Manhattan's fortifications, Sir Henry Clinton had been contemplating a major offensive in the South, intended to build on recent British gains in Georgia. As so often before, everything hinged on the arrival of reinforcements from Britain, and, of course, on the outcome of the Franco-American siege of Savannah. The troops had finally arrived in late September, but it was not until November 18 that Sir Henry learned that Savannah was safe. Once certain that the bloodied d'Estaing and his fleet really were bound for the West Indies, Clinton pushed ahead with assembling a powerful task force of his own, aimed at recovering South Carolina for the Crown.

Given the formidable logistical challenges of mounting an expedition of more than 7,000 men, along with their accompanying siege artillery, supplies, transport ships, and escorting men-of-war, it was only on December 26, 1779, that Clinton and Admiral Arbuthnot sailed from New York: their objective was Charleston, the chief settlement of South Carolina. If that state was restored to royal control, the American secretary Lord George Germain now believed, it could become the base for a British thrust northwards, harnessing resurgent Loyalists to methodically overrun and pacify the remaining rebel states. British hopes also rested on a belief that the rebellion could be ruptured internally—not simply by maximizing the support of active crown sympathizers, but by exploiting the obvious impotence of Congress, and reports of widespread discontent among the Revolution's erstwhile supporters. If even the celebrated Benedict Arnold was eager to defect, then surely others must be thinking like him?

With ice thickening around Manhattan, Clinton's fleet only just cleared New Jersey's curling Sandy Hook to reach open sea before yet another snowstorm struck. The movements of troops and shipping involved in such a major operation were impossible to conceal, and had been duly noted and reported by Washington's spies. By 1780, the American commander-in-chief could count on intelligence not only from a steady trickle of British and Hessian deserters, but also from an expanding network of agents. Back in the fall of 1778, when d'Estaing was refitting his squadron at Boston following the Rhode Island fiasco, he had appealed to Washington for credible information about the strength and intentions of the British fleet at New York. Washington used the Frenchman's request as a pretext to upgrade his existing intelligence service, laying the foundations for what would become known as the "Culper Ring."

Using the alias of "Samuel Culper" (often given as plain "Culper"), Abraham Woodhull, a farmer of Setauket, Long Island, acted as the network's chief intelligence officer. By late spring of 1779, the ring had been strengthened through the recruitment of the merchant Robert Townsend (alias "Samuel Culper Junior") who lived in New York city. Both of these agents

were managed by Major Benjamin Tallmadge ("John Bolton") of the
Continental Light Dragoons: he assessed their reports and then forwarded
them directly to George Washington, who took a keen interest in espionage,
and acted as his own intelligence officer, or "spymaster." In instructions issued
to Tallmadge in October 1779, Washington had left no doubt of his primacy:
all dispatches, and likewise "any verbal intelligence that may be obtained," were
to be transmitted "to no one but the Commander-in-Chief." With the help of
trusted and sharp-witted young aides like Alexander Hamilton and Tench
Tilghman, Washington processed not only reports from the Culper Ring, but
also from agents serving other senior officers whose zones of command
adjoined New York. Washington took a close interest in the technicalities of
spy-craft; for example, he controlled supplies of the widely used invisible, or
"vanishing," ink, and was thoroughly familiar with its application.[15]

From direct observation of British troops, shipping, and fortifications,
and by monitoring gossip in coffee-houses and taverns, such operatives
provided much valuable intelligence. But there were limits to what they
could discover—and crucially, to the speed with which they could transmit
potentially vital information. Here, the Culper Ring was especially limited,
as even after the appointment of Townsend in New York, all of its intelligence was processed by Woodhull on Long Island—more than fifty miles
off. From Woodhull, information was forwarded by whaleboat across Long
Island Sound, under the supervision of another Continental officer, Captain
Caleb Brewster, and then inland from the Connecticut shore by dragoon
dispatch rider to Washington's headquarters; as they were typically in the
Hudson Highlands, or even farther distant, in New Jersey, this involved a
roundabout journey of well over a hundred miles, which meant that intelligence often arrived several days after it was sent. In March 1779, a frustrated Washington wrote to Tallmadge wishing that "C—— could fall upon
some more direct channel by which his letters could be conveyed, as the
efficacy of his communications is lost in the circuitous route." Even after
Townsend started operating in New York city, the far shorter alternative
routes—northwards from Manhattan via King's Bridge, or across the
Hudson to the Jersey shore—were closely watched by the British, and too
risky.[16]

While well aware that a major shift of British manpower was afoot, even
after the vast flotilla had made sail Washington lacked confirmation of
where it was headed, which regiments were embarked, or whether General

Clinton was on board. It was not only Washington who was puzzled. Even among the British, all except an inner circle of senior officers were ignorant of their destination. A week before the fleet sailed, Captain Peebles noted the "various opinions about this change of front," with speculation extending to such northerly targets as Rhode Island or Boston. Or perhaps the redeployment was simply a move to keep "out of the way" of the ice solidifying in the Hudson River?[17]

Although unsure of Clinton's objective, in response to the jarring defeat at Savannah, Washington had already received Congress's orders to send the regiments of his Virginian division to bolster General Lincoln's hard-pressed forces in South Carolina. Obliged to maintain the conflict with an army that was typically far under strength, Washington could scarcely afford to spare such veterans. On a personal level, their departure was an emotional wrench: as a reserved Virginian gentleman surrounded by blunt-speaking Yankees, Washington was loath to part with the officers and men of the Old Dominion. But leave they must. The Virginians marched briskly to Head of Elk, Maryland, and before Christmas were already aboard ship and on their passage down Chesapeake Bay, heading for their native state. After disembarking at Williamsburg, Portsmouth, and Suffolk, they were expected to head farther south by road. According to a report from Baltimore, which had either second-guessed Clinton or had more reliable intelligence than Washington himself, they were ultimately headed for Charleston, "for the better defense of that important place" against an expected British attack.[18]

* * *

At Morristown, the "deplorable" shortage of provisions continued to cause Washington "the most anxious and alarming fears." Yet even though his men were "half starved, imperfectly clothed, riotous, and robbing the country people of their subsistence from sheer necessity," as Washington contemplated the bleak, frozen landscape he increasingly recognized "a field opened for enterprise." Despite all the discouraging circumstances, in the absence of Clinton's task force he was drawn toward the possibility of exploiting the ice to attack the depleted British garrison of Staten Island. Explaining this idea to Brigadier-General William Irvine, who commanded his outlying troops, Washington emphasized that success would depend on two factors: a "firm and solid" bridge of ice between the island and the New Jersey shore, and reliable intelligence of the enemy's strength.[19]

After Irvine confirmed that the ice was thick enough, Washington entrusted the mission to Major-General William Alexander, a middle-aged New York landowner who persisted in using the title "Lord Stirling," despite the House of Lords' firm rejection of his claim to a lapsed Scottish earldom. Whether or not Stirling's rank was real, he displayed an aristocrat's pomposity and appetite for the finer things in life. Even in an age of hard drinkers, Stirling was a noted toper; as the madeira flowed, he enjoyed nothing more than regaling his dinner guests with stories of his previous wartime exploits. His finest hour had been Washington's worst—the disastrous defeat at Brooklyn Heights on August 27, 1776. There, thanks to Henry Clinton's bold plan, the raw rebels had been outflanked and routed. But Stirling staged a gallant stand against overwhelming odds, before being cornered and captured. Exchanged soon after, he had since proved a loyal subordinate to Washington, partici-pating in most of his battles from Trenton to Monmouth Court House. While lacking the judgment and flair for effective senior command, Stirling was a staunch and optimistic upholder of the revolutionary cause. His services were all the more valued because, by January 1780, such committed Patriots were in increasingly short supply.[20]

Allocating some 2,600 men to the raid, Washington outlined Stirling's objectives: to capture the estimated 1,000 British troops on the island, and to carry off or destroy all stores and livestock. Success hinged on surprise, and every possible stratagem should be deployed to achieve it by seizing the enemy's outlying guards and patrols, and by feeding false information to their agents in New Jersey.[21]

Despite this warning, Stirling's raid was compromised by faulty intelli-gence and lax security. Held by 1,800 royal troops, including Lieutenant-Colonel John Graves Simcoe and his Queen's Rangers, Staten Island's garrison was almost twice as strong as the Americans believed. The defenders also knew that an attack was imminent. Not only was it "univer-sally rumored," but, as Simcoe noted, "several of the rebel generals had been [seen] openly measuring the thickness of the ice." When Stirling's troops crossed the frozen sound early on January 15 and split into two columns, the British fell back behind their well-sited fortifications—now strength-ened by an accumulated "abatis of snow, near ten feet high, all around them"—and awaited attack. Under these unfavorable circumstances, as

Stirling reported, "an assault was deemed undesirable." In fact, the raiders themselves now risked being cut off and captured. Contrary to expectations, unfrozen channels still allowed communication by water with New York city. As soon as Stirling's raiders appeared, the British sent a boat for help, and by evening several large ships had arrived to reinforce the defenses. Harassed by Simcoe's dragoons, the Americans withdrew next morning, suffering several killed and many more frostbitten, some so badly that they could not walk and had to be hauled off in sleighs. Beyond burning nine abandoned vessels and taking a handful of prisoners, the raid achieved nothing.[22]

The British were soon contemplating a counter-blow across the ice, aimed at capturing General George Washington. Given the precarious health of the patriot war effort, and the extent to which "His Excellency" was now personally responsible for keeping it alive, such a coup could have tilted the conflict in Britain's favor. If Washington were to be eliminated, there was no obvious candidate of equal stature to take his place. In such a scenario, Washington had apparently indicated that the Rhode Islander Major-General Nathanael Greene should assume his mantle. Ten years younger than Washington, Greene was a gifted, self-taught soldier who had evolved into a competent administrator and a canny strategist—both essential prerequisites for high command. Like Washington, he was hungry for action and military glory. But for all Greene's many virtues, Washington was a hard act to follow: by 1780, he was not merely Congress's unchallenged commander-in-chief, but the embodiment of the revolutionary cause. The consequences of his capture would be difficult to exaggerate.[23]

There were precedents for such an operation. Back in December 1776, for example, a patrol of British light dragoons had swooped down on the unsuspecting rebel Major-General Lee, who had foolishly taken lodgings several miles away from his division in New Jersey. A former British army officer who had served alongside Washington in 1755 during the French and Indian War, Lee was seen by many—and above all by himself—as a rival candidate for the position of American supreme commander. Given his inflated reputation, the British rated Lee's capture as a spectacular success. Weary after riding more than sixty miles in a day, one of the general's captors, young Banastre Tarleton, could scarcely credit "a most miraculous event" which seemed more "like a dream" than reality. Cornet Tarleton, who would go on to make a reputation as the brutally effective colonel of a crack loyalist unit, the British Legion, became a close friend of John André; as a brigade major at Philadelphia, he had been one of the Mischianza knights, his shield bearing the device of a light dragoon, his motto "swift, vigilant, and bold."[24]

In March 1778, Washington had himself given serious thought to a plan to abduct Sir Henry Clinton from his New York headquarters. As Number 1 Broadway lay close to the waterside, and had been isolated by the fire that devastated much of the city during the late summer of 1776, Washington was sure that nothing save "want of secrecy" could prevent "an enterprising party" from fulfilling its mission. It could be conveyed in whaleboats from King's Ferry on the ebb tide, then carry Sir Harry and his official papers back up the Hudson on the flood. As a finishing touch, Washington suggested, the snatch squad could be dressed in red, like the enemy. Colonel Samuel Webb's regiment of Connecticut Continentals (whose captured British uniforms had fooled Clinton's unlucky courier Daniel Taylor in October 1777) would be perfect for the job. In the event, that attempt was postponed until Christmas Day 1780, when the boats' crews were blown past their objective by gusting winds.[25]

The "very important enterprise" of capturing Washington had occurred to Simcoe soon after Lord Stirling's failed raid in mid-January 1780. Based on intelligence from deserters and other sources, Simcoe learned that, like Charles Lee in 1776, Washington was quartered "at a considerable distance from his army." From studying detailed maps of the country, he believed "that it would not be difficult to carry him off." Simcoe's plan to abduct the rebel commander would involve eighty Rangers, with an officer to every six hand-picked men. Marching by "very secret ways, made more so by the inclement season," they were to approach within striking distance of Washington's quarters by daybreak, tie up their horses in an adjoining swamp, then rush the guards on foot. Simcoe was sure his scheme would work: his only "apprehension" was how to take Washington alive if he proved determined to "personally resist" arrest. As the rebel commander was over six feet tall, and still fit and active, this was a valid question.

On January 31, Simcoe had outlined his plan to his local commander, Brigadier-General Thomas Stirling, who gave his "full approbation." But before Simcoe could seek higher approval, the "Hussar" troop of the Queen's Rangers was ordered to join a convoy crossing the ice to New York city. It transpired that Simcoe was not alone in noting Washington's vulnerability.

Captain George Beckwith, who was aide-de-camp to Clinton's deputy, the Hessian Lieutenant-General Wilhelm von Knyphausen, had proposed a remarkably similar design, and was concentrating a formidable force of cavalry to execute it. To provide a distraction for Beckwith's troopers, who were to ride inland from Paulus Hook on the Jersey shore, three other parties would attack at different points across the ice from Staten Island.

The columns set out before daylight on February 11. Simcoe, who commanded one of the supporting forces, led 200 infantry as far as Woodbridge without encountering any enemy. Determined to help his friend Beckwith by stirring up the rebels, he had pushed on to the Amboy–Elizabethtown crossroads before finally meeting opposition. With the New Jersey militia now gathering to oppose him, Simcoe conducted a fighting retreat, deploying his Rangers to skirmish from behind trees bordering the road. They were hounded all the way back to the frozen sound, where accurate cannon fire from Staten Island, and an ambush artfully placed "behind ridges of ice heaped up by the tide," rebuffed the militiamen.[26]

Although the covering parties did their utmost to create a diversion, Beckwith was defeated by the weather. Heavy rainfall encrusted the snow with sharp ice, which "cut the fetlocks of the horses" and made it "absolutely impossible" to push on toward Morristown. Without the unexpected downpour, the audacious plan might well have succeeded. Reporting events to Washington, a relieved Major-General Arthur St. Clair estimated the raiders at 300 horsemen. From Hackensack they had ridden "some distance into the country." From their route and repeated inquiries about the location of Washington's quarters, their objective was clear enough. Had they not been turned back by the state of the roads, St. Clair believed, the consequences could have been serious: the enemy's diversionary forces were strong enough to have distracted attention from a cavalry strike at Washington, and there were too few troops nearby to have protected him.

Next day, the unflappable Washington was characteristically dismissive of his recent peril and satisfied that the vigilance of St. Clair's men had frustrated the enemy, "whatever might have been their intentions." Yet the lesson did not go unheeded: the commander-in-chief had "now taken precautions against such a party as might be reasonably supposed to reach this [place] in the course of a night."[27]

* * *

Inclined to downplay fears for his own safety, Washington remained alive to the possibility that the British might yet take advantage of the ice to launch further offensives. In particular, as the Hudson River was now frozen solid as far north as West Point—some sixty miles above New York city—there were concerns that this smooth, unbroken highway would compromise the security of that vital fortress. Writing to his commander in the Hudson Highlands, Major-General William Heath, Washington warned: "This may tempt the enemy to undertake something against you by surprise, by carrying up their men in sleighs, of which they have lately collected a large parcel." Of course, it was possible that the sleds had been stockpiled for nothing more sinister than hauling firewood, but it would all the same be wise to "guard against every possible event." To minimize the risk to West Point, every fortification that was capable of sheltering men from the elements had to be permanently garrisoned, with the gates barred each night. Heath was already alert to the dangers of a surprise attack on the Highlands: aware that the enemy might "more expeditiously pass up on the ice than by the roads," he had ordered his men "to keep a sharp look out" at King's Ferry.[28]

In his *Memoirs*, William Heath cheerfully described himself as "of middling stature, light complexion, very corpulent, and bald-headed." French officers who served alongside him later that year noted his striking resemblance to one of the age's most celebrated soldiers, John Manners, marquess of Granby. As a dashing cavalry commander during the British army's German campaigns of the Seven Years' War, Granby had become a household name on both sides of the Atlantic. In an age when even men with a good head of hair often wore wigs, Granby was unusual in flaunting his bald pate. It was conspicuous at the battle of Warburg in 1760, when he led his charging troopers with such gusto that his tricorne hat was whipped off by the wind, inspiring the saying "to go at it bald-headed." Granby was painted hatless and wigless by the leading British artists Allan Ramsay and Sir Joshua Reynolds, and his distinctive appearance was familiar from the popular engravings and pottery figurines their portraits inspired. Above all, Granby's ruddy countenance beamed down on bleary-eyed drinkers from the sign-boards of the many inns named after him, not least by the grateful veterans whom he had helped to establish as publicans.[29]

Heath was clearly flattered by comparisons with Granby. Born into a family of gentlemen farmers at Roxbury, near Boston, from boyhood he had been fascinated by military life, devouring every book about strategy and tactics that he could find. Heath put all this theoretical knowledge to practical use when the long-anticipated fighting between redcoats and rebels flared up in Massachusetts on April 19, 1775. There, amid the rock-studded New England pastures, Heath was active in motivating and directing the swarming, sniping militiamen who harassed the British regulars as they retreated along the road from Concord to Boston.[30]

Nothing in Heath's subsequent military career had matched that impressive debut. He proved to be a dependable brigadier under Washington during the campaign of 1776, but soon after made a blunder that cost him his commander's confidence. In February 1777, Heath was sternly rebuked after making a feeble attempt to recapture Fort Independence, which guarded the only road onto Manhattan Island, via King's Bridge. Heath had sent the British garrison a blustering warning to surrender or take the consequences. It was a threat that Heath was unable to enforce; instead of launching an assault, he retired in confusion. Acutely sensitive for his army's reputation, Washington wished that the summons had never been sent, "as I am fearful it will expose us to the ridicule of our enemies." This lapse led Washington to distrust Heath's competence as a combat leader, and he was never again assigned an independent field command.[31]

But the affable and tactful Heath proved his worth in other ways. After Burgoyne's army capitulated at Saratoga in October 1777, Heath was sent to Boston with responsibility for overseeing the 5,000 British and German prisoners of war held nearby. As Congress welched on the surrender terms conceded by Gates, deciding that Burgoyne's troops should not be shipped home after all, the officers and men of the "Convention Army" were understandably surly. Impounding them at Cambridge, cheek by jowl with the fiercely rebel Bostonians, risked friction or worse. Through a combination of firmness, patience, and interminable paperwork, Heath contained the volatile situation for a year, until the captives were finally marched south to new quarters at Charlottesville, Virginia.

In early June 1779, following Clinton's lunge up the Hudson against the King's Ferry forts, Heath was recalled from Boston to rejoin Washington's "Grand Army." On November 27, after the British had regrouped at New York, he was appointed to command the Hudson Highlands. From the outset, this was an assignment that required all of Heath's patience: 1780 started inauspiciously when sixty of West Point's garrison suddenly "slung their packs and went off with arms and accoutrements complete." As Heath informed Washington, these deserters had "entertained a most absurd and groundless opinion" that their three-year terms of enlistment had *all* ended on January 1, 1780, even though they had joined up at different times. He had ordered a captain's command of one hundred men in pursuit, with instructions "to bring them back dead or alive." Slogging through the snow drifts on the west bank of the Hudson, the runaways had only covered some six miles before they were overhauled at New Windsor, and brought back to the point. Most of them were set at liberty, although the ring-leaders were confined to face a court martial.[32]

To add to Heath's anxieties, West Point suffered a succession of mysterious fires. At dusk on January 9, the stout dove-tailed timbers of the North Redoubt, across the Hudson from the main fortifications, were found ablaze. A detachment was ordered over the frozen river to help, but the flames persisted and crept toward the powder magazine. Fearing an explosion violent enough to blow them all sky high, the firefighters were about to sprint for cover when a courageous sergeant dashed alone into the magazine and "did not quit until he had thrown out every cask of powder, and box of ammunition deposited in it." Just before midnight on January 26, another fire consumed the quartermaster's barracks. Several sleepers were lucky to escape in their shirts before the building was reduced to ashes. An adjoining structure was saved, although "scorched to a coal." Had it continued to burn, West Point's main magazine would have been in "great danger," and Heath believed the garrison would have quit the fort "from the apprehensions of instant destruction."

Then, in the early hours of February 1, the North Redoubt was discovered to be on fire *again*. This time the blaze was so hard to reach that, without a proper "water engine" fitted with a flexible leather hose capable of playing directly on the flames, it took two days to extinguish. Damage was extensive, and the redoubt would have been totally destroyed, save for the "unwearied exertions of the troops, day and night." Heath assured Washington that while these repeated fires might seem extraordinary, no steps had been neglected to guard against them. Indeed, as West Point's outlying redoubts and various other buildings were built of wood, and the stone barrack chimneys were shoddily constructed, in such a gusty season it was all too easy for a trapped spark to be "fanned to a flame." In consequence, the exhausted garrison were "almost afraid to close their eyes should fire break out."[33]

Yet for all these worrying distractions, Heath's greatest dilemma in the Highlands mirrored Washington's at Morristown: how to gather supplies for

his men when the roads were clogged by snowdrifts and local farmers stubbornly refused to part with their produce for depreciated Continental currency,
especially when the army's commissaries still owed them for what they had
already supplied. Heath warned New York's state governor George Clinton
that the situation of his troops was "truly alarming." Instead of accumulating
the stockpiles necessary to sustain a siege, West Point's garrison was struggling
to find its "daily bread." Despite their "scanty allowance"—which often meant
no bread at all—the soldiers had been "on almost constant fatigue, dragging
materials for their barracks and all their fuel on hand sledges more than a
mile." Facing heavy snowstorms and cutting winds, some of them were still
under canvas. While Heath's cold and hungry men had endured their dismal
lot "with a patience scarcely to be conceived," that quality was not unlimited.
Appealing for immediate relief from the New York legislature, Heath warned
that if this was not forthcoming, the troops would have no choice but to
disperse. In that case, "the most important posts in the United States, and the
only barrier for the security of this State, will be left open to the enemy."[34]

Worn out by just three vexing months at West Point, Heath obtained
Washington's permission to take a spell of leave back in Roxbury. On
February 18, he handed over command of the Highlands to Brigadier-
General Howe. By then, Heath was at least confident that the garrison
would be supplied with bread. But he cautioned that the fortifications
necessary to secure such an important position were still far from complete.[35]

* * *

Since the end of the previous summer, Benedict Arnold's negotiations with
the British had stalled, although he had already left Clinton and André in
no doubt of his determination to join them. Ensuing months had given him
little cause to regret his decision to change his allegiance.

Even before the humiliating outcome of his court martial, Arnold had
suffered an affront that only increased his alienation from Congress and the
patriot cause. During the fall of 1779, as inflation spiraled and food prices
rose, many of Philadelphia's poorer citizens faced acute hardship. On
October 4, city militiamen marched through the streets in protest, turning
their anger against merchants suspected of exploiting army contracts to
amass personal fortunes, and forcing them to take shelter in the home of the
jurist James Wilson. As the two sides traded musket and pistol fire, Joseph

Reed called out cavalry to disperse the militia; the troopers scattered them with much "cutting and slashing." Although Arnold was no longer military commander of Philadelphia, he had also intervened in an effort to end the fracas. But to many humble Philadelphians, the high-living general was no better than the hated war profiteers and speculators he was trying to protect. Jostled in the streets by a "mob of lawless ruffians," he only escaped a beating by holding them at bay with a brace of loaded pistols. When a hostile crowd subsequently assembled outside his own home, Arnold sent a message to Congress: as there was no protection "to be expected of the state for an honest man," he requested a guard of twenty Continentals, under a steady officer. Despite the seriousness of the situation, which had already resulted in bloodshed, Congress refused to act: once again, it was wary of kindling a dispute with the Supreme Executive Council of Pennsylvania, to whom Arnold should have applied for protection. The riot eventually subsided, yet the "Fort Wilson" affair was a worrying eruption of crowd violence, and another indication of how far notions of American liberty had strayed from those that Arnold had set out to uphold in 1775.[36]

The depreciating currency that fueled such discontent only worsened Arnold's own financial problems. Whatever his long-term plans with the British yielded, he needed an urgent injection of cash. In the spring of 1780, after his trial had cleared the way for a return to active service, he revived his hopes of a naval command, and with it, the prospect of prize money. In early March, he informed Washington that the Board of Admiralty was contemplating an expedition involving several frigates. It would depend on securing a detachment of 300 to 400 men from the army; if trained seamen could be drafted instead of soldiers, so much the better. Arnold, who had told his friend Silas Deane that the expedition was his own idea, mentioned that it would probably embark from the Connecticut port of New London, and last for "about two months." No specific destination was mentioned, but Arnold believed that once he had had a chance to lay the scheme before Washington, the latter would agree that it was "an object of importance." As Arnold was familiar with the West Indies, which had become an important theater of the expanded war, they are the likeliest target. In offering himself as commander, Arnold explained, he had heeded the advice of his surgeons, who still believed that his wounded leg and stiff ankle ruled out an army command for "some time to come." By contrast, a naval posting would allow him to fulfill his wish "to render my country every service in my power."[37]

It is intriguing to speculate how a well-known officer like Benedict Arnold would have executed such an operation in the wake of his secret overtures to the British; it was scarcely the kind of command that Sir Henry Clinton had expected him to assume. Perhaps, if pressed, Arnold could have justified it as a short-term solution to his personal money problems, with no bearing on his previous decision to turn his coat; and as Sir Henry and Arnold's chief contact, Major André, were both far to the south preparing to besiege Charleston, such awkward questions might not even have arisen. In the event, like Arnold's attempt to secure a naval commission in 1778, the proposal was never tested. Already weakened by detachments sent south, and with veterans going home every day as their enlistments expired, Washington could spare no more men from Morristown.[38]

Anticipating that possible outcome, Arnold had already requested "a leave of absence for the ensuing summer, or until my wounds are so well as to admit my riding and walking with some degree of ease, and of course, being able to take command of a division in the army." Arnold had been assured that a "voyage to sea, and bathing frequently in salt water" would work wonders, strengthening his leg and relaxing the muscles, which were "greatly contracted." Washington had agreed to Arnold's request for leave, though he had hoped and expected to see him join the army. In his letter to Deane, Arnold had spoken of his intention—if the proposed expedition was blocked—of traveling to Boston "to take command of a private ship." When he granted Arnold leave, Washington had emphasized that any "voyage" beyond the United States would require the permission of Congress. If Arnold had hoped to skipper a privateer in quest of rich prizes, then that scheme was wrecked, too.[39]

When replying to Arnold, Washington had taken the opportunity to offer his congratulations, and those of "Mrs. Washington," on a "late happy event": on March 19, Peggy had been safely delivered of a boy, who was named Edward. But for all the couple's joy, the birth only increased the family's expenses. With no chance of a naval command, Arnold looked elsewhere to augment his funds. In April 1779, Congress had referred his military accounts to the Board of Treasury. These proved so difficult to unravel that when the board reported back in October, they were handed on to a special committee of five. The committee members fared no better, and on February 14, 1780, the accounts were returned to the Treasury. That outcome angered Arnold, who believed the board was ill disposed toward him. It reported back to Congress on April 27, 1780, with a detailed (though still baffling) ruling. By this, virtually all of Arnold's public accounts for the Canadian campaign of 1776 were cleared, even though much of the money that he had been advanced was not fully accounted for. But £2,000 to which Arnold believed himself entitled was disputed and withheld. Half concerned a sum that Arnold claimed to have already paid to the commissary of provisions, John Halstead; but that officer denied receiving the money, and the board insisted that it could not credit the sum to Arnold unless he could produce a voucher. Despite a search, no evidence was found that such documentation had ever been lodged with the Treasury. The other £1,000 concerned Arnold's 4 percent commission on the £25,000 he had handled while acting as his own commissary and quartermaster in Canada, a rate that he argued was lower than a specialist would have charged. When Arnold appealed, Congress appointed another committee of three to consider both the contested sum and the report itself.[40]

As Arnold's biographers have noted, the determination with which he sought to secure such a relatively small amount testifies to the dire state of his finances. In the spring of 1780, it was later claimed, he was desperate enough to seek a loan from Gerard's replacement as French minister to the United States, Anne-César, the chevalier de La Luzerne. Evidence for the episode rests largely on the recollection of La Luzerne's secretary, François, marquis de Barbé-Marbois. Although he was in America from the fall of 1779 to 1784, Barbé-Marbois composed his colorful narrative of Arnold's treason many years later, and only published it in 1816, after a remarkable diplomatic career spanning the French Revolution, the Napoleonic regime, and the restoration of the Bourbons. While including much anecdotal background material, his knowledge of the plot was limited. For example, like the historian Stedman, he assumed that Arnold's treason only commenced *after* his court martial; he also believed that "the English commander" had sent "emissaries" to exploit Arnold's resentment of his countrymen, and that he had eventually opened his correspondence with Sir Henry Clinton via the prominent Loyalist, Colonel Beverly Robinson. More seriously, the credibility of Barbé-Marbois's account is undermined by his technique of adding entirely fictitious material for dramatic effect: for example, he invented a more flowery version of Washington's reprimand to Arnold. As his American translator admonished: "The interpolation into a professed history of speeches and letters—however apposite they might be in tenor, or eloquent in the fabrication—although conformable to the practice of the ancients, is still a reprehensible license." Despite this caveat, Barbé-Marbois's account is worth careful examination, especially when it deals with events in which the chevalier de La Luzerne (and thereby his personal secretary) was closely involved.[41]

According to Barbé-Marbois, the chevalier "had been charmed with the talents and bravery of Arnold, and took pleasure in testifying a particular predilection for him." But when Arnold sought to take advantage of this good opinion to secure a loan from the French government, explaining that he would otherwise be forced to retire from the army, the chevalier had loftily rejected his approaches as unworthy of them both. Here, as customary, Barbé-Marbois put his own polished prose into the chevalier's mouth; but some support for the episode comes from a report in the *Pennsylvania Packet* after Arnold's treason was exposed. Papers seized at his Philadelphia home had included "private correspondence" employing the "most sarcastic and contemptuous expressions" about "the French nation and . . . an eminent personage of that nation." In his narrative, Barbé-Marbois claimed that the letters in question, in which La Luzerne's character was "roughly handled," were found in the "apartment of Mrs. Arnold." The chevalier had burned the papers without even deigning to read them. This incident, which seems to have at least some basis in fact, has been cited as providing the "earliest hints" of the strong anti-French prejudice that figures in Arnold's later justifications for his treason. Yet it can only have reinforced existing sentiments: as already seen, Sir Henry Clinton maintained that Arnold had expressed such opinions when he first approached him, in May 1779.[42]

* * *

Increasingly frustrated by circumstances, during the spring of 1780 Benedict Arnold picked up where he had left off the previous summer, and reactivated his treasonable correspondence with the British. In early May, he renewed contact with the Crown's commanders in New York via his old agent, Joseph Stansbury. With Henry Clinton and John André both still in the South, besieging Charleston, Arnold now dealt with General Knyphausen and his aide, Captain George Beckwith. It was the capable Beckwith, an officer with a real aptitude for intelligence work, who handled the correspondence with "Mr. Moore."[43]

Arnold made it clear that he remained ready to undertake a "decisive part"—provided he received assurances "of certain indemnifications for himself and family, in case of emergency." Indeed, Arnold declared that "were it not for his family . . . he would join the army without making any terms." He was especially keen to confer with a trustworthy officer, to establish a "regular mode of communication," and to arrange a "token" as a means of preventing fraud. In Sir Henry's absence, Knyphausen felt unable to give a full answer. However, he would certainly represent "Mr. Moore's offers" to him at the "first opportunity," and meanwhile "be happy in cultivating the connection, and in giving . . . every testimony of his regard from the persuasion he entertains of his rectitude and sincerity." As a sign of good faith, "trifling expenditures" incurred in forwarding intelligence were to be "readily reimbursed," while a meeting would be arranged whenever Arnold deemed it practicable. Meanwhile, Beckwith would procure two identical rings as a means of verifying identification, along with a pair of pocket dictionaries for communication by cypher.[44]

Until Clinton returned, Arnold could do little more than feed information to Beckwith. But that task received his close attention. On June 7, for example, he sent prompt notice of intelligence that he believed to be of the highest significance: it concerned plans for a Franco-American assault on Quebec. In late April, the marquis de Lafayette had disembarked at Boston, following a mission to obtain fresh military aid from France. He informed Washington: "I have affairs of the utmost importance that I should first communicate to you alone." Two weeks later, when they met at Morristown, Lafayette revealed that a powerful French fleet and army was on its way to fight alongside the Americans. His dogged lobbying in Paris had helped persuade Louis XVI and his ministers that troops allocated for an aborted invasion of England could be usefully employed in America. These well-disciplined, white-coated regulars were commanded by the veteran comte de Rochambeau, who was instructed to act under Washington's orders; the troops would be convoyed by a fleet under another highly experienced officer, the chevalier de Ternay.[45]

The first division of what was codenamed the *Expédition Particulière* sailed from the Breton port of Brest on May 2, 1780. British agents had long since noted the bustling preparations there, and the expedition's purpose was soon known in London. While besieging Charleston, Clinton received a report, written by Germain to the Lords of the Admiralty, and then urgently forwarded by them, that a "very considerable armament" of twelve ships of the line was sailing from Brest for North America. It was not known precisely where the French were headed, although Quebec was a possibility. Germain's letter was dated March 15, and stated that the French were expected to quit port by the end of that month; it reached Clinton in mid-May, by which time the flotilla might be nearing American waters. Faced with this looming threat, and still unsure of its target, Clinton and Admiral Arbuthnot were both understandably anxious to conclude the siege operations and return to their vulnerable base at New York without delay.[46]

On June 4, 1780, Washington entrusted Arnold with a copy of a proclamation for distribution among the French inhabitants of Canada, informing them of their countrymen's forthcoming expedition against Quebec. This should be given to a printer "whose secrecy and discretion may be depended on"; he was to strike off a proof-sheet in French for correction at headquarters. Washington added: "The printer is to be particularly charged not on any account to reserve a copy himself or suffer one to get abroad." Three days later, Arnold replied to Washington from Philadelphia, explaining that he had experienced problems in finding a trustworthy printer who understood French. Eventually, "Mr. Claypole" in Second Street had undertaken the job; when forwarding copies to Morristown, he was to be sure to observe "the greatest caution and secrecy." Meanwhile, the original draft had been sealed up and left with "Mrs. Arnold," to be delivered as Washington directed. That same day, June 7, Arnold sent the proclamation to Stansbury, to be forwarded to Captain Beckwith. Unknown to Arnold, this tempting information was false, deliberately spread by Washington in the hope that it would reach the British and deceive them as to his true intention: when the French arrived, he hoped to join them in a combined assault on New York city, not Quebec.[47]

Arnold's belief that the manifesto was genuine was bolstered by the chevalier de La Luzerne, who had assured him that no fewer than 8,000 French troops were destined for Canada. Oblivious of Arnold's treasonable dealings, Washington could not have suspected that his misinformation would be transmitted to the enemy so promptly. The British took the intelligence seriously: Sir Henry Clinton forwarded a translation of the proclamation to Germain. Years later, Arnold still believed it was legitimate and worth recalling when he listed his activities on behalf of the Crown: he had informed Sir Henry "of the expedition intended against Quebec, in which the French fleet and forces were to attack that place, while the marquis de

Lafayette made a diversion in Upper Canada, by the way of Connecticut River and St. Johns."[48]

Soon after he unwittingly helped to spread Washington's fake news, Arnold picked up bona fide intelligence that the American commander had hoped to keep secret at all costs. On June 12, while traveling to New Haven on private business, Arnold broke his journey at Washington's Morristown headquarters. There he gleaned information of such significance that he immediately sent it on to New York. He wrote: "six French ships of the line, several frigates, and a number of transports with 6,000 troops are expected at Rhode Island in two or three weeks to act under General Washington." Although Arnold still believed that the expedition's ultimate objective was Quebec, his accurate intelligence of its strength, timing, and port of arrival was of exceptional importance. He had already tried to wheedle this information out of his friend La Luzerne, but without success. According to Barbé-Marbois, the chevalier had informed Congress under the "most profound secrecy" that the French armament was on its way. An "inconsiderate member" let it slip to Arnold, who approached La Luzerne and "tried every means to learn where the army would debark, and when it would form a junction with Washington." Now, Arnold had exactly the intelligence that he had been seeking: if the British high command acted on it, here was a chance to destroy the French before they had even set foot on North America's mainland.[49]

When Arnold renewed his correspondence with the British, he was increasingly confident of securing a position that would allow him to play a decisive role in ending the American rebellion. Sometime in early May, he had a conversation in Philadelphia with his old friend Philip Schuyler, who was now in Congress, during which he seemingly suggested himself as commandant of West Point. On May 25, he certainly wrote to Schuyler, asking "who was to have the command of the North River." Replying on June 2, Schuyler said that he had discussed the matter with Washington, who had expressed his desire to do what was "agreeable" to Arnold. During their conversation, Schuyler wrote, Washington had dwelled on Arnold's abilities and sufferings, and his "well-earned claims" on his country. Rather than any definite promise of West Point, there was talk of "an important post" or a field command. Schuyler added: "Your reputation, my dear sir, so established, [and] your honorable scars, put it decidedly in your power to take either."[50]

After Arnold became a hated traitor to the patriot cause, Washington was adamant that he had never spoken about him to Schuyler in terms of such "affection and approbation." Writing to Joseph Reed, he recalled that Schuyler had mentioned receiving a letter from Arnold "intimating his intention of joining the army and rendering such services as his leg would permit": although still incapable of active service, he could "discharge the duties of stationary command without much inconvenience or uneasiness." Washington would have been glad of Arnold's "aid and assistance"; as he envisaged "an active and vigorous campaign" in which the whole army would be mobilized in an attack on New York, leaving West Point "to the care of invalids and a small garrison of militia," there was little prospect of Arnold obtaining that posting. But if, for the reasons given, command of West Point would be "more agreeable and convenient" to Arnold than a field role, then Washington would "readily indulge him." He had been more inclined to take that course because it was clearly desirable to New York— the state most immediately interested in the safety of the post. Here, Washington was referring to a letter from another Arnold admirer, New York congressman Robert Livingston, who had expressed doubts about the "military character" of the current commander in the Hudson Highlands, Brigadier-General Robert Howe. Livingston wondered whether West Point "might not be most safely confided to General Arnold, whose courage is undoubted, who is the favorite of our militia, and who will agree perfectly with our governor." Washington had no immediate concerns about Howe, but conceded that he might be replaced when the onset of a new campaign provided the opportunity for a "general arrangement" of responsibilities. It is likely that Arnold discussed the Hudson Highlands command with Washington himself when he attended headquarters at Morristown on June 12; by that evening, he was sure of being offered the West Point command on returning to Philadelphia from his trip to Connecticut.[51]

Lauded as a trusty guardian of West Point, Arnold had already provided the British with detailed intelligence about the fort. His report, which highlighted the strongpoint's vulnerability to a surprise attack, was written at nearby Fishkill on June 16. Although Arnold had stayed at the Robinson House in May 1778, this was the first time that he had inspected the fortress at close quarters. Touring the defenses in company with Brigadier-General Howe, he was unimpressed by what he saw. Arnold observed: "It is surprising a post of so much importance should be so totally neglected."

Numbering just 1,500 men, the garrison was less than half of what was needed to man its extensive defenses; General James Clinton's brigade of 1,200 New Yorkers had been ordered as reinforcements, and were marching down from Albany; the Americans hoped that they would arrive before the British could attack—a move which was believed to be under consideration. While the defenses were well built, they were "most wretchedly planned," if their object was to "stop the passage of the river." The point itself was on relatively low ground, compared to the chain of hills behind it. All of the fortifications, including the strong Fort Putnam, were dominated by the highest point of all, Rocky Hill. That eminence was defended by nothing more than a small redoubt holding 200 men and a couple of 6-pounder cannon. Open "at the back," the Rocky Hill redoubt was also "wretchedly executed . . . and might be taken by assault by a handful of men." Arnold was told that "the English may land three miles below and have a good road" to haul up heavy cannon to Rocky Hill. During his tour of the fortifications, Arnold had spoken "so particularly" about the weakness of the "Rocky Hill Work" and "with what care it could be taken" that his host, Brigadier Howe, later remembered thinking it somewhat strange, although he "had not the least suspicion" of the real reason for such intense interest. Arnold was also convinced that the "boom or chain thrown across the river to stop the shipping" was weaker than it looked: it could be broken by a large, heavily laden vessel, riding the momentum of a strong wind and tide.[52]

* * *

When Arnold revived his negotiations with the British, the fortunes of the young United States were at low ebb. Congress was now an ineffective and discredited body, stuffed with mediocrities and enfeebled by its inability to extract funds from the states. After barely surviving the worst winter in memory, the Continental Army was starving, penniless, and on the brink of disintegration. Mounting hardships had eroded morale and spread resentment and discontent among officers and ordinary soldiers alike. On the evening of May 25, such feelings boiled over at Morristown, when two famished regiments of the Connecticut line mutinied and were barely restrained by their officers and steady Pennsylvanian troops. Their gripes were all too common. On the day after the unrest, Major Sebastian Bauman, who commanded the artillery at West Point, wrote to his friend General

Henry Knox. The major was worried about "the suffering of the army" and the poor state of his guns. Something had to be done, although he had little faith that Congress would act. Indeed, Bauman had lost all respect for that body. He wrote: "The troops have half a pound of bread per day, but no meat, and when meat, no bread. A scorching sun, hard labor, and no rum . . . and no pay for fighting, for who? For a set of retrogrades?" No one understood the underlying problem better than Washington. He believed that only a stronger Congress could save the cause of liberty. In the wake of the Connecticut mutiny, he assured Virginian congressman Joseph Jones: "Certain I am, unless Congress speaks in a more decisive tone; unless they are vested with powers by the several States competent to the great purposes of war, or assume them as a matter of right; and they, and the States respectively, act with more energy than they hitherto have done, that our cause is lost."[53]

Just days later, on May 30, Washington learned of the fall of Charleston; under heavy bombardment, and facing the prospect of a bloody storm, General Lincoln had surrendered on the 12th. In their greatest success of the war, the British captured 5,000 men and much sorely needed equipment. News of Clinton's triumph reached New York soon after reports of the upheavals at Morristown, and General Knyphausen saw an opportunity to strike against Washington with the troops at his disposal. "Old Knyp" was egged on by the embittered hardline Loyalists who clustered in New York city, not least the former royal governor of New Jersey, William Franklin, the estranged illegitimate son of Benjamin Franklin. Unknown to Knyphausen, Sir Henry Clinton had intended to launch just such an offensive himself when he returned from the South, and his premature thrust upset that plan. On the night of June 6, Knyphausen invaded New Jersey, crossing over from Staten Island with 5,000 men under generals Edward Matthew and Thomas Stirling. Pushing inland, they soon faced stubborn resistance from the New Jersey militia, stiffened by a brigade of Continentals. When Washington advanced from Morristown, Knyphausen burned the village of Connecticut Farms, then withdrew to Elizabethtown Point. This became a base for future operations, linked to Staten Island by a pontoon bridge across the narrow Arthur Kill.[54]

By June 18, Sir Henry Clinton was back in New York. News of his return, and ominous reports of British shipping hovering off Verplanck's Point, rekindled Washington's abiding fears for the Hudson Highlands. On June

21, he once again marched his foot-sore troops north toward King's Ferry. Major-General Greene remained at Springfield with 1,000 Continentals and the New Jersey militia. They were soon obliged to fight again. On June 23, and now acting on Clinton's orders, Knyphausen advanced from his bridgehead. The outnumbered Greene fell back before him, then rallied his troops in a strong defensive position behind Springfield. Here, a hard contest took place for control of the bridge, which was flanked by swamps. Ensign Jeremiah Greenman of the 2nd Rhode Island Regiment was in the thick of the action. Greenman, who had served as a humble private soldier under Arnold in his 1775 expedition to Quebec, and was captured during the chaotic assault on December 31, described the stubborn engagement in his journal. He recorded that the enemy's

> infantry was not more than a musket shot from us, and advancing very fast for the bridge; their light troops, chiefly Jäger, advanced for the brook and each flank which they soon gained, the musketry at the same time playing very smartly on the bridge; they being so far superior in number they crossed it, and soon [were] considerable in the rear of the right wing.

But they made little further progress. As Ensign Greenman continued: "the left wing having advantageous ground, fought them at a retreat forming at every fence and knoll." Stalled by these defensive tactics, the invaders withdrew, burning as they went. Next morning, June 24, Greenman heard that "the enemy had all left the Jersey Shore."[55]

Knyphausen's retreat relieved the pressure on Greene in New Jersey, but Sir Henry Clinton now hoped to follow up his victory at Charleston with another. His plan hinged on the latest intelligence forwarded by Benedict Arnold, which awaited him on his return to New York. Convinced that the report was credible, Sir Henry resolved to exploit it. By now, he clearly trusted Arnold, assuring his London correspondent, the diplomat William Eden, that his information was "received from such authority as I would have risked an action upon."[56]

According to Arnold, the French might be expected to reach Rhode Island in late June or early July. Working to that schedule, by June 22, while operations in New Jersey were ongoing, Clinton had "prepared a select corps" of 6,000 troops; they were encamped and ready to embark within a few hours. Sir Henry had originally hoped to pre-empt the French by reoccupying Newport before they landed. But unlike Clinton, Admiral Arbuthnot was unconvinced of the enemy's destination: he wanted confirmation, and the support of an expected reinforcement of six ships of the line under Rear-Admiral Thomas Graves. Despite Arbuthnot's caution, Clinton planned to attack the French as soon as they landed—if the admiral had not already intercepted their fleet before it reached port.[57]

For all his thorough preparations, Sir Henry's bold plan was doomed by Arbuthnot's habitual indecisiveness and his reluctance to offer whole-hearted cooperation to the army. The admiral's frigates spotted the French flotilla off Virginia on July 5, but then lost track of its whereabouts. It was only on the 18th that Clinton received word, from one of General Robertson's scouts on Long Island, that the French had already been ashore at Newport for a week, and were busy fortifying themselves: Arbuthnot had missed his chance of destroying de Ternay's squadron at sea, while Sir Henry's hopes of a swift attack on Rochambeau's army were diminishing.

But the French were far more vulnerable than their enemies realized. Cooped up aboard their transport ships during an unusually protracted Atlantic crossing, they had finally disembarked at Newport in a pitiful state. According to the artillery officer Jean-François-Louis, comte de Clermont-Crevecoeur, many were suffering from scurvy. They were in no condition to repel a determined attack by Clinton's veterans, who were spoiling for a fight with their traditional enemy. Among the Britons keen to test their mettle against the French regulars was Lieutenant-Colonel Simcoe. He lobbied Clinton to ensure that his Queen's Rangers would be included in any attack on Rhode Island. His friend Major André replied in language which suggested that the war was a duel writ large: "The General assures you, that the Rangers shall be pitted against a French regiment the first time he can procure a meeting."[58]

Although the French were now too well established to succumb to a *coup de main*, Sir Henry Clinton was determined to arrange the "meeting." There remained the possibility of a landing on the shore north of Newport, covered by Arbuthnot's massed broadsides. This was the kind of elaborate amphibious operation in which the British were uniquely experienced. Admiral Graves arrived off New York on July 13; his ships required some refitting, but with Arbuthnot's help he was ready to put to sea again within six days. After the combined squadrons sailed, it was agreed that Sir Henry should embark his troops and make for Huntington Bay, on the north shore of Long Island, and await the navy's assessment of the French position.

All of this activity did not go unnoticed by Washington's spies. On July 21, Colonel Elias Dayton wrote to headquarters from Elizabethtown, New Jersey. That morning he had received dependable intelligence that Arbuthnot and Graves had sailed two days earlier, while "fifty sail of transports" had followed them up Long Island Sound, "expecting to take troops on board at Whitestone, from whence 'tis said, they are immediately to proceed to Rhode Island." According to Dayton's information, the British intended "to attempt the reduction of that post with the French troops now there, which only consist of five or six thousand, and those sickly and unfit for active service." As Washington was temporarily absent from camp, his quick-thinking aide Alexander Hamilton immediately forwarded the intelligence to Lafayette, who was acting as liaison officer with his countrymen at Rhode Island: "Though this may be only a demonstration," Hamilton explained, "I think it best to forward it without waiting the general's return."[59]

That same day, British warships were already menacing Rhode Island. Their sudden appearance caused consternation in the French camp. Baron Ludwig von Closen observed:

> This unexpected visit was tremendously disturbing to our generals and the whole army, which did not feel strong enough as yet to receive such a formidable enemy, since only half our troops were in condition to fight and oppose a landing; moreover, we had brought ashore only a very little of our artillery and munitions at that time.

Another infantry officer, Jean-Baptiste-Antoine de Verger noted in his journal: "Our situation was such that we had great cause to fear that we should be taken by storm."[60]

But the storm never broke. Although the French assumed that Clinton's troops were aboard the fleet hovering off Rhode Island, they had not even embarked. Arbuthnot was to blame. He had found fresh water for Admiral Graves' crews by emptying the casks on the army's transport ships. By the time the butts were refilled, the wind was unfavorable. It was only on July 28 that the troop ships finally anchored in Huntington Bay. On the 30th, Clinton's aide-de-camp Captain Henry Savage brought pessimistic tidings from Arbuthnot: the French were well fortified and reinforced by American militia; a direct assault was not viable, although the admiral made no mention of Clinton's alternative plan for a landing farther north. By now, after so much dithering, Clinton was becoming concerned for the security of New York, which Washington was reported to be threatening. He summoned a council of war, which advised sailing back to cover Manhattan.

The sudden danger to the French at Rhode Island had placed George Washington in a quandary. Ever since Lafayette told him that Rochambeau and de Ternay were on their way, he had hoped that they would join forces with him in an all-out assault on New York city. But Washington had scarce learned of their arrival at Newport than it became clear that they feared being trapped by Clinton, and that he must take steps to help *them*. Rochambeau grew so anxious that his American colleague at Rhode Island, Major-General Heath, mobilized militia to support him. Lafayette believed that his countrymen would be greatly reassured if Washington could send Continental troops to their aid, or make a diversion. But that was easier said than done. To prepare for his anticipated attack on Manhattan, Washington had appealed to the states for both supplies and manpower. But the response had been bitterly disappointing, and he despaired of obtaining the "men or means" he needed.[61]

In addition, Rhode Island was too distant for Washington to reach swiftly with his Continentals. The only way to relieve pressure on the French was to threaten New York, although even that strategy would involve a massive logistical effort in assembling the supplies and transportation necessary to move his army from New Jersey and West Point. It was not until July 27 that Washington could begin shifting his troops, and it was July 31 before they started crossing the Hudson at King's Ferry. By then, Clinton had already decided to turn back. Although a concern for New York played a part in this decision, he maintained that his primary reason for aborting the Rhode Island offensive was Arbuthnot's discouraging advice.[62]

At Newport, the French were elated at their deliverance, and happy to attribute it to Washington's canny maneuvering. On July 30, Baron von Closen wrote in his journal: "If the enemy had been able to land during the first six days after the appearance of his fleet, we would not have been able to put up very strong opposition, and our army would have risked a great deal." He shrugged: "But with these endeavors, as with the fair sex, if the first moments of surprise are lost, all is over: the favorable moments never return." The British were correspondingly frustrated. Young Lieutenant George Matthew

of the Coldstream Guards rued the lost opportunity: "It was reported, sometime after, that the French were in such consternation at being blockaded by
a superior fleet, that had we proceeded, they would, at our arrival, have run
their ships aground and thrown their guns overboard," he wrote.[63]

Clinton's hopes had been dashed by a combination of bad luck and
Arbuthnot's bloody-mindedness. He found it difficult to contain his disappointment at the factors that had prevented "such a stroke . . . as would have
totally demolished the French armament." With hindsight, Sir Henry realized that the failure to act decisively on Arnold's intelligence, and eliminate
Rochambeau's groggy and scorbutic whitecoats, was a costly error that
Britain would "ever have reason to lament . . . as there is little doubt that our
not being able to crush this reinforcement immediately on its arrival gave
additional animation to the spirit of rebellion, whose almost expiring
embers began to blaze up afresh on its appearance."[64]

Arnold was understandably irate that his revelations had been squan-
dered. When he compiled a résumé of what he considered to be his most
important "services" to the British, he recalled that he had "informed Sir
Henry Clinton of the exact number of French troops and ships . . . the time
appointed from their sailing from France, and when they might be expected
at Rhode Island." Referring to himself in the third person, he claimed:

> . . . the time so pointed out by General Arnold proved to be exact to a
> day, and had Admiral Arbuthnot seconded the exertions of Sir Henry
> Clinton, and co-operated cordially with him in his intended attack on
> the French fleet and army, the whole might have been easily captured on
> their first arrival at Rhode Island, which [would] in all probability have
> eventually put a favorable period to the American war.

Looking back, Arnold exaggerated the precision of his intelligence, yet there
was no doubting its quality.[65]

Sir Henry Clinton agreed with Arnold's assessment. He testified that
the information he had sent him "on many occasions" was undoubtedly
important:

> But that which he gave me of the expected arrival of the French arma-
> ment in 1780 was such, that if the good old Admiral Arbuthnot had
> fortunately placed the same confidence in it that I did, and had met the

French fleet and army ... at their landing at Rhode Island, and before their army could have been reinforced and entrenched, most complete success might have been expected.

In a related memorandum, Clinton observed that if the plan had succeeded, placing the entire French force "in a critical situation," he would "have been at a loss to name the sum such service had merited."[66]

* * *

In early July 1780, Arnold returned to Philadelphia from Connecticut. Despite his best efforts, he had been unable to complete the sale of his New Haven mansion. To add to his frustrations, he had heard nothing from his British contacts. Having supplied such prime intelligence, he was irritated that his most recent letters had not been answered, or even acknowledged. Of course, Arnold's correspondents Captain Beckwith and Major André had both been busy on active service; and it was his information of June 12 from Morristown that had launched Sir Henry Clinton's expedition against the newly arrived French. With such distractions, it was scarcely surprising that the negotiations had been neglected. But on July 7, Arnold wrote impatiently for "a very explicit answer" to his letter to Captain Beckwith of a month earlier, in which he had requested a meeting. He wanted "an interview with Major-General Phillips, or some other proper officer, as nothing more can be done without it." He was now more confident than ever that he would command West Point soon, and certainly before the end of the month. He had a French engineer's plan of the fortifications on both sides of the Hudson River; if a meeting could be fixed, Arnold believed he could "settle matters" so that the fort could be captured by the British "without loss."[67]

Arnold was so restless that he sent off two more letters on July 11 and 12, reiterating his hopes for a personal conference "with some intelligent officer in whom a mutual confidence could be placed." His urgency was heightened by a conviction that the patriot war effort was in crisis: "The mass of the people are heartily tired of the war, and wish to be on their former footing," Arnold claimed. Great expectations had been raised for Washington's planned attack on New York in conjunction with the French; if they were disappointed, the British had "only to persevere and the contest will soon be at an end."[68]

Arnold finally received a reply from André on July 13. This expressed Sir Henry's appreciation of the "useful intelligence" contained in his June letters from Morristown and Fishkill. Clinton agreed that Arnold's command of West Point "would afford the best opportunities," and that an interview was "absolutely necessary." Arnold could rely on Clinton's promise that "effectual cooperation" would secure him "the full measure of the national obligation." On July 15, Arnold wrote back with a definite demand: he asked for £10,000, for him or his heirs, in the event of loss of property, plus compensation for his lost pay. If he supplied "a plan of cooperation" by which Clinton could possess West Point and its garrison, he considered £20,000 a "cheap purchase for an object of so much importance." He wanted £1,000 to be paid to his agent, and expected "a full and explicit answer."[69]

Before leaving Philadelphia to assume the command that he now expected to be awaiting him in the Hudson Highlands, Arnold tried to wring whatever cash he could out of Congress. On July 17, he mentioned that his pay was now nearly four years in arrears, and also asked for an advance of another four months' salary to buy field equipment for the coming campaign. Arnold did not specify that he expected to be in a fixed garrison, where such an allowance was not justified. Accepting a report from the Board of Treasury, on July 21 Congress authorized him an advance of $25,000, "on account of his pay."[70]

Years later, Washington recalled meeting Arnold on July 31, 1780, as the army was crossing King's Ferry on its way to menace Manhattan. When Washington informed Arnold that he was to have "command of the light troops, which was a post of honor," he was perplexed that the only response was glum silence. It is unlikely that Washington offered Arnold the light infantry assignment: that active command demanded physical fitness, and had already been promised to Lafayette; here, Washington's memory deceived him. The next day, August 1, general orders from Peekskill announced that Arnold would have the army's left wing. It was now that Arnold went to headquarters to protest his unsuitability for a field command. Ironically, he was spurning the recognition and responsibility that he had always sought, and his first chance to serve under Washington's personal command. But for Major-General Benedict Arnold, that glorious opportunity had come too late: he had long since decided that his loyalties lay with the British, and was now intent on handing them the strategic objective that would earn him their eternal gratitude, and satisfy his own ambition to "deliver his country" from civil war.[71]

Washington's "great movement" against New York had strained patriot resources to the limit, and his trusted subordinate Nathanael Greene believed it would be wise to explain its purpose "to the Army, and through them to the country." The short-lived offensive had been both "very rapid" and "very fatiguing." Such exertions had not only "harassed" the army, but subjected the public to a "most enormous expense." To justify the herculean effort, and reconcile the troops to future labors, it was necessary to demonstrate that the "enterprise was great, the object noble; and the end for which it was under-taken . . . partly answered, if not fully so." There was no need to boast, Greene added, "but I think we may with great reason suppose the enemy's return to be in consequence of our movements; and that gives us the reputation of having saved our allies from an injury, and subjected the enemy to the morti-fication of having being obliged to relinquish their project."[72]

Greene's arguments were persuasive: on August 3, general orders from Peekskill announced that the army would next day resume its old position, "having moved to the present ground in consequence of the enemy's disposi-tions to make a combined attack upon our allies at Rhode Island"—a threat that they had "probably" thwarted. Patriot newspapers spread an even more positive interpretation of events, informing readers that "Sir Henry no doubt relinquished this project in consequence of this movement of our army." As Washington's weary troops prepared to re-cross the Hudson River in the morning, "After Orders" added a terse but significant announcement: "Major General Arnold will take command of the garrison at West Point and Major General Lord Stirling succeeds to the command of the left wing." Some weeks earlier, Arnold had assured Major André that American resistance to Britain would soon be at an end. "The present struggles are like the pangs of a dying man, violent but of short duration," he wrote. By betraying West Point to the British, Benedict Arnold intended to administer the *coup de grâce*.[73]

CLINCHING THE DEAL

By August 5, 1780, Major-General Benedict Arnold had established his headquarters at the Robinson House, situated two miles downriver from West Point, on the opposite bank of the Hudson. It was a remote spot, described as a "dreary situation, environed with mountains" and dark forests; there was not another house "in view, and but one within a mile." Arnold was untroubled by such isolation or the wild surroundings: writing to his predecessor, Brigadier-General Robert Howe, he regarded his quarters as both secure and suitably appointed for an "invalid." Arnold had cause to be content: West Point was the essential cornerstone of his plan to help Sir Henry Clinton smash the American rebellion. Besides Clinton and Major André, no one else understood this better than his wife: at a recent dinner hosted by Colonel Robert Morris, "a friend of the family came in and congratulated Mrs. Arnold that her husband was appointed to a different but more honorable command" than West Point. Probably echoing Washington's orders of August 1, which had assigned Arnold to the army's left wing, this news had thrown the twenty-year-old Peggy into "hysteric fits." To the astonishment of everyone, efforts to pacify her with assurances that the general had been "selected for a preferable station . . . produced no effect."[1]

Arnold's command included not only the fortress of West Point, which was intended to be garrisoned by 1,500 Massachusetts militia, but its "dependencies." It embraced the zone from Fishkill down to King's Ferry, where the redoubts at Stony Point and Verplanck's Point were manned by Colonel James

Livingston's regiment, and also the outposts facing the enemy's positions on the eastern side of the Hudson. Unlike the opposite bank of the river, which was dominated by Washington's "Grand Army," the swath of Westchester County stretching from British-held King's Bridge to the American lines at White Plains was disputed territory. By 1780, this "Neutral Ground" had been thoroughly scoured, both by officially approved foraging expeditions and by gangs of freelance plunderers. These marauders included the loyalist "Cowboys," who specialized in rustling cattle to feed the garrison of New York, and the less discerning "skinners"; although "professing attachment to the American cause," in the opinion of Major William Hull of the 8th Massachusetts Regiment, who had patrolled the ravaged zone in 1779, they were "devoted to indiscriminate robbery, murder, and every species of the most brutal outrage."[2]

Secured at long last after persistent lobbying, Arnold's new posting complicated his communications with the British. Until a more efficient system was established, any correspondence still had to be transmitted back and forth between Philadelphia and New York city, before finally being forwarded to Arnold at West Point. In late July, when he was handling the correspondence during André's absence on Clinton's Rhode Island expedition, Captain Beckwith had grappled with the problem but had been unable to "fix a direct mode of communication by the *Hudson.*" Although "certain," the alternative of corresponding via Philadelphia was inevitably "tedious," he observed.[3]

The pitfalls that Beckwith anticipated were soon apparent. On August 14, Stansbury wrote to Odell: "Mr. Moore commands at West Point, but things are so poorly arranged that your last important dispatches are yet in her hands, no unquestionable carrier to be found." The unnamed female was Peggy Arnold, to whom her husband continued to send information about military operations, embedded within personal letters, on the assumption that she would ensure that the essential data reached the British; even if intercepted, these would seem innocuous enough—nothing more than a husband keeping his wife abreast of camp gossip. Stansbury was confident that once Odell had opened a communication with Arnold "on the spot," unnecessary delays would be avoided. By now, Stansbury had been increasingly sidelined by Arnold in favor of another Philadelphia-based agent, the Quaker merchant Samuel Wallis. Born in Maryland, Wallis had worked for Sir William Howe during the British occupation of the city; familiar with Pennsylvania's frontier "Indian country," in the summer of 1779 he had volunteered to supply André with a "perfect knowledge of everything" concerning Major-General John Sullivan's expedition to chastise Britain's Iroquois allies. Although John Rattoon ("Mercury") still acted as a courier, it was Wallis who was entrusted with carrying Arnold's impatient letters of July 11 and 12 to New York, where he received 200 guineas from Beckwith to cover expenses.[4]

With the treason poised to enter its final stage, as both Beckwith and Stansbury had emphasized, it was imperative for Arnold to establish his own direct line of contact with Major André. An increasing sense of urgency now prompted him to take steps to infiltrate existing patriot spy networks. Rather than immediately exposing American agents to the British, Arnold's intention was to exploit them to expedite his own conspiracy. Arnold enjoyed the perfect cover for his inquiries: as incoming commander of the strategically vital Hudson Highlands, it was only natural that he should seek to maintain an efficient intelligence service of his own. Indeed, it was a sign of commendable diligence, to be expected of an officer of Arnold's proven zeal in the patriot cause.

Although they aroused no suspicion, Arnold's determined efforts to identify and recruit existing American agents were frustrated. An approach to the marquis de Lafayette at headquarters was rebuffed, because the Frenchman regarded his pledge of secrecy as sacrosanct. With his immediate predecessor at West Point, Arnold was more tenacious. The efficiency of Robert Howe's spies had been obvious earlier that summer, when they had provided prompt and accurate information of British activity around New York. Arnold was also aware that Howe employed double agents. In July, he had informed André: "Two or three persons in whom you confide as spies on General Howe are in his pay, and often give him important information." No sooner had Arnold taken up residence in the Robinson House than he sent a perfectly reasonable request to Howe: "As the safety of this post and garrison in a great measure depends on having good intelligence of the movements and designs of the enemy, and as you have been fortunate in the agents you have employed for that purpose, I must request (with their permission) to be informed who they are, as I wish to employ them, for the same purpose." Arnold added: "I will engage upon my honor to make no discovery of them to any person breathing."[5]

Howe replied to Arnold in the friendliest possible language; but, like Lafayette, felt unable to divulge the identities of his agents. His explanation gives a glimpse into the hazardous business of espionage during the Revolutionary War. Howe had recruited his "two most intelligent and confidential" agents with difficulty; they had only agreed to serve him "with the greatest reluctance, and not without my pledging in the most solemn manner my honor not to inform any person upon earth of their names, or of their acting in the capacity of emissaries." Both were "persons of character and property, who cannot without utter ruin get out of the enemy's power." They were true Patriots, "devoted to America," and prepared to serve her in the only way they could—however much they might dislike it. Howe had written to his agents, urging them to let him pass on their addresses to Arnold; but when he had previously made a similar request, "they in the most positive terms refused," and there was little likelihood that they would change their minds now. Howe could not blame them, "as their life, and the ruin of their families must be the certain consequence should any accident happen to them." Arnold hoped that Howe's "emissaries" would "think better of the matter" and "resume their friendly offices" for him. But they did not, and Arnold was obliged to explore other options.[6]

The assumption that Major-General Arnold had every right to improve his own intelligence network deflected suspicion from another strategy intended to expedite communications with André, and contrive a meeting with him: the major, under his alias of "John Anderson," could himself adopt the role of exactly the kind of secret agent it was now known that Arnold was keen to recruit. With this strategy in mind, Arnold boldly approached Colonel Elisha Sheldon, who commanded the outlying cavalry outposts from Lower Salem. Arnold knew that the colonel employed a spy, Elijah Hunter, who operated in New York, and mentioned that there was a person in the city with whom he wanted to open a regular channel of intelligence. He hoped that Hunter could be employed to fix a meeting with him. Although Arnold did not know it, Hunter was a double agent, loyal to the American Patriots. In 1776, he had been a captain in the 2nd New York Militia, and since "retiring" that December had become one of Washington's most trusted agents; by early 1779, the mixture of false and genuine information that he was permitted to "feed" to the unsuspecting British had gained him the confidence of both Sir Henry Clinton and New York's governor, General William Tryon. In the event, and fortunately for Arnold, Hunter was delayed on Manhattan; it would be necessary to keep looking for a messenger to André.[7]

* * *

As that frustrating summer dragged on, news of unexpected events across the Atlantic gave George Washington cause to hope that Lord North's battered administration was finally about to crack under the strain of waging a long, costly, and unpopular war. In mid-August, the British packet ship *Mercury* was intercepted by American privateers while on passage from Falmouth to New York, and brought into Philadelphia. Like the frigate *Alliance*, which arrived in Boston from France, she bore tidings of a "great mob in England."[8]

Newspapers soon spread accounts of serious disorder in London, at the very heart of Britain's embattled empire. The lurid anecdotes of fire, destruction, and mayhem were not exaggerated: between June 2 and 8, 1780, in what became known as the Gordon Riots, London suffered the worst breakdown of law and order in memory. Combined with other favorable developments in Europe, as Washington later confided to John Cadwalader, these "English disturbances" had encouraged him to start believing that the tide of conflict was turning against Britain, and "that the hour of deliverance was not far distant."[9]

What has been described as "perhaps the most violent and savagely repressed of all the riots in London's history" originated in anti-Catholic agitation stirred up by Lord George Gordon, a former naval officer and vocal opponent of the American war. According to Thomas Irving, whose letter to New York was captured aboard the *Mercury*, Gordon was "little better than a madman" who belonged "in a straight-jacket [sic]." Mad or not, he had emerged as a leader of resistance to the government's Catholic Relief Act of 1778, legislation that was itself a response to the strains of a global conflict. Intended to swell the ranks of Britain's overstretched army by attracting recruits previously barred on religious grounds, the act offered limited concessions to Catholics willing to take an oath of allegiance to King George.[10]

During 1779, Gordon's parliamentary speeches had used increasingly inflammatory language. His rantings against Catholics tapped into a tradition of anti-popery which had been reinvigorated by the intervention of those old enemies, the Bourbon powers of France and Spain, in the American war; such ingrained antipathy toward Catholics was no less a part of the ideological fabric of Britain's former American colonies. In addition, many Britons were uneasy about sending newly recruited "Papist" troops to fight against Protestant Americans, a factor highlighting the widespread sympathy the rebels enjoyed among opposition politicians, and the extent to which the war had split British opinion.

Events escalated during the summer of 1780. On June 2, Gordon summoned a mass meeting on London's St. George's Fields, with the aim of presenting a "Protestant Petition" to Parliament. Some 20,000 marchers were expected, but an estimated 60,000 turned up: by the time they reached Westminster, the original contingent of respectable working folk had been swollen by opportunistic criminals. Shocked at the size of the crowd, Parliament refused to consider the petition. The mood of Gordon's frustrated supporters now turned ugly. When magistrates failed to respond firmly by reading the Riot Act and ordering the marchers to disperse, some of them began to wreck and loot. The *Gentleman's Magazine* blamed this "desperate attack upon the lives and properties of the inhabitants of this metropolis" on "a set of miscreants, who, after assuming the character of men heated with zeal for their religion, and mingling with them, proceeded to commit the most horrible acts of unprovoked desolation that are to be met with in any history."[11]

Yet this was no mindless rampage: objectives were carefully targeted, with rioters focusing their attentions on the wealthy rather than the poor, and on bricks and mortar, not flesh and blood. Specific buildings were "pulled down" and their contents burned in the street to prevent uncontrolled blazes. Despite such discrimination, when the rioting peaked on the night of Wednesday, June 7, it seemed to horrified observers that all of London was ablaze. Indeed, "more than twenty dreadful conflagrations in different parts of the desolated and afflicted metropolis were to be seen raging, licking up everything in the way," a sight that drew comparisons with "the burning of Rome by the emissaries of Nero."[12]

During that week, six London prisons, including the notorious Newgate, were torched and their inmates freed. Many Catholic chapels, schools, and dwellings were destroyed; but it is significant that the property of non-Catholics among the political elite, such as the home of Chief Justice Lord Mansfield, was also targeted. For several days, the London and Westminster magistrates appeared panic-stricken and paralyzed: mindful of the potentially lethal consequences of summoning soldiers against civilians, they were reluctant to act. But as the rioting escalated, the government's resolve finally stiffened. Exasperated by the weakness of his ministers, George III showed strong personal leadership, calling a privy council meeting which authorized the military to open fire without first securing the customary permission from the magistrates. On June 7, a royal proclamation announced that all necessary force would be used to suppress "such rebellious and traitorous attempts, now making against the peace and dignity of our Crown, and the safety of the lives and properties of our subjects."[13]

Next day there were 10,000 troops in the capital—manpower that Sir Henry Clinton could have put to good use across the Atlantic. The redcoats' unfettered license to shoot to kill enabled them to repel two attacks on the Bank of England. Colonel Charles Stuart, who was in London on leave from America, viewed the crisis as a purely military operation, and noted with approval that "the soldiers dealt death about pretty freely." As more regulars and militia were deployed to the capital, the last mobs were cowed and dispersed. Large concentrations of troops remained encamped in St. James's Park and Hyde Park until mid-August. They stirred civilian fears of impending military rule, although Colonel Stuart believed their presence was justified, considering "the seeds of the late insurrection too deeply sown not to produce a crop if the military should be removed."[14]

The outbreak cost the lives of an estimated 300 rioters shot by the troops, crushed by falling debris, or burned alive as they lay stupefied after guzzling raw, unrectified spirit looted from Thomas Langdale's gin distillery in Holborn; unlucky bystanders added to the toll. In the draconian crackdown that followed the restoration of order, twenty-six convicted rioters were hanged in batches close to the scenes of their crimes. They included William McDonald, a one-armed former soldier; Charlotte Gardiner, "a black" from New York; and fourteen-year-old Richard Roberts, who, being a "slender lad" and therefore likely to suffer an unusually prolonged death by strangulation on the gallows, had weights placed in his pockets "that he might be sooner out of his pain."[15]

By contrast, the disturbances caused the death of just one soldier, and that was only indirectly the consequence of mob action. Seventy-year-old General William Belford of the Royal Artillery had remained on horseback day and night to prevent the rioters reaching his precious guns in the arsenal at Woolwich Warren, exertions that burst a blood vessel in his lungs and led to a fatal fever. Belford, who was "esteemed one of the best artillery officers in the British service," had begun his long career on the Spanish Main at the siege of Cartagena in 1741. But it was five years later, as a major in command of "Butcher" Cumberland's cannon at Culloden, that he had really made his mark. As his obituary recalled, "by his spirit, boldness and activity on that day," he "checked the vigor of the clans," so helping to thwart rebellion that had come close to toppling the Hanoverian dynasty.[16]

Lord George Gordon was tried for treason, but acquitted on the grounds that he had never envisaged such violence, and attempted to curb the excesses of his supporters. At first, government informers fostered a false belief that French and American agents had helped to foment the rioting: Colonel Stuart's brother, Lord Mountstuart, was convinced that "American emissaries" whipped up the mob for their own "diabolical purposes." But while the attacks on the homes of prominent politicians certainly suggest a readiness to express disapproval against the unpopular American war, the original and overriding motivation of Gordon's supporters was deep-seated suspicion of Catholics, and foreigners in general.[17]

Like Washington, Alexander Hamilton took heart from news of the riots. Writing to his fiancée Elizabeth Schuyler, the daughter of the former general, he observed: "The affairs of England are in so bad a plight that if no fortunate events attend her this campaign, it will seem impossible for her to proceed in the war." Hamilton reflected: "But she is an obstinate old dame, and seems determined to ruin her whole family, rather than let Miss America go on flirting with her new lovers, with whom, as giddy young girls often do, she eloped in contempt of her mother's authority."[18]

George Washington's hopes that domestic upheaval would undermine the North ministry's resolve to subdue America dissipated more swiftly than the smoke hanging above the smoldering rubble of Newgate. Writing to his French colleague Rochambeau in late August, he was obliged to acknowledge that owing to the ministry's "vigorous measures to punish the rioters," rather than materially aiding the cause of American independence, the "internal ferments and insurrections which have taken place in England" would prove nothing more than an embarrassment to Britain.[19]

Besides its tidings of the "Gordon Riots," the *Alliance* had brought other intelligence that finally quashed Washington's hopes for a great offensive against the British in New York city: when she had left Lorient six weeks earlier, the anticipated second division of the French reinforcement was blockaded at Brest by a British fleet; even if it fought through the cordon, it could not be expected to reach North America before October, by which time supplies stockpiled for the projected Franco-American attack on Manhattan would long since have been consumed.

In any event, the first wave of the French were still in no condition to fight; according to an American deserter who had left Rhode Island in mid-August, they now had a "yellow fever among them that carries off eight or ten a day"; and save for two frigates, de Ternay's warships remained bottled up in Newport harbor by the Royal Navy, their sails furled. With no realistic prospect of an offensive that summer, the short-service militia were sent home, and the Continentals marched farther back to Hackensack, New Jersey; there, they would be nearer to the Hudson Highlands, which Robert Howe's agents believed to be as vulnerable as ever to British attack. Howe told Washington that his spies were certain "offensive measures" were being contemplated, and that "Clinton was under positive orders to act vigorously and make you his object." While Tryon kept Washington at bay, it was possible that Clinton would lunge against West Point, as the "militia at that post would be an easy conquest." But other intelligence from New York suggested that Washington's understrength field army had become the prime British objective. One of the general's emissaries reported: "officers of high rank are continually saying that Washington was America, and that every risk should be run to subdue him." Now was the time to strike, when "his army consisted of . . . raw boys, hardly able to wield a flintlock."[20]

* * *

Now, as Washington reluctantly reconciled himself to an inglorious defensive campaign, Arnold learned that Sir Henry Clinton had finally agreed to his price for delivering up West Point. André's letter of acceptance was written on July 24 but, owing to the convoluted line of communications, only reached Arnold a month later, on August 24. The major informed Arnold that if he surrendered the fortress, with its guns, magazine of stores, and 3,000 men, "the sum even of 20,000 pounds" would be his. This was an indication of the high value that Clinton placed on West Point, and a vindication of Arnold's determination, worthy of a wily trader, to accept nothing less than his asking price. Such generosity reflected the risks involved; but as André emphasized, payment was strictly conditional on "services done." As for "an absolute promise of indemnification" of £10,000, plus an annuity of £500, whether or not the plan actually succeeded, that could never be given.[21]

To earn his money, Arnold must keep his side of the bargain: as the Highlands' command was currently under strength, it had to be reinforced to the required level of manpower. Yet at the same time, Arnold somehow needed to weaken his position, leaving it vulnerable to a surprise attack: that paradox could be resolved by ensuring that even though his command increased in numbers, its effectiveness was undermined by sending detachments on duties where they would be useless in defending West Point. On August 16, for example, general orders from the Robinson House announced that a total of 220 men, officers included, were to be drafted from the militia of the Massachusetts Brigade "to cut firewood for the garrison." Of course, adequate stockpiles of fuel were essential to survive the harsh Highlands winter; but these sturdy soldiers—all "good axmen"— would no longer be on hand to help repel any sudden assault: they were to march for Fishkill, a settlement across the Hudson and some eleven miles north of West Point.[22]

Arnold's old Quebec comrade Colonel John Lamb, who was commandant of West Point itself, questioned this movement. He had already obeyed orders to send 200 men to Fishkill as a guard, although why so many were needed there he could not "possibly conceive." Now contemplating another detachment, he warned Arnold: "If such drafts ... are made from the garrison we shall neither be able to finish the works that are incomplete nor [be] in a situation to defend those that are finished." This, of course, was Arnold's objective, and the men marched anyway. Totally unaware that Arnold was intent on delivering West Point to the enemy, the scar-faced gunner had already warned him that if the British learned that the fortress was defended by nothing but militia, it might "become an object" for them. But there was one small group of men that Arnold was determined to keep close at hand, and with good cause. When Washington ordered that the eight soldiers employed as bargemen by Howe at West Point should be returned to their regiment, Arnold took the liberty of retaining them, as it was "not otherwise possible to procure a proper crew" for his own barge. Washington saw no reason to object.[23]

Now, more than ever, it was vital for Arnold to arrange a face-to-face meeting with Major André, so that the plan's details could be finalized. The cautious Sir Henry Clinton was also keen to establish beyond the slightest doubt that "Gustavus" really *was* the celebrated patriot hero Major-General Benedict Arnold, and that his advances were genuine, and not some elaborate deception to tempt *him* into a trap. As a precaution, during Arnold's recent trip into Connecticut, his movements had been monitored by two spies sent by the local Loyalist, Joseph Chew, who was acting on instructions from Major André.[24]

Arnold's continuing quest for a reliable intermediary led him to renew an acquaintance with the lawyer Joshua Hett Smith, whom he had previously met in 1778 while commandant in Philadelphia. A Whig landowner, that year Smith had married a South Carolinian in Charleston, where he encountered Robert Howe. In 1780, Smith and his wife had returned to his family home at Haverstraw, on the west bank of the Hudson, some three miles below King's Ferry. As commander of the Highlands, Howe had used Smith as a go-between for his own network of spies in New York, whose identities he had politely but firmly refused to reveal to Arnold. Perhaps as a sign of goodwill, when Arnold took over in the Highlands, Howe recommended Smith's services to him.[25]

Yet other Patriots disliked and distrusted Smith. Even in a war where political differences split families, such suspicions were understandable: Joshua was the brother of William Smith, the influential loyalist chief justice of New York, who was a close associate of Sir Henry Clinton. Within Arnold's own military "family," Smith drew the undisguised disdain of Lieutenant-Colonel Richard Varick, who had recently joined the general's staff. With increased responsibilities, Arnold had invited Philip Schuyler's former secretary to assist his long-serving aide, Major David Franks. A staunch supporter of Arnold against Horatio Gates during the Saratoga campaign, Varick accepted eagerly, particularly because he understood that his staff duties would not be onerous, allowing him time to pursue his legal studies. Another incentive was the promised presence of Peggy Arnold, who, Varick gallantly observed, "will certainly make our situation in the barren Highlands more agreeable, and I am persuaded will more than compensate for every deficiency of nature."[26]

As Varick's official deskwork kept him busier than expected, allowing little time for study, he was determined to have "no connection" with Arnold's family arrangements, or his stores, which had become a subject of controversy. Soon after his arrival, Varick had heard Major Franks express his disapproval that Arnold had brought "so many stores to Robinson's House, saying that in case the enemy should come expeditiously either our baggage or the stores must be lost." Varick had replied that the stores could "go to the Devil" before he lost his own baggage, and that he had no interest in Arnold's conduct in that respect.[27]

That summer, Arnold gained small injections of cash by selling off his personal stockpile of surplus rations—pork, salt, wine, rum, and other goods—issued by the commissary. This petty penny-pinching disgusted Varick, who must have rolled his eyes at orders issued from headquarters on August 29, 1780, which threatened punishment to the "great number" of sutlers who sold liquor to the garrison. Any offending civilian would be "turned off the Point," while a soldier could expect to receive "one hundred lashes on his bare back without court martial." Arnold added: "The General expects that no officer of any rank will either directly or indirectly be concerned in the business of sutling, as is unbecoming the character of an officer and a gentleman." But the more that Arnold's black-market profiteering revolted his upright subordinates, the better for his trading with the British. It provided the perfect blind, and bolstered a belief that his shady dealings with Joshua Hett Smith probably involved private business ventures—deplorable to be sure, but not treasonable.[28]

* * *

Arnold wrote his acceptance of Clinton's deal on August 30, under the alias "Gustavus." This time he framed his reply in carefully disguised mercantile language: West Point's supplies became "goods at market," its garrison "speculators." But while the message's true meaning might be lost on anyone unacquainted with the plan, it would be clear enough to André. "Gustavus" said that he expected to fix an interview between Mr. Anderson and "Mr. M[oor]e" (another of Arnold's codenames) "when you will be able to settle your commercial plan I hope agreeable to all parties." Indeed, Mr. Moore "flatters himself that in the course of ten days he will have the pleasure of seeing you."[29]

Lieutenant-Colonel Varick knew about this letter, and mentioned it to Franks when the major returned from Philadelphia, where he had gone to collect Peggy Arnold and her infant son. Although he had not actually read the letter, Varick was aware that it was written "in a mercantile style to a person in New York whose fictitious name was John Anderson"; its object, he understood, was "to establish a line of intelligence of the enemy's movements." In response, Franks said that he "thought Arnold had corresponded with Anderson or some such name before from Philadelphia, and had got intelligence of consequence from him." This raises the intriguing possibility that Franks had previously stumbled across one of the treason's first letters, without appreciating its significance. Now reassured by Franks, Varick had no doubt that Arnold's correspondence with "Anderson" was "proper, in discharge of his duty, and commendable if he could procure intelligence in that way." Arnold's decision to mask his treasonous negotiations beneath what appeared to be legitimate attempts to recruit agents was proving highly effective in deceiving his "family" of staff, who were busy enough with their own interests. Colonel Varick admitted: "I never was solicitous to know the real characters or names of his emissaries, further than he chose to communicate them to me . . ."[30]

The messenger selected to deliver Arnold's response to Clinton's offer was William Heron, a native of Cork who lived at Redding, Connecticut. Heron had served as a member of the state assembly, and was a neighbor of Major-General Samuel Holden Parsons. As far as Parsons knew, and as he would later assure Washington, Heron was a trusty Patriot—"a consistent, rational Whig." Indeed, for "several years" Heron had exploited his "very intimate acquaintance" with a fellow Irishman at British headquarters to feed Parsons "important and very interesting intelligence."[31]

On about August 27, 1780, General Parsons recalled some weeks later, Heron had asked him to help arrange a "flag" so that he could go into New York and collect a debt. Parsons forwarded the request to Arnold, and on the morning of August 30 Heron waited on him at the Robinson House. After several hours, as Heron remembered, Arnold asked his secretary Varick to make out the necessary permit, and then signed it. Retiring to his own room, Arnold sent word for Heron to join him. As soon as he entered, Arnold asked Heron whether the person with whom he expected to transact his "business at the enemy's lines" could be relied on to deliver a letter "from a friend of his," addressed to "Mr. John Anderson, Merchant, New York." Arnold told Heron that he had inspected the letter's contents, "at the same time pointing [out] that it had been sealed with a wafer which he had broken, and afterwards sealed with wax." Heron subsequently maintained that he was immediately suspicious: Arnold had expressed himself in a "very particular and significant manner"; the "superscription" seemed to be in a "feigned hand"; and most strangely of all, while the general claimed that the letter had been opened, examined, and then resealed, its wafer remained perfectly intact.

According to Parsons, Heron went to New York and conducted his business, but "the extraordinary precaution which Arnold had used" when handing over the letter "excited his curiosity to examine the manner in which it was sealed, and finding the wafer had not been broken, as Arnold had told him, he suspected it might contain something illicit." Instead of delivering the letter, he had therefore brought it back, handing it over to Parsons on September 10. Unaware of its true significance, Parsons assumed that the letter referred "merely to commerce." Rather than informing Washington immediately by courier, he resolved to "make it a subject of private conversation" when they next met.[32]

If the letter had been forwarded promptly to Washington's headquarters, it's *possible* that Arnold's conspiracy would have been uncovered then. However, even if Arnold's own connection with the mysterious Anderson had been established, there was nothing to implicate him in anything more than the kind of dubious trading for which he was notorious and had already been reprimanded: the letter might have provided grounds for an inquiry, or even another court martial, but it would not necessarily expose Arnold's treason.

Writing to Washington in 1782, Parsons cited Heron's interception of Arnold's letter as proof of his "fidelity." In 1790, when Washington was president of the United States of America and Heron approached him for a government post, he based his appeal for patronage on the significance of that same "event," which "may have been attended with more salutary consequences to the public than many actions of greater brilliancy." Heron maintained that, "notwithstanding the ambiguity and darkness" of the letter's language, and Arnold's popularity as a "military character," he had not hesitated to disclose his "fears and apprehensions" to Parsons.[33]

But when William Heron made his claim, Parsons was long dead and unable to contradict him. Had he actually revealed such suspicions in September 1780, the general would surely have entrusted the incriminating letter to a dispatch rider and sent him galloping off to Washington without delay. Documents among Sir Henry Clinton's papers reveal that Heron's role in Arnold's conspiracy was more complex and ambiguous than he claimed. While his ultimate allegiance and motivation remain unclear, Heron was undoubtedly operating as a double agent, simultaneously supplying intelligence to both the Americans and the British.

On September 4, 1780, when Heron was in New York to settle his "business," he made a detailed verbal report to the American-born British army intelligence officer Major Oliver De Lancey, in the presence of Chief Justice

William Smith. Heron told his listeners what they wanted to hear—and what Arnold had recently assured them: the revolutionary cause was rotten and ready to collapse. Citing his contacts among the rebel generals, Heron emphasized the low morale and poor condition of Washington's under-strength army: even if further French reinforcements arrived, it would be incapable of assaulting New York. Civilians were no less disillusioned: "The people are in general tired of the whole business of war, and become beggarly and distressed, as well as exceedingly suspicious of all who are for continuing it." Indeed, De Lancey noted: "Mr. Heron is confident that the whole rebellion must fall soon." In his journal Smith wrote: "I spent three hours with Mr. Heron of Redding in Connecticut, and took notes after he was gone of what he had communicated. It was most material." Next day, Smith delivered a copy of Heron's "information" to Tryon's successor as New York's governor, Lieutenant-General Robertson.[34]

A report that Heron sent to British headquarters some weeks later leaves no doubt that his decision to forgo delivering Arnold's "Gustavus" letter to André was based on self-preservation and a concern to maintain his "cover" as a double agent. Handing the letter to Parsons, he calculated, would bolster his patriot credentials and help deflect any suspicion that he might be a British spy. He assured De Lancey: "By a precaution which I may say I was Providentially influenced to make use of, I have retained the confidence of those in high office [and] consequently can be useful unless I am rendered otherwise through the means of those from your quarter."[35]

Although the "Gustavus" letter was blocked by Heron's ploy, it was not long before Arnold's answer reached the British. He wrote another letter on September 3, and the opportunity to deliver it may have stirred memories of his glory days as an intrepid defender of American liberty. Charles McCarthy of His Majesty's 9th Regiment of Foot had been captured with Burgoyne at Saratoga, becoming one of the "Convention Army" incarcerated first at Cambridge, Massachusetts, and then Charlottesville, Virginia. That summer, as the intelligence files of Clinton's headquarters reveal, determined redcoats from Burgoyne's captive army managed to reach British lines: in late August, for example, Edward Byrn of the Royal Artillery, John Morris of the 20th Foot, and Richard Morris of the 34th all came in. They had escaped from "Chandler Vale" (Charlottesville), then made their way north, helped by a "great many friends in the country." Private McCarthy was not so lucky: while "endeavoring to make his escape from the Rebels to New York," he was recaptured amid the rocky terrain of the Hudson Highlands. Once more in enemy hands, he was joined by his wife Mary, who had been left at Quebec when Burgoyne's army went south in 1777. Soon after, as Mrs. McCarthy later testified, she was "intrusted by General Arnold with his dispatches to bring to New York."[36]

Oblivious as ever to Arnold's real intentions, Lieutenant-Colonel Varick promptly wrote to West Point for an officer to escort Mrs. McCarthy down the Hudson. Although Varick never saw the letter which she was given, Arnold revealed that "he had written [it] to a friend of his in New York, under fictitious characters." Arnold himself wrote the instructions issued on September 4 to Lieutenant Isaac Barber: "You are to proceed in a barge with a flag, one sergeant, and seven privates to Fort Washington or other British post on the river, taking with you Mary McCarthy and her two children, late of Quebec, who have my permission to pass into the British lines, where you are to leave them and return without delay." Despite these precautions, it was a nerve-racking mission; but "at the greatest hazard of her life," Mrs. McCarthy brought the correspondence safely into New York, and personally delivered it "to his excellency General Robertson in the presence of Colonel Beverly Robertson [sic]." Arnold's letter was forwarded to Major André, and his reply would soon be forthcoming.[37]

* * *

Even as his plot to confound the cause of American liberty moved inexorably toward its climax, Arnold continued to rage against Congress for breaking faith with its defenders. He was incensed to learn that it had rejected a memorial from seventeen general officers requesting an increase in pay and requisites that would allow them to maintain the dignity of their rank, especially when serving alongside their newly arrived French allies who had ready access to hard cash. Instead, and reaffirming the position it had adopted in May 1778, Congress responded by offering seven years' half-pay, plus grants of land—1,100 acres for major-generals—when the war was over. Always keen to maximize his funds, Arnold had naturally hoped that Congress would settle a pay rise *before* he defected to the British. But the bitterness of his disappointment also reflected grievances that had long since nudged him along the path to defection, and which, after more than a year of treasonable negotiations, still rankled. It was, he wrote to

Nathanael Greene, "A very encouraging gratuity indeed, from the public to men who have sacrificed their fortunes, time, constitutions, and who have so often bled in the cause of their country." Arnold's rants against Congress were not some smokescreen to blind his fellow officers, but a sincere expression of deeply held beliefs: they were intertwined with his treasonous designs, and, by his own reasoning, went far to justify them. Here, as with his outspoken court martial defense statements in January, Arnold saw no dishonorable contradiction between his public utterances and his private dealings.[38]

Arnold's resentment was certainly shared by other major-generals, including Samuel Parsons. After reading the congressional resolution that Arnold had forwarded to him, Parsons considered himself to be a model "of patience and self-denial" in "giving it two or three readings before I stamped it in earth." While Parsons would never forsake his country's "just and glorious cause," he considered that the "wretches who have crept into Congress are almost below contempt." Indeed, America would "never prosper in their hands."[39]

But the neglect of Congress was felt most severely by the rank and file of the Continental Army, who now deserted to the British on Manhattan in ever-increasing numbers. On September 12, Clinton's aide, Major James Cramond, forwarded his esteemed friend Major André intelligence of two men who had left Washington's camp just a few hours before. Both reported that "desertion is very frequent, and much favored by the country people, who are much exasperated at the cavalier treatment they have met with from their republican friends." The statements of many other deserters interrogated at headquarters by the meticulous Captain Beckwith also corroborated Arnold's contention that American morale was at rock bottom. Their testimonies provide a remarkably consistent picture, and highlight two major grievances. Edward McDonnell, who quit the 11th Pennsylvania Regiment, voiced the most common gripe of all: his daily ration was just "one pound of bread," with "one pound of meat sometimes." Others fared even worse: Joseph Goldsmith of the 9th Connecticut had "not had any meat for four days," while Tobias Wrightman, whose unit was not specified, reported that Washington's main army at Tappan had been "eight days without meat." But Beckwith's informants had another recurring complaint: distrust of the French. For example, Samuel Kenny of the 3rd New Jersey Regiment, who had served in the light infantry corps commanded by Lafayette, said that the marquis's decision to present his men with "French colors" caused much dissatisfaction. Another unnamed "rebel deserter," who came over to Long Island on August 26, concurred: the Light Infantry had received "new colors— white, a flower de luce [fleur-de-lis] and small stripes," but maintained they would not fight under the French flag; indeed, they "would rather fight against the French." According to John Graham of the 2nd Pennsylvanians, the "French laws" caused "great discontent"; in particular, the "old countrymen" born in Britain—who had always formed a significant proportion of the Continental Army—"don't like it."[40]

As such testimony demonstrates, the deep-seated anti-Catholic prejudices that had recently fueled the Gordon Riots in London also existed within the Continental Army. Even its officers could be ambivalent about their new allies. Before the French arrived at Newport, Major Samuel Shaw had rejoiced, "as an American citizen . . . in the prospect of so speedy, and I hope an effectual aid." But as a soldier, Major Shaw, who was aide-de-camp to General Henry Knox, resented having to rely on foreign help when the United States was populous enough to win its independence. He declared to Colonel Lamb: " 'Tis really abominable, that we should send to France for soldiers, when there are so many sons of America idle." A month later, the major's opinions had not mellowed. He told his brother Nathaniel: "It is painful to think that our country, instead of exerting the powers God has given her to work out her own salvation, should be under the necessity of calling in foreign troops." He added: "It is a disgrace we shall not easily get over."[41]

The simmering discontent among Washington's veterans in the summer of 1780 can only have reinforced Arnold's belief that his decision to defect was not only justified by the failure of Congress to provide effective government, but would ultimately serve the best interests of his long-suffering comrades. His response to Parsons proposed radical action: "The Army . . . are fully convinced that [Congress's] wish and intention is to disgust and disband us in detail . . . I have [been] recommending a thousand or fifteen hundred men of all ranks to [visit] Congress to present a spirited but decent memorial setting forth their claims."[42]

Of course, at the very time he advocated such bold measures, Arnold was refining a plan that would not simply browbeat Congress into meeting its soldiers' reasonable demands, but overthrow its authority entirely. There is no doubt that Arnold's contempt for Congress was genuine, and that it was shared by many other American soldiers, from the cold, hungry, and shabby privates who looked up to him as a hero, to his grumbling fellow generals. But if Arnold's complaints were all too common, his remedy was exceptional. By turning over himself and his command to the British, he intended to deliver a shock to the Continental Army that would breach the dam of its misguided loyalty to an undeserving Congress, unleashing hoarded resentments and swelling the stream of disgruntled deserters into a flood.

* * *

On September 4, as Mary McCarthy made her hazardous voyage down the Hudson and the wily William Heron spilled out his intelligence to Major De Lancey, Washington received more bad news: it confirmed ominous rumors that Major-General Horatio Gates had sustained a crushing defeat at the hands of Lord Charles Cornwallis, who had been left to command the British forces in South Carolina when Clinton returned to New York. Their armies had met near Camden on the still, hazy morning of August 16. Although Gates's force of around 4,000 outnumbered Cornwallis by more than two to one, he was rash to offer battle: many of his men were skittish militia, and he made the mistake of concentrating them on the left wing of his army, placing his reliable, disciplined Continentals on the right. This unbalanced array proved disastrous. When the British advanced, the militia promptly crumbled, leaving the regulars to face simultaneous assaults from the front and flank.

Cornwallis's seasoned units included the 23rd Foot, or Royal Welch Fusiliers, a regiment Sir Henry Clinton knew well from his earlier German campaigns; it had distinguished itself at the battle of Minden on August 1, 1759—the same day that Lord George Sackville (as Germain was then known) had brought disgrace on himself by stubbornly ignoring orders to bring up the British cavalry. Clinton received a vivid report of the latest "gallant services" of his "Old Mindonian Regiment." Formed on the right of the British line, it faced the rebel militia. According to Lieutenant Thomas Barrette, the enemy was "drawn up four deep, shoulder to shoulder and we only two deep, with open files, so as to occupy as great a front as opposed to us." After giving "three huzzas," the fusiliers received the rebels' volley, gave their own, and then, as Barrette reported, "rushed in upon them with our bayonets before they could load a second time, which made such an impression on them, that they fled precipitately into swamps and thick brush wood," throwing away their weapons and packs.

Barrette conceded that his comrades on the left, who confronted veteran Virginian and Maryland Continentals, had a far tougher fight of it. But even such dogged resistance could only postpone the inevitable outcome. Reporting to Germain, Cornwallis described how the "dead calm" prevented the smoke of the musketry from blowing away, making it "difficult to see the effect of a very heavy and well supported fire on both sides." But despite the choking darkness, the British line "continued to advance in good order ... keeping up a constant fire or making use of bayonets as opportunities offered." After an "obstinate resistance for three quarters of an hour," the enemy were thrown into "total confusion" and obliged "to give way in all quarters."[43]

Victory over Gates gave especial satisfaction to Sergeant Roger Lamb of the 23rd, who'd had the dangerous honor of carrying one of his regiment's standards during the battle. Three years earlier, as a corporal in the 9th Foot, he had fought at Saratoga alongside Charles McCarthy, and been captured with him. After the "Convention Army" marched to Virginia, Lamb led several comrades in a successful escape to New York. They were interviewed at headquarters by Major André, who, Lamb remembered, "received us with great affability and kindness." Promoted to sergeant, Lamb blessed "the Providence" which had inspired his escape and preserved him to share in a victory "obtained in the hard-fought field over a general whose former success at Saratoga, had been trumpeted from one end of America to the other."[44]

In New York, the British were elated at the tidings from the South. Captain Peebles supposed that they would leave "Mr. Washington ... in the dumps." On September 8, the scale of Gates's defeat was made clear when Congress's account of the disaster was circulated via handbills: it acknowledged the loss of 1,000 Continentals, even more militia, and 8 cannon. To cap it all, as Peebles noted, Gates's own report to Congress made it clear that he had fled with the first of the militia, leaving the Continentals "to make the best of it and get out of the scrape as well as they could"; under those shameful circumstances, he deserved "every infamy and disgrace that can happen to him." In Peebles' estimation, Camden was the "severest blow" that the rebels had yet sustained; Cornwallis had won the "handsomest and most complete affair that has been done this war."[45]

Gates's discomfiture was scarcely less satisfying for his critics within the Continental Army. They included his old antagonist, Benedict Arnold. In the last letter he ever wrote to his friend Nathanael Greene, Arnold could not resist gloating. "It is an unfortunate piece of business to that hero and may possibly blot his escutcheon with indelible infamy," he observed. Arnold added: "It may not be right to censure characters at a distance, but I cannot avoid remarking that his conduct on this occasion has in no wise disappointed my expectations, or predictions on frequent occasions."[46]

* * *

Nothing underlines Arnold's unswerving conviction of his "rectitude" more than his ready resort to a phrase like "indelible infamy" without any apparent awareness of its irony. Yet the time when Arnold would indelibly "blot" his own "escutcheon" in the eyes of his erstwhile comrades was rapidly approaching. It was soon apparent that Arnold's letter of September 3, taken into New York by the redoubtable Mary McCarthy, had reached Major André. On September 7, Arnold wrote to Colonel Sheldon, explaining that since they had met, he had had an opportunity of "transmitting a letter to the person in New York, of whom I made mention, and am in expectation of procuring a meeting at your quarters." If, as he hoped, he was able to arrange the rendezvous, Arnold would be able to "open a channel of intelligence that will be regular, and may be depended upon." That same day, September 7, André—as "John Anderson"—wrote to Colonel Sheldon asking his indulgence in allowing a meeting between himself and his friend, "Mr. G[ustavus]," at Dobbs Ferry at noon on September 11; this crossing of the Hudson was fifteen miles downriver from King's Ferry, and in neutral territory. The puzzled cavalryman forwarded this letter to Arnold, commenting that he had never previously heard of Anderson. Because André's letter had casually mentioned an "officer who is to command the escort," Arnold worried that this phrase would raise Sheldon's suspicions by suggesting official British sanction of Anderson's trip. In an effort to deflect any suspicion from himself, Arnold's reply to Sheldon speculated that the letter he had sent by Mrs. McCarthy had been intercepted, and that the "John Anderson" who had written to him might be an impostor. But regardless of that possibility, Arnold still intended to go to Dobbs Ferry to meet the flag of truce.[47]

Arnold was now becoming increasingly anxious, and beginning to show signs of strain. On September 10, he wrote to André; in case this letter fell into the wrong hands, he once again maintained the fiction that his message of September 3 had been intercepted, since he could not suppose that "John Anderson" would be "so imprudent as to trust a British officer, commanding a flag" with their "private concerns," even though they were only of a "commercial nature." To avoid a British "snare," it would be necessary for Anderson to come himself, or to send someone whom he trusted, to Sheldon's headquarters, without revealing his real intentions to the colonel or anyone else. But if, as Arnold well knew, André had himself written the letter to Sheldon, he should attempt to get into the American lines "by stealth": once there, Arnold wrote, "I will engage you shall be perfectly safe."[48]

Despite the continuing confusion, Arnold decided to barge downriver to Dobbs Ferry, in the hope that André would be able to keep the appointment. As a cover for his presence at the ferry, he wrote to Washington on September 11, explaining that—like any diligent commander—he was there to establish signals in case the enemy came upriver, and to fix a warning beacon on a nearby mountain.[49]

But this plan was foiled, and in the most alarming way. Guard boats from the fourteen-gun British sloop HMS *Vulture* were patrolling the Hudson. Unapprised of Arnold's negotiations, they had not been informed that he intended to meet a British flag at Dobbs Ferry; they fired on his barge, forcing it over to the west bank. On the eastern shore, meanwhile, André waited for Arnold in company with Colonel Beverly Robinson; in this instance, Clinton's orders suggest that Robinson, the older, local man and the senior ranking officer, was to be Arnold's primary contact, with André tagging along.[50]

As neither Arnold nor the two British officers were now willing to risk crossing the river under a flag of truce, all returned with their business unfinished. Looking back, Arnold identified this bungled meeting, which almost cost him his life, as a key factor behind the failure of the entire conspiracy. He angrily blamed "the mismanagement of those employed by Sir Henry Clinton, who failed in their appointment of meeting General Arnold in a flag of truce, on the North River, which had nearly proved fatal to him."[51]

Back at the Robinson House, the frustrated Arnold prepared to try again. To the outpost commander at North Castle, Major Benjamin Tallmadge, he wrote that if a John Anderson from New York should turn up, he was to send him to headquarters under escort of two dragoons, and if possible, accompany him. Tallmadge was Washington's intelligence expert, and ran the Culper Ring of spies, but Arnold's request raised no suspicions. There was no reason why it should. Indeed, the major, who was most grateful for the attention that the famed general and former horse trader had given to ensuring that his troopers were well mounted, was only too happy to oblige. The same notification went to Tallmadge's immediate superior officer, Lieutenant-Colonel John Jameson, who had now replaced Sheldon at Lower Salem. In what would prove to be a fortunate development for Arnold, the competent Sheldon had been temporarily removed from command while under arrest on a bogus charge of selling off cavalry horses for his own profit.[52]

On September 15, Arnold wrote to André that if there were objections to his coming by land—despite escorts provided by the unsuspecting Tallmadge and Jameson—he would send him "a person" whom he could trust "by water," to meet him at Dobbs Ferry on Wednesday, September 20, between 11 p.m. and midnight. That "person"—the naive but willing Joshua Smith—was to conduct André to "a place of safety," where Arnold would meet him. Arnold cautioned that it would be necessary for André to be disguised. If Arnold did not hear from the major, he could still rely on the contact being at Dobbs Ferry at the specified time. It is likely that Arnold had made these arrangements with Smith the day before, when Peggy and little Edward Arnold had stopped at his house on their journey from Philadelphia. Using commercial terms, Arnold then passed on intelligence regarding the strength of Washington's army and his own command: he now had "about £1,000"—1,000 men—already "on hand" at West Point, but could "collect £1,500 more in two or three days." This was approaching Clinton's requirement of 3,000 troops.[53]

That same day, Arnold received a note from Washington that instantly attracted his attention. Given the unpromising strategic situation in the aftermath of Gates's defeat at Camden, it was clearly necessary for Washington to meet with General Rochambeau and Admiral de Ternay, "to combine some plan of future operation which events will enable us to execute." Scheduled for September 20, the conference was to be held at Hartford, Connecticut, a town roughly midway between the allies' armies in New Jersey and on Rhode Island. His Excellency informed Arnold that he would be at Peekskill on the evening of Sunday, September 17. Arnold was to send down a captain's guard of fifty men, and to provide a night's forage for about forty horses. Washington cautioned: "You will keep this to yourself, as I want to make my journey a secret." At once, Arnold dashed off a note to André, raising the possibility of capturing Washington during the river crossing, if it proved possible to act on the information in time.[54]

At noon on Sunday, Arnold was dining with his family, his aides, officers over from West Point, and the Smiths. A messenger arrived with two letters from Colonel Beverly Robinson, who, the day before, had come upriver on the *Vulture* and was anchored off Teller's Point, below King's Ferry in Haverstraw Bay. One was addressed to Major-General Israel Putnam, seeking an interview to settle "some particular business ... of a private nature, and only interesting to myself"; as Putnam had left the Highlands long since, this was simply a means of delivering the letter in which it was enclosed, addressed to Arnold. Its purpose was to arrange a meeting, once again ostensibly to settle Robinson's private business, but actually intended to discuss the West Point plan. The colonel's language was designed to avoid arousing suspicion if read by anyone else. He wrote to Arnold: "I am persuaded (from the humane and generous character you bear) that could I be so happy to see you, you would readily grant me the same request I should make to him [Putnam], but for prudential reasons I dare not explain the matter further until I have some assurance that it shall be secret if not granted." To make doubly sure that Arnold took the hint, Robinson mentioned that, instead of leaving the letter with the officer at Verplanck's Point, he had originally intended sending it to Arnold by his servant James Osborne, under a flag of truce: as Arnold would know, "James Osborne" was one of the pseudonyms adopted by his emissary Stansbury's New York correspondent, Jonathan Odell.[55]

Arnold had glanced at the letter before pocketing it with a brief remark to the assembled company that Robinson wanted to see him. Gruff Colonel Lamb immediately protested that to grant such an interview would invite suspicion of an improper correspondence. Indeed, any communications about Robinson's private affairs should go to the state governor. Lamb was adamant that Arnold should inform Washington when he next saw him.[56]

Later that day, as expected, Washington broke his journey to Hartford by stopping for dinner at Smith's house. Paying his respects as commander of the Highlands, Arnold joined Washington there, and then accompanied him to King's Ferry and over the Hudson to Peekskill. Despite Arnold's tip-off, the crossing was uninterrupted by the British: the *Vulture* did not swoop, and no column of dragoons spurred up to intercept Washington and his escort as they rode inland; but if all went to plan, there would be another opportunity to eliminate His Excellency soon enough.

If Lafayette's memory can be credited, the crossing was not without incident for Arnold. Despite reports from agents in New York that more British warships had arrived there ahead of French reinforcements, Lafayette still hoped that the commander of the French West Indies fleet, the comte de Guichen, would make an appearance. Knowing that Arnold sent flags of truce to New York, the keen young Frenchman turned to him in the boat and blithely asked: "since you have communication with the enemy, you must ascertain as soon as possible what has become of Guichen." At this, the startled Arnold had gasped: "What do you mean?" Before Lafayette could clarify his request, they landed, and talk turned to other matters.[57]

Whether or not he actually received that worrying jolt, Arnold soon recovered his composure. At Peekskill, he informed Washington of the request that he had received from Robinson, and asked his advice about it. Washington's stance was unequivocal: Arnold should grant no interview to Robinson, and instead inform him by letter that he must approach the civil authorities. Next day, Arnold drew up a reply for Robinson, and after the officious Varick observed that it sounded overly friendly, dutifully modified its language. But the diligent secretary failed to notice when Arnold slipped in another sealed letter. This repeated his pledge to dispatch a person to Dobbs Ferry on the night of Wednesday, September 20, with a boat and a flag of truce; it was possible that his contact would seek out the *Vulture*. Robinson could depend on that man's secrecy and honor, and that his business, "of whatever nature shall be kept a profound secret." Meanwhile, the *Vulture* must maintain her station "until the time mentioned." Arnold added a "P.S." which revealed that he expected General Washington to lodge with him at the Robinson House on the night of Saturday, September 23; when planning any attack on West Point, Sir Henry Clinton could take the enemy commander's absence into account; or perhaps his presence would offer another chance to kidnap him.[58]

Inside his covert message to Colonel Robinson, Arnold enclosed yet another, for "a gentleman in New York from one in the country." Intended for André, this included a copy of Arnold's message of September 15, proposing the meeting at Dobbs Ferry on the 20th. The letters were sent by flag of truce, and reached Robinson, aboard the *Vulture*, on September 19. Replying to Arnold, the colonel maintained his credible cover of attempting to settle "private business" regarding his confiscated estate; had he known that Arnold was meeting Washington, he would have applied to him, "as I flatter myself I should be allowed every reasonable indulgence from him." Robinson begged that his "best respects" be presented to his old friend, but had nothing further to say to Arnold: he would await "a more favorable opportunity" to "do something" for his family. By the enclosure which Robinson forwarded to André, the major would be left in no doubt that the original proposal for a meeting was to be taken seriously, and that Arnold's agent might now come directly to the *Vulture*. Both of the surreptitious messages were inside a sealed cover, addressed to William Smith at New York, but inscribed with a note that Robinson could open it; this may have been a means of hinting that André would be met by Smith's brother, Joshua.[59]

* * *

By now, Sir Henry Clinton was finalizing his preparations for the attack on West Point. As first envisaged, this was to form one element of a broader plan intended to succeed where his Rhode Island expedition had failed, and eradicate the French. Clinton explained this strategy to Lord George Germain: "My idea of putting into execution this concerted plan with Mr. Arnold with most efficacy was to have deferred it until Mr. Washington, co-operating with the French, moved upon this place to invest it"; to sustain the effort, the "rebel magazines should have been collected and formed into their several depots, particularly that at West Point." Had Arnold surrendered himself and the Highland forts at that instant, Clinton would have been "given every advantage which could have been desired." Under that scenario, Sir Henry believed, Washington would have been obliged to fall back from his advanced position above King's Bridge, on the northern boundary of Manhattan, leaving the French troops waiting on Long Island an easy prey. To execute that ambitious plan, Sir Henry had made careful preparations, with "vessels properly manned and of a particular draft of water ready to have improved the designed stroke to the utmost."

But on September 14, the unexpected arrival of Admiral Sir George Brydges Rodney with ten ships of the line and two frigates had changed Clinton's thinking. As fond of fighting as of prize money, the sixty-one-year-old Rodney had served at sea since the age of fourteen. Lean and vigorous, he was the antithesis of the sluggish Arbuthnot, and exactly the kind of naval colleague that Sir Henry Clinton needed to help implement his revised plan. With the balance of sea power now overwhelmingly favoring the British, it was "highly probable that Mr. Washington would lay aside all thoughts" of attacking New York; in fact, even before Rodney's arrival, given the lack of American manpower and supplies, a siege was unrealistic. While

Clinton's original strategy was ruled out, the idea of striking at West Point was not; the long-anticipated blow must now be delivered without delay. As Sir Henry recalled in his memoirs, the "juncture" with Rodney seemed "most peculiarly, and critically favorable": it followed hot on the heels of Gates's defeat at Camden, which had "spread terror and dismay through the country." The timing was propitious in another critical respect: "the attention of everyone within and without" the British lines at New York "was closely drawn to an armament that I was just then assembling for an expedition to the Chesapeake."[60]

Before leaving for the Hartford summit, Washington had called on his spies to provide "a particular account of the embarkation that is talked [of]." He wanted to know "when it will take place, where destined, and what corps will it consist of." The agents answered the call, but, as Sir Henry had calculated, their intelligence agreed that the expedition was bound for the South—"the object of which (having been for some time talked of and known) lulled suspicion to sleep with respect to any other." In Philadelphia, for example, James Madison reported that between 5,000 and 6,000 troops would embark at New York on September 25, "either for Virginia or South Carolina." Those duped by Clinton included Major Tallmadge; still utterly unaware of Arnold's scheming, on September 21 he happily forwarded him the latest "private accounts" that he had received from his agents in New York. Although some believed the expected embarkation was intended to "dispossess the French of Rhode Island," and others doubted whether it would embark at all, Tallmadge told Arnold that he was "convinced they are destined to Virginia," to "establish a post there." Tallmadge had already forwarded intelligence to Washington from "Samuel Culper"; "according to the best information," he also believed that the force assembling at New York was bound for Virginia, with the "principle [sic] view" of rescuing the "Convention Army."[61]

As Clinton explained to Lord George Germain, he could "no longer defer the execution of a project" which promised "such considerable advantages, nor to lose so fair an opportunity." Under cover of the "mask" offered by the southern expedition, "which every person imagined would of course take place," Sir Henry prepared his move up the Hudson River: "I laid my plan before Sir George Rodney and Lieutenant-General Knyphausen, when Sir George—with that zeal for His Majesty's service which marks his character—most handsomely promised to give me every naval assistance in his power." Clinton later claimed that "he had everything ready for seizing the

Highlands, and putting an end ... to the war." His preparations included assembling "boats of all drafts for proceeding to Albany."[62]

The troops eventually embarked aboard transport ships, as if headed for the south but actually intended for West Point, totaled about 2,800 rank and file; including drummers, sergeants, and officers, their effective strength rose to 3,000. This approximated the compact task force that Clinton had led up the Hudson three years earlier, with such conspicuous success. Like that expedition, it was a mixture of British, German, and loyalist troops. There was the elite Brigade of Guards, formed of volunteers detached from each of the three venerable regiments who traditionally guarded the monarch and who were collectively nicknamed "the Bodies"; despite such ceremonial duties, they were now veterans of four years' hard service in America. By contrast, the 82nd Foot was a "young" regiment raised in 1778, although it had already been instrumental in rebuffing the American expedition against Penobscot, Maine, during the previous summer. The 84th had originated in 1775 as the Royal Highland Emigrants, formed as a loyalist unit by the old Jacobite Allan Maclean. It had served so well that it was adopted onto the regular establishment; the men of its 2nd Battalion were "chiefly recruits," but "commanded by an excellent officer"; and as highlanders, they were considered natural fighters. The Hessian regiment of von Bose likewise met with approval, while the Provincial Light Infantry of Lieutenant-Colonel John Watson ("a well-officered and commanded" corps) and Colonel Edmund Fanning's King's American Regiment ("of great service, reckoned hitherto one of the best" loyalist battalions) were both considered potentially worthy of acceptance as regular units. Specialists included a detachment of riflemen from the Hessian Jäger corps, and another of troopers of the 17th Light Dragoons, both rated "as good as any" in their parent units. There were also men of the Royal Artillery ("of course good"), along with guides and pioneers to deal with obstructions.[63]

Colonel Simcoe's Queen's Rangers received orders to "hold themselves in readiness for embarkation" at the same time as the Guards. As Simcoe recalled, the Rangers were "generally supposed" to be destined "for the expedition being in forwardness to the southward." As he had made clear during the aborted Rhode Island campaign, Simcoe would much have preferred to stay with the main army, where there was a chance of fighting Washington and the French. As adjutant-general, his good friend Major André did his best to reassure him, without revealing the true objective. On September 12, when Simcoe was still in the dark about Clinton's intention of striking West Point, André wrote to him: "Rely upon it, your alarms are vain." Either Simcoe or Colonel Watson, "one or other," would not embark for the South. André added: "I should have been happy to have seen you and hinted that apparent arrangements are not always real ones, but I beg you to seek no explanations. I should not say what I do, but I cannot without concern see you in any uneasiness I can remove."[64]

Years later, when compiling his history of the Queen's Rangers, Simcoe maintained that he became privy to the "great design" against West Point, and that Sir Henry had "informed him on what service he would eventually employ him if it took effect." This was a claim that Clinton left unchallenged when Simcoe invited him to comment on the manuscript of his book before publication. But given André's cryptic message, the colonel can only have been fully briefed at a late stage. That one of the army's best officers—and André's personal friend—remained oblivious of the plan for so long testifies to the secrecy cloaking the entire operation, which was maintained despite the best efforts of the Culper Ring and Robert Howe's agents.[65]

Sir Henry was keeping his cards close to his chest. Chief Justice Smith, who missed little that occurred on Manhattan, was completely unaware of the West Point plan: on September 17, Smith noted in his diary that the general continued with his "daily rides for an airing," excursions that encouraged hardcore Loyalists to believe him an indecisive time-waster. "What can he mean?" Smith pondered. "We know nothing of his designs." That same day, Clinton informed Rodney of the West Point operation. Besides his second-in-command Knyphausen, few other British officers were in on the secret: André, of course, had been involved in the negotiations with Arnold from the start, and expected to play his part in their culmination; Knyphausen's efficient aide, Captain Beckwith, had handled the correspondence with Arnold when Clinton and André were off besieging Charleston; Colonel Beverly Robinson and Lieutenant-General James Robertson had also been aware of Arnold's plotting; Stansbury and Odell, too, who had deciphered and encoded much of the correspondence, must have guessed what was finally in the offing. But most crown soldiers and sailors, high and humble alike, knew no more about the proposed plan than Washington and his agents. Unsurprisingly, Clinton decided to keep the bumbling Arbuthnot in the dark: the operation he envisaged would require decisiveness and activity—precisely the qualities that the "good old Admiral" lacked.[66]

* * *

By Tuesday, September 19, 1780, Sir Henry Clinton's forces were poised to move up the Hudson. All that remained was to fix a meeting with Arnold to finalize the details of the operation. On receiving the letter that Arnold had sent via Colonel Robinson on Monday, reiterating his hopes of a meeting at Dobbs Ferry on the night of the 20th, Sir Henry Clinton agreed to Major André going to the proposed rendezvous with a flag of truce. André was to write to Captain Andrew Sutherland of the *Vulture*, with instructions to bring his sloop downriver from its mooring place off Teller's Point, and collect him at the ferry. Sir Henry later maintained that before André departed on his mission, he gave him "every caution that prudence suggested": he was not to go within enemy lines or change out of his British uniform, and "on no account" to accept papers; if intercepted, either of these last actions would leave him vulnerable to an accusation of spying.[67]

From the conspiracy's infancy, André had known that this day must come. Back in June 1779, when setting out the ground rules for their negotiations, he had explained that Arnold's cooperation with Sir Henry Clinton would be "arranged by my meeting you as a flag of truce or otherwise as soon as you come near us." Like his general, André was conscious of the risks that the mission involved. Yet they were balanced by the likely rewards, which would surely secure his position within Britain's American army. On August 31, Clinton had formally requested royal approval of André's elevation to the status of full adjutant-general. Writing to his mother next day, André cheerfully reported his continuing "good fortune" in being raised to "the first office with the army, if that of most confidence and least profit is to be styled so." The post was usually accompanied by the rank of lieutenant-colonel, and he had hopes of obtaining that, too. Looking back over his recent career, the "steep progress" that the major had made left him feeling "giddy"; yet he believed that his responsibilities had given him "a greater confidence in myself than I should else have."[68]

There are grounds for believing that once he had settled the plan's details by his conference with Arnold, Major André would play an active part in its execution. Given his leading role in the protracted negotiations, he deserved to be in at the kill. It was later reported that he was promised the honor of leading an elite force in the assault on West Point. "Military glory was all he sought," while the "thanks of his general, and the approbation of his king" would be a "rich reward for such an undertaking." But such conspicuous service must inevitably bring fortune as well as fame: if he succeeded, it was said, the major had been promised promotion to brigadier-general, a jump in rank that would have been remarkable even by André's standards. Given the likely consequences of so "splendid an achievement" as storming "the American Gibraltar," a grateful King George III could surely have offered little less.[69]

According to tradition, the eve of André's departure on his mission to meet Arnold was marked by a sentimental send-off party hosted by his brother officers. There is no hard evidence for this, and given the priority of maintaining secrecy the story is improbable. That day André is known to have joined Sir Henry Clinton in a social call on Friederike Charlotte, Baroness Riedesel, whose husband had commanded the Brunswick contingent under Burgoyne in 1777, and who had shared the hardships of that ill-fated campaign. In the summer of 1780, Sir Henry had placed "his delightful country seat" of Mount Pleasant at the family's disposal; it was surrounded by meadows and peach orchards leading down to the East River. The Riedesels had four daughters; when Clinton and André visited, the youngest—christened "America"—was still a baby of six months. Sir Henry desperately missed his own children back in England, and the domestic surroundings must have offered a welcome distraction from André's impending mission.[70]

That same day, September 19, André also called on James Rivington, publisher of New York's *Royal Gazette*, with the third and final installment of a mock-heroic poem, "The Cow Chase," which he had been working on in his spare time over the past two months. Inspired by the popular old ballad "Chevy Chase," which commemorated a celebrated Anglo-Scottish clash during the late fourteenth century, André's offering satirized a more recent fight. On July 21, as adjutant-general, he had forwarded Sir Henry Clinton's approbation for the gallant behavior of seventy Loyalists under Colonel Abraham Cuyler, who had defended a blockhouse near Bull's Ferry, New Jersey, against a 2,000-strong rebel force. Led by Brigadier-General Anthony Wayne, the raiders had been intent on rustling cattle to feed Washington's hungry troops, but became distracted by a costly and futile attempt to dislodge Cuyler's "Refugees" from their strongpoint. In civilian life, "Mad Anthony" Wayne had reputedly been a tanner, a connection that seems to have sparked André's mischievous parody. The first canto of "The Cow Chase" was published by Rivington on August 16, and its opening verses provide a fair sample of the rough wit that entertained André's comrades, and enraged his American opponents:

> To drive the kine, one summer's morn,
> The Tanner took his way,
> The calf shall rue, that is unborn,
> The jumbling of that day.
>
> And Wayne-descending steers shall know,
> And tauntingly deride;
> And call to mind, in every low,
> The tanning of his hide.

In retrospect, the major's final flippant verse would be seen as strangely prophetic:

> And now I've closed my epic strain,
> I tremble as I show it,
> Lest this same warrior-drover Wayne,
> Should ever catch the poet.[71]

8

TREASON OF THE BLACKEST DYE

At 7 p.m. on September 20, 1780, a small boat came alongside HMS *Vulture*, moored off Teller's Point, about fourteen miles downstream from Benedict Arnold's headquarters at the Robinson House. Wearing his scarlet uniform, Major André clambered aboard, to be greeted by Captain Andrew Sutherland and Colonel Beverly Robinson. As the "tide was favorable," André wrote to Clinton, rather than send on the general's letters to the *Vulture*, he had decided to deliver them himself. Clinton had intended Sutherland to bring his ship downriver to Dobbs Ferry, where André was expected to rendezvous with Arnold's agent. By going *upriver*, the major had disobeyed his explicit instructions; and by shifting the proposed meeting from neutral ground into rebel-controlled territory, he had already increased its risks.[1]

Colonel Robinson nonetheless agreed with André that the contact they were expecting was more likely to meet them at their present anchorage; after all, Arnold had advised that the *Vulture* should remain where she was "until the time appointed" for the assignation. But that night nobody appeared. Arnold had undoubtedly intended Joshua Hett Smith to keep the promised appointment, and had issued him a pass dated September 20. It read: "Permission is given to Joshua Smith, Esquire, [and] a gentleman, Mr. John Anderson, who is with him, and his two servants, to pass and repass the guards near King's Ferry at all times." Arnold was calculating that his authority as commander of the Hudson Highlands would satisfy any awkward questions, and remove all difficulties. He also authorized Smith to draw a light boat from Major Edward Kierse, the quartermaster at King's Ferry. Smith received Arnold's order that afternoon, yet he did nothing to procure a boat or a crew.[2]

Joshua Smith was crucial to the success of Arnold's plan, but his lackadaisical approach to his task hardly suggests a dedicated conspirator. His lethargy gives strong support to his own contention—first made when he was charged with complicity in the treason, and maintained while an exile in England—that he had never known Arnold's true intentions. From both the official record of Smith's trial and the narrative of events that he wrote many years later to ingratiate himself with the British, it is reasonable to conclude that he was not told the real reason for André's visit, but believed that it might involve a business proposition, or discussions regarding a peace settlement that would benefit America. This was an outcome that Smith was known to favor: at the Robinson House, he had recently angered the fiercely patriotic Colonel Varick by maintaining that an honorable peace could have been made with the Carlisle Commissioners in 1778. But Smith's services had earned him the gratitude of General Robert Howe, who had recommended him to Arnold. Given Smith's uncertain loyalties, Arnold's reluctance to confide in him is understandable; but this lack of trust left André's fate in the hands of an intermediary who was unaware of the high stakes at play, and who failed to act with the necessary urgency.[3]

Waiting aboard the *Vulture*, as Captain Sutherland recalled, André had "expressed much anxiety" when the flag of truce failed to arrive on schedule; next day, he was "full of fears lest anything should have happened to prevent its coming." André reported his dilemma to Clinton. As this was now the second "excursion" that he had made "without an ostensible reason," and both times in company with Robinson, another would "infallibly fix suspicions." The amiable major was a well-known character in New York city, and his absence would be swiftly noted by enemy agents. Rather than return to Manhattan, and then make a third trip up the Hudson, André confided to Sir Henry that he had resolved to remain on board the *Vulture*, telling Robinson and Sutherland that he had caught a bad cold coming upriver and was suffering from a stomach disorder. Meanwhile, he would try "further expedients" to fix the vital clandestine meeting. One idea was prompted by an episode that had occurred the previous morning, before he had reached the sloop. Seeing a white flag on shore, a ship's boat had pushed off to investigate under its own flag of truce, only for the crew to be fired on by a dozen men sheltering behind rocks. At the urging of André and Robinson, Captain Sutherland sent another flag-boat to General Arnold to complain about this "violation of the customs of war." André used that opportunity to make his presence clear: the captain's letter of protest was in the major's familiar handwriting and was countersigned "John Anderson." In addition, Robinson used the same "flag" to express his disappointment at "not seeing Mr. Smith at the time appointed, being very anxious to conclude our business, which is necessary should be done without delay." Robinson had clearly taken the hint given on the covering envelope of Arnold's last message, that the chief justice's brother Joshua was the intended emissary. The colonel added: "If Mr. Smith will come here, we will attend him to any convenient and safe place."[4]

Irked by Smith's lethargy, on September 21 Arnold traveled to King's Ferry, determined to expedite matters in his own forceful way. When he reached Verplanck's Point, Colonel Livingston passed on Sutherland's message of protest and Robinson's letter, which had both arrived there under the flag of truce; Livingston noticed that Arnold seemed "a good deal reserved." Crossing over to Stony Point, Arnold learned from Major Kierse that no boat was available, so he ordered his own barge back upriver to bring one down to Haverstraw Bay, close to Smith's spacious home, the two-story "White House." Arnold rode there himself, arriving in time to help Smith browbeat his tenants, the brothers Samuel and Joseph Colquhoun, into rowing to the *Vulture* that night. Tired and wary, both were reluctant to go, and only agreed after Arnold threatened to expose them as "Tories" unwilling to aid the patriot cause.[5]

Accompanied by Smith's unnamed black servant and a spare horse for André, Arnold followed the river road to a spot opposite the *Vulture*, while the surly Colquhouns rowed Smith out to the ship, their oars muffled in sheepskin. In case of interception by an American guard boat, Arnold had written Smith a new pass that morning, giving him permission to go to Dobbs Ferry with three men and a boy "with a flag to carry some letters of a private nature for gentlemen in New York and to return immediately . . . as the tide and business suits." A second pass—the one already given by Arnold to Smith on September 20—authorized him to proceed with two servants and "Mr. John Anderson." Smith also carried an unsealed letter addressed to Robinson. Couched in suitably vague terms, it read: "This will be delivered to you by Mr. Smith who will conduct you to a place of safety." It continued: "Neither Mr. Smith or any other person shall be acquainted with your proposals. If they (which I doubt not) are of such a nature that I can officially take notice of them, I shall do it with pleasure. If not, you shall be permitted to return immediately." Arnold added: "I take it for granted Colonel Robinson will not propose anything that is not for the interest of the United States as well as himself." Finally, Smith carried a scrap of paper inscribed "Gustavus to John Anderson": the message that Arnold was waiting on shore for André would be clear enough.[6]

At around midnight, the skiff ground alongside the *Vulture* and Smith came aboard. André, who had been resting in his cabin, instantly "started out of bed and discovered the greatest impatience to be gone." It had never been in doubt that André should go ashore to meet Arnold, rather than the American general come aboard the *Vulture*. André also understood that if the interview dragged on too long to allow his return to the ship before daylight, Smith would lodge him in a safe place until the next night.[7]

Although Arnold's letter to Colonel Robinson had suggested that he, too, might come ashore, "Major André thought it best for him to go alone." Robinson explained to Clinton that as none of the various papers mentioned them both, "it appeared to him (as indeed it did to me) that Arnold wished to see him." Arnold later claimed that either André *or* Robinson was to come ashore; but crucially, there was no pass made out in the colonel's name. If, as Smith later maintained, Arnold really had expected Robinson, and not André, to meet him, the oversight is puzzling. However, "not being named in the flag," Robinson "did not attend Major André"; in words that hint at some reluctance, he told Clinton that he had "submitted to be left behind."[8]

In his published *Narrative*, Smith claimed that "Colonel Robinson pleaded indisposition, and said Mr. Anderson could as effectually answer all the purposes of going on shore as himself." He continued: "For my own part, it made no difference to me who bore me company, so that the object of my mission was fully answered, and the great national ends obtained, which Arnold assured me would be the result of the affair." As André would be going ashore under an assumed name, Captain Sutherland suggested that he should shed his uniform, and offered him civilian clothes of his own. Mindful of Clinton's specific instructions, André refused, accepting only a large blue greatcoat; flapping open, this scarcely hid his regimentals. The major, Sutherland recalled, "had not the smallest apprehension on the occasion," saying "that he was ready to attend General Arnold's summons, when and where he pleased." The captain added: "nor did he in any instance betray the least doubt of his safety or success." Before they left, Robinson remarked that, as Smith's large boat was unwieldy for just two oarsmen, it should be towed by one of the *Vulture*'s armed boats. Smith and André both objected strongly that this was inconsistent with the "character of a flag of truce"—even though Smith's craft was not even displaying one.[9]

Sometime before 1 a.m. on Thursday, September 22, the boat moved off toward the rendezvous with Arnold. Smith had told the anxious Robinson that Arnold would be waiting at Haverstraw, at a place called "the old Trough," with a spare horse to carry him "to Mr. Smith's house at a few miles from the shore." A row of around two miles brought the boat to the west shore of the Hudson, about six miles below Stony Point. Samuel Colquhoun later testified that he heard the noise of a man on the bank above. Smith went up, then returned immediately. Then the "person" who had been brought ashore climbed the bank, while Smith stayed with the boat. Now, at last, André finally met Arnold, who "was hid among firs." What they said remains a mystery, although once the introductions were over, it seems they discussed Arnold's remuneration: he certainly claimed so later to Clinton.[10]

* * *

Without doubt, the two soldiers must also have settled the details of the military operation to capture West Point, clarification that Sir Henry Clinton insisted on before moving his troops upriver. According to General James Robertson, who came to know Arnold well and probably received his information from him, André "met him to concert the proper movements, so that no men might be lost, nor opposition made." While no official plan of attack has ever been discovered, other sources give valuable clues as to what it may have involved. As Robertson informed Sir Jeffery Amherst, the basic premise was a surprise in force: "The troops of our army embarking for an expedition supposed for the southward were to be conducted in one tide to take possession," he wrote. As already noted, it is likely that Major André was promised a leading role in the first assault. Although that conclusion rests on a conversation with André that Major Benjamin Tallmadge recalled more than half a century later, the evidence is vivid and convincing. The British officer had pointed out "a table of land on the west shore, which he said was the spot where he should have landed, at the head of a select corps." André had then "traversed in idea the course up the mountain into the rear of Fort Putnam, which overlooks the whole parade of West Point." And as "Arnold had so disposed of the garrison, that little or no opposition could be made ... André supposed he should have reached that commanding eminence without difficulty." All of this strongly suggests an attempt to exploit the specific intelligence that Arnold had sent to André on June 16, 1780, which highlighted the importance of storming the vulnerable Rocky Hill redoubt to secure the heights overlooking the other defenses.[11]

Young Lieutenant George Matthew of the Coldstream Guards, who was with the assembled assault force, subsequently heard reports of another, more elaborate plan: as aide-de-camp to his uncle, Major-General Matthew, it's likely he had the details from him. The lieutenant reported: "Sir Henry Clinton, on a certain day agreed upon between him and General Arnold, was to lay siege to Fort Defiance." At that stage, Arnold "was immediately to send to Washington for a reinforcement, and before that could arrive was to surrender the place." Clinton, meanwhile, was "to make a disposition to surprise" the relief column. As the reinforcements would "probably have been commanded by General Washington in person," had the stratagem succeeded "it must have put an end to the war." Patriot sources mention a similar ruse. Lafayette maintained: "The plan was to come up suddenly before West Point and to present all the appearance of an attack," and "Arnold intended to say that he had been surprised by a superior force." Congressman William Churchill Houston likewise told Governor William Livingston of New Jersey how it "was concerted with Clinton that an attack should be made on the fort, which Arnold, with the best face he could put on the matter, would have given up." While "an ostensible prisoner" of the British, Arnold would have "received his wages as a traitor," before eventually disposing of himself "as he pleased." The brisk assault outlined by André and the stealthier stratagems reported by Matthew, Lafayette, and Houston may well have been separate components of the same overall plan, calculated to maximize the chances of success.[12]

One matter for settlement between André and Arnold was the timing of the proposed attack. It is possible that a provisional date had already been set, but remained subject to final confirmation. The whereabouts of Washington was clearly an important consideration. Based on what he knew of his itinerary, Arnold had originally expected him to arrive at West

Point on September 23, and to lodge overnight at the Robinson House; but that date was subsequently adjusted to Sunday, September 24, presumably because the Hartford summit had lasted longer than anticipated. It would be difficult, although not impossible, for André to return to New York and activate the plan before Washington's scheduled arrival. Under the circumstances, a later date would have offered greater flexibility. As early as the 19th, James Madison in Philadelphia had heard that the troops in New York believed to be headed for "Virginia or South Carolina" were to embark "on the 25th instant." This date tallies with several other American sources, which subsequently reported that the operation was intended for the night of September 25–26. By then, Washington might be gone from the fortress and back with his main army encamped around Tappan (Orange Town), twenty-five miles downriver, on the Hudson's west shore, close to Dobbs Ferry. But it was also possible that Washington would stay longer at West Point. That scenario offered another means of securing the great prize mentioned by Lieutenant Matthew, and capturing Congress's commander-in-chief.[13]

Although the self-effacing Washington subsequently sought to play down his own significance in Clinton's plan, there is compelling evidence that he was a prime objective. Within the American army, it was widely believed that Arnold, in full Judas mode, envisaged nothing less than betraying "His Excellency" to the British. Of course, Arnold had already tried to do so, without success, when he forwarded intelligence of Washington's journey to Hartford. As Colonel Hamilton recalled soon after the treason's discovery: "There was some color for imagining it was part of the plan to betray the general into the hands of the enemy." He added: "Arnold was very anxious to discern from him the precise day of his return; and the enemy's movements seem to have corresponded to this point." As a bonus for the British, an abduction of Washington would be likely to snare his accompanying entourage, too. Captain William Stevens of the Continental Army's 2nd Regiment of Artillery reported to his wife Betsy that Arnold had negotiated not only the surrender of West Point and its dependencies, but also "the capture of His Excellency General Washington, General Marquis de Lafayette, General Knox, and the French ambassador." Captain Stevens maintained that all of them were "to be taken at General Arnold's quarters at Robinson House on their return from Hartford." There is strong corroborative evidence that Arnold's old friend, the French envoy

La Luzerne, was in his sights. Soon after, when the chevalier was at Rhode Island, he assured Ezra Stiles, the president of Yale College, that "passing through West Point in his way hither on the 24th [September] ... General Arnold importuned him even to indecency to tarry and rest there four or five days"; significantly, this disclosure implies that Arnold expected Clinton to strike by September 29 at the latest. Stiles added that "Arnold also knew General Washington would meet there at the same time on his return from an interview with the French officers at Hartford." It was probably La Luzerne, and not the French general, who was intended when William Smith reported Sir Henry's comment that, had his plan succeeded, he "should have had both Washington and Rochambeau prisoners."[14]

A circumstantial account of "the most cursed plot ever formed by man, for the seizing of the person of his Excellency General Washington, with his family, on their return from the eastward" soon appeared in a newspaper that was already familiar with Benedict Arnold, the *Pennsylvania Packet*. According to an officer writing from the American camp at Tappan, the abduction was planned for the night of September 25. Appropriately enough, the omnipresent *Vulture* would play a central role: it was "prepared for the reception" of Washington and his staff, and carried Colonel Beverly Robinson "with a sufficient number of picked men, for the purpose aforesaid." The officer added: "The plan was to have surprised his Excellency and family, with the Marquis de La Fayette, in the dead time of the night, in the above mentioned Robinson's House, which was the quarters of Arnold, and where his Excellency was to have lodged that night." The correspondent claimed that Colonel Robinson was "pitched upon to execute" the scheme, "being best acquainted with the avenues leading thereto." If the kidnapping plan succeeded, "the garrison at West Point was next to be given up." With his local knowledge, expertise in intelligence, and proven combat record, Robinson would have been a logical choice to manage such a raid; it also explains his presence on the *Vulture*, which is otherwise difficult to justify. In addition, the isolated Robinson House was the perfect spot for such a covert operation. Too distant from West Point for swift support from the garrison, it was defended by no more than a hundred men of Arnold's personal "life guard"; drafted from the Massachusetts militia, they were accommodated nearby in tents and barracks. Even when reinforced by Washington's own escort, such part-time soldiers could not have been expected to fend off a surprise attack by veterans.[15]

* * *

But any British move against West Point depended on the prompt return of Major André. The wary Clinton had sent him upriver for sound reasons: as he explained to Lord George Germain, he had wanted the secret negotiations to be "rendered into certainty, both as to the person being Major General Arnold" and so that "the manner in which he was to surrender himself, the forts, and troops to me ... should be so conducted under a concerted plan between us ... that the King's troops sent upon this expedition should be under no risk of surprise or counter-plot." Only André could give Sir Henry the assurances of "perfect security" that he needed before committing his forces.[16]

The several hours that the major spent conferring with Arnold on the banks of the Hudson should have given ample time to settle the main issues, but they were still talking when Smith interrupted them at about 4 a.m. to warn that dawn was imminent. The question now was what to do with André. Smith later claimed that Arnold tried to persuade the exhausted Colquhoun brothers to row the major back to the *Vulture*; but they maintained that they saw neither Arnold nor their passenger once he had stepped ashore. Samuel Colquhoun declared that it was Smith who tried to get them to make the return trip, but they refused because of tiredness and approaching daylight. In response, Smith told them to do as they liked. He said nothing about them returning André to the sloop that night, once they had rested, and was clearly oblivious of the real risks he faced.[17]

Those dangers were all too soon apparent. As the long-suffering Colquhoun brothers rowed Smith to Haverstraw Creek, Arnold and André headed for the White House on horseback. It was there, in a "place of safety," that André was to remain concealed until nightfall. Riding to Smith's house, they were hailed by an American sentry: it was, André admitted, "a guard I did not expect to see." Contrary to Clinton's instructions, the major was now inside enemy lines, with his situation becoming more perilous by the hour. This was the first baleful consequence of the major's decision to arbitrarily shift the meeting from the relative safety of Dobbs Ferry; another, far worse, soon followed.[18]

At the White House, as Arnold and André talked upstairs and Smith arranged breakfast, they were alerted by a succession of thudding cannon shots. From an upstairs window, they saw the *Vulture* under fire from Teller's

Point. After observing the sloop for almost a week, the feisty Colonel Livingston had become exasperated by her presence offshore; on his own initiative and without consulting Arnold, he took action. While Arnold and André were meeting on the west bank, across the river Livingston had been busy emplacing a 4-pounder cannon and a howitzer, and had secured ammunition from Colonel Lamb at West Point. As a professional gunner, Lamb doubted whether a bombardment with such relatively puny ordnance would have any effect, deeming it a "waste of powder." But he was wrong. At daylight on Thursday, September 22, Livingston's gun crews opened up on the *Vulture*. Colonel Robinson testified to Clinton that they endured a "very hot fire" for two hours before the Americans' powder magazine fortunately exploded. The *Vulture* had returned fire, but before she could get out of range her hull was punctured six times, once perilously "between wind and water." Two shells lobbed from the howitzer were also on target, and a splinter nicked Sutherland's nose. It was a windless day, but the *Vulture* was finally towed out of range by her boats. At about 8.30 a.m., her log records, she dropped anchor some two miles downriver, off Sing Sing in the Tappan Zee.[19]

Livingston's unilateral decision to cannonade the *Vulture* had unforeseen consequences. It thwarted Arnold's plan to get André back to New York the way he had come, via the Hudson. Now, a land route seemed more viable. To cover *both* eventualities, Arnold prepared two passes for Smith, addressing them from his official headquarters. One pass gave Smith permission to go by boat with three men and a flag to Dobbs Ferry and return; the other authorized him to travel overland to White Plains and back. Arnold also inscribed a personal pass for André. This read: "Permit Mr. John Anderson to pass the guard to the White Plains or below, if he chooses, he being on public business by my direction."[20]

Yet André still believed that he would somehow regain the security of the *Vulture*. At about 10 a.m., Arnold left for the Robinson House by way of Stony Point. Before he departed, André recalled, there had been "some mention" of "my crossing the river, and going by another route." At this, the major objected strongly, "and thought it was settled that in the way I came I was also to return." That belief was reinforced after Arnold gave him six documents, mostly detailing West Point's defenses and garrison; all but one were in his own handwriting. When he sought an assurance that they would be destroyed in the event of interception, André replied that he had taken the necessary precautions, "as when I went into the boat I should have them tied about with a string and a stone" to sink them rapidly. The documents introduced a further element of risk, and flouted another of Clinton's injunctions. Yet there was no need for André to even carry them, as the British already had excellent intelligence of West Point, and the salient facts could have been memorized by the major. But André recalled that Arnold was insistent, and "himself made me put the papers I bore between my stockings and my feet."[21]

Arnold went upriver in his personal barge, now presumably confident that the conspiracy was heading toward a satisfactory conclusion. Smith accompanied him to King's Ferry, then returned to André, who was still hiding at the White House and increasingly impatient to be away. But Smith proved as tardy and indecisive as ever, making no attempt to get André to the *Vulture*. Smith contended that his "ague" prevented him from spending hours out on the cold river; more likely, after that morning's brisk cannonading, he was disinclined to risk himself in a boat. Whatever his reason, Smith chose the land route. But instead of forging ahead, he waited until late afternoon before setting off. André, who was still expecting to return by water, was now mortified to learn of Smith's determination to go overland instead. That decision finally made it necessary for André to swap his uniform for civilian clothing. Smith gave him an un-cocked beaver hat and one of his coats: this was purple or brown, with worn gold lace and buttonholes bound in vellum. André kept his own nankeen breeches and waistcoat, his distinctive white-topped boots, and the caped blue watch-coat that Captain Sutherland had loaned him. By shedding his uniform, André had now infringed all three of Clinton's directives.[22]

At last, as the sun began to set on September 22, they departed, accompanied by Smith's black servant, with André riding the horse left behind by Arnold. Usually so convivial and talkative, the young officer was now morose and silent. They crossed the Hudson at King's Ferry. In contrast to André, Smith was verbose, bantering with officers at Stony Point and with Colonel Livingston at Verplanck's Point. He explained that they were traveling northwards, to the Robinson House. In a tense moment for André, Livingston—who had once studied law with William Smith—invited Joshua to stay for supper, or at least to take a glass of "grog" (watered rum). Smith declined, explaining that his companion had urgent business and wished to push on. By now it was dark, and, as Livingston later declared, the night and the fact that Smith's companion had ridden ahead precluded a proper sight of him.[23]

Smith and André now headed downriver, toward the British lines, and the major grew more cheerful. Sometime between 8 and 9 p.m., they were challenged by New York militia, commanded by Captain Ebenezer Boyd. When he demanded to see their credentials, Smith produced Arnold's pass and explained that they were heading to White Plains to gather intelligence for him. Keeping up a bold front, Smith asked the best route; Boyd replied that the safest way ran farther east, via North Castle, as enemy partisans were known to be prowling the Tarrytown Road closer to the Hudson. Becoming increasingly inquisitive, Boyd now positively insisted that the travelers spend the night at a neighboring house. André was reluctant, but had no choice when Smith refused to argue the point. That night they shared a bed. Smith did not get much sleep: the anxious André never stopped tossing, turning, and sighing.[24]

Next morning, Saturday, September 23, the trio were up before sunrise. André was now relaxed and chatty, although he was not yet safe. At Strang's Tavern, near Crompond Corner, they were halted by another rebel picket: its commander, Captain Ebenezer Foote, scrutinized Arnold's pass; but finding nothing amiss, he let them proceed. Soon after, André had a far closer shave when he passed by an American officer he had met before: Colonel Samuel Webb of the Connecticut Continentals had been a prisoner of the British in New York since December 1777, but was now out on parole. Webb stared long and hard at the major, whose hair stood on end while "his heart was in his mouth"; but he did not stop him. Mightily relieved, André now "thought himself past all danger."[25]

Soon after, when the riders stopped for breakfast at a farmhouse near the crossing of the Croton River at Pine's Bridge, Smith suddenly dropped a bombshell: he was turning back. Henceforth, the major would be on his own. Smith, who had already increased André's risks by refusing to ferry him to the *Vulture*, now abandoned him in unfamiliar territory. Smith knew the roads himself, but was fearful of the dangers lurking in the desolate "Neutral Ground" beyond the Croton, the lawless zone ranged by the pro-British "Cowboys" and the more ambivalent "Skinners." As Smith was known to many of the "Skinners," if he had stayed with André he could probably have got him out of any trouble with them, and so safely home. Had they encountered Tory "Cowboys," the British officer André—and through him, Smith—would have had nothing to fear.

But Smith returned to report developments to Arnold at the Robinson House, leaving André to ride on through a depressing and forbidding no man's land of dark, dismal woods and abandoned farmsteads, where crops lay unharvested and fallen fruit rotted on the ground. He still had about twenty miles to go before reaching British lines, and was, as he put it, "left to the chance of passing that space undiscovered." The major had now violated all of Clinton's specific orders: he was in enemy territory, out of uniform, and with bulky packages of incriminating documents stashed inside his boots.[26]

Initially, all went well for André. But sometime between 9 and 10 a.m., after crossing a little bridge over a brook scarcely half a mile north of Tarrytown, he encountered a band of seven "volunteer militiamen." Without an officer, their precise purpose on the road was a matter for debate; according to Lafayette's aide, Major Shaw, they were "freebooters, who live by the plunder they pick up between the lines." Whatever their intent, their presence that morning was providential for the patriot cause. Three of them—John Paulding, Isaac Van Wart, and David Williams—had been lying in wait amid bushes on the south side of the bridge, playing cards. Struck by André's "gentlemanlike" appearance, and noticing his handsome boots, the trio emerged from cover. With his musket leveled, Paulding challenged him to halt.[27]

André's first response was ill-considered and ultimately disastrous. He cheerfully hoped that the men belonged to his "party." "What party was that?" they asked. "The lower party," he replied, meaning the British farther down the Hudson. To André's relief, Paulding said that they, too, were of that party. Paulding had escaped from prison in New York just four days before, and was wearing the green jacket of a Hessian Jäger; this encouraged André to reveal himself as a British officer. He was horrified when Paulding stated that he and his companions were in fact Americans, and ordered him to dismount. Now, too late, André produced Arnold's pass. Paulding—who alone of the three could read—waved it aside. "Had he pulled out General Arnold's pass first," he soon after testified, "I should have let him go."[28]

The trio frisked André thoroughly. Taking his gold watch and some paper Continental dollars, they rummaged through his clothes and saddlebags for coins and other concealed valuables. André was ordered to strip. He responded with warnings of Arnold's displeasure, and then resorted to bribery, offering money and goods if they would let him go. Neither approach worked. Taking off André's boots, and noticing the sagging soles of his stockings, Paulding and Williams soon found the hidden documents.

By now, Paulding at least was alert to their significance: here was a spy. It was agreed to hand André over to Lieutenant-Colonel Jameson of the 2nd Light Dragoons at North Castle, which they did that "forenoon." By an extraordinary coincidence, the last canto of André's poem "The Cow Chase," with its final stanza about catching "the poet," was published in Rivington's *Royal Gazette* that same day.

* * *

Colonel Jameson already knew that Arnold was expecting a "John Anderson" from New York, so he decided to send André to *him* under escort, along with a covering letter explaining the circumstances of his arrest and the discovery of the papers. Given the contents of the documents, it is hard to credit that Jameson did not immediately suspect Arnold. If the sharper Colonel Sheldon had remained in command, he would surely have considered Arnold's authorship of the papers sufficient grounds for detaining him. But Jameson's attitude reflected a reluctance to believe that his revered superior officer could be guilty of treachery; once again, Arnold's enduring reputation as a champion of the revolutionary cause worked its magic. Yet Jameson clearly had some reservations, and his response was a compromise. He wrote to Arnold: "I have sent Lieutenant Allen with a certain John Anderson taken going into New York. He had a pass signed with your name. He had a parcel of papers taken from under his stockings, which I think of a very dangerous tendency." The colonel went on: "The papers I have sent to General Washington."[29]

Jameson's covering letter to Washington mentioned that Anderson "had offered the men that took him one hundred guineas and as many goods as they would please to ask." The colonel explained that he had already sent on the prisoner to Arnold, then added a comment that suggests André had rapidly recovered his wits and tried hard to salvage the situation. Jameson wrote that Anderson had been "very desirous of the papers and everything being sent with him." From this, it seems that André persuaded Jameson to send him to Arnold; if the colonel had allowed himself to be swayed further, the major would have embarked on his journey in possession of all the incriminating evidence. But here at least Jameson exercised caution, thinking it "most proper" that Washington should see the documents. Without appreciating its significance, Jameson included intelligence from

New York: "No Troops have embarked as yet that I can learn. The shipping lies ready and [there is] much talk in York about an embarkation."[30]

That evening, after André had gone on his way to Arnold, the espionage specialist Major Tallmadge rode in from a patrol. On learning the circumstances of the prisoner's arrest, he "was very much surprised to find that he had been sent by Lieut-Col Jameson to Arnold's head-quarters at West Point, accompanied by a letter of information respecting his capture." When Tallmadge heard that Jameson had also "dispatched an express with the papers found on John Anderson, to meet General Washington then on his way to West Point," he pointed out "the glaring inconsistency of this conduct" to the colonel, "in a private and most friendly manner." Tallmadge then suggested a measure of his own, which he later declined to reveal—but which presumably involved arresting Arnold—at which Jameson "appeared greatly agitated." Although the major offered to shoulder all responsibility, his superior officer considered the proposed action "too perilous to permit." Tallmadge finally obtained Jameson's "reluctant consent to have the prisoner brought back to our head-quarters." But when the order was about to be sent for Lieutenant Allen to return with Anderson, "strange as it may seem, Lieut-Col Jameson *would persist* in his purpose of letting his letter go on to General Arnold." Writing to Washington within days of André's arrest, Jameson made no mention of any dissension about the letter to Arnold, maintaining that Tallmadge and other officers "were clearly of opinion that it would be right" until he received further orders.[31]

Jameson rationalized the change of plan in a letter to Allen: "From some circumstances I have just heard, I have reason to fear that a party of the enemy are above; and as I would not have Anderson retaken or get away, I desire that you would proceed to Lower Salem with him and deliver him to Captain Hoogland." Accompanied by one man, Allen should then resume his journey to West Point and deliver Jameson's letter to Arnold; he was also to show him his own note from the colonel, "that he may know the reason why the prisoner is not sent on."[32]

By next morning, Sunday, September 24, André had been retrieved and delivered to Lower Salem, where he was guarded by Major Tallmadge. When the young dragoon observed André pacing back and forth, turning crisply on his heel to retrace his steps across the floor, he had suspected that he was a military man, "bred to arms." Tallmadge was constantly in the same room as André, who "soon became very conversable and extremely interesting."

That afternoon, the prisoner, who had grown agitated and anxious, "asked to be favored with a pen, ink, and paper."[33]

With no prospect of escape, André now wrote a long and remarkably candid letter to General Washington. With evident relief, he confessed his true identity, and admitted that his mission was "to meet upon ground not within the posts of either army, a person who was to give me intelligence." The major did not reveal that his contact was Benedict Arnold; indeed, he had nothing to declare, save for what related to himself. André described his departure from the *Vulture* and concealment ashore. At that time, he admitted: "I was in my regimentals, and had fairly risked my person." But, against his intentions, he had been conducted within the American lines, and was "betrayed (being adjutant-general of the British Army) into the vile condition of an enemy in disguise within your posts." He continued: "Thus become a prisoner, I had to concert my escape." While adamant that he was not a spy, more than anything else André was concerned to establish that he had behaved properly, like an officer and a gentleman. Though certainly "unfortunate," being only "involuntarily an impostor," he hoped to be "branded with nothing dishonorable, as no motive could be mine but the service of my King." Now, as he read the major's unsealed letter for Washington, Tallmadge was amazed to discover his true identity—and to deduce his purpose.[34]

André had been returned to American lines long after the messenger with the papers found in his stockings set off to deliver them to Washington. But the courier had lost valuable time; he had already traveled some way toward Hartford when he learned that Washington was returning by a different route than that taken on his outward journey. Instead of the "lower road" via Danbury and Peekskill, he was following the "upper," which led to West Point through Fishkill. Turning back and then cutting across country, the dispatch rider arrived at Salem late on Sunday afternoon, added André's letter to his package of papers, and headed for Arnold's headquarters at the Robinson House, where he hoped to find Washington. Meanwhile, Lieutenant Allen was already on his way to West Point, with Jameson's letter for Arnold. There was no way of telling which of them would arrive at their destination first.[35]

* * *

Throughout that weekend, Benedict Arnold remained oblivious of André's capture. From what Smith had reported after parting with the major on

Saturday, all being well he should have reached the safety of Manhattan that morning; a message from him might be expected soon, and by Monday at the latest. Or perhaps it had been arranged that Arnold should simply be ready for the onset of whatever plan they had finally agreed on, and play his pre-arranged role when the redcoats came upriver.

During this tense interlude, Arnold's mood was not improved by an ugly quarrel that erupted during dinner on Saturday, September 23. Colonel Lamb and Joshua Smith had sat down as guests with the Arnolds, and the general's disgruntled aides, Varick and Franks. Both remained suspicious of Smith, and disapproved of Arnold's continuing association with him. Varick had previously told Lamb that Smith was "a damned Tory and a snake in the grass." When Smith made a sarcastic jibe about the depreciation of the Continental currency, it sparked a furious row with Varick that only subsided when the distraught Peggy Arnold, who was concerned at her husband's mounting anger, begged them to stop bickering. After Smith left for Fishkill, Arnold tongue-lashed his truculent subordinates: if he had asked the Devil himself to dine, then the gentlemen of his family should be civil toward him, he growled. The unrepentant Franks stormed out, leaving Varick to assure Arnold that they were only concerned to protect his reputation from contamination by Smith, who was "a damned rascal, a scoundrel, and a spy." Finally, after both Varick and Franks asked to be relieved of their staff duties, Arnold promised to distance himself from Smith.[36]

That evening, after the atmosphere had calmed, the Arnolds played host to the chevalier de La Luzerne and three companions. They had stopped at the Robinson House on their way to a meeting with the French commanders at Rhode Island. It was now that Arnold tried to persuade the chevalier to extend his stay, hoping to add him to his prospective haul of captives for Clinton; but he left early on Sunday morning. Of course, other notables were due soon. Colonel Varick, who had spent a sleepless night, informed a correspondent: "we this evening expect His Excellency, the Marquis de Lafayette, and General Knox on a visit in their return to camp." But in another unforeseen development, Washington was prevented from arriving on schedule. Accompanied by his staff and an escort of dragoons, he had passed through Fishkill and was already heading down the Albany Post Road when he met La Luzerne, traveling in the opposite direction. As the chevalier insisted on discussing the Hartford conference, Washington felt obliged to turn back and spend the night with him at Fishkill, instead of pushing on for Arnold's headquarters, as planned. His party lodged at the home of Dr. Charles McKnight; by coincidence, Joshua Smith—who, like Arnold, was unaware that André had been arrested—also dined there.[37]

On the morning of Monday, September 25, 1780, Washington informed his staff that they would ride the remaining twelve or so miles to the Robinson House before breakfast. As Washington wanted to take a short detour to inspect a pair of redoubts, two young aides, Dr. James McHenry and Major Samuel Shaw, were sent ahead to tell Peggy Arnold to start the meal without them. They arrived to find Arnold already at the table, and told him that Washington "would dine there." Arnold politely invited them to breakfast, and they readily accepted. As they were just sitting down to eat, Arnold left the room to issue some orders. He now met Lieutenant Allen, who handed over Colonel Jameson's letters revealing the capture of John Anderson, who had been in possession of a pass signed in Arnold's name and papers revealing information of West Point's defenses: these, as he read with growing alarm, had been sent directly to Washington, who was expected at any moment. McHenry recalled next day: "Arnold, I think, must have received the advice while we were present, as I observed an embarrassment which I could not at that time account for."[38]

Washington's arrival was imminent, and if Jameson's other messenger had already reached him, the game would be up. For all Arnold knew, Washington was already in possession of the damning papers—copied in his own handwriting. He was unaware that the express rider had initially taken the wrong road and had still not overhauled the commander-in-chief. Within minutes, so Arnold believed, he would be confronted with the hard, unavoidable evidence of his treason, and would face the drum-head retribution that must inevitably follow. But he quickly mastered himself. According to his other breakfast guest, Major Shaw, "His Excellency was then in sight, and coming directly to Arnold's quarters, who desired one of his family to excuse him to the General, as he was absolutely obliged to go immediately to West Point, but should be back in two hours."[39]

It was now about 10 a.m. What happened next is described in the vivid account that Arnold gave soon after to the lieutenant-governor of New York, Andrew Elliot. After instructing Allen to wait for an answer, he "ran out and ordered an horse saddled, and sent a servant down the hill to order his barge's crew to man the boat." Luckily for Arnold, they had "just returned from buying a new suit of sails." Arnold then went to his wife. She had been with the two aides, but fortunately they had just gone into the garden to pick peaches for her. Elliot reported: "He told her he must fly to save his life without having time to explain." Arnold mounted his horse, but as he rounded the stable, he came face to face with four light dragoons "who told him His Excellency was just coming up the road." With remarkable presence of mind, Arnold told the troopers to stable their horses, "then galloped down almost a precipice"—the "short road"—to the Hudson; at the landing place, he "threw his saddle with his pistols into the boat, and desired the men to pull away as he was obliged to go to Stony Point and was anxious to return to meet his Excellency." The image of Arnold coolly pausing to unbuckle his saddle and holstered pistols recalled strikingly similar incidents at St. Johns in 1776 and at Ridgefield a year later. Repeated at this latest moment of crisis, the gesture was pure Arnold, combining thrift with deliberate defiance.[40]

Arnold had been wise to insist on retaining the services of his experienced personal bargemen; without them, he would have been forced, like André, to undertake a far riskier journey by land. They were just setting off when an armed boat from West Point arrived at the landing. According to his statement to Elliot, Arnold "called to the crew to go up to the house for refreshment, and when Washington arrived, to tell him that he would be back before dinner." However, Arnold's barge "was not three hundred yards from the wharf when he saw the armed vessel put off after him." Hoisting their new sails, Arnold's crew soon left it behind.

As his boat approached the choke point of King's Ferry, Arnold "hoisted a flag" to "deceive his bargemen," and "pretended he had public business to negotiate with a British officer" on board the *Vulture*. As it passed downriver, Arnold's barge was spotted by Colonel Livingston at Verplanck's Point. By taking the unilateral decision to open fire on the *Vulture* three days earlier, Livingston had unknowingly deranged Arnold's entire plan. Now, or so he assured the chevalier de Chastellux two months later, "he had such a suspicion" of the general, "that had his guard boats been near, he would have gone after him instantly, and asked him where he was going." Chastellux assumed such a question would have "embarrassed the traitor" and led to his arrest. But it is just as likely that Arnold would have bluffed his way out of the predicament by spinning Livingston the same plausible yarn that he had told his crew—or cocked his pistols and threatened to blow the colonel's brains out. As Arnold had promised his bargemen two gallons of rum, they pulled their oars with a will, and the boat sped downriver toward the *Vulture,* now moored off Sing Sing.[41]

* * *

Less than an hour after Arnold's departure, Washington and his escort arrived at the Robinson House; it was dry, militiaman Alpheus Parkhurst remembered, and the "great rumbling and trampling" of hooves kicked up a pall of dust. As instructed, Major Franks informed Washington that Arnold was over the river at West Point, but would be back soon, adding that Mrs. Arnold and Colonel Varick were both unwell. Unperturbed, Washington told Franks to order breakfast. After the meal, Washington, Lafayette, Knox, and their aides crossed to West Point. A two-hour tour of inspection left Washington shocked at the poor state of the defenses. He was likewise puzzled by Colonel Lamb's statement that Arnold had not been seen that day. Washington later recalled: "The impropriety of his conduct when he knew I was to be there, struck me very forcibly, and my mind misgave me; but I had not the least idea of the real cause." With growing concern, he re-crossed the Hudson.[42]

It was only now that Jameson's other messenger reached the Robinson House. "On our return," Major Shaw wrote, Washington "was presented by an express with a letter informing him of the capture of André, and inclosing the papers taken with him." The major added: "This disclosed the whole, and the absence of Arnold was no longer a mystery." The package from Jameson had also included Major André's letter to Washington. Like Arnold, His Excellency disguised whatever emotion he felt at the shocking revelation. As a first response, Hamilton and McHenry were ordered to mount up and gallop to Verplanck's Point. Perhaps, if American shore batteries or guard boats had stopped Arnold's barge it might still be possible to catch him there? But, as Lafayette commented next day, "since no one suspected his flight, no one from the posts could have thought to arrest him."[43]

By the time Hamilton and McHenry reached King's Ferry, Arnold's barge had long since passed. When it came under the *Vulture*'s guns, Arnold informed his astonished crew that "he had quit the rebel service and joined the standard of his Britannic Majesty." As he expected to raise a brigade for King George, he assured the eight privates, "if you will join me my lads, I will make sergeants or corporals of you all." To his coxswain, Corporal James

Lurvey, he promised "something more." Lurvey, a five-year veteran of Rufus Putnam's Massachusetts Regiment, described by General Heath as "a man of strict integrity, the most unshaken bravery, and the warmest attachment to his country," gave an indignant reply: "No, Sir, one coat is enough for me to wear at a time." The corporal's uncompromising reaction was the first indication of just how badly Arnold had misjudged the mood of his countrymen; grumbling was one thing, outright defection quite another.[44]

Arnold had escaped by the skin of his teeth, through a combination of circumstances scarcely less incredible than those which had uncovered his plot. Many years later, his relief was still evident. Indeed, that day he was "subjected . . . to the most imminent hazard of his life, which was only saved by the most fortunate accident, and almost miraculous escape." The "accident" was undoubtedly the timely arrival of the letter from Jameson that alerted Arnold to André's arrest—and his own mortal danger—just minutes before Washington's outriders drew rein at the Robinson House. Washington was convinced that he would have caught Arnold "but for the egregious folly, or the bewildered conception of Lieut. Colo. Jameson who seemed lost in astonishment and not to have known what he was doing." Alexander Hamilton believed that Arnold had been warned owing to an "ill-judged delicacy," but other officers were less forgiving; for example, Colonel Richard Butler observed that "Arnold escaped by the stupidity of one Colonel Jameson, of the Dragoons." In New York, the British assumed that as Jameson had clearly recognized the general's handwriting, he "must have been Arnold's friend," and deliberately warned him of his peril.[45]

Arnold was safe, but Major André remained in American hands and would be tried for his life as a spy. Waiting anxiously aboard the *Vulture*, Colonel Robinson had received no word of him since he had left the ship with Joshua Smith four days earlier. On Sunday, the colonel had written to Sir Henry Clinton with the "greatest concern," promising to do everything in his power "to come at some knowledge of Major André." Now, Arnold's arrival aboard the *Vulture* "unfolded all." Before the sloop headed downriver, the staunch Corporal Lurvey was sent to Verplanck's Point with letters for Washington. One, from Arnold, was a terse vindication, and opened in typically forthright fashion: "The heart which is conscious of its own rectitude, cannot attempt to palliate a step which the world may censure as wrong," he declared. Another letter, from Robinson, marked the start of a determined effort to save Major André, demanding that he be "set at liberty, and allowed

to return immediately." Reminding Washington of their "former acquaintance," and marshaling arguments that would become a mantra in coming
days, Robinson wrote that "every step" that the major had taken "was by the
advice and direction of General Arnold"; in consequence, he was "not liable
to censure" and could not be detained "without the greatest violation of
flags, and contrary to the custom and usage of all nations."[46]

* * *

In his unrepentant letter from the *Vulture*, Arnold had appealed to
Washington's "known humanity" to ask his "protection for Mrs. Arnold
from every insult and injury that a mistaken vengeance of my country may
expose her to." He implored: "It ought to fall only on me; she is as good and
as innocent as an angel." Keen to absolve his wife of any involvement in the
plot, Arnold maintained the same fiction after he joined the British in New
York; Elliot noted down his statement that "she was ignorant of all." Peggy's
innocence went unquestioned by those who lacked inside knowledge of the
conspiracy. Rather than being subjected to scorn and suspicion, she was
pitied, not least because the sudden flight of her husband had apparently
triggered a prolonged bout of hysteria.[47]

It was assumed that Peggy's breakdown had commenced when Arnold
first delivered the shocking news that the conspiracy was exposed, and he
must flee for his life. Alexander Hamilton helped to spread that version of
events in an eloquent and widely published letter to his close friend and
fellow aide, Colonel John Laurens. This maintained that Peggy "fell into a
swoon" as soon as her husband went to her apartment and revealed that
"some transactions had come to light which must forever banish him from
his country"; the traitor left her in that condition "to consult his own safety."
In a letter to the chevalier de La Luzerne, the marquis de Lafayette likewise
claimed that Arnold had absconded, leaving his wife "lying unconscious."[48]

According to Colonel Varick, however, Peggy's hysterics only began
"about an hour" *after* Washington and his party—which included both
Hamilton and Lafayette—had breakfasted and crossed the Hudson to West
Point. Varick left his sickbed to pay them his respects, then retired again. In
a letter to his sister Jane, written less than a week later, he told how that
"good woman" and "amiable lady" Mrs. Arnold, who had tended him during
his high fever of the previous evening, had asked the housekeeper how he

was faring. Soon after, Varick was startled by a sudden shriek. Summoning enough strength to leave his bed and run upstairs, he encountered "the miserable lady ... raving distracted." Peggy's hair was "disheveled and flowing about her neck; her morning gown with few other clothes remained on her—too few to be seen even by a gentleman of the family, much less by many strangers." Wild-eyed, she seized his hand and made a startling accusation: "Colonel Varick, have you ordered my child to be killed?" She then fell to her knees at Varick's feet, offering "prayers and entreaties *to spare her innocent babe.*" Deeply shocked and still gripped by a burning fever, the colonel tried in vain to raise her up. When Major Franks and Dr. William Eustice arrived, the three of them managed to carry Peggy to her bed "raving mad." After finally becoming more composed, Peggy "burst again into pitiable tears," telling Varick "that she had not a friend left here." When he sought to reassure her that Arnold would soon be back from West Point with Washington, she exclaimed: "No, General Arnold will never return, he is gone; he is gone forever, there, there, there"—pointing up to the ceiling— "the spirits have carried [him] up there, they have put hot irons in his head." At this, the loyal Varick finally began to suspect that Peggy's "hysterics and utter frenzy" signified "something more than ordinary." When Washington soon after returned without Arnold, Varick concluded that "all was not right." Peggy now maintained that there was a hot iron on *her* head, and as only General Washington could remove it, she must see him. But when Varick brought Washington to Peggy's bedside, she refused to believe it was him. Despite the general's assurances, "she exclaimed no, that is not General Washington; that is the man who was going to assist Colonel Varick in killing my child." Varick added: "she repeated the same sad story about General Arnold. Poor distressed, unhappy, frantic, and miserable lady."

When he saw Peggy Arnold, Washington had already received the bulky packet from Colonel Jameson that left no doubt of her husband's treason. At around 4 p.m., with the distraught Peggy still upstairs and Major Franks looking in on her, Washington and the company "sat down to dinner in a strange manner." Despite his high fever, Varick officiated over the meal. He recalled: "Dull appetites surrounded a plentiful table."[49]

That evening, when Colonel Hamilton returned from his fruitless mission to intercept Arnold, Peggy was still "frantic with distress for the loss of a husband she tenderly loved—a traitor to his country and to his fame, a disgrace to his connections." Writing next day to his fiancée Elizabeth

Schuyler, the twenty-three-year-old Hamilton left no doubt that he was among Peggy's devoted band of sympathetic admirers:

> It was the most affecting scene I was ever witness to . . . one moment she raved; another she melted into tears; sometimes she pressed her infant to her bosom and lamented its fate occasioned by the imprudence of its father in a manner that would have pierced insensibility itself. All the sweetness of beauty, all the loveliness of innocence, all the tenderness of a wife and all the fondness of a mother showed themselves in her appearance and conduct.

Next morning, when Hamilton paid Peggy another visit, she was calmer. Despite his best efforts to soothe her, she was "not easily to be consoled." She was now "very apprehensive the resentment of her country will fall upon her (who is only unfortunate) for the guilt of her husband."[50]

Lafayette was no less touched by the plight of the "unhappy Mrs. Arnold," and equally certain that "she did not know a word" of the conspiracy. The day after Arnold's flight, he assured the chevalier de La Luzerne that "General Washington and everyone else here sympathize warmly with this estimable woman, whose face and whose youthfulness make her so interesting." As Mrs. Arnold intended to go to Philadelphia, Lafayette implored the ambassador to exert all his influence to "prevent her from being visited with a vengeance she does not deserve."[51]

Given the stress she must have endured as the conspiracy approached its nail-biting climax, coupled with the undoubted shock of its sudden exposure, it is possible that Peggy Arnold's hysterics were genuine; if not, she delivered a performance that the amateur thespian Major André would have applauded. Real or feigned, Peggy's "madness" was an opportune distraction, calculated to appeal to the protective instincts of Washington and his young officers. In combination with Arnold's letter from the *Vulture*, it removed any suspicion that she was implicated in her husband's plotting.

Peggy Arnold made a remarkably swift recovery. On September 26, she was well enough to send a brisk note to Lieutenant-Colonel Varick regarding household matters: "You will be so obliging as to receive any monies which may be due to General Arnold and transmit the same to me," she wrote. On the reverse, Peggy tallied 12.5 pounds of butter at $12 per pound, and

31 quarts of milk at $4 each—a total claim of $274 to supplement the Arnold family finances.[52]

Next day, with Washington's approval, Mrs. Arnold left for Philadelphia, escorted by Major Franks. On the second night, they stopped at Paramus, New Jersey, as the guest of Mrs. Theodosia Prevost. Although married to a British lieutenant-colonel, Mrs. Prevost's sympathies were ambivalent: while Jacques Marcus Prevost of the Royal American Regiment was away fighting the rebels in the South, she entertained patriot officers, including Washington and Hamilton, at convivial French-style salons held in her home, named "The Hermitage" after the cottage of the *philosophe* Jean-Jacques Rousseau. By 1780, Mrs. Prevost was conducting an affair with Aaron Burr; they married two years later, after her husband died of wounds. Theodosia Burr was a highly intelligent woman, not given to tittle-tattle, but she told Burr a remarkable story concerning Peggy Arnold's brief stay with her. When Peggy arrived at Paramus, the "frantic scenes" of her recent hysteria resumed, "and continued as long as strangers were present." But once they were alone, Mrs. Arnold became "tranquilized" and assured her hostess that "she was heartily sick of the theatrics she was exhibiting." Peggy then confided that "she had corresponded with the British commander, that she was disgusted with the American cause and those who had the management of public affairs; and that, through great persuasion and unceasing perseverance, she had ultimately brought the general into an arrangement to surrender West Point to the British." This "confession" only surfaced in 1837, long after Peggy's death, on the publication of Burr's posthumous *Memoirs*. The Shippen family sought to rebut it with an anecdote of their own: Burr had tried to seduce their virtuous Peggy, and when rebuffed, exacted a petty vengeance by seeking to blacken her reputation. This was pure speculation, based on nothing more than Burr's well-earned reputation as a womanizer. Although Peggy's role was exaggerated, in essence the story related by Theodosia Burr to her husband and then published by his editor is plausible enough, especially given the subsequent documentary revelations of Peggy's involvement in her husband's treasonable correspondence; years later, Colonel Varick ruefully admitted that he had come to believe that her memorable hysterics at the Robinson House were "a piece of splendid acting." Burr's motive in revealing the story is itself significant, and suggests a lingering admiration for America's most notorious turncoat. At the age of nineteen, Burr had served as a volunteer under

Arnold on his celebrated expedition to Quebec; in his opinion, the "gay, accomplished, artful, and extravagant" Peggy Arnold had "contributed greatly to the utter ruin of her husband, and thus doomed to everlasting infamy and disgrace all the fame he had acquired as a gallant soldier at the sacrifice of his blood."[53]

* * *

The *Vulture* and its unexpected passenger arrived in New York city on Tuesday, September 26, "to the amazement of all." According to Lieutenant-Governor Elliot, Clinton "was thrown into the greatest distress from the failure of so well concerted a plan, so near ending the rebellion." Sir Henry was no less distraught at the plight of André, and immediately wrote to Washington, enclosing a letter that he had received from Arnold. Following the stance already taken by Robinson, Arnold had assured Clinton that André could not justifiably be detained,

> . . . as he was invited to a conversation with me, for which I sent him a flag of truce, and finally gave him passports for his safe return to your Excellency; all of which I had then a right to do, being in the actual service of America, under the orders of General Washington, and commanding general at West Point and its dependencies.

Quite apart from its failure to acknowledge the small matter of his own treasonous intent—which stripped him of all legitimate authority as commander of the Hudson Highlands—Arnold's statement misrepresented the crucial question of the flag of truce: when André came ashore in Haverstraw Bay with Joshua Smith, he had enjoyed no such protection.[54]

The New Yorkers surprised by the sudden arrival of General Arnold included Chief Justice William Smith. He had had no inkling of Clinton's West Point plan; but now that "the secret" was out, he recollected how Sir Henry had claimed back in July that "the rebellion would end suddenly in a crash," while he had maintained "it would die of a consumption." In his diary, Smith noted: "If he was in treaty with Arnold at that time he had authority for what he said." But the plan had miscarried, and Smith believed that either Major André or Sir Henry himself must have committed some "great error." Perhaps, he speculated, Clinton had been "too slow in collecting his troops to ascend the river." Yet as Sir Henry soon after told him, "every-thing had been ready for seizing the Highlands and putting an end, he owned, to the war." The plan's fatal flaw was its reliance on cast-iron proof that the correspondent on whom it depended really *was* Benedict Arnold, and that the celebrated Patriot was not playing a double-game: Clinton told Smith that "the interview with Arnold was absolutely necessary" to verify his identity. Just months earlier, Clinton had acted without hesitation on receiving Arnold's intelligence of the French arrival at Rhode Island; but now he was more cautious. If he had trusted Arnold and gambled on an attack without waiting for Major André, Clinton might have landed the devastating blow that he had contemplated for so long. But by its very nature, treason sows suspicion, and it played on Sir Henry's own insecuri-ties: distracted by fears for the young officer he had sent upriver, he was unable to overcome his doubts, and the opportunity was lost.[55]

Even though Arnold's plot had been uncovered, Washington had no way of knowing whether Sir Henry would abandon his designs against West Point, or attack regardless. The fortress remained vulnerable: Washington's main army was downriver at Tappan, too far away to respond in time if a British flotilla suddenly came upriver; the wind, which blew from the south on the night of September 25–26, favored such a move. Washington had found the post's defenses "in the most critical condition"; but in his usual unflustered fashion, that evening he issued a stream of orders from the Robinson House intended to "give it security." There was nothing to suggest that Colonel Livingston at King's Ferry was implicated in the conspiracy, but as a precaution, Colonel Lamb was sent to relieve him. Lamb's replace-ment as commandant of West Point, Colonel Nathaniel Wade of the Massachusetts militia, was warned to be "as vigilant as possible" and make the "best disposition" of his men, "as the enemy may have it in contempla-tion to attempt some enterprise, even tonight." Deliberately weakened by Arnold, from whom the enemy would have "acquired a most perfect knowl-edge of the defenses," West Point's garrison consisted only of militia and a few companies of regular artillerymen.[56]

What Washington needed more than anything was veteran Continentals. Thanks to the quick-witted Colonel Hamilton, reinforcements were soon heading north. Still at Verplanck's Point after his futile attempt to catch Arnold, that evening he acted on his own initiative and wrote to Major-General Greene, advising him to put the army under marching orders, and "detach a brigade immediately this way." Hamilton explained: "There has just been unfolded at this place a scene of the blackest treason." Arnold had gone to the enemy, and the British adjutant-general was being held as a spy. The colonel added: "West Point was to have been the sacrifice; all the dispositions have been made for the purpose and 'tis possible, though not probable, tonight may still see the execution."[57]

Hamilton's express, which was soon followed by another from Washington, reached Greene about 11 p.m., and he swiftly issued the necessary orders. Years later, Baron von Steuben's aide-de-camp, Major William North, remembered the hectic scene at midnight, as horses were hastily saddled, and officers went along the tent lines "ordering their men, in a suppressed voice to turn out and parade." No drums were beaten, and the troops formed up in darkness, and—as North reported—"in consternation." Under the circumstances, he believed, some trepidation was understandable, "for who in such an hour, and called together in such a manner and in total ignorance of the cause but must have felt and feared the near approach of some tremendous shock." That night, Ensign Greenman heard, the British intended to attack both West Point *and* the main American army at Tappan.[58]

As a first response, Greene ordered the Pennsylvania division upriver toward King's Ferry. As Brigadier-General Anthony Wayne proudly reported, the 1st and 2nd Brigades marched off, leaving their tents still standing. They had quit camp at 2 a.m. on the 26th, and by sunrise had reached Haverstraw, "distant from our former camp 16 miles, the whole performed in a dark night without a single halt or a man left behind." Wayne's men were positioned to dispute "inch by inch" the same "strong ground" over which Sir Henry Clinton's troops had launched their successful assaults on Fort Clinton and Fort Montgomery three years earlier. "Mad Anthony" now believed that his Pennsylvanians had saved West Point from a similar fate. With his flair for melodrama, he reported: "Our army was out of protecting distance, the troops in possession of the works a spiritless *Miserabile Vulgus* in whose hands the fate of America seemed suspended." Wayne continued: "In this situation, His Excellency (in imitation of Caesar and his Tenth Legion), called for his *veterans*." They had reached King's Ferry very "much fatigued for want of sleep," but if the enemy came upriver, they would march onwards to West Point. By the morning of September 27, as Wayne informed Washington, the wind had changed and was now blowing "strong down the river." Although Washington remained wary, and the new commander of the Hudson Highlands, Major-General St. Clair, was warned to evacuate the posts at King's Ferry and reinforce West Point should the enemy come upriver in force, by October 1 the threat had receded.[59]

Even as they responded to Washington's directives, Arnold's former comrades tried to comprehend his betrayal. Writing at 9 p.m. on Monday, September 25, Brigadier-General Henry Knox struggled to contain his disbelief. His orders to West Point's chief gunner, Major Bauman, began: "The strangest thing in the world has happened. Arnold has gone to the enemy . . ." Next day, at Tappan camp, Brigadier-General Robert Howe was equally flabbergasted, but articulated his feelings in a letter to Washington:

> How poignant is my anxiety, my dear General, that a man of a character so exalted, to whom by all accounts his country owes so much, and from whom so much more might have been expected . . . should to the ruin of his own glory, the disgrace of the army, and the dis-basement of human nature sink into a degree of treachery so black that expression has not coloring to paint it properly.

He voiced another, worrying thought: "How painful and embarrassing this affair must be to your Excellency—for who shall be confided in, if Arnold could not be trusted?" Howe recalled that sometime before, one of his "emissaries" had assured him "that a general officer high up was in compact with the enemy." Whatever the spy's information, it was too vague to expose the traitor, who would earn "eternal infamy" and the scorn of his countrymen: "Little did I think then that Arnold was the man, but since he was, how providential is his detection."[60]

That same day, September 26, Nathanael Greene's general orders had likewise highlighted "the providential train of circumstances" that exposed the treason and proved that the cause of American liberty enjoyed "divine protection." As a confirmed believer in destiny, Washington was quick to acknowledge the intervention of some unseen benefactor. "In no instance since the commencement of the war," he wrote to his aide John Laurens, "had the interposition of Providence appeared more conspicuous than in the rescue of the post and garrison of West Point from Arnold's villainous perfidy." That deliverance resulted from a "combination of extraordinary circumstances," not least an "unaccountable deprivation of presence of mind in a man of the first abilities, and the virtuous conduct of three militiamen." But the "concurrence of incidents" that had baffled the conspiracy were even more "extraordinary" than Washington conceded. By banning Arnold from meeting Colonel Robinson under a flag of truce, he had himself set the scene for André's far more hazardous rendezvous with the traitor. Even then, the major might have got safely back to New York, were it not for Colonel Livingston's unauthorized decision to displace the *Vulture*—and his own penchant for fancy, and eye-catching, white-topped boots.[61]

* * *

With West Point secured, Washington turned his attention to the captive Major André. On the evening of September 25, he had already dispatched orders for the contrite Colonel Jameson to send him on to the Robinson House under a heavy escort, in order to prevent any attempt at escape; by now Joshua Smith, who was suspected of aiding Arnold's treason, had also been arrested. In the days after Arnold's defection, disquieting information about Major André and his likely fate filtered into New York via deserters from Washington's army. George Hobly of the 1st New Jersey Regiment was interrogated by Captain Beckwith on September 28. Two days earlier, Hobly had been at Tappan Meeting House when his regiment was paraded to hear Nathanael Greene's ringing announcement that "Treason of the blackest dye" had been uncovered. Hobly added: "they likewise told them that there were two gentlemen taken at Stony Point who were spies from the British Army." Another deserter, Jeremiah Hopkins, who had served in the British 34th Foot before enlisting in Colonel Proctor's Regiment of Artillery, heard more ominous reports at Tappan. Washington was now back in camp, and they intended to "hang the officer they have in their possession as a spy."[62]

Lieutenant-Colonel John Graves Simcoe was frantic to help his friend by mounting the rescue operation that Washington anticipated. Writing to headquarters "in the greatest anxiety and distress," Simcoe volunteered his Queen's Rangers for the mission. Simcoe wrote: "I fear some misadventure has happened to André; I have to offer myself and my corps for any coup that might assist him; I have forty cavalry, as gallant men as ever were in the field; and horses capable of marching seventy miles without halting." He added: "I have often risked my life, but never can with so much pleasure, [than] in a case where attachment to my General, private friendship and public duty, all call upon [me] in the most feeling manner." Meanwhile, he had sent men to watch the road between Washington's camp at Tappan and Philadelphia, reasoning that the rebel commander "would not proceed to extremities" without the agreement of Congress, and would probably send Major André to them, "in which case he might possibly be retaken on the road thither."[63]

But Major André remained at Tappan, closely guarded around the clock; and soldiers alone would decide his fate. Even though André "was taken under such circumstances as would have justified the most summary proceedings against him," Washington informed Clinton, his case had been referred "to the examination and decision of a Board of General Officers." The fourteen members, with Major-General Greene as president, assembled at Tappan church on September 29. André was charged that: "He came within our lines in the night, on an interview with Major General Arnold, and in an assumed character; and was taken within our lines, in a disguised habit, with a pass under a feigned name, and with the enclosed papers concealed upon him." The names of the board were read to the prisoner: they included Brigadier-General Henry Knox, with whom he had shared a convivial evening, and a bed, near Ticonderoga in 1775. Anthony Wayne, whom the major had lampooned so mercilessly in "The Cow Chase," was not among them. John Laurance, the judge advocate general, laid several papers before the board, including the frank letter that André had written to Washington from Salem on September 24, and the pass and other documents that he had been carrying when intercepted. The major readily admitted to assuming the name John Anderson and concealing the papers. In an additional statement, he made a telling admission: "That the boat he came on shore in carried no flag." Asked to elaborate, the major replied: "That if he came on shore under that sanction, he certainly might have returned under it." As Washington observed to Clinton, "it is evident Major André was employed in the execution of measures very foreign to the objects of flags of truce and such as they were never meant to authorize or countenance in the most distant degree." In view of André's own statements, there was no need to summon witnesses. Having maturely considered all the papers, the facts of the case, and André's "confession," the board pronounced that he "ought to be considered as a spy from the enemy, and that, agreeably to the law and usage of nations, it is their opinion he ought to suffer death."[64]

This stark verdict was forwarded to Sir Henry on September 30. With his own hands, Washington handed the packet to Captain Aaron Ogden of the 1st New Jersey Regiment, who was to proceed with an escort under a flag of truce and deliver it to the nearest British post, at Paulus Hook. Washington's public letter was accompanied by a strictly private message. Acting on "special instructions" issued by Lafayette, Captain Ogden was to assure the post commander "that if Sir Henry Clinton would in any way suffer General Washington to get within his power General Arnold, then Major André would be immediately released." Clinton's intelligence officer, Captain Beckwith, also knew of this offer from American deserters: John Needham, of Colonel Crane's 3rd Regiment of Artillery, told him that the captured adjutant would be hanged if the British "did not send out General Arnold" in exchange for him. When he arrived at Paulus Hook, Ogden was "politely offered accommodation for the night." At supper, seated next to the commanding officer, he discreetly mentioned Washington's proposition. The Briton immediately rose from the table and crossed the Hudson to New York city. He returned about two hours later with a "laconic answer" from Sir Henry that "a deserter was never given up."[65]

Clinton faced a cruel dilemma. The only chance of saving André was to trade him for Arnold. Yet if Arnold was handed over to face the retribution of his countrymen, not only would the British be guilty of a gross breach of faith, but there would be precious little incentive for other disillusioned American Patriots to follow his lead. Unable to relinquish Arnold, Sir Henry remained determined to retrieve his adjutant-general. He swiftly wrote another letter to Washington, questioning whether the board that condemned André had known "all the circumstances on which a judgment ought to be formed." He added: "I think it of the highest moment to humanity, that your Excellency should be perfectly apprised of the state of this matter, before you proceed to put that judgment in execution." He was therefore sending Lieutenant-General Robertson, along with Lieutenant-Governor Elliot and Chief Justice Smith, to present a "true state of the facts." The delegation would set out for Dobbs Ferry next day, October 1, "as early as the wind and tide will permit," and await Washington's permission to meet him or his representatives.[66]

Clinton still believed that André could be saved; but the major had no such illusions. After his judges delivered their sentence, he obtained Washington's permission to write to Sir Henry, absolving him of all blame for his misfortunes. André emphasized that the events that had led to his "present situation . . . were contrary to my own intentions, as they were to your orders." He added: "I am perfectly tranquil in mind, and prepared for any fate, to which an honest zeal for my King's service may have devoted me." It was an emotional farewell: "With all the warmth of my heart," the major assured Clinton, "I give you thanks for your Excellency's profuse kindness to me; and I send you the most earnest wishes for your welfare, which a faithful, affectionate, and respectful attendant can frame." He had a final favor to ask: as the income of his mother and sisters had been "much affected" by the French capture of Grenada, the major hoped that the value of his commission, which would otherwise be lost at his death, might go to them.[67]

Major André assured Sir Henry that he had received "the greatest attention from His Excellency General Washington, and from every person under whose charge I happen to be placed." Cheerful and composed in the face of impending death, the major had quickly won the friendship and admiration of his captors, especially young officers like Benjamin Tallmadge and Alexander Hamilton. Described by Tallmadge as a "young fellow of the greatest accomplishments," and by Hamilton as uniting a "peculiar elegance of mind and manners, and the advantage of a pleasing person," he personified the gentlemanly code of honor that they aspired to. André chatted freely with the officers who guarded him; he had "unbosomed his heart" to Tallmadge, and it was while traveling downriver with him from West Point to King's Ferry that he had outlined the proposed assault. Now that the plan was uncovered, André had no reservations about discussing it; as no other prisoners with comparable knowledge were in rebel hands, it is likely that he was the source of information that soon surfaced in letters and newspapers—for example, the date of the operation and the plan to abduct Washington and his staff. Yet the same affable "frankness" that won André such admiration from his captors had detracted from his effectiveness as a spy, and contributed to his fate.[68]

André's openness now raised concern among craftier espionage specialists. The double agent William Heron, who, in the interests of self-preservation, had recently blocked Arnold's efforts to communicate with the major under the alias of "Gustavus," grew increasingly anxious that he would be exposed to the Patriots. "This affair of Arnold being frustrated will I fear be attended with ill consequences," he fretted to Major De Lancey. "Major André being deficient in point of fortitude makes him disclose matters which in my opinion a man of honor would rather suffer death than be guilty of, drawing into ruin those who he knew to be engaged in the same cause with himself." Heron added: "such conduct in a person of his rank makes those of your friends here shudder, and in their present fright conclude themselves in danger by holding any correspondence with any person short of the commander-in-chief." In Heron's opinion, Major André would "not suffer" death, but would "probably be exchanged."[69]

Here, as in his assessment of the major's "fortitude," Heron was misinformed. General orders for October 1 announced that André would be executed at 5 p.m. The major received the news calmly, and penned a note to Washington: he requested to be shot, as befitted a soldier, not hanged like a common felon. André wrote: "Buoyed above the terror of death, by the consciousness of a life devoted to honorable pursuits, and stained with no action that can give me remorse, I trust that the request I make to your Excellency at this serious period, and which is to soften my last moments, will not be rejected." He continued: "Let me hope, Sir, that if aught in my character impresses you with esteem toward me, if aught in my misfortunes marks me as a victim of policy and not of resentment, I shall experience the operation of these feelings in your breast, by being informed that I am not to die on a gibbet."[70]

What Major André characterized as a "professional death" was typically administered by six musketeers from a range at which they could not miss, and was intended to provide an awful warning that spectators would never forget. The crashing volley of heavy lead balls inflicted massive damage on tissue and bone. Shockingly bloody, execution by firing squad was at least swift. In 1780, before the widespread adoption of the trap-door "drop," intended to mercifully break the victim's neck, hanging involved a more prolonged ordeal. In both Britain and America, the condemned were typically obliged to stand on a horse-drawn cart directly below the gallows, with the rope tied to the beam above and the noose placed around their neck; at the appointed signal, the executioner whipped the horse to pull away the cart, leaving the victim dangling and strangling. To minimize suffering, the positioning of the halter was crucial. This had been clear at the execution of one of the Gordon rioters, twenty-two-year-old Theophilus Brown. As the cart was about to be driven off, "the constables observing [that] the rope was not properly placed, spoke to the executioner to alter it." The hangman insisted that everything "would come right" after Brown was "turned off"; when the constables persisted that it would not, the expert replied, "Who ought to know best—you or I?" But instead of falling behind Brown's ear, the knot went under his chin, and he "was full twenty minutes in dying." Even without such callous bungling, hanging was a distinctly undignified business: in their death struggles, the hanged often kicked and twitched in a grim jig, involuntarily losing control of their bodily functions. For a debonair officer and gentleman like Major André, it would be hard to imagine a more ignominious fate.[71]

Washington did not respond to André's plea. Documents published by Congress to demonstrate the impartiality of the major's treatment in custody explained: "The practice and usage of war were against his request, and made the indulgence he solicited, circumstanced as he was, inadmissible." Alexander Hamilton, who could see no harm in complying with André's wishes, informed Miss Schuyler that it was decided "to evade an answer, to spare him the sensations which a certain knowledge of the intended mode would inflict."[72]

* * *

As arranged, Clinton's delegation went upriver in the *Greyhound* schooner early on October 1. News of their coming caused André's execution to be postponed until the next day. As the meeting was considered to be a strictly military matter, only Robertson was permitted to land and confer with Major-General Greene. On the vital question of the flag of truce, Robertson now argued that whether or not one was flying "was of no moment," because, as Arnold had maintained, André "landed and acted" under his directions. Greene retorted that "they would believe André in preference to Arnold." Robertson nonetheless depended on Greene's "candor and humanity" to relay all the facts to Washington. Before they parted, Greene raised a final point of his own. Robertson informed Clinton: "Greene now with a blush, that showed the task was imposed and did not proceed from his own thought, told me that the army must be satisfied by seeing spies executed; but there was one thing would satisfy them—they expected if André was set free, Arnold should be given up." He had answered this offer "with a look only, which threw Greene into confusion."[73]

Despite General Robertson's refusal to countenance an exchange of Arnold for André, the meeting provided the opportunity for another covert approach to Sir Henry Clinton. A note proposing a swap, dated September 30, 1780, and signed "A.B.," articulated prevailing sentiments among the American officer corps. Although André was an enemy, its author wrote, "his virtues and his accomplishments are much admired." In addition, as "Arnold appears to have been the guilty author of the mischief," he "ought more properly to be the victim." The author alleged, without foundation, that Arnold had meditated "a double treachery," arranging his interview with the major in such a way that, if they were discovered, he could sacrifice him "to his own safety." A "P.S." emphasized: "No time is to be lost."[74]

Sir Henry Clinton believed that the note was written by "Hamilton, W[ashington's] aide-de-camp." That attribution was rejected by the editors of Hamilton's *Papers*, on the grounds that the "disguised hand" in which the note is written was not otherwise used by him, and because he had assured Elizabeth Schuyler that while it was proposed that he suggest to André "the idea of an exchange for Arnold," he could never have acted on that suggestion for fear of forfeiting the major's esteem. But while Hamilton clearly bridled at personally brokering a deal, that does not rule out his authorship of the letter. He was in the perfect position to hand it over, as he had accompanied Greene to the conference. While the generals talked, Robertson's aide-de-camp, Major Thomas Murray, "walked elsewhere" with Hamilton and "two other Rebel officers." As Hamilton strolled with Murray, he could easily have passed on the letter. Colonel Simcoe also knew about the note, and was certain that Hamilton had written it. "Amongst some letters which passed on this unfortunate event," he wrote, "a paper was slid in without signature, but in the handwriting of Hamilton, Washington's secretary, saying 'that the only way to save André was to give up Arnold.' "[75]

Still anchored off Dobbs Ferry, that night Robertson wrote confidently to Clinton, assuring him that he hoped "to carry Mr. André, or at least Mr. Washington's word for his safety," back to New York next morning. He added: "I am persuaded André will not be hurt." As promised, Greene relayed Robertson's comments to Washington: but they "made no alteration in his opinion and determination." Greene also handed his commander two letters that Robertson had forwarded from Arnold. In the first, Arnold made "grateful acknowledgement and thanks" for the "polite attention" shown by Washington and his staff to his wife during her recent distress. He then repeated points he had already raised in his letter to Clinton—that André should not be considered a spy, because he had acted throughout under Arnold's directions. However, he continued with an abrupt change of tone, if the board of officers was insistent and "that gentleman should suffer the severity of their sentence, I shall think myself bound by every tie of duty and honor to retaliate on such unhappy persons of your army as may fall within my power, that the respect due to flags, and to the law of nations, may be better understood and observed." If the warning went unheeded, and Washington allowed "an unjust sentence to touch the life of Major André," Arnold called on "Heaven and earth to witness, that your Excellency will be justly answerable for the torrent of blood that may be spilt in consequence." In the other, much shorter letter, Arnold informed Washington: "I no longer consider myself acting under the commission of Congress." He added a statement that would be dismissed by Washington and his officers as the worthless words of a villain and scoundrel, but which nonetheless reflected sentiments which he had expressed to Sir Henry Clinton in May 1779 and would maintain for the rest of his life: "At the same time, I beg leave to assure your Excellency, that my attachment to the true interest of my country is invariable, and that I am actuated by the same principle, which has ever been the governing rule of my conduct in this unhappy contest."[76]

Washington did not deign to respond to Arnold's attempts at justification, and his blunt threats had no more influence on him than Robertson's convoluted arguments. Aboard the *Greyhound*, Robertson and his colleagues were unaware that Washington's "Evening Orders" had included a stark announcement: "Major André is to be executed tomorrow at twelve o'clock precisely. A battalion of eighty files from each wing to attend the execution."[77]

* * *

Sir Henry Clinton only replied to André's emotional letter of September 29 on October 1, after his delegation had already gone upriver. He had read the major's words in "astonishment," as he remained convinced of his innocence. Clinton was sure that General Robertson and the "other respectable friends" sent to plead André's cause had evidence "which I flatter myself General Washington will in justice admit." Sir Henry added: "God knows how much I feel for you in your present horrid situation, but I dare hope you will soon be relieved from it." He signed off: "believe me Dear André ever your faithful affectionate humble servant, H. Clinton." But it's unlikely that André ever read his general's letter.[78]

On the morning of Monday, October 2, Major André was served breakfast, as usual, from General Washington's own table. At the appointed time, he came down the steps of the stone house where he had been confined, and fell in with his escort, linking arms with an officer to either side. André was "most elegantly dressed in his full regimentals"—the scarlet, gold-laced coat of a British staff officer, faced in the gay popinjay green of the 54th Foot, with buff breeches and waistcoat, and polished boots. Tallmadge recalled that the major "marched to the destined ground with as much ease and cheerfulness of countenance as if he had been going to an assembly." Captain John Van Dyke of Lamb's artillery heard André praise the "good discipline" of his guards, and the "excellence" of the fifers and drummers who set the pace with "lively tunes." When he first saw the high gallows, as one of his guards, eighteen-year-old Eli Jacobs of the Massachusetts Continentals, remembered, he "started backward." In response to something said by one of the officers, Jacobs "distinctly heard André say, 'I detest the mode.'" His last request had been denied, but he quickly recovered his poise and marched on.[79]

The major's courage was all the more impressive because, as he waited during the final macabre arrangements, he was clearly struggling to master the physical symptoms of fear. With the cold, clinical detachment of a trained medical man, Dr. James Thacher noted how André swallowed uneasily, and absently rolled a pebble with his foot. Another witness remembered that the major's first effort to spring onto the wagon beneath the gallows failed when his legs crumpled under him; but he tried again, and clambered up. André had recently lost his composure on the road to White Plains, but he kept it now. With thousands of eyes fixed upon him, the major prepared to give his last and most memorable performance. When the hangman, whose face was hideously disguised with black grease, placed the noose around his neck, André fended him off and did the job himself; the major knew what he was about, tugging the knot snugly behind his right ear. He then produced a handkerchief and "hood-winked" his eyes. The officer supervising the execution was the Continental Army's own adjutant-general, Colonel Alexander Scammell. When Scammell asked André for any last words, he raised his blindfold and said in a firm voice: "All I request of you, gentlemen, is that you will bear witness to the world that I die like a brave man." By now, many in the crowd were weeping. It was too much for Major Tallmadge, who turned away "in a flood of tears." Scammell's lowered sword gave the signal, and as the wagon jerked away, its momentum gave André a "great swing." Within minutes he hung still. After the major's servant removed his outer clothing and boots, his body was placed in a black-painted coffin and buried at the foot of the gallows.[80]

News of André's execution reached New York on October 5. Captain Peebles of the Black Watch reported that General Clinton was "much afflicted," while "the whole army was sorry for the untimely death of that promising young man." Sir Henry was more distraught than his soldiers knew: when an American officer who had witnessed the execution confirmed the details, he exclaimed "oh my God, can it be possible—and wept." The American spy Robert Townsend ("Samuel Culper Junior") maintained that "General Clinton was inconsolable for some days." Even Townsend, who had naturally taken a keen interest in André's activities, regretted his fate. He wrote to his handler, Major Tallmadge: "I never felt more sensibly for the death of a person whom I only knew by sight, and had heard converse, than I did for Major André. He was a most amiable character." As William Smith noted, Arnold, too, was "vastly disconcerted" by the news.[81]

Denied a chance to save his friend, John Graves Simcoe took André's death especially hard. In a mark of esteem, he gave directions that the Queen's Rangers "should immediately be provided with black and white feathers as mourning for the late Major André, an officer whose superior integrity and uncommon ability did honor to his country, and to human nature." While they would "never sully their glory in the field by any undue severity," it was nonetheless Simcoe's "most ardent hope, that on the close of some decisive victory, it will be the regiment's fortune to secure the murderers of Major André, for the vengeance due to an injured nation, and an insulted army." In his official orders of October 8, Clinton formally announced the death of his adjutant-general, a gentleman "of the highest integrity and honor, and incapable of any base action and unworthy conduct." He added: "Major André's death is very severely felt by the commander-in-chief, as it consequently will be by the Army, and must prove a sad loss to his country and to His Majesty's service." Sir Henry used that same opportunity to make another announcement: he had been pleased to appoint "Benedict Arnold Esq., colonel of a regiment with the rank of Brigadier General." Now wearing the red coat of King George, Arnold longed for an opportunity to avenge Major André. Serving alongside Simcoe, he would soon have his chance.[82]

9

THE RECKONING

On the evening of Saturday, September 30, 1780, Philadelphia was thronged with the "greatest concourse of people" that Congressman Benjamin Huntington of Connecticut had ever seen. Surging through the city's wide, straight streets, the crowd followed an illuminated procession that moved slowly toward the wharves fronting the broad Delaware River. The cavalcade was led by several gentlemen on horseback, backed by a line of Continental Army officers on foot. Then came a score of the city's own militiamen, with flickering candles thrust into the muzzles of their shouldered muskets. Behind them marched drummers and fifers playing the "Rogue's March," a jaunty tune long used by the British army when casting out disgraced miscreants, and since adopted by its opponents.[1]

The martial music reverberated from the handsome buildings that lined the route, mingling with the shouts, jeers, and cheers of the spectators. Their attention was focused on the parade's center-piece: a horse-drawn cart carrying a stage, on which a striking tableau of two life-like effigies had been arranged. One was immediately recognizable as General Benedict Arnold, the erstwhile hero of the revolutionary cause. His effigy was appropriately clad in a blue and buff uniform, and was posed sitting on a chair, with one leg stretched out and resting on a cushion; this realistic touch recalled the turncoat's favored method of easing the pain of the crippling wound he had sustained at Saratoga, in defense of American liberty. But the emphasis that night was on Arnold's recent apostasy, not his past glories.

Accordingly, his effigy was two-faced to reflect his double-dealing. To underline Arnold's duplicity, an ingenious mechanism operated by a hidden boy kept his Janus-like head revolving continuously, as the cart trundled along. In its left hand, the dummy-Arnold held a mask; in its right, a letter from the fallen angel Beelzebub, "telling him that he had done all the mischief he could do, and now must hang himself."[2]

Looming behind the seated general was a truly grotesque figure of "his friend the Devil," decked out in black robes and with a goat's horns on his head. Lucifer dangled a bulging purse at Arnold's left ear. His right hand hefted a pitch-fork "ready to drive him into Hell as the reward due for the many crimes which his thirst for gold had made him commit." Arnold's misdemeanors were detailed on a "large lanthorn of transparent paper," which swung before his effigy. Its inscription concluded: "The treachery of this ungrateful General is held up to the public view, for the exposition of infamy; and to proclaim with joyful acclamation another instance of the interposition of bounteous Providence."[3]

This was the second time in three days that Arnold's effigy had been paraded through Philadelphia. A makeshift papier-mâché figure had already made its appearance on the evening of Thursday, September 28, the day after the shocking news of his conspiracy first reached the city. On that occasion, the Quaker Samuel Fisher had been "alarmed with the noise of drums and fifes and much shouting of the mob in the street." As a pacifist, jailed by Philadelphia's revolutionaries for his loyalist sympathies, Fisher at first feared that the rowdy crowd intended violence against his fellow "Friends." He was relieved to learn that its wrath was directed toward "an effigy of Arnold hanging on a gallows, the body of which was made of paper hollow and illuminated, and an inscription in large letters thereon, which they conveyed through many parts of the city."[4]

This first spontaneous gibbeting of Arnold by Philadelphia's "mob" was eclipsed by the far more orderly and elaborate procession orchestrated soon after, with the blessing of Pennsylvania's Supreme Executive Council. The sophisticated effigies paraded during the second event were created by the acclaimed local artist Charles Willson Peale. A Philadelphia radical and ardent Patriot, who had fought against the British in New Jersey as a militia lieutenant, by 1780 Peale had already secured his professional reputation by making portraits of the Revolution's leading soldiers and statesmen. His prolific output included the impressive full-length 1779 portrait of "George

Washington at Princeton." This iconic image of the Continental Army's revered commander-in-chief, depicted in the aftermath of his most celebrated victory, won such widespread praise that Peale had been kept busy ever since, making copies for admirers.[5]

Regrettably for posterity, Peale never painted Arnold's portrait, although he was certainly familiar with the general from his days as Philadelphia's military governor. In now preparing Arnold's likeness for public exhibition and abuse, Peale drew inspiration from a long-established tradition in Britain's former North American colonies, in which figures of the Pope and the Devil were burned amid celebrations every November 5. This anti-Catholic "Pope Day" ritual had itself originated in the bonfires kindled in England on that same date, to commemorate the detection in 1605 of Guy Fawkes, a conspirator in the "Gunpowder Plot" to blow up the House of Lords, and with it Britain's monarch, James I. In addition, the parading of effigies of those deemed guilty of transgressing society's accepted codes of behavior, exposing them to the communal scorn of crowds making "rough music" on improvised instruments, was a feature of traditional shaming rituals, or "skimmingtons," which had even deeper roots in British folk culture.[6]

Like these precedents, the tableau paraded through Philadelphia on September 30, 1780, fulfilled specific functions and conveyed unmistakable messages. It gave spectators an opportunity to vent their rage, and to express gratitude for the divinely ordained "Providence" that had baffled Arnold's "hellish plot" at the eleventh hour, just as it was about to be implemented. The relief of Patriots was palpable, and with good reason: disaster had been averted by only the narrowest of margins. Major Samuel Shaw, who had witnessed the conspiracy's extraordinary climax, exclaimed: "Great Heaven! What an escape we have had!" In Shaw's opinion, the loss of even "three capitals on the continent would not have been a misfortune of equal magnitude" to the fall of West Point. To Shaw, the Hudson Highland fortifications were the "palladium of American independence . . . this grand link in the chain of our union being once broken, we may bid adieu to peace, liberty, and safety." Had the treason succeeded, the major added, the enemy would have gained possession of the entire Hudson corridor, from New York city to Fort Ticonderoga on Lake Champlain. Following on the heels of British victories in the South, Shaw believed, it would have "reduced us to an extremity from which nothing, in the present spirit of the times, but a creating power could have extricated us."[7]

The sense of salvation was all the greater because it was widely credited that Arnold's plot envisaged something even deadlier to the patriot cause than the capture of West Point. As Congressman John Hanson noted: "our worthy General was also to have been put into their hands." That double blow would have "affected us more than any other stroke we have received since the war [began]," making "such an escape . . . equal to a small victory." Congratulating Washington on the "timely discovery" of Arnold's "infernal machinations," New Jersey's governor, William Livingston, believed that if the "plot to captivate your person" had succeeded, it would have been "more regretted by America" even than the fall of the fortress itself. The loss of *either* West Point or Washington would undoubtedly have been a major setback for the patriot cause: the elimination of *both* might have forced Congress to capitulate. With typical modesty, Washington made light of the kidnap scheme, arguing that Arnold would not have wished "to hazard the more important object of his treachery by attempting to combine two events, the lesser of which might have marred the greater." But as even Washington acknowledged, "there were circumstances which led to a contrary belief." His countrymen remained convinced that he had enjoyed a providential escape from the clutches of his enemies. On the day after the treason's discovery, Major Sebastian Bauman observed: "it does plainly appear that there is a guardian angel who watches over this country and his Excellency." Congress agreed, and felt justified in decreeing "a day of public thanksgiving throughout the United States."[8]

Peale's realistic effigies also offered a clear, visual explanation for Arnold's shocking conduct: innately evil and corrupt, he had been tempted by the Devil and English gold. However simplistic, this interpretation reflected prevailing opinion that fall, and ever since. In the wake of Arnold's treason, patriot newspapers were full of letters, many written by serving Continental Army officers, which reveal the rapid emergence of the widespread belief that his underlying motivation was greed: "Lost to every sentiment of honor," it was reported, "the infamous General Arnold" had been corrupted and disgraced by his insatiable desire for money.[9]

One of the most outspoken denunciations of Arnold's assumed avarice, first published in the *New-York Packet* and then reprinted by other newspapers, came from an author with the classically inspired pseudonym of "Publius." That nom de plume had been used by Alexander Hamilton when he wrote three articles for the same newspaper two years earlier. As Hamilton was closely involved in the aftermath of Arnold's defection, it is possible that he played at least some role in preparing this essay, too. Whoever wrote the piece certainly yearned to see Arnold suffer horribly for his crimes. He asked: "What species of punishment can be inflicted equal to the demerits of the poor, sordid wretch, who for the base-born passion, love of gold, can deliberately bring upon his country, for which he has fought and bled, such a complication of horror, devastation, and war!" "Publius" had a gruesome suggestion: ". . . were it possible to convert his breast into a living furnace, and his heart into a nervous crucible, to be forever employed in melting and refining his beloved gold . . . the days of eternity would be too few to atone for his crime."[10]

Such lurid fantasies highlight another function of Peale's effigy—perhaps the most important of all. In the absence of the flesh-and-blood Arnold, who had narrowly escaped retribution thanks to his own share of Providence, his likeness provided a substitute upon which spectators could unleash their pent-up resentment, enjoying the illusion of vengeance, if not the reality. Staged as the climax to the orderly procession of September 30, the dramatic fate of Peale's Arnold manikin left a strong impression on witnesses, not least the timid hypochondriac Daniel Newton, who made space in a diary typically dominated by reports of his own ill health to describe that evening's exciting events. When the procession finally reached the Delaware riverfront at Market Street Wharf, and after Arnold's effigy had been subjected to the derision of "the populace who showed the highest resentment of such a traitor," it was tossed onto a bonfire "amidst thousands of spectators" who gave "loud huzzas and acclamations . . . rejoicing to think that his traitorous plot was discovered so soon, and thousands of lives saved." And so, as the *Pennsylvania Packet* wrapped up its coverage of the spectacle, having committed the traitor to the flames, the crowd "left both the effigy and the original to sink into ashes and oblivion."[11]

The Philadelphia processions were only the first of many such public demonstrations of disapproval for Arnold and his treachery. In coming months, as the *New Jersey Journal* recalled more than a year later, "the streets of every city and village in the United States . . . rung with the crimes of General Arnold." The outcry was so prolonged and intense because Arnold was no ordinary turncoat: not only was he the most senior American officer to defect to the British, but he had previously made a vital contribution to the patriot cause. On the day after his defection, Lafayette expressed his feelings to La Luzerne: "In the course of a revolution such as ours, it is natural that a few traitors should be found, and every conflict which resembles a civil war of the first order ... must necessarily bring to light some great virtues and some great crimes." But that Arnold, who had given "proof of talent, patriotism, and, especially, of the most brilliant courage, should at once destroy his very existence and should sell his country to the tyrants whom he fought against with glory," was an event that confounded, distressed, and humiliated Lafayette to a degree he could not express. Arnold's swift plummet to disgrace was proportionate to his giddy fame. "Never since the fall of Lucifer has a fall equaled his," observed Nathanael Greene. Men who had fought beside Arnold were mortified by his betrayal. Writing to his fellow Quebec veteran Colonel Lamb, Arnold's former secretary Eleazer Oswald delivered a bitter verdict:

> ... let his name sink as low in infamy, as it was once high in our esteem. Happy for him, and for his friends, it had been, had the ball which pierced his leg at Saratoga, been directed thro' his heart; he then would have finished his career in glory, but the remainder of his wretched existence, must now be one continued scene of horror, misery, and despair.[12]

Feelings against Arnold ran especially high in his home state of Connecticut, whose inhabitants were now naturally keen to distance themselves from a celebrated local hero so suddenly transformed into a detested national traitor. On the evening of October 26, 1780, a procession through New Milford culminated in a grimly realistic mock execution. As before, Arnold's effigy was suitably dressed in uniform, and shadowed by the Devil, "who seemed however ashamed of so unprofitable a servant." Like a condemned felon going to the gallows, the effigy rode in a horse-drawn cart, and was posed sitting on a coffin, with arms pinioned. Once the effigy had toured the town, it "was brought under strong guard to the place of execution, where, in the view of some hundreds of spectators, he was formally hanged, cut down and buried." As the language of this report indicates, amid such a heightened emotional atmosphere it was all too easy to imagine that Arnold in person, and not some inanimate dummy, was dangling at the end of a rope.[13]

* * *

The focus of all this concentrated hatred settled comfortably into his new role as a soldier of King George. From Manhattan, the American spy Robert Townsend reported that Sir Henry Clinton had formally introduced him to the other general officers on the parade "as General Arnold in the British service." Townsend, who was relieved that Arnold remained unaware of his activities as a mainstay of the Culper Ring, noted that the newcomer was "much caressed" by New York's governor, Lieutenant-General James Robertson. Like Clinton, General Robertson was viewed in a dim light by committed Loyalists, who believed that Britain's high command was too soft on the rebels, and more interested in an easy life than in fighting. One of Robertson's bitterest critics was Judge Thomas Jones, who ridiculed him for pursuing a lifestyle ill-suited to a man in his early sixties. Jones maintained that the veteran Scot was "the laughing stock of the citizens," chasing after teenaged strumpets and "waddling about town" with a brace of "pretty little misses" under each arm. But there was more to Robertson than such scandalous stories suggest. Whatever creature comforts he enjoyed had been hard earned in a military career that had begun forty years earlier, at the siege of Cartagena; the catastrophic casualties of that campaign had helped the Highlander to rise swiftly from private soldier to junior officer. During the French and Indian War, Robertson had become the army's quartermaster-general and indispensable right-hand man of General Jeffery Amherst, the conqueror of Canada. Now, some twenty years later, Sir Jeffery was the British army's commander-in-chief and an influential figure at the heart of government.[14]

On October 6, 1780, Robertson wrote to his old chief, explaining that "Arnold, the boldest and most enterprising of the rebel Generals, lives with me and sits by me while I write." Surveying Arnold's military career and his recent attempt to deliver up West Point, Robertson characterized his guest as a man "who does nothing by halves." He informed Amherst that Arnold had been denied his old Continental Army rank of major-general because it would have offended the British brigadiers. However, when Robertson told Arnold that "it would be more honorable" for him to earn his promotion "after performing some service of moment," he had agreed, and now longed for the opportunity to distinguish himself in the royal cause. In fact, Arnold had already proposed a plan that was especially close to his heart: besides "driving the Congress from Philadelphia," he advocated destroying the stores there and the ships in the Delaware River, and occupying a ten mile-wide swath of land to provide forage and provision for the British army.[15]

Another British veteran who also enjoyed the finer things in life, the hard-fighting Admiral Rodney, was no less impressed with Arnold's aggressive energy, which contrasted sharply with Sir Henry Clinton's caution. In a private letter to Lord George Germain, Rodney reported that after first coming into New York, Arnold had assured both him and Clinton that "he would answer with his head" that West Point could still have been captured within ten days. "But to my infinite surprise," Rodney continued, "cold water was immediately thrown upon it," even though just days before Arnold's arrival he had been told that the fortress "was of infinite consequence, and if taken would ruin the rebels." Rodney added: "Believe me, my Lord, this man Arnold, with whom I had many conferences, will do more towards suppressing the rebellion than all our generals put together." But the admiral doubted whether he would be given the chance to prove himself: "Jealousy, my Lord, unless commands from home signifies His Majesty's pleasure, will prevent Arnold being employed to advantage."[16]

While Arnold enjoyed the esteem of senior British officers, including Sir Henry Clinton himself, he was less well received among their juniors. From a "gentleman" who had left New York on November 2, one leading London newspaper heard "that General Arnold is a very unpopular character in the British army, nor can all the patronage he meets with from the commander-in-chief procure him respectability." The report continued: "General Clinton, from obvious and just motives of policy, gives this signal convert great encouragement ... but the subaltern officers have conceived such an aversion to him, that they unanimously refused to serve under his command."[17]

Even allowing for exaggeration, it is clear that Arnold faced considerable resentment and suspicion. It was his misfortune that André had been so well liked within Britain's American army; and while he had forfeited his life, Arnold was granted the £6,000 that the major had been authorized to promise him should the plan misfire, plus £315 for expenses. With ill-timed insensitivity, Arnold had tried to convince the grieving Sir Henry Clinton to increase this sum to the £10,000 that he had proposed himself. If André, too, had escaped from rebel hands, Arnold's own reception would likely have been warmer. Captain Ewald of the Jäger corps, who had befriended André in Germany before the war, was among those officers who regretted his loss and regarded Arnold with distaste; as a professional soldier who had grown to grudgingly respect the American rebels during four years of fighting them, the one-eyed Hessian disapproved of what he deemed to be a cynical betrayal of their cause. Yet British officers who had been far closer to Major André, and who might have been expected to dislike Arnold even more strongly, became his champions: notably, neither John Graves Simcoe nor Sir Henry Clinton ever wavered in their support for him, or changed their belief that he had defected for sincere, ideological reasons, to reunite Britain's broken Atlantic empire.[18]

While many of Arnold's former comrades now hated him with a passion, such animosity was not reciprocated: in New York, he had no qualms about praising their exploits against the British. Another of Germain's correspondents, the Honorable George Damer, reported: "There is a freedom as well as a propriety in General Arnold's conversation and behavior." Damer elaborated: "He speaks handsomely of Washington, and of the officers of the rebel army in general." However, Arnold made some exceptions, and they included Horatio Gates. As blunt, tactless, and opinionated as ever, besides lauding the American Patriots, Arnold could not help lecturing the redcoats on their past blunders, especially the failure to act on his own sound intelligence. Damer told Lord George: "He does not scruple to mention the inactivity of our army at certain periods in former campaigns, and in this he very strongly expressed his astonishment upon his arrival at our not having attacked the French upon their disembarking at Rhode Island."[19]

Soon after coming into New York, Arnold had sought to broadcast his views on the American conflict more widely. In his published address "To the Inhabitants of America," which was dated October 7, 1780, and first appeared in the Royal Gazette four days later, he aimed to justify his actions to rebels, Loyalists, and neutrals alike. This was drafted with the help of Chief Justice Smith, and was heavily laced with the tropes of loyalist propaganda—for example, equating Congress with "the tyranny of the usurpers in the revolted provinces." On the question of Arnold's motivation, the ghost-written address offers little insight; yet it is possible to identify passages where his voice can be distinguished from Smith's, and these deserve further consideration.[20]

In two areas in particular, Arnold's post-treason arguments can be anchored on opinions that he is known to have expressed from his very first approach to Sir Henry Clinton, via Joseph Stansbury, in May 1779. Concerning what Clinton had characterized as his "displeasure at the French alliance," Arnold assured his readers in October 1780 that he had aimed to make his preferences for Great Britain clear by retaining his command in the Continental Army until he had an opportunity of surrendering it, "and in concerting the measures for a purpose, in my opinion, as grateful as it would have been beneficial to my country." Here, in light of Carl Van Doren's claims that Arnold "took no final steps until his price had been accepted," it is worth re-emphasizing that he had offered to join the British when he first contacted them; West Point only became an objective after he was instructed to remain with the Continental Army.

The second key issue—the extent to which, in Sir Henry's words, Arnold proposed his "assistance for the delivery of your country"—arose when his later address tackled the thorny problem of the timing of his switch of allegiance. Loyalists might think that Arnold had taken too long to make up his mind; Patriots that he had abandoned them too soon. But he rounded on those "censurers whose enmity to me originates in their hatred to the principles by which I am now led to devote my life to the reunion of the British Empire, as the best and only means to dry up the streams of misery that have deluged this country." Such personal critics could rest assured—and here the phrase is unadulterated Arnold—"that, conscious of the rectitude of my intentions, I shall treat their malice and calumnies with contempt and neglect."

In late October, once again with Smith's help, Arnold prepared a detailed assessment of the military situation, including both a report giving the "Present State" of the Americans' armed forces and finances, and a more general expression of his thoughts on winning the war for King George. Arnold provided an accurate overview of problems that dogged Washington: many of his best officers were disillusioned and resigning; Congress and the Continental Army were at loggerheads; the American navy amounted to little more than a trio of frigates; and funds were exhausted. To exploit this crisis, Arnold suggested winning over the disillusioned American officers and soldiers by offering to settle their arrears of wages, with half-pay continuing for seven and a half years after the war, and land grants ranging from 200 acres for privates to 10,000 acres for major-generals. All this, Arnold estimated, would cost less than a few months of usual war expenses. Alternatively, all private soldiers and NCOs might be offered fifteen or twenty guineas—half paid immediately, and the rest when the war ended. If such incentives were authorized, Arnold was confident that he could soon enlist between 2,000 and 3,000 turncoats. As for George Washington himself, perhaps "a title ... might not prove unacceptable." Neither proposal was tested. The prospect of hard cash and land might have tempted some desperate Continentals, but Arnold's suggestion that His Excellency could be won over by honors from the state that he had opposed so tenaciously was utterly fanciful.[21]

Alongside such recommendations of unsubtle bribery, Arnold gave Lord George Germain his own trenchant thoughts on strategy. A reinforced British army, in which he would fight to earn his old rank of major-general, was the best means of crushing the rebellion, he believed. To maximize manpower, Arnold advocated that the loyalist provincials should be relieved of garrison duty and sent on active service as light infantry. Given sufficient force, there were two options to achieve victory. First, Washington could be pursued remorselessly, run to ground, and forced to fight; as an initial objective, Arnold's old command in the Hudson Highlands should be targeted in the spring. Alternatively, all troops (save for those left to hold New York) should head south, seizing the Chesapeake region. Once Virginia and Maryland had been overawed, and British civil government restored, their resources—both of men and supplies—could be harnessed for an advance north through the rebel states of Pennsylvania, New Jersey, and ultimately New York. Significantly, Arnold opposed starting a campaign farther south, using South Carolina as a base to attack Virginia; this was a strategy that Lord Cornwallis would soon implement, with disastrous consequences.

On October 25, before Arnold's letter to Germain was dispatched, he published a direct appeal intended to encourage the mass defection of Washington's long-suffering troops. His "Proclamation to the Officers and Soldiers of the Continental Army," which was also distributed as a broadside, offered "the most affectionate welcome and attention to all who are disposed to join me in the measures necessary to close the scene of our afflictions." Sir Henry Clinton had authorized Arnold to "raise a corps of cavalry and infantry," to be "clothed, subsisted, and paid" like other units in British service. As a further incentive to deserters, any man who brought in "horses, arms, or accoutrements" would be "paid their value or have liberty to sell them." Each NCO or private would receive a bounty of three guineas, while Arnold had authority to nominate his officers himself. Arnold aimed to head a "chosen band of Americans." He declared: "I shall with infinite satisfaction embrace this opportunity of advancing men whose valor I have witnessed and whose principles are favorable to a union with Britain and true American liberty."[22]

That same day, Brigadier-General Arnold made a personal appeal to Major Benjamin Tallmadge, the American cavalry officer and intelligence specialist. Young Tallmadge had admired Arnold, and only became aware of his plot when it was uncovered by pure chance; yet there was nothing to suggest that he was ripe for seduction. Arnold's approach to the major, like his proposal that Washington could be bought by "a title," reveals his utter failure to comprehend the reality of a conflict in which other men had long since decided where their own allegiance lay, and were fully committed to their cause. He wrote: "As I know you to be a man of sense, I am convinced you are by this time fully of opinion that the real interest and happiness of America consists in a reunion with Great Britain." To achieve that "happy purpose," Arnold had accepted a commission in the British army, and now invited Tallmadge to join him "with as many men as you can bring over with you." Arnold would press no arguments, as the major's "own good sense will suggest everything I can say on the subject." As Tallmadge was preoccupied with military duties, for which he received the praise of Washington and Congress, he only received Arnold's invitation on January 28, 1781. The major, who was affronted that the notorious renegade should single him out, immediately sent a copy to Washington, expressing his determination "to treat the author with the contempt his conduct merits" and ignore him. Washington, who had already condemned Arnold's "Proclamation" as an "unparalleled piece of assurance," which only added to his men's "detestation" of the traitor, had "consoled" Tallmadge "abundantly on the occasion."[23]

* * *

In the aftermath of Arnold's defection, some dedicated Patriots hoped that the extraordinary outpouring of shock and anger it provoked could be harnessed to energize the flagging cause of American liberty, and bring the protracted war with Britain to a victorious conclusion. Major Shaw had quickly sensed an opportunity "to use the means Providence has intrusted to us ... to see the end happily accomplished." "For shame!" he appealed. "Let us bestir ourselves, as a people worthy the blessings for which we contend." In his published address, "Publius" fused his fulsome denunciation of the traitor with a comprehensive rallying cry: "let us invoke the genius of liberty to revisit us, and inspire us with sentiments suitable to the dignity of freemen," he urged. "Publius" exhorted his countrymen to support the Continental Army "with cheerfulness and alacrity, not of necessity but of choice." In addition, they must be "careful and diligent in detecting every species of villainy . . . especially the dangerous and fatal practice of sinking the value of our currency" and in "choosing men of known integrity and abilities for our representatives both in civil and military concerns." "And above all things," "Publius" declared, "let us study unanimity, which gives firmness and strength." Shaw and "Publius" were both close to the geographical center of the drama; but in distant Virginia, Edmund Pendleton also shared their hopes that recent events would finally rouse the supporters of American independence from their apathy before it was too late.[24]

It has been widely accepted that such appeals fell on receptive ears, and that, as a most ironic consequence, Arnold's treachery revived the patriot cause when it was at its nadir. Logical enough, this interpretation has a long pedigree. Within weeks, British critics of the American war were suggesting that, amid the furor, Arnold's defection might indeed achieve the opposite of what it had intended. One newspaper commentator observed: ". . . as the detection of treason gives strength to the cause meant to be betrayed, Arnold's desertion can only be made a matter of triumph to the favorers of American Independence." Modern historians and writers have gone further, arguing that Arnold's treason had an unforeseen, and momentous, impact on the course of the Revolutionary War. Carl Van Doren, who first uncovered the conspiracy's full details, observed: "No event in the course of the whole Revolution did so much to intensify patriotic sentiment." He added: "Arnold as traitor helped fix a powerful new image of the United States in the minds of its people." Arnold's sympathetic biographer Willard Wallace concurred: "What neither Arnold nor the British perceived was that the treason had an effect contrary to what they anticipated. The treason shocked the country into a semblance of unity." This interpretation has continued to gain acceptance. James Kirby Martin, the author of a scholarly study of Arnold's pre-treason career, commented: "his audacious course had the ironic effect, at least for him, of reigniting faltering sensations of popular support for the rebel cause." More recently, the argument that Arnold became an unwitting savior of the Revolution has been spread among a wider readership by the prominent non-fiction author Nathaniel Philbrick. In his interpretation, Arnold's treason "saved" Americans "from themselves." By his treachery, Arnold "succeeded in galvanizing a nation." Philbrick emphasized that the renegade had jolted his countrymen to their senses in the very nick of time: "Just as the American people appeared to be sliding into apathy and despair, Arnold's treason awakened them to the realization that the War of Independence was theirs to lose." In turning traitor, Arnold "had alerted the American people to how close they had all come to betraying the Revolution by putting their own interests ahead of their new-born country's."[25]

At first glance, subsequent events would seem to justify such judgments. Scarcely a year after Arnold's defection, in October 1781, a British army under General Charles Cornwallis was isolated and captured at Yorktown, Virginia; this was a devastating defeat, from which Lord North's administration never recovered, and which effectively ended British efforts to subdue America. By any assessment, it was a remarkable turnaround. Yet Yorktown was not the outcome of some Arnold-inspired revival of patriotic fervor. On the contrary, the downfall of Cornwallis only resulted from an extraordinarily fortuitous combination of events, which were every bit as "providential" as those responsible for exposing Arnold's treason. When all factors are considered, the American victory at Yorktown owed little to a revitalized patriot war effort, and much to muddled British strategy and the unexpected but timely arrival off Virginia of a powerful French fleet from the West Indies.

Long into the summer of 1781, the scenario that unfolded at Yorktown would have seemed fanciful; and before patriot fortunes finally revived, they reached their lowest point. Far from improving, in the aftermath of Arnold's defection morale continued to fall. Above all, there was no post-Arnold surge of volunteers to swell the Continental Army: it was one thing to heap execrations on an effigy of the reviled turncoat; quite another to enlist and fight against him. The historian Charles Royster was surely correct in suggesting that the civilians who eagerly participated in such demonstrations were using Arnold as a scapegoat upon whom to offload their own sense of guilt at betraying the "highest revolutionary ideals," and failing to give the cause of American liberty the enthusiastic support that it had originally enjoyed.[26]

The fall of 1780 saw no slackening in the steady stream of deserters to the British in New York. The grievances voiced by Sergeant John Porter of the 6th Massachusetts Regiment, who came in on October 30, were typical. Congress was struggling to raise recruits willing to serve for the duration of the war, he said. Porter claimed that once the "six-months men" in his company had served out their time, most of the remaining sixteen aimed to desert. As ever, Porter and his comrades were hungry: in theory, the daily ration was half a pound of bread and the same of unsalted beef; but there were many days without meat. When the exasperated sergeant warned that "he would desert if he was not treated better," his officer had answered: "he could not blame him." With approaching winter, the crisis intensified: interrogated on November 26, Michael Lane of the 1st New Jersey Regiment said it was "very common to hear the soldiers say that they will not stay any longer, but they will go to the British Army." It was now "confidently reported that the Pennsylvanians were deserting from Mr. Washington's army by fifty at a time." Although unfounded, there were rumors that General Greene had "gone over to Lord Cornwallis with 700 men." It was also said that attempts to raise recruits "for the war" had sparked violent riots in Fishkill; that Vermont's Ethan Allen and his Green Mountain Boys intended to secede and join the British; and that the talk in camp was of joining General Arnold in New York at "the first opportunity."[27]

There are other indications that Benedict Arnold's offers to his former comrades were encouraging their desertion. In early October, Ensign Benjamin Gilbert of Massachusetts assured his parents that Arnold had publicly declared that "he will have a brigade of Continental troops with him before spring." Gilbert heard that he had distributed hand bills offering "ten guineas bounty, to any American that will come and join him." He added: "It has so much influence that many have deserted and daily are deserting." It was not just the rank and file who were dissatisfied. Soon after, Gilbert reported that the Massachusetts Line were in "a dubious and precarious situation," because officers were resigning every day. Even though the number of Continental regiments was reduced by order of Congress from eighty to fifty-nine, there would not be enough officers left to staff them. If the reorganized regiments were filled up with short-service men, then Gilbert would himself resign, "for I am determined not to be a drill sergeant always": no sooner were the levies disciplined than their time was up, and the drudgery of training began all over again, making the officers "perpetual slaves."[28]

Disaffection among the American officer corps extended to the highest levels. In London, pro-government newspapers reveled in publishing intercepted "rebel letters" that proclaimed "to the world in terms not to be contradicted, the deplorable state to which the Americans are reduced." One of the documents was an address from seven New England generals to their parent states. Headed by Rhode Island's Nathanael Greene, they sought "to represent the distressing conditions of their officers in the army." They drew a pessimistic picture, reflecting the failure of Congress to orchestrate an effective war effort, and the Royal Navy's continuing confinement of the French to Rhode Island: "The war appears to us as far from an honorable issue as it has ever done," they stated. "Our allies, however generous their intentions, have not been able to give us the expected assistance." The other published letter, from Alexander Hamilton to the privateer Isaac Sears, reinforced the strong impression that the patriot cause was in terminal crisis. Weeks after Arnold's defection, he had written: "I am sorry to find that the same state of indifference to public affairs prevails." Hamilton concluded: "My fears are high, my hopes low." An editorial crowed: "What now will Opposition say of this same America, that is never to be conquered?"[29]

* * *

Pro-ministry newspapers in London had initially heralded Arnold's defection as a turning point; *Lloyd's Evening Post* believed that as he was "a brave, gallant and experienced officer," his loss "must be severely felt by the Americans, and his known probity will make that cause appear very bad, which he could no longer support with honor." The *Morning Herald* was confident that Arnold's "return to his allegiance would be followed by that of thousands." But the opposition press told a different story. As the *London Courant* noted: "Not one man has come over with General Arnold to the British standard."[30]

Despite the flow of deserters from Washington's army, Arnold's own loyalist regiment, the American Legion, struggled to fill its ranks. By December 11, there were eight officers, but only thirty-two men. One of them, however, was a fine specimen, and exactly the kind of recruit that Arnold had hoped to attract. Sergeant-Major John Champe was a Virginian who had deserted from Major Henry Lee's own legion in New Jersey on October 20; three days later, he was questioned at British headquarters by Captain Beckwith. When Champe chanced to meet Arnold on the streets of New York, the general listened to his story and invited him to join his regiment. But the strapping dragoon was not all he seemed: on instructions from Lee, and with the full approval of Washington, he was to kidnap

Arnold and bring him back to face justice for his crime. Washington was most insistent that the turncoat should be taken alive. He told Lee: "No circumstance whatever shall obtain my consent to his being put to death." That action would promote the idea that "ruffians had been hired to assassinate him." Instead, Washington declared, "My aim is to make a public example of him."[31]

According to Lee's colorful *Memoirs*, compiled many years later, Champe made a thorough study of Arnold's routine, noting that he generally returned home around midnight, and before retiring always visited the garden— presumably to use the privy. Champe hatched a plan to surprise the general under cover of darkness, gag him, and with the help of a companion, bundle him through the garden fence and down an alley to a boat waiting at the Hudson quayside. The sergeant and his accomplice were to prop Arnold between them; if questioned, they would explain that they were lugging a drunken soldier to the guard-house. Everything was ready, but on the very day before the night designated for the enterprise, the American Legion, including Sergeant Champe, was ordered aboard ship. They were bound for Virginia, as part of an expedition commanded by Arnold himself.[32]

Brigadier-General Benedict Arnold sailed from Sandy Hook on December 20, 1780, at the head of about 1,500 men: half of them were British and Hessian regulars, the rest Loyalists, including Simcoe's Queen's Rangers. Clinton intended that the expedition should help to relieve the growing pressure on Cornwallis in the Carolinas, where British setbacks had stiffened patriot resistance. Sir Henry later explained that he had selected Arnold "for this service from the very high estimation in which he was held among the enemy for active intrepidity in the execution of military enterprises, and from a persuasion that he would exert himself to the utmost to establish an equal fame with us in this first essay of his capacity." However, "as a precaution," Clinton had sent along two experienced officers—Lieutenant-Colonel Simcoe and Lieutenant-Colonel Thomas Dundas—whom Arnold was "to always consult previous to his engaging in any operation of moment." Clinton also issued both officers with a "blank dormant commission," authorizing them to assume command in the event of Arnold's "death or incapacity," a step of which he remained unaware.[33]

Arnold's convoy was scattered by storms, and a third of his force missed the appointed rendezvous; but as the new year began, he pushed up the James River without them. On January 4, Arnold landed his troops at

Westover, and marched on to Richmond. In the heart of enemy territory, he embarked on a brisk and comprehensive program of devastation. As Arnold was proudly to recall:

> ... with only one thousand men he effected the destruction of the American magazines designed for their Southern army, took their park of artillery, a large quantity of arms and ammunition, captured and destroyed upwards of twenty of their ships, which several British officers sent previously for the purpose did not think it prudent to attempt with three thousand men.

Clinton was delighted, and readily acknowledged that by "spreading terror and alarm through the country," Arnold had done "most essential injury to the enemy and their allies." In an overview of Arnold's operations with the British, Sir Henry stated: "As he had been by much the most active and successful general when against us, so he had done most essential service with us." In Virginia, Arnold had proved himself as effective and energetic as ever—too much so for some of his new redcoat comrades. Deputy Adjutant-General Frederick Mackenzie believed that Arnold's "success with so small a body of troops" would cause the previous expedition sent to the Chesapeake under Major-General Alexander Leslie "to appear in a very unfavorable light." Mackenzie observed: "I am almost sorry ... that such a man as Arnold should have executed with an inferior force, what a British general did not even attempt with a superior one." Rounding off his professional assessment, Mackenzie noted: "Arnold is bold, daring and prompt in the execution of what he undertakes."[34]

While Arnold's raiders rampaged through the Old Dominion, Washington was helpless to intervene. A shocked Major Shaw explained why. "The accumulated distresses of the army have at length produced most dreadful effects," he informed the Reverend Eliot. On New Year's Day 1781, the Pennsylvanian regiments stationed at Morristown, New Jersey, had mutinied, and were headed for Philadelphia, determined "to demand redress of their grievances from Congress." These were Wayne's veterans, the same men who had marched at midnight to save West Point; but they had finally had enough. They defied their officers, and even "Mad Anthony" himself could not dissuade them from their purpose. As Shaw explained, the mutineers were exasperated by the "many and complicated injuries" they had "groaned under for so long," but the final straw was their state's decision to offer bounties to every short-term "six-month" man willing to re-enlist: men who had already served for three years, and were told they must remain until the war ended, felt cheated. By menacing Congress, the disgruntled Pennsylvanians were taking the very course that Arnold had recommended during the previous summer. But British attempts to exploit the unrest, and encourage large-scale defections, fell on deaf ears: the mutineers spurned the "idea of turning *Arnolds*." Intelligence sifted at Clinton's headquarters revealed that the seasoned Continentals had declared that if the British invaded New Jersey "to take advantage of them 'while they were seeking their rights,' they would turn out and fight them heartily as ever under General Wayne." Through an elected board of sergeants, they negotiated with Joseph Reed, who was still the president of Pennsylvania's Council. Complaints were addressed, and discharges granted to men who swore that their time was up.[35]

On January 20, New Jersey regiments at Pompton followed the Pennsylvanians' lead. They told one of Sir Henry's agents that "they were determined, unless they got redress, to join the British." Washington reacted swiftly and firmly. He informed Congress: "Unless this dangerous spirit can be subdued by force there is an end to all subordination in the Army, and indeed to the Army itself." Given 300 steady Massachusetts men and 4 field pieces, Brigadier Howe was ordered to "quell the rioters." Ensign Gilbert went with the detachment. After "finding themselves surrounded on every side," he reported, the mutineers surrendered. Three ring-leaders were immediately tried and sentenced to death. One was pardoned at the inter-cession of his officers. The other two were executed by a firing squad drawn from "those who were their seconds in the mutiny"; they obeyed with tears streaming down their cheeks. This ruthless action ended the disorder. But it had been a severe shock, and with many of the discharged Pennsylvanians reluctant to re-enlist, Washington's army was weaker than ever.[36]

Now, in another manifestation of Providence, a great storm battered and dispersed Admiral Arbuthnot's blockading squadron off Newport, giving the French a momentary naval superiority. De Ternay had succumbed to illness, but at Washington's suggestion, his successor, the chevalier Destouches, prepared to sail against Arnold. At the urging of ambassador La Luzerne, the chevalier had already sent a small squadron to harass Arnold, under Le Gardeur de Tilly; consisting of just one sixty-four-gun man-of-war and a few smaller vessels, this force had obliged him to take a safer position at Portsmouth, up the Elizabeth River, which was too shallow for the French ships to follow. With his allies active at last, Washington decided to send 1,200 Continentals overland under Lafayette; in Virginia, the marquis would cooperate with the local commander, Baron von Steuben.[37]

By now, Brigadier-General Benedict Arnold had a price on his head: Virginia's governor, Thomas Jefferson, offered 5,000 guineas for his capture, hoping that hardy frontiersmen "from the Western side of the mountains" might be induced to "bring off the greatest of all traitors." If Arnold could only be delivered dead, the bounty would fall to 2,000 guineas—"in proportion as our satisfaction would be reduced," and "America [would] be deprived of seeing him exhibited as a public spectacle of infamy, and of vengeance." Intelligence received by the British in New York also left no doubt that Arnold was a marked man. Joseph Batty, who had left Rhode Island on February 26, reported that a thousand French troops were due to sail for the Chesapeake with "the first easterly wind." He added: "The conversation in general was that they wanted to take General Arnold, who they seemed to make personally their object." Another informant, who had come through Philadelphia on March 7, had seen the "troops under La Fayette ... go down the river, as they said against Arnold, who [he] was informed was their only object." Months earlier, Arnold's former comrade Eleazer Oswald had remarked that "as a punishment for the enormity of his crimes, the mark of Cain is branded on him in the most indelible characters." It was: "A mark by which 'every one he meeteth shall know him, and slay him.'" This was a harsh creed that Washington was now happy to follow: he instructed Lafayette to "do no act whatever with Arnold that directly or by implication may screen him from the punishment due to his treason and desertion, which if he should fall into your hands, you will execute in the most summary way."[38]

Even before substantial French and American forces began converging to snare him, Arnold had been alerted to the risks he faced. When he first appeared in the James River, the Hessian Captain Ewald reported, Arnold sent a naval officer ashore under a flag of truce, warning the local militia to lay down their arms. The Virginian officer who received the flag wondered whether the general in question was "the traitor Arnold." If so, then any request should be made under the name of the next ranking British officer, "for the American officer would not and could not give up to a traitor." But there was more: the Patriot declared that "if he was to get hold of Arnold, he would hang him up by the heels, according to the orders of Congress." Ewald observed: "The English officer delivered the message word for word, and Arnold was obliged to make a very wry face."[39]

This episode is echoed by an anecdote of Arnold's "military speculations in Virginia" that achieved wide circulation in patriot newspapers. Arnold had taken a captain prisoner and, "after some general conversation," had asked him "what the Americans would do with him if they caught him." At first the officer had evaded an answer, "but upon being repeatedly urged to it, he said, 'Why, Sir, if I must answer your question, you must excuse my telling you the plain truth: if my countrymen should catch you, I believe that they would first cut off that lame leg, which was wounded in the cause of freedom and virtue, and bury it with the honors of war, and afterwards hang the remainder of your body in gibbets.' " In modern renderings, the final phrase is typically given as "on a gibbet"; but "in gibbets" is correct, and conveys a very specific meaning: Arnold would not simply be hanged and decently buried, like Major André, but once dead, his corpse would be encased in a set of "gibbet irons," and then suspended from a gallows until it rotted away. Gibbeting, or "hanging in chains," was as an exemplary punishment reserved for especially heinous crimes. Common in England long before it was officially placed on the statute book in 1752, like other old-country customs it spread to the New World; on both sides of the Atlantic it was used in an unsuccessful effort to deter pirates, and in the American colonies to stigmatize slaves who had poisoned their masters. Faced with such a grim fate, as Captain Ewald noted, even the resolute Arnold became "very restless," and "always carried a pair of small pistols in his pocket as a last resource to escape being hanged."[40]

But Washington was denied the vengeance he craved. In an unusual burst of energy, Admiral Arbuthnot quickly refitted his damaged ships; on March 16, he clashed with Destouches off the Virginia Capes. It was an indecisive engagement, but the French returned to Newport, leaving the British to make for the Chesapeake. The "good old admiral" had saved Arnold; short of provisions, he could not have held out much longer. On March 31, a fleet of transports arrived with 2,200 reinforcements. They were commanded by Major-General Phillips, who had fought against Arnold at Saratoga and now assumed command. By another coincidence, at the battle of Minden in 1759, Phillips had commanded the artillery battery that killed Lafayette's father. Bitterly frustrated, the marquis was obliged to relinquish his efforts to trap Arnold. In conjunction with Phillips, Arnold resumed his energetic campaign to destroy the logistical base of the rebellion in the South. On May 5, the New Englander Benjamin Gilbert had the "mortification" to watch their "formidable army" burn and plunder unopposed along the James River. He complained: "the country appears to be devoted to their services, and it is as hard a matter to find a sincere friend to his country in this part of the state as to find a Tory in the state of Massachusetts Bay." When Phillips died of fever on May 21, Arnold briefly resumed command; but he was soon superseded by General Cornwallis, and by early June was back in New York, reputedly "as rich as a nabob" from the prize money accumulated by plundering Virginia.[41]

Washington was deeply disappointed at the failure of the "enterprise on Arnold," and with good reason. Writing to John Laurens, who was in France to seek fresh financial support, he explained that "a successful blow in that quarter, would, in all probability, have given a decisive turn to our affairs in all the southern states." The venture had involved "considerable expense," and placed Virginia under the inconvenience of calling out its militia. In addition, the setback was regrettable "because the world are disappointed at not seeing Arnold in gibbets." Above all, Washington continued, the failure rankled "because we stood in need of something to keep us afloat ... day does not follow night more certainly, than it brings with it some additional proof of the impracticality of carrying on the war without the aids you were directed to solicit." The commander-in-chief gave his friend a frank assessment of the continuing crisis: "As an honest and candid man ... whose all depends upon the final and happy termination of the present contest ... without a foreign loan our present force, which is but the remnant of an army, cannot be kept together in this campaign, much less will it be increased and in readiness for another." Washington added: "we are at the end of our tether ... now or never our deliverance must come."[42]

* * *

British expectations that Arnold's example would trigger a mass defection among the American rank and file were disappointed, but they continued to hope that his lead would be followed by other jaded patriot generals. They were encouraged in this belief by the canny double spy William Heron, who had now adopted the pseudonym "Hiram." During 1781, he exploited his friendship with the unwitting Major-General Samuel Holden Parsons to create the impression among the British that he, too, was ready to turn his coat. On April 25, Major Oliver De Lancey, who was now Clinton's adjutant-general and head of intelligence, made a memorandum of his conversation with Heron, which shows that the British still believed in cultivating a defector with the ability to win the war. "Hiram" had promised to obtain information from Parsons: "He is to let me know what P——s wish is, how we can serve him, and the methods he means to put out himself." Hiram was to tell Parsons, "he can no way serve us so well as continuing in the army; that the higher his command, the more material service he can render; he is to promise great rewards for any services he may do us." The major elaborated: "He is to hold up the idea of Monk to him, and that we expect from his services an end to the war. That during the time he continues in their army, he shall have a handsome support, and should he be obliged to fly, to remind him of the example and situation of Arnold." Although Parsons did supply Heron with intelligence regarding American troop dispositions, which the artful "Hiram" forwarded to the British to bolster his own credentials, there is no evidence that the general had any idea that he was being touted as another Monck or Arnold. Heron did his best to inflate Parsons' influence and abilities, but he was an undistinguished officer, with none of Arnold's natural flair for leadership.[43]

Meanwhile, Arnold hoped to prove himself on active service as a soldier of the king. He continued to lobby Clinton to assault the Hudson Highlands, and while still in Virginia had joined General Phillips in proposing an attack on Baltimore or Philadelphia; both were weakly defended and beyond reach of Washington's army. Sir Henry was receptive to the plan: as Lord George Germain had criticized his lack of aggression, he needed to demonstrate decisive action; in addition, although Clinton was as skeptical of far-fetched loyalist claims as most British officers, there were indications that a raid into Maryland and Pennsylvania would enjoy solid support from crown sympathizers.[44]

Sir Henry's loyalist advisers included William Rankin. Like Arnold, the Pennsylvania-born Rankin had originally opposed oppressive British policies for the colonies, and sided with those seeking "a redress of grievances." But as an opponent of American independence—"a separation of the two countries which in his opinion would be equally fatal to the welfare of both"—he resolved "to take an active and zealous part in favor of Great

Britain." In spring 1778, after Congress had been driven from Philadelphia to York, Rankin formed an "Association" of 600 loyalist militia, pledged to "engage in any enterprise, however hazardous, to assist in restoring the peace of the Crown." Rankin, who lived near York, proposed to kidnap the members of Congress, and deliver them as prisoners to General William Howe; but "he received for answer that the service proposed could not be carried into execution." Encouraged by the Pennsylvanian Loyalist spokesman Joseph Galloway, Rankin nonetheless worked to expand his network of "Loyal Associates." After Clinton replaced Howe, he communicated with him by "many confidential messengers," and later made the extraordinary claim that he had eventually recruited "upwards of twenty thousand" who were willing to aid the king's troops.[45]

Whatever their real numbers, Rankin's followers were never mobilized. Although detailed plans for a major raid on Philadelphia, to be commanded by Arnold's admirer General Robertson, had been drawn up by early June, the enterprise was abandoned after Cornwallis refused to contribute the requested contingent from his army. From harsh experience, his Lordship had learned to put little faith in promises of zealous loyalist assistance. Explaining his stance to Clinton, he wrote: "I have too often observed, that when a storm threatens, our friends disappear." Instead, Cornwallis committed himself to a campaign in Virginia, and the establishment of a stronger base than Portsmouth, at Yorktown. Following a second conference at Wethersfield, Connecticut, on May 22, 1781, Washington and Rochambeau had agreed to focus their attention on the British forces in and around New York city. Even after he heard that a French fleet from the West Indies under François Joseph Paul, comte de Grasse, would be heading for North America that summer, Washington remained fixated on Manhattan. When Rochambeau's troops joined his own army on the Hudson in early July, New York was still the objective. It was only when de Grasse decided to head for the Chesapeake, where Cornwallis was now dangerously isolated, that Washington and Rochambeau marched south in the operations that would lead to their great victory at Yorktown.[46]

It was partially to stage a diversion aimed at relieving the growing pressure on Cornwallis that Clinton sent Arnold to raid the coast of his native Connecticut. His objective was the leading seaport of New London, a haven for the privateers licensed to attack British shipping. In command of about 1,500 men, Arnold was to impound or destroy the vessels and stores that he found there. His flotilla arrived off the harbor early on September 6; an offshore wind prevented him from landing, but when it suddenly changed, the American privateers in port began to slip away up the Thames River. Arnold split his force in two: his own division disembarked near New London, while Lieutenant-Colonel Edmund Eyre landed on the Groton side. Arnold's first objective, Fort Trumbull, offered little resistance, but its garrison escaped across the river to Fort Griswold; as intelligence suggested that its defenses were weak, Arnold sent orders for Eyre to take possession, so that its guns could be trained on the fleeing shipping.[47]

But when he reached higher ground above New London, Arnold saw that Fort Griswold was far stronger than he had first thought. He sent an officer by boat to countermand the attack. But it was too late. Captain George Beckwith, who was serving as a volunteer, approached under a flag of truce, but his summons to surrender was "peremptorily refused, and the attack commenced." The assault force consisted of the 40th Foot (which had held the Chew House at Germantown in 1777) and the 54th—Major André's old regiment. With high stone walls, numerous cannon, and about 150 determined defenders under the resolute Lieutenant-Colonel William Ledyard, Fort Griswold was a hard nut to crack. The redcoats attacked with fixed bayonets, climbing up onto each other's shoulders in order to reach the embrasures. The garrison used long spears—naval "boarding pikes"—to fend them off. Out of an attacking force of 766 men, 180—including a disproportionate number of officers—were killed or wounded. Having inflicted heavy casualties, the defenders decided to surrender; but they had waited too long, and men who had clawed their way over the bodies of their comrades were disinclined to grant quarter. The defenders were slaughtered: "85 men were found dead in Fort Griswold, and 60 wounded, most of them mortally." Although Arnold had not overseen the assault, as commander of the raid he was held responsible; and when the stores in New London were burned, the explosion of an unsuspected powder magazine and a change of wind spread the flames, so that part of the town was "unfortunately destroyed." To outraged Patriots, the vindictive Arnold had acted in character: besides massacring the gallant defenders of Fort Griswold, he had wantonly torched New London, just miles from his Norwich birthplace. Bloody and fiery, the New London raid was a suitably controversial end to Arnold's Revolutionary War career.[48]

* * *

Arnold's foray to Connecticut did nothing to relax Washington's grip on Cornwallis, who was obliged to capitulate on October 19, 1781. For the British, Yorktown was a disaster to rank alongside Burgoyne's defeat at Saratoga. Yet Benedict Arnold still believed that the war could be won for King George. He had staked everything on that outcome, and was determined to do his utmost to achieve it. In November, he secured Sir Henry Clinton's permission to leave for England. There, as his adviser William Smith put it, he would promote "all measures of vigor" and the "practicability of restoring the King's interest in this country." On December 15, he and Cornwallis sailed from New York aboard the *Robust* man-of-war, as part of a fleet strong enough to fend off interception. Peggy Arnold went, too, in a more comfortably appointed vessel. Meeting an understandably frosty reception in Philadelphia following the exposure of her husband's plot, she had soon joined him in New York; besides the infant Edward, they now had another son, born on August 28, 1781, and named James Robertson, after Arnold's benefactor, the old Scottish general.[49]

After a stormy winter voyage, the Arnolds arrived in London, unsure of what awaited them. Exhaustive newspaper coverage of the trial and execution of Major André had been accompanied by some far less flattering character sketches of his collaborator, General Arnold, and this had influenced opinion, especially among critics of the war. Back in November 1780, the prolific man of letters Horace Walpole had written that Arnold's treachery "had cost the life of a much better man." In February 1782, he noted the arrival in the capital of Cornwallis, "and that man of wretched fame, Arnold." Walpole, like the Hessian Captain Ewald, disapproved of Arnold's betrayal of his comrades; but other, more influential, figures were keen to recognize a celebrated rebel who had now returned to his true allegiance. Arnold was introduced at court on the arm of one of his former enemies, General Sir Guy Carleton, while Lord George Germain, who had received extremely favorable reports of his abilities, treated him with conspicuous respect. Crucially, the king himself was most sympathetic and attentive, while Queen Charlotte showed equal favor to the poised and elegant Peggy Arnold. Like true Americans, neither of them was intimidated by royalty. As Clinton's informant John Bull reported, "they both seemed quite at home when they were presented" at St. James's Palace. In Paris, Benjamin Franklin had heard "much of the audiences given" to Arnold, "and of his being present at councils." Franklin scoffed: "He seems to mix as naturally with that polluted court as pitch with tar."[50]

George III believed that Benedict Arnold was a man worth listening to. At the king's request, he compiled a detailed paper, entitled "Thoughts on the American War." It is possible that this incorporated notes that William Smith had given him in December to help answer "questions that may be put to him." This document maintained that, even after seven years of conflict, "a great majority of the Americans" remained opposed to a separation from Great Britain. Of course, if this was true, then it was natural to ask why the royal generals had not proved more successful in harnessing loyalist support. Rather than engage in the "tedious and invidious task" of remarking "upon the inactivity and misdirection of the King's arms," Arnold had his own proposals for exploiting "the friends of the Restoration." Wherever the crown forces made headway in subduing the "usurpation," it would be vital to establish a civil government: this was preferable to military rule, imposed by an army whose indiscriminate plundering alienated friend and foe alike. Without that first step, he argued, "the Loyalists in general" would not be willing or able to "give any essential assistance to the Royal Arms." Perhaps surprisingly, Arnold advocated moderation: any "restored legislature" would only injure the "conciliatory designs of the Crown," if it showed "too vindictive a spirit." With Congress so weak, and the departure of most of the French forces leaving the rebels as helpless to "undertake any enterprise" as before their arrival, the time was ripe for a negotiated settlement. Arnold considered a new peace commission to be "indispensably necessary," and felt it should be composed of statesmen, rather than soldiers. Alongside talk, there remained the option of force: Arnold believed that by "the complete detachment of Vermont from the rebel interest," and the reduction of that perennial objective, the Hudson Highlands, "early in the spring," much might be expected from another military campaign.[51]

But the proposals put forward by Arnold, which were as viable as any that had gone before, were now several years too late; once again, he had been overtaken by realities that he stubbornly refused to recognize. A decade later, Arnold claimed that the commander-in-chief Lord Amherst, the mentor of his good friend General Robertson, had signified the king's pleasure that he should immediately return to New York, whereupon he would be promoted to major-general. "I informed his Lordship that I was

ready to embark at the shortest notice, and for some time waited in expectation of a frigate being provided to carry me out," he recalled, only to be
detained in England "by order of Lord Shelburne."[52]

Recently appointed as prime minister, William Petty, earl of Shelburne,
was more interested in negotiating a favorable peace settlement than
prolonging a costly and unpopular war: Arnold had missed his chance of
leading a fresh campaign to reunite the empire. By 1782, there was no realistic prospect of denying American independence. Instead of fresh initia-
tives to subdue rebellion, 1783 brought British recognition of a sovereign
United States of America. For Benedict Arnold, and for thousands more
Americans who had actively opposed that outcome and were now exiles
from their homeland, there remained the question of securing compensation from the Crown. In 1784, the American Loyalist Claims Commission
began the herculean task of assessing Britain's financial obligations to
"memorialists" now scattered from the shires of England to the islands of
Nova Scotia. They included William Rankin, who had looked in vain for a
chance to mobilize his underground army of loyal Pennsylvanians; Joshua
Hett Smith, who had been acquitted of complicity in Arnold's treason after
a lengthy trial, and had then fled to British New York from fresh patriot
charges that he was a danger to the state; and Colonel Beverly Robinson,
whose "particular services and unwearied exertions . . . in His Majesty's
cause" had led not only to the confiscation of "his real and personal estate,"
but also to his conviction for high treason against the state of New York. In
support of Robinson's application, Sir Henry Clinton had observed that his
"zealous and active services rendered him very obnoxious to the enemy,
insomuch that of all other men he is, perhaps, the least likely to receive any
favor now at their hands."[53]

But there was one man on whom the new American republic would
look even less kindly. In March 1784, Benedict Arnold, "late of the Province
of Pennsylvania in America, and now of the city of London," submitted his
own lengthy memorial to the commissioners. Arnold acknowledged the
£6,000 that he had received from Sir Henry Clinton in October 1780 "on
account of his losses, risks, and services rendered government," but hoped
for some further compensation, reflecting the sacrifices he had made in
consequence of "his loyalty to His Majesty and his attachment to the British
government." Arnold humbly prayed that the honorable board would take
his case into consideration, as he and his family had been "banished

America," while his own "decided conduct precluded a possibility of their return."[54]

Arnold's application traced his remarkable personal journey from staunch opponent of "unjust" British claims on America, to a realization that "the rulers of his countrymen were blind to their real interests," and his subsequent decision to employ "every means in his power" to thwart a separation from Great Britain. Then came the West Point plan, "which, had it succeeded, would in all probability have put a favorable end to the war in America." However, "by the most unfortunate circumstances it having failed, the memorialist was in the most imminent danger of losing his life, was obliged to make a precipitate flight, and very narrowly escaped from the Americans." All that was accurate enough, but Arnold's "true account" of his losses was more economical with the facts. At a "moderate computation," he reckoned that his real and personal property forfeited in Connecticut and Pennsylvania amounted to £16,125. Among his claims was £5,000 for Mount Pleasant—although he glossed over the fact that his father-in-law, Edward Shippen, had already bought back the confiscated estate on his behalf. He also maintained that Congress had promised him land worth £5,000, and that his half-pay pension as a wounded officer, commuted to ten years' full pay, amounted to another £4,500. His most extraordinary claim was that his prior "engagements with Sir Henry Clinton" led him to refuse Washington's offer to command the rebels' Southern Army, an assignment that went instead to Nathanael Greene, who, Arnold reported, received £20,000 from Virginia and the Carolinas in reward for his labors. This was a gross distortion of reality: Arnold was never offered the southern command, and Greene did not receive anything like the sum mentioned (and what he did obtain was also intended to support his troops). Some of the confiscated property for which Arnold sought compensation is revealing of his lavish lifestyle in Philadelphia, and his broad interests: there was a pair of horses, for which he had refused £200; a carriage, "almost new," worth £100; "books, electrical machine, microscope, etc." with china and glass valued at £200; and "a valuable Negro man-slave, 22 years old," price £100.

A year later, after making no headway with the commissioners, Arnold had a change of heart and withdrew his claim. For a man so often accused of avarice, this is a puzzling step; but Arnold justified it on the grounds that he had already "in a great measure" received compensation from Sir Henry Clinton for the loss of his personal estate, while Mrs. Arnold had an annual pension for life, of about £360. While all of this was not a full compensation for lost real estate, risks run, and services rendered, because of the expense of staying in London to prosecute his claim, he had requested that his documents be returned.[55]

Peggy Arnold's pension is a more revealing document than a first reading suggests. Amounting to £500 before fees, the annuity was authorized at the court of St. James on March 19, 1782, and was a personal award from King George III. It was made "unto Margaret Arnold, wife of our trusty and well beloved Brigadier General Benedict Arnold," but it recognized Peggy's personal contribution to the royal cause. As Sir Henry Clinton testified, in her own right she had rendered "very meritorious" services. Her husband was more specific, and his statements surely remove any lingering doubt that she was heavily involved in forwarding the treasonable correspondence of 1779–80. In 1792, when outlining his circumstances to Prime Minister William Pitt the Younger, Arnold explained: "On my first arrival in England I applied to Lord North for some provision for Mrs. Arnold (in consequence of her sufferings and the imminent danger she had experienced) when His Majesty was graciously pleased to grant her the pension that she now enjoys." He had already made it clear that Peggy's pension could not be considered as any compensation for *him*, "as it was expressly given in consideration of the sufferings she endured, the hazards she run [*sic*], and her being banished from her friends, and country in consequence of her loyalty."[56]

As Arnold explained in 1792, when he revived the subject of his "losses and claims on government," after withdrawing his memorial to the commissioners he had spent six years in various "exertions in business," by which he hoped to provide for his family and remove the need for future applications. During that time, he had pursued trading ventures among the loyalist communities of New Brunswick, but had proved both unpopular and unsuccessful. For Arnold, the life of a merchant skipper and trader was a poor substitute for his enduring dreams of military glory. Arnold's real gift was for soldiering, and even some of his former comrades in the Continental Army remained fiercely protective of his fighting reputation. Several years after the treason, Arnold's old friend Colonel Lamb dined at General Putnam's headquarters, along with an officer who had served as a brigadier under Horatio Gates at Saratoga. When Arnold's name was mentioned, the company readily drank "confusion to the traitor." Lamb had "remarked that it was a pity so good a soldier, and a man of such consummate courage, should become so despicable a villain." At this, "Gen. G"—who may have been John Glover—questioned whether Arnold had ever given "proof of such quality." When Lamb cited his personal experience of Arnold's exploits at Quebec and Compo Hill, and mentioned "the storming of the German entrenchments" on October 7, 1777, they were dismissed as "mere Dutch courage," imbibed from the rum bottle. Lamb's response was withering: "let me tell you, that drunk or sober, *you* will never be an Arnold, or fit to compare with him in any military capacity." As tempers flared, and with them the prospect of a "meeting" to satisfy honor, "Old Put" swiftly calmed the situation by proposing Washington's health in a well-filled "brimmer."[57]

Ironically, Arnold's hopes of a renewed military career in British service were blighted by his decision to uphold King George; a man who had turned his coat once might do so again. That harsh reality had been spelled out in 1784, when he sought an appointment with the East India Company, whose troops were safeguarding and expanding the largest remnant of Britain's drastically truncated overseas empire. Such a posting to the far-flung subcontinent could have recast his prospects on an upward trajectory, and provided ample scope to acquire both glory and booty. Arnold's charismatic leadership and willingness to take on the heaviest odds were exactly the qualities needed to inspire the heavily outnumbered soldiers of "John Company" as they faced the massive armies of local rulers like the implacable Tipu Sultan, the "Tiger of Mysore." Heading a force that was largely composed of local sepoys who knew nothing of his American past, he might have rivalled the fame and fortune gained a generation earlier by the former East India Company clerk, Robert Clive. But "Arnold of India" was not to be. Rejecting Arnold's request as tactfully as he could, George Johnstone, the former Carlisle Commissioner who was now a director of the Company, made a telling argument in justification of his decision: "Under an unsuccessful insurrection all actors are rebels: crowned with success they become immortal patriots. A fortunate plot holds you up as the savior of nations, a premature discovery brings you to the scaffold, or brands your fame with dark and doubtful suspicions." Johnstone, who had brazenly proffered a bribe to Joseph Reed in 1778, cited Arnold's own role model General George Monck as an example of the "best men from the best motives obliged to change sides." His lecture on ethics continued:

It is inglorious in a great mind, who has taken a leading part, to retire until the scene is settled, and in the multiple difficulties in which the most virtuous may be environed, he must trust his conscience for the rectitude of his conduct and appeal to the honor of his life to prove that the general good was his motive . . .

In seeking Johnstone's patronage, Arnold had emphasized that his actions during the war between Britain and America had been driven by a desire "of rendering the most essential service to both countries by bringing about a reunion." But while Johnstone was satisfied with the "purity" of Arnold's conduct, "the great vulgar herd" thought otherwise. However blunt, such reasoning was irrefutable. George Washington had been a rebel, but after leading his countrymen in a *successful* war of independence, his reputation was unassailable; he was now lauded as a triumphant hero, not condemned as a misguided traitor. By contrast, Benedict Arnold had picked the losing side. His plot had failed, and irrespective of his underlying motives, posterity would judge him accordingly.[58]

In the spring of 1792, after his return from New Brunswick, Arnold reminded William Pitt that he had frequently "urged to be employed in any service, however difficult or hazardous," but without success, even though "many junior officers (with more interest, but perhaps less zeal for the service) have been promoted, and reaped the advantages of being employed, when I have been totally neglected." That summer, Arnold once again tendered his services to "the British armies in India." As the expansion of British territory on the subcontinent would require "a sufficient body of cavalry," Arnold, who was a skilled horseman, hoped that his "poor abilities" would be worthy of acceptance. As usual, this latest offer was ignored. In December, Arnold tried another ploy, asking Pitt to propose him to fill the vacant governorship of Dominica: it was a post for which he believed himself well qualified, having "braved every danger in the service of the public," and being "well acquainted in the West Indies." But there was still no place for him.[59]

When he persistently sought Pitt's patronage, Arnold was struggling to "educate, and provide for a numerous family of children." As he reminded Sir Henry Clinton, who gladly supported his claims, he was dependent on his half-pay as a colonel: that pension, and his wife's, only lasted during their own lifetimes, and on their deaths, their four youngest children might be left "totally destitute." In his appeals to Pitt, Arnold harked back to his service in the long-lost American war; since then, "the decided part" he had taken in favor of the British government had subjected him to "the most unmerited and mortifying abuse, not only from my own countrymen, but from many persons in England." Previously, Arnold had attributed such "illiberal" slurs to the prevailing misconception that his conduct in America was influenced by "mercenary" rather than "just" motives, and treated them with the contempt they deserved; should it prove "necessary to appeal to the public" in his justification, he hoped that Clinton would confirm that he had always "acted from principle," and that his conduct was "perfectly disinterested." Soon after he wrote to Pitt, Arnold was obliged to defend his reputation against aspersions cast by James Maitland, earl of Lauderdale. Arnold issued a challenge to a duel, and a meeting was fixed for Kilburn Wells on July 1, 1792. Lord Edward Hawke, whom Peggy Arnold characterized as "a most respectable peer and our particular friend," was Arnold's second. Lauderdale was seconded by the celebrated Whig politician, Charles James Fox. When Fox signaled, Arnold fired his pistol, but missed; Lauderdale stubbornly refused to return the shot. Eventually, he conceded that he had never intended to injure Arnold's character, which was accepted as an apology. Honor was satisfied, and Peggy, who had been sick with worry, was delighted to "find the General's conduct so much applauded." If, twelve years after he had attracted opprobrium for turning his coat, Arnold still believed such attacks on his character to be "unmerited," and worth rebuffing on the dueling field, it was surely because *he* considered that his actions had been honorable all along.[60]

Arnold's repeated approaches to Pitt that year may have fallen on deaf ears because the prime minister was increasingly preoccupied with the prospect of war with revolutionary France. The upheavals that brought down the old regime and cost Louis XVI his head were in large part a consequence of the vast debts France had amassed in helping the American rebels to gain their independence; and King Louis and his ministers had been prompted to provide direct military assistance as a result of Burgoyne's surrender at Saratoga, an event which Arnold had done much to bring about. When a fresh French war erupted in 1793, Arnold took the risky decision to buy a ship and follow his old trade in the West Indies, which once again became a zone of conflict. While awaiting his vessel at the Cornish port of Falmouth, Arnold chanced to meet the French diplomat Charles Maurice de Talleyrand, who was bound for America. Years later, Talleyrand retained a vivid memory of their "rather striking" encounter. Hearing that an American general was a fellow lodger, he asked his innkeeper for an introduction. The soldier evaded the politician's questions, and when asked for letters of introduction to his countrymen, blankly refused. After some minutes, he explained why: "I am perhaps the only American who cannot give you letters for his own country." Talleyrand remembered: "He dared not tell me his name. It was General Arnold." The Frenchman's recollection chimes with a bleak assessment that Arnold had recently sent to Pitt. "I am totally precluded from returning to America, which most other Loyalists may do," he had written. Talleyrand was a guileful survivor, with a knack for ingratiating himself with the winners; but even he was moved by Arnold's plight. He felt obliged to "confess that I felt much pity for him, for which political puritans will perhaps blame me, but with which I do not reproach myself, for I witnessed his agony."[61]

When Arnold finally reached Guadeloupe, he revealed flashes of his old character. The island had been captured in May 1794 by British troops under the Revolutionary War veteran Lieutenant-General Sir Charles Grey, whose tactics exploited the bayonet charges that had proved so brutally effective against the American rebels. But the French soon counter-attacked, and Arnold was trapped in the port of Pointe-à-Pitre when it fell to republican forces. Adopting Major André's alias of "Anderson," he initially posed as a neutral American seeking a cargo, but was soon apprehended and imprisoned aboard a ship in the harbor. When a sympathetic sentry revealed that he was destined for the guillotine, which had already decapitated scores of local royalists, Arnold contrived a "masterly" escape. After lowering his clothes and valuables inside a cask, he used a crude raft to reach a canoe, in which he paddled past the French guard boats at the harbor mouth, and then "pushed for the British fleet." According to the expedition's historian Cooper Willyams, who was chaplain of HMS *Boyne*, "the celebrated Brigadier-General Arnold" came aboard in the early hours of June 30, 1794. Reporting Arnold's close shave with the "republican razor," a correspondent to the *Gentleman's Magazine* noted that "a similar presence of mind saved him when he deserted the American cause." Arnold promptly attached himself to General Grey, and with "amazing assurance" requested to serve under him as senior brigadier, on the strength of his old British army rank. Such presumption irritated Grey, who may have nursed a lingering resentment at Arnold's ill-fated involvement with his lamented aide-de-camp, Major André. Yet it was later reported that Arnold rendered Grey "great services"; although not specified in the general's official dispatches, these were significant enough to be recognized in a resolution of thanks from the "Standing Committee of the West India Planters and Merchants." On August 1, 1795, the members expressed their obligations for his actions, taken at the commander-in-chief's request, "which were attended with such beneficial effects, in covering the retreat of the troops at Guadeloupe." It was a tribute that Arnold considered "highly gratifying." His "very gallant and meritorious service at Guadeloupe" also brought more concrete rewards: in 1798, King George granted him and his family 13,400 acres of crown land in Upper Canada. John Graves Simcoe, who had served as the territory's first lieutenant-governor, and who remembered Arnold's "great personal kindness and civility" during their Virginian service, had readily backed the award "in his hour of distress."[62]

Ground down by sickness and disappointment, Benedict Arnold died on June 14, 1801, aged sixty. Within three years, Peggy succumbed to cancer of the womb, comforted in the knowledge that her children and stepchildren had all been provided for. According to an anecdote recorded by Arnold's first sympathetic biographer, as "death drew near" and "his mind wandered," he pleaded to be dressed in his "old American uniform," in which he had won his battles and his fame. When this last request was met, he is said to have uttered: "God forgive me for ever putting on any other." Based as it is on unverified "tradition," there is no way of telling whether the story is genuine, or simply reflects a hope that even the arch-traitor Benedict Arnold might have expressed contrition for his misdeeds, and sought some belated redemption.[63]

It is certainly likely that Arnold kept the uniform in which he had escaped to the *Vulture* on the afternoon of September 25, 1780, complete with the epaulettes and sword-knots that Washington had presented to him as a signal mark of honor two years before, at the height of his fame; as he expected to welcome the commander-in-chief to the Robinson House that day, he would surely have dressed appropriately. Arnold may even have called for his old uniform on his deathbed; it was in the Continental Army that he had established his reputation as an outstanding soldier, and there's nothing to suggest that he ever lost his admiration for Washington and his old comrades, or his love for his native country.

But it is hard to credit that Arnold would ever have asked forgiveness for abandoning the cause of American liberty. Such an act would have betrayed the unswerving, egoistical self-belief that had always governed his behavior. By his own lights at least, in turning his coat from Continental blue to British scarlet, Benedict Arnold had acted from the very best of reasons; for the rest of his life, he never deviated from the justifications that he had first given to Sir Henry Clinton in May 1779. While Arnold surely regretted his failure to achieve his great ambitions, and to win fame, honor, and wealth as the visionary soldier whose bold action had ended a futile civil war and reunited the fractured British Empire, an individual so strongly convinced of his own "rectitude" could never have acknowledged himself wrong all along. For a man who did "nothing by halves," regret was one thing, remorse quite another.

NOTES

Abbreviations used in the notes

AA	*American Archives*, ed. Peter Force, 4–5th Series, 9 vols. (Washington, DC, 1837–53)
AO	Audit Office Papers, National Archives, Kew, London
CL	William L. Clements Library, University of Michigan, Ann Arbor
CP	Henry Clinton Papers, William L. Clements Library, University of Michigan, Ann Arbor
FO	Founders Online (Early Access Documents), National Archives, Washington, DC, http://founders.archives.gov/
GLC	Gilder Lehrman Collection, New-York Historical Society, New York
GWP	George Washington Papers (Series 4: General Correspondence), Library of Congress, Washington, DC
JCC	*Journals of the Continental Congress, 1774–1789*, ed. Worthington C. Ford et al., 34 vols. (Washington, DC, 1904–37)
LDC	*Letters of Delegates to Congress, 1774–1789*, ed. Paul H. Smith et al., 26 vols. (Washington, DC, 1976–2000)
MSS	manuscripts
NA	National Archives, Kew, London
NDAR	*Naval Documents of the American Revolution*, ed. William Bell Clark, William James Morgan, et al., 11 vols. to date (Washington, DC, 1964–)
N-YHS	New-York Historical Society, New York
NYPL	New York Public Library, New York
PCC	Papers of the Continental Congress, National Archives, Washington, DC
PMHB	*Pennsylvania Magazine of History and Biography*
PRO 30/8	Chatham Papers, National Archives, Kew, London
PRO 30/55	Carleton Papers, National Archives, Kew, London
PWRW	*Papers of Washington, Revolutionary War Series*, ed. Philander D. Chase et al., 24 vols. to date (Charlottesville, 1985–)
WMQ	*William and Mary Quarterly* (3rd Series)
WW	*The Writings of George Washington from the Original Manuscript Sources, 1745–1799*, ed. John C. Fitzpatrick, 39 vols. (Washington, DC, 1931–44)

Introduction

1. Greene to Washington, West Point, July 27, 1779, in Richard K. Showman (ed.), *The Papers of General Nathanael Greene*, 12 vols. (University of North Carolina Press, Chapel Hill, NC, 1976–2002), IV, p. 271. **In all quotations, eighteenth-century spellings, capitalizations, and abbreviations have been modernized.**

2. George Clinton to Parsons, Poughkeepsie, NY, March 26, 1778, in S. Hall (ed.), *Life and Letters of Samuel Holden Parsons* (Binghamton, NY, 1905), p. 161.
3. Marquis de Chastellux, *Travels in North America in the Years 1780, 1781, and 1782*, ed. Howard C. Rice, Jr., 2 vols. (University of North Carolina Press, Chapel Hill, NC, 1963; first English edition published London, 1787), I, p. 89 (entry for November 21, 1780).
4. Hoffman Nickerson, *The Turning Point of the Revolution: or, Burgoyne in America* (Houghton Mifflin, Boston, 1928), pp. 334–5; Evelyn M. Acomb (ed.), *The Revolutionary Journal of Baron Ludwig von Closen, 1780–83* (Institute of Early American History and Culture, Williamsburg, VA, 1958), p. 60; James Thacher, *A Military Journal During the Revolutionary War from 1775 to 1783* (Cottons and Barnard, Boston, 1827), pp. 131–2 (June 10–12, 1778).
5. William Abbatt (ed.), *Memoirs of Major-General William Heath* (New York, 1901; first ed., Boston, 1798), p. 271; Acomb, *Journal of von Closen*, p. 60.
6. Thacher, *Military Journal*, p. 211.
7. Chastellux, *Travels*, I, p. 91; "General orders," Peekskill, NY, August 3, 1780, in *WW*, XIX, p. 313.
8. Washington to Arnold and to Schuyler, Cambridge, MA, December 5, 1775, *PWRW*, II, pp. 493, 498.
9. Washington to Pierre Penet, Valley Forge, April 30, 1778, *PWRW*, XIV, p. 684; Washington to Arnold, Valley Forge, May 7, 1778, in *WW*, XI, pp. 359–60.
10. Dave Richard Palmer, *The River and the Rock: The history of Fortress West Point, 1775–1783* (Greenwood Publishing Corporation, New York, 1969), pp. 164–5; Burgoyne to Sir Henry Clinton, Albany, October 25, 1777, CP, Vol. 25/file 36.
11. Charles Royster, *A Revolutionary People at War: The Continental Army and American character, 1775–1783* (University of North Carolina Press, Chapel Hill, NC, 1979), p. 284.
12. "General orders," Peekskill, August 1, 1780, in *WW*, XIX, p. 302; "Extract from a diary kept by Mr. [Tobias] Lear at Mount Vernon, in 1786" (entry for October 23), in Richard Rush, *Occasional Productions, Political, Diplomatic and Miscellaneous* (J.P. Lippincott & Co., Philadelphia, 1860), p. 80.
13. Rush, *Occasional Productions*, p. 81; Nathanael Greene to Governor William Greene of Rhode Island, Camp at Tappan, NY, October 2, 1780, in Showman, *Papers of Greene*, VI, p. 328.
14. "General Greene's orders," Headquarters, September 26, 1780, ibid., p. 314.
15. Gilbert to his parents, Orange Town [Tappan], October 6, 1780, in CL, "Benjamin Gilbert Letter Book." On the impact of Greene's orders, see John A. Ruddiman, "'A record in the hands of thousands': Power and negotiation in the orderly books of the Continental Army," *WMQ*, LXVII, 4 (October 2010), pp. 747–74; 762.
16. Edward Field (ed.), *Diary of Colonel Israel Angell, Commanding the Second Rhode Island Continental Regiment during the American Revolution, 1778–1781* (Preston and Rounds Company, Providence, RI, 1899), p. 123; Thacher, *Military Journal*, p. 210.
17. *Norwich Packet*, October 17, 1780; Russell to Lieutenant Jasper Mead, Camp Tappan, September 30, 1780, CL, Miscellaneous Collections.
18. Pendleton to James Madison, [Edmundsbury, VA], October 17, 1780, GLC, MSS 00099-050.
19. Greene to Catherine Greene, Tappan, September 29, 1780, and to Governor William Greene, Tappan, October 2, 1780, in Showman, *Papers of Greene*, VI, pp. 321, 330.
20. Chastellux, *Travels*, I, p. 91.
21. Cited in "Memoir of the author," in *Simcoe's Military Journal: A history of the operations of a partisan corps, called the Queen's Rangers, commanded by Lieut. Col. J.G. Simcoe, during the War of the American Revolution* (Bartlett & Welford, New York, 1844), pp. ix–x.
22. William Renwick Riddle, *The Life of John Graves Simcoe: First lieutenant-governor of the Province of Upper Canada, 1792–96* (McClelland and Stewart, Toronto, 1926), pp. 82–4.
23. Chastellux, *Travels*, II, pp. 378–9.
24. John Graves Simcoe, *A Journal of the Operations of the Queen's Rangers* (printed for the author, Exeter, 1787), p. 234; see also Lafayette to Nathanael Greene, Tyre's Plantation, June 27, 1781, in Banastre Tarleton, *A History of the Campaigns of 1780 and 1781, in the Southern Provinces of North America* (London, 1787), p. 347; Henry Phelps Johnston, *The Yorktown Campaign and the Surrender of Cornwallis 1781* (Harper & Brothers, New York, 1881), pp. 55–6.
25. Simcoe's letter to Chastellux, dated 20 January, *The Gentleman's Magazine*, 1787 (January), pp. 36–9.
26. Anon [John Graves Simcoe], *Remarks on the Travels of the Marquis de Chastellux* (London, 1787).
27. Simcoe, *Journal of the Operations of the Queen's Rangers*, p. 102.
28. Simcoe, *Remarks*, pp. 50, 53.
29. Ibid., p. 50.
30. Carl Van Doren, *A Secret History of the American Revolution* (Viking, New York, 1941).
31. On the American legacies of British victory in the Seven Years' War, see Colin G. Calloway, *The Scratch of a Pen: 1763 and the transformation of North America* (Oxford University Press, New York, 2007).

32. For the estimated breakdown of Patriots, Loyalists, and neutrals, see Alan Taylor, *American Revolutions: A continental history, 1750–1804* (W.W. Norton & Company, New York, 2016), p. 212. On the role of the Continental Army as a factor behind the growth of American national identity, see Stephen Conway, *The War of American Independence* (Edward Arnold, London, 1992), pp. 174–5.

33. Otis quoted in Thacher, *Military Journal*, p. 17; "An Officer of the Army," *The History of the Civil War in America* (London, 1780). Authorship of this perceptive but little-used book has been tentatively assigned to Captain William Hall of the 28th Foot.

34. Johann Ewald, *Diary of the American War: A Hessian journal*, ed. Joseph P. Tustin (Yale University Press, New Haven, CT, 1979), p. 309.

35. The Royal Proclamation of Rebellion is given in Peter D.G. Thomas, *Revolution in America: Britain and the colonies, 1763–1776* (University of Wales Press, Cardiff, 1992), pp. 86–7; Washington to Gage, Cambridge, August 11, 1775, and Gage to Washington, Boston, August 13, 1775, *PWRW*, I, pp. 289, 301; Henry J. Young, "Treason and its punishment in revolutionary Pennsylvania," *PMHB*, XC, 3 (July 1966), pp. 287–313, 287–8.

Chapter One

1. "Some interesting particulars relative to General Arnold," *The British Mercury and Evening Advertiser* [London], November 28, 1780; Isaac N. Arnold, *The Life of Benedict Arnold: His patriotism and treason* (Jansen, McClurg, and Company, Chicago, 1880), p. 18.

2. For Arnold's pride in his ancestry, see Joshua Hett Smith, *An Authentic Narrative of the Causes Which Led to the Death of Major André* (Mathews and Leigh, London, 1808), p. 169. Joshua Smith was Arnold's emissary to André during the climax of his conspiracy to betray West Point, and as an attempt to absolve himself from blame for the major's death, his *Narrative* must be treated with caution when dealing with the treason. However, it includes unique material, such as Smith's recollections of his conversations with Arnold, that merits close attention.

3. Arnold, *Life of Arnold*, p. 18.

4. Willard M. Wallace, *Traitorous Hero, The Life and Fortunes of Benedict Arnold* (Harper and Brothers, New York, 1954), pp. 7–8.

5. "Extract of a letter from a gentleman, dated Tappan, October 2, 1780," in *Boston Gazette*, October 16, 1780; Jared Sparks, *The Life and Treason of Benedict Arnold* (first ed., Boston, 1835; Harper & Brothers, New York, 1865), pp. 5–6; Arnold, *Life of Arnold*, p. 22.

6. Arnold, *Life of Arnold*, p. 26.

7. On the strong possibility of Arnold's militia service in 1757, see James Thomas Flexner, *The Traitor and the Spy: Benedict Arnold and John André* (Harcourt, Brace, and Company, New York, 1953), pp. 8–9.

8. For acceptance of the desertion stories, see, for example, Wallace, *Traitorous Hero*, pp. 11–13; Willard Sterne Randall, *Benedict Arnold: Patriot and traitor* (William Morrow & Co., New York, 1990), pp. 32–4; Van Doren, *Secret History*, p. 145. For the contrary view, see Flexner, *Traitor and Spy*, p. 410; James Kirby Martin, *Benedict Arnold, Revolutionary Hero: An American warrior reconsidered* (New York University Press, New York, 1997), pp. 27–9, 444–5, notes 41–5.

9. *PMHB*, XXII, 1 (1898), pp. 124–5.

10. "Genuine history of Gen. Arnold, by an old acquaintance," *The Political Magazine*, I (1780), p. 690; see also Joshua Hett Smith's recollection of his conversation with Arnold in 1780, in his *Authentic Narrative*, p. 167.

11. The sign survives in the collections of the New Haven Colony Historical Society.

12. Arnold's conversation of 1780, as reported in Smith, *Authentic Narrative*, p. 167.

13. Wallace, *Traitorous Hero*, p. 26; "Genuine history of Gen. Arnold," p. 690.

14. Chastellux, *Travels*, I, December 22, 1780, pp. 193–4.

15. See Arnold, *Life of Arnold*, p. 29; Parkhurst, in John C. Dann (ed.), *The Revolution Remembered: Eyewitness accounts of the War for Independence* (University of Chicago Press, Chicago, 1980), p. 57; Ewald, *Diary of the American War*, p. 295. Another telling reason against identifying the "Benidick Arnold" listed on the New York provincial muster rolls in 1760 as the future general is his given height of five feet nine inches, which was tall for the era.

16. Gordon S. Wood, *Empire of Liberty: A history of the early republic, 1789–1815* (Oxford University Press, New York, 2009), pp. 50–1.

17. For the seduction story, see "Some account of Benedict Arnold, brigadier-general in the British army," *European Magazine and London Review for 1783* (February), pp. 83–5. While plagiarizing much of the "Genuine history" published in 1780, this essay also includes other details.

18. On the integration of dueling within the political system, see Joanne B. Freeman, *Affairs of Honor: National politics in the new republic* (Yale University Press, New Haven, CT, 2001).

19. The details were given to biographer Isaac Arnold by Thomas Waterman, from the family of Arnold's mother, Hannah Waterman. See *Life of Arnold*, pp. 30–2.
20. For Arnold's account of the Boles episode, see his letter in *Connecticut Gazette*, February 14, 1766; also, Lawrence Henry Gipson, *American Loyalist: Jared Ingersoll* (Yale University Press, New Haven, CT, 1920), pp. 233–6.
21. See "Written complaint lodged with the New Haven Custom House by Rutherford Cooke and Caleb Comstock, New Haven, 5 February 1767," manuscript letter offered for sale by William Reese Company, New Haven, CT, March 2017.
22. Arnold to B. Douglas Esq., New Haven, from "St. George's Key," June 9, 1770, *Historical Magazine, with Notes and Queries*, I (April 1857), p. 119.
23. See Arnold to Margaret Arnold, St. Croix, July 25, 1768, GLC, MSS 03301.
24. Arnold to Margaret Arnold, [West Indies], January 21, 1774, *The Magazine of History, with Notes and Queries*, III (April 1906), p. 259.
25. For gossipy anecdotes, see "Genuine history of Gen. Arnold," p. 690; balanced discussions are in Wallace, *Traitorous Hero*, pp. 28–9, and Martin, *Benedict Arnold, Revolutionary Hero*, p. 52. Professor Martin speculates that Arnold's pleas for letters from his wife may have been a coping mechanism for his feelings of guilt at such conduct.
26. Wadsworth's comment was passed on to Benjamin Tallmadge by Timothy Pickering in 1822. See Henry Phelps Johnston (ed.), *Memoirs of Colonel Benjamin Tallmadge* (Gillis Press, New York, 1904), pp. 135–6.
27. On the creditors led by Corbyn, see the detailed descriptions and extracts given in "Archive of letters relating to the early business endeavors (and disreputable conduct therein) of Benedict Arnold," offered for sale in March 2017 by William Reese Company, New Haven, CT. Photocopies of the documents are in the British Library, London (RP 9607). For background, see Martin, *Benedict Arnold, Revolutionary Hero*, pp. 46–7; Wallace, *Traitorous Hero*, pp. 23–4; also, "Genuine history of Gen. Arnold," p. 690.
28. Arnold's letters to Remsen cited in Martin, *Benedict Arnold, Revolutionary Hero*, p. 48.
29. Smith, *Authentic Narrative*, p. 167; "Genuine history of Gen. Arnold," p. 690; Miller's "declaration," dated London, March 5, 1784, was made in support of Arnold's "Memorial" to the American Loyalist Claims Commission, outlining his grounds for compensation. See AO, 13/96A, fols. 75–80; *Proceedings of a General Court Martial for the Trial of Major-General Arnold* (Francis Bailey, Philadelphia, 1780; reprinted in a private edition, New York, 1865), p. 102.
30. The most detailed account of the episode was written by Samuel Peters himself, in his *General History of Connecticut* (originally published 1781), pp. 262–9; the same episode is highlighted in the "Genuine history of Gen. Arnold," which suggests that Peters is the author of that prejudiced, but revealing, article (see *Political Magazine*, I (1780), p. 746). For a discussion of the episode which weighs the credibility of Peters' account, see Wallace, *Traitorous Hero*, pp. 32–4.
31. On the footguards, see Wallace, *Traitorous Hero*, pp. 34–5.
32. Arnold to the Massachusetts Committee of Safety, Cambridge, April 30, 1775, and "Orders to Benedict Arnold," Cambridge, May 3, 1775, in *AA*, 4th Series, II, 450, 485; also, Richard Frothingham, *Life and Times of Joseph Warren* (Little, Brown & Company, Boston, 1865), p. 474.
33. Hall, *Life and Letters of Parsons*, pp. 24–5; Parsons to Joseph Trumbull, New London, June 2, 1775, in *Collections of the Connecticut Historical Society*, I (1860), p. 182; "Journal of Captain Edward Mott," in ibid., pp. 166–8.
34. Edward Mott to the Massachusetts Provincial Congress, Shoreham, May 11, 1775, in *AA*, 4th Series, II, 557–60.
35. Ethan Allen, *A Narrative of Col. Ethan Allen's Captivity* (originally published Philadelphia, 1779; 6th ed. Thomas & Thomas, Walpole, NH, 1807), pp. 16–20.
36. Allen to the Massachusetts Provincial Congress, in *AA*, 4th Series, II, 556; Feltham to Gage, New York, June 11, 1775, cited in Allen French, *The Taking of Ticonderoga in 1775: The British story* (Harvard University Press, Cambridge, MA, 1928), p. 44. French's book provides an excellent analysis of the conflicting evidence.
37. "Journal of Mott," *Collections of the Connecticut Historical Society*, I (1860), p. 172; Arnold to the Massachusetts Committee of Safety, Ticonderoga, May 11, 1775, in *AA*, 4th Series, II, 557; "Benedict Arnold's regimental memorandum book," *PMHB*, VIII, 4 (December, 1884), pp. 363–75; 366.
38. "Benedict Arnold's regimental memorandum book," pp. 367–8; Arnold to the Massachusetts Committee of Safety, Crown Point, May 19, 1775, and "Journal kept by Eleazer Oswald on Lake Champlain," in *NDAR*, I, pp. 364–6, 358.
39. *JCC*, II, p. 56 (May 18, 1775); Allen and Arnold to Continental Congress, and Arnold to Massachusetts Committee of Safety, all from Crown Point, May 29, 1775, in *AA*, 4th Series, II, 732–5.
40. Allen et al. to Continental Congress, June 10, 1775, in *AA*, 4th Series, II, 957–8; "Benedict Arnold's regimental memorandum book," p. 373.

41. "Benedict Arnold's regimental memorandum book," pp. 367, 373.
42. Freeman, *Affairs of Honor*, pp. 172–5.
43. *AA*, 4th Series, II, 1,085–7.
44. Arnold to the Continental Congress, Crown Point, June 13, 1775, ibid., 976–8.
45. *JCC*, II, pp. 73–4 (May 31, 1775); Massachusetts Provincial Congress to Arnold, June 1, 1775, and to Walter Spooner et al., June 13, 1775, Arnold to Continental Congress, Ticonderoga [Albany], June 23, 1775, and Spooner Committee report to Massachusetts Provincial Congress, Cambridge, July 6, 1775, in *AA*, 4th Series, II, 1,382–3, 1,407–8, 1,066–7, 1,596–7; "Benedict Arnold's regimental memorandum book," p. 375.
46. Arnold, *Life of Arnold*, p. 47. On Arnold's accounts, see Martin, *Benedict Arnold, Revolutionary Hero*, pp. 105–6.

Chapter Two

1. *JCC*, II, pp. 109–110 (June 27, 1775).
2. See John H.G. Pell, "Philip Schuyler: The general as aristocrat," in George A. Billias (ed.), *George Washington's Generals* (William Morrow & Company, New York, 1964), pp. 54–78. On Montgomery, see "Journal of John Joseph Henry," in Kenneth Roberts (ed.), *March to Quebec: Journals of the members of Arnold's expedition* (Doubleday, Doran & Company, New York, 1938), p. 363.
3. For a good overview of Montgomery's campaign, see Willard M. Wallace, *Appeal to Arms: A military history of the American Revolution* (Harper & Brothers, New York, 1951), pp. 68–72.
4. Allen, *Narrative*, pp. 28–35; also, Brown's memorial of his services to Schuyler, Albany, August 27, 1776, in *AA*, 5th Series, I, 1,218.
5. *Pennsylvania Packet*, Monday, December 25, 1775 (under "Philadelphia").
6. See Paul David Nelson, *General Sir Guy Carleton, Lord Dorchester: Soldier-statesmen of early British Canada* (Farleigh Dickinson University Press, Madison, NJ, 2000), p. 74.
7. Deane to Schuyler, Headquarters, Cambridge, August 20, 1775, in *LDC*, I, pp. 704–5.
8. Washington to Schuyler, Camp at Cambridge, August 20, 1775, *PWRW*, I, pp. 331–4.
9. On the genesis and course of the Quebec expedition, see J.H. Smith, *Arnold's March from Cambridge to Quebec* (New York, 1903); Gates to Colonel Arnold, Headquarters, August 25, 1775, *Historical Magazine*, I (1857), p. 372. Gates remains a controversial figure, but for a balanced assessment, see Paul David Nelson, *General Horatio Gates: A biography* (Louisiana State University Press, Baton Rouge, LA, 1976).
10. "Instructions to Reuben Colburn," Headquarters, Cambridge, September 3, 1775, *PWRW*, I, pp. 409–10.
11. Washington to Arnold, and "Instructions to Arnold," Cambridge, September 14, 1775, *PWRW*, I, pp. 455–60.
12. "General orders," Cambridge, September 5, 1775, *PWRW*, I, p. 415; "Account of Brigadier General Morgan," *Political Magazine*, II (1781), pp. 173–4; Don Higginbotham, *Daniel Morgan: Revolutionary rifleman* (University of North Carolina Press, Chapel Hill, NC, 1961), pp. 4–5.
13. See Arnold to Washington, "Fort Weston," September 25[–27], 1775, in *PWRW*, II, pp. 40–4.
14. Arnold to Washington, "Second portage from Kennebec to Dead River," October 13, 1775, in *PWRW*, II, pp. 155–6.
15. Arnold to Washington, "Chaudier Pond," October 27[–28], 1775, in *PWRW*, II, pp. 244–6; Arnold to Enos, Dead River, 30 miles from Chaudière Pond, October 24, 1775, in *Collections of the Maine Historical Society*, I (1831), p. 474.
16. Arnold to ——, Pointe-Aux-Trembles, November 27, 1775, in *Collections of the Maine Historical Society*, I (1831), p. 495; Arnold to Washington, Point Lévis [Quebec], November 8, 1775, in *PWRW*, II, pp. 326–7.
17. Dann, *Revolution Remembered*, p. 17. Vining was granted his pension in 1833; "Journal of Captain Simeon Thayer," in Roberts, *March to Quebec*, pp. 258, 261.
18. "Journal of Henry Dearborn," in Roberts, *March to Quebec*, p. 137.
19. Arnold to Washington, Chaudière Pond, October 27–28, 1775, and Washington to Arnold, Cambridge, December 5, 1775, *PWRW*, II, pp. 244–6, 493–4; also Arnold to Montgomery, "St. Marie, 2 and half leagues from Point Lévis," November 8, 1775, in *Collections of the Maine Historical Society*, I (1831), p. 481.
20. Schuyler to Hancock, Ticonderoga, November 22, 1775, in *NDAR*, II, p. 1,100. A native of Maine, Roberts based his fictional account on exhaustive research, which he published in his *March to Quebec*; see also *Annual Register*, 1776, given in David H. Murdoch (ed.), *Rebellion in America: A contemporary British viewpoint* (Clio Books, Santa Barbara, 1979), p. 302. Because of the sheer quantity of American news, the 1776 volume was only published on September 25, 1777 (Murdoch, *Rebellion in America*, p. 294).

21. Arnold to Montgomery, "St. Marie, 2 and a half leagues from Point Lévis," November 8, 1775, in *Collections of the Maine Historical Society*, I (1831), pp. 480–1.

22. For Maclean, see Stephen Brumwell, "The Scottish military experience in North America, 1756–83," in Edward M. Spiers, Jeremy A. Crang, and Matthew J. Strickland (eds.), *A Military History of Scotland* (Edinburgh University Press, Edinburgh, 2012), pp. 383–406, 388–9; "Lt. John Starke's sketch of the war in Canada," in *NDAR*, II, p. 1,075.

23. Arnold to Cramahé, November 15, 1775, in *Collections of the Maine Historical Society*, I (1831), p. 486.

24. See Captain John Hamilton to Vice-Admiral Samuel Graves, November 20, 1775, and "Lt. John Starke's sketch of the war in Canada," in *NDAR*, II, pp. 1,074–5.

25. See Arnold to ——, Pointe-Aux-Trembles, November 25, 1775, in *Collections of the Maine Historical Society*, I (1831), pp. 493–4.

26. Montgomery to Philip Schuyler, Holland House "near the Heights of Abraham," December 5, 1775, and from Montreal, November 13, 1775, in *NDAR*, II, pp. 1,277, 1,007.

27. Arnold to the Continental Congress, "Camp before Quebec," January 11, 1776, in Roberts, *March to Quebec*, p. 109; Wallace, *Traitorous Hero*, p. 80.

28. Montgomery to Carleton and to Wooster, Holland House, December 16, 1775, in *NDAR*, III, pp. 120–1.

29. See "Journal of John Joseph Henry," in Roberts, *March to Quebec*, pp. 375–6. The seventeen-year-old rifleman Henry was with Arnold's column, but all faced the same problems with the weather.

30. Wallace, *Appeal to Arms*, p. 82.

31. Higginbotham, *Daniel Morgan*, pp. 44–9; "Journal of Henry," in Roberts, *March to Quebec*, pp. 376–9.

32. See Arnold to Wooster, "General Hospital," Quebec, December 31, 1775, and Campbell to Wooster, Holland House (Quebec), Saturday, December 31, 1775, both in GWP (MSS 44693, Reel 035). Both letters informed a report in the *New-York Packet*, February 1, 1776, given in Frank Moore (ed.), *Diary of the American Revolution, from Newspapers and Original Documents* (Charles Scribner, New York, 1860), I, pp. 185–7.

33. "Journal of Senter," in Roberts, *March to Quebec*, pp. 234–5.

34. Arnold to Washington, "Camp before Quebec," January 14, 1776, in *PWRW*, III, pp. 81–2.

35. Wooster to Hancock, Montreal, February 11, 1776, in *AA*, 4th Series, IV, 1,001; Wooster to Washington, Montreal, February 25, 1776, *PWRW*, III, pp. 361–2; Washington to Lt.-Col. Joseph Reed, Cambridge, January 31, 1776, *PWRW*, III, pp. 225–9; *JCC*, IV, p. 47 (10 January 1776); "Richard Smith diary" (January 8, 1776), in *LDC*, III, p. 61; Arnold to Hancock, "Camp before Quebec," February 12, 1776, in *AA*, 4th Series, IV, 1,017.

36. Arnold to Washington, "Camp before Quebec," February 27, 1776, in *PWRW*, III, p. 382; Dann, *Revolution Remembered*, p. 21. Sabin was granted his pension in 1832.

37. Montgomery to Schuyler, "Camp before St. John's," October 20, 1775, in *NDAR*, II, p. 531.

38. Arnold to Hancock, "Camp before Quebec," February 1, 1776, in *AA*, 4th Series, IV, 907–8; Brown's "Petition and Memorial" to Congress, June 26, 1776, in *AA*, 5th Series, I, 1,219–20. See also Wallace, *Traitorous Hero*, pp. 89–90, 106.

39. Arnold to Schuyler, Montreal, April 20, 1776, in *AA*, 4th Series, V, 1,098–9.

40. Arnold to Gates, Chambly, May 31, 1776, in *AA*, 4th Series, VI, 649; *Annual Register*, 1776, cited in Murdoch, *Rebellion in America*, p. 374.

41. Arnold to Sullivan, Chambly, June 13, 1776, in Otis G. Hammond (ed.), *Letters and Papers of Major-General John Sullivan*, I, in *New Hampshire Historical Society Collections*, XIII (1930), pp. 237–338.

42. James Wilkinson, *Memoirs of my Own Times*, 3 vols. (Philadelphia, 1816), I, pp. 48–9; for Wilkinson's career, see Andro Linklater, *An Artist in Treason: The extraordinary double life of General James Wilkinson* (Walker and Company, New York, 2009).

43. Wilkinson, *Memoirs*, I, pp. 54–5; Burgoyne to Germain, Montreal, June 22, 1776, and Germain to Burgoyne, Kew Lane [London], August 23, 1776, in *Historical Manuscripts Commission: Stopford-Sackville Manuscripts*, 2 vols. (HMSO, London, 1904–10), II, pp. 37, 39.

44. Piers Mackesy, *The War for America, 1775–1783* (1964; new ed. University of Nebraska Press, Lincoln, NE, 1993), pp. 43, 60.

45. Schuyler to Washington, Fort George, May 31, 1776, *PWRW*, IV, pp. 409–11; also, Russell P. Bellico, *Sails and Steam in the Mountain: A maritime and military history of Lake George and Lake Champlain* (Purple Mountain Press, Fleischmanns, NY, revised ed., 2001), pp. 135–9.

46. Arnold to Schuyler, St. Johns, June 13, 1776, in *AA*, 4th Series, VI, 1,039; Arnold to Washington, Albany, June 25, 1776, *PWRW*, V, pp. 96–7.

47. Gates to John Hancock, Ticonderoga, July 29, 1776, in *AA*, 5th Series, I, 649; "Extract of a letter from an officer at Ticonderoga," August 1, 1776, *Maryland Journal*, August 28, 1776.

48. See "The case of Lieutenant John Starke," in *NDAR*, VI, p. 55; Douglas to Mr. Stephens, Quebec, October 21, 1776, in *AA*, 5th Series, II, 1,178.

49. Arnold to Schuyler, Montreal, June 10, 1776, in *AA*, 4th Series, VI, 927; Arnold to Sullivan, Chambly, June 13, 1776, in Hammond, *Sullivan Papers*, I, p. 238. For a detailed discussion of this affair, and the identification of "Major Scott" as Captain John Budd Scott, see Ennis Duling, "Arnold, Hazen, and the mysterious Major Scott," in *Journal of the American Revolution, Annual Volume 2017* (Westholme, Yardley, PA, 2017), pp. 143–53; Wilkinson, *Memoirs*, I, pp. 45–6.

50. Arnold to Schuyler, St. Johns, June 13, 1776, in *AA*, 4th Series, VI, 1,038; Hazen to Sullivan, Chambly, June 13, 1776, in Hammond, *Sullivan Papers*, I, p. 240; see "General Arnold's protest" and "Minute of the court," in *AA*, 5th Series, I, 1,272–3.

51. See Arnold's letter to the court martial, Ticonderoga, August 1, 1,776, and the court members to Gates, August 6, 1776, in *AA*, 5th Series, I, 1,273–4.

52. Wilkinson to Varick, Mount Independence, Ticonderoga, August 5, 1776, in *NDAR*, VI, p. 61; Gates to Hancock, Ticonderoga, September 2, 1776, in *AA*, 5th Series, I, 1,268.

53. Gates to Hancock, Ticonderoga, July 29, 1776, and Schuyler to Gates, German-Flats, August 3, 1776, in *AA*, 5th Series, I, 649, 747; Washington to Gates, New York, August 14, 1776, *PWRW*, VI, pp. 20–2.

54. "B. Arnold Brigadier General & Commander in Chief of the Fleet of the United States of America on Lake Champlain" to Jacobus Wynkoop, Crown Point, August 17, 1776, N-YHS, Benedict Arnold Collection, 1772–80, MSS 2958.286, Folder 1.

55. See Arnold to Gates, Isle la Motte, September 18, 1776, and Arnold's "Memorandum of Articles which have been repeatedly wrote for, and which we are in the extremest want of," Valcour, October 1, 1776, in *NDAR*, VI, pp. 884, 1,082.

56. See Arnold to Gates, Schuyler Island, October 12, 1776, and Carleton to Burgoyne, on board the *Maria* off Valcour Island, October 12–15, 1776, ibid., pp. 1,235, 1,272.

57. Arnold to Gates, Schuyler Island, October 12, 1776, ibid., p. 1,235; "Journal of Captain George Pausch" (October 11, Windmill Point, Lake Champlain), ibid., p. 1,259.

58. Burgoyne to Douglas, Camp at River La Cole, October 12, 1776, and Carleton to Burgoyne, October 12–15, 1776, ibid., pp. 1,230, 1,274.

59. See Arnold to Gates, Schuyler Island, October 12, 1776, ibid., p. 1,235, and to Schuyler, Ticonderoga, October 15, 1776, ibid., p. 1,276; Carleton to Burgoyne, off Valcour Island, October 12–15 [14th], 1776, ibid., p. 1,274.

60. Arnold to Schuyler, and Gates to Schuyler, both from Ticonderoga, October 15, 1776; Varick to Gates, Albany, October 17, 1776; and Gates to Governor Trumbull, Ticonderoga, October 22, 1776, in *AA*, 5th Series, II, 1,079–80, 1,102, 1,192.

61. Maxwell to Governor William Livingston of New Jersey, Ticonderoga, October 20, 1776, ibid., 1,144; Lee to Thomas Jefferson, Philadelphia, November 3, 1776, in *LDC*, V, p. 431.

62. Christie to Germain, Montreal, October 26, 1776, in *Stopford-Sackville Manuscripts*, II, p. 46; *Annual Register*, 1776, in Murdoch, *Rebellion in America*, p. 423.

63. Arnold to Schuyler, Ticonderoga, October 15, 1776, in *AA*, 5th Series, II, 1,079–80.

64. Carleton to Germain, on board the *Maria* off Crown Point, October 14, 1776, in *NDAR*, VI, pp. 1,257–8; Bellico, *Sails and Steam in the Mountains*, pp. 159–60; Samuel Stringer to William Knox, Fort George, October 28/November 3, 1776, GLC, MSS 020437-00477.

65. Gardner W. Allen, *A Naval History of the American Revolution*, 2 vols. (Boston, 1913), I, p. 179.

66. Arnold to Schuyler, Providence, February 7 and March 8, 1777, NYPL, Philip Schuyler Papers (MSS Col 2701/Microfilm ZL-444), Reels 15 and 16.

67. Washington to Arnold, Morristown, March 3 and April 2, 1777, *PWRW*, VIII, p. 493 and IX, pp. 45–6; Henry to Lucy Knox, Morristown, New Jersey, March 23, 1777, GLC, MSS 02437-00557.

68. Arnold to Washington, Providence, March 11, 1777, *PWRW*, VIII, pp. 551–3.

69. Arnold to Lucy Knox, Watertown, MA, March 4, 1777, GLC, MSS 02437-00543; and Lucy to Henry Knox, Boston, April 3, 1777, in GLC, MSS 02437-00565.

70. For the official British account of the raid, see *New-York Gazette*, May 5, 1777. Other details are given in a dispatch from Captain G. Hutchinson, who spoke to the raiders shortly after they re-embarked, published in *The London Gazette*, June 5, 1777.

71. Washington to John Hancock, Morristown, April 28, 1777, *PWRW*, IX, pp. 293–4.

72. John Adams to Abigail Adams, April 30, 1777, in *LDC*, VI, p. 687; Joseph Plumb Martin, *A Narrative of a Revolutionary Soldier: Some of the adventures, dangers, and sufferings of Joseph Plumb Martin*, new ed. (New York, 2001), p. 55.

73. "A British officer's account of the Danbury Raid, April 21–28, 1777," in *NDAR*, VIII, p. 456.

74. *The Connecticut Courant*, April 30, 1777. This report was republished in full alongside the British account, from the *New-York Gazette* of May 5, 1777, in several London newspapers, for example, *The General Evening Post*, June 7–10, 1777. See also "Some account of Benedict Arnold," *European Magazine and London Review for 1783* (February), p. 85. For the punctured horse hide, see Arnold, *Life of Arnold*, p. 131 (note).

75. See Isaac Q. Leake (ed.), *Memoir of the Life and Times of General John Lamb* (Joel Munsell, Albany, NY, 1850), pp. 149–53; Wallace, *Traitorous Hero*, p. 123.

76. "An Officer," *History of the Civil War in America*, I, p. 279; William Tryon to [Henry Clinton?], on board the *Richard and Ann* transport, St. Cast Bay, September 12, 1758, in William S. Powell (ed.), *The Correspondence of William Tryon, and Other Selected Papers*, 2 vols. (North Carolina Division of Archives and History, Raleigh, NC, 1980), I, pp. 1–3.

77. Leake, *Life of Lamb*, pp. 161–2.

78. *London Gazette*, June 5, 1777; "An Officer," *History of the Civil War in America*, I, p. 279; Knox to Nicholas Everleigh, Morristown, May 5, 1777, GLC, MSS 02437-00587.

79. Arnold to General McDougall, "Paugatuck [Saugatuck], 3 miles east of Norwalk," April 28, 1777, 6 p.m.; Hughes to General McDougall, Saugatuck Bridge, 9.30 a.m./1.30 p.m., April 28, 1777, in PCC, "Transcripts of letters from George Washington," III, pp. 197–8; 195.

80. *Annual Register*, 1777, cited in Murdoch, *Rebellion in America*, p. 456.

81. John Adams to Nathanael Greene, May 9, 1777, in Showman, *Papers of Greene*, II, pp. 74–5.

82. John to Abigail Adams, May 2, 1777, in *LDC*, VII, p. 12; *JCC*, VII, p. 323; Washington to John Hancock, Morristown, May 5, 1777, in *PWRW*, IX, p. 349.

83. *JCC*, VII, pp. 372–3.

Chapter Three

1. *JCC*, V, pp. 618, 626 (July 30 and August 1, 1776); see also J.E.A. Smith, *The History of Pittsfield*, 2 vols. (Lee and Shepard, Boston, 1869–76), I, pp. 267, 270.

2. See Brown to Gates, Albany, December 1 and December 2 (twice), and Gates to Brown, December 2, 1776, and Brown to John Hancock, December 10, 1776, in *AA*, 5th Series, III, 1,158–9; *JCC*, VI, p. 1,040 (December 26, 1776).

3. Smith, *History of Pittsfield*, I, pp. 272–3, and William L. Stone, *Life of Brant*, 2 vols. (George Dearborn & Co., New York, 1838), II, pp. 116–19. I have been unable to locate a copy of the original handbill to verify the quoted passages, but as given by William Stone (p. 116) they have been accepted as genuine by Arnold's leading biographers.

4. Arnold to Hancock, Philadelphia, May 20, 1777, in PCC, "Letters from general officers, 1775–89," I, p. 86; *JCC*, VII, pp. 371–3 (May 20, 1777).

5. Lee to Thomas Jefferson, Philadelphia, May 20, 1777, and Adams to Abigail Adams, May 22, 1777, in *LDC*, VII, pp. 95, 103; *JCC*, VII, p. 382 (May 23, 1777).

6. This overview of a complex subject draws heavily on the analysis in Wallace, *Traitorous Hero*, pp. 132–3. Arnold's efforts to clear his accounts were hampered by his belief that essential official documents from the Canadian campaign were destroyed when the *Royal Savage* was burned at Valcour Island. In fact, Arnold's papers were salvaged by the British and survive in Laval University, Quebec. In the estimation of Willard Sterne Randall, they show that Arnold made "a serious attempt … to keep track of his expenses" and "document that he had scrupulously carried out" his instructions to pay rather than pilfer the Canadians. See Randall, *Benedict Arnold*, p. 337.

7. Hancock to Arnold, Philadelphia, June 11, 1777, Francis Lightfoot Lee to his brother, Richard Henry Lee, Philadelphia, June 17, 1777, and John Adams to Abigail Adams, June 18, 1777, in *LDC*, VII, pp. 182–3, 202, 207.

8. Arnold to Hancock, Philadelphia, July 11, 1777, in PCC, "Letters from general officers, 1775–89," I, pp. 106–7.

9. Washington to John Hancock, Morristown, NJ, July 10, 1777, *PWRW*, X, pp. 240–1.

10. For Burgoyne's campaign, see especially J.F. Luzader, *Saratoga: A military history of the decisive campaign of the American Revolution* (Savas Beatie, New York, 2008); an older, but still useful, study is Nickerson, *The Turning Point of the Revolution*.

11. See Arnold to Washington, Snook Kill, New York, July 27, 1777, *PWRW*, X, pp. 433–5.

12. *JCC*, VIII, pp. 623–4 (August 8, 1777); Adams to Abigail Adams, May 22, 1777, in *LDC*, VII, p. 103; see also the detailed discussion in Martin, *Benedict Arnold, Revolutionary Hero*, pp. 356–8. The "radical Whig" opposition to "standing armies" has generated much literature. For a useful overview, which cautions against exaggerating anti-military sentiment, see Don Higginbotham, "The early American way of war: Reconnaissance and appraisal," *WMQ*, XLIV, 2 (April 1987), pp. 230–73; 245–53.

13. William B. Willcox (ed.), *The American Rebellion: Sir Henry Clinton's narrative of his campaigns, 1775–1782, with an appendix of original documents* (Yale University Press, New Haven, CT, 1954), p. 66.

14. For a detailed eyewitness account of Bennington by a patriot "gentleman," see *Pennsylvania Evening Post*, September 4, 1777, given in Moore, *Diary of the American Revolution*, I, pp. 479–81.

15. See, for example, *The Morning Post and Daily Advertiser*, November 17, 1777.

16. Gansevoort to Arnold "or the officer commanding their army in the march to Fort Schuyler," Fort Schuyler August 22, 1777, and Arnold to Gates, "10 miles above Fort Daton [Dayton]," August 23, 1777; also intelligence regarding Fort Schuyler, from Col. Peter Gansevoort, Kingston, September 18, 1777, in *The Remembrancer; or, impartial repository of public events for the year 1777* (J. Almon, London, 1778), pp. 444–8. In some accounts, Fort Schuyler is known by its original name, Fort Stanwix.

17. *Remembrancer, 1777*, pp. 447–8 (note); Thacher, *Military Journal*, pp. 89–91. For a later version incorporating oral history, see Stone, *Life of Brant*, I, pp. 255–61.

18. Arnold to Gates, Fort Schuyler, August 24, 1777, in *Remembrancer, 1777*, p. 445; Arnold to Washington, Snook Kill, July 27, 1777, *PWRW*, X, p. 435.

19. For an excellent analysis of Freeman's Farm, see Eric H. Schnitzer, "The tactics of the battles of Saratoga," in William A. Griswold and Donald W. Linebaugh (eds.), *The Saratoga Campaign: Uncovering an embattled landscape* (University Press of New England, Hanover, NH, 2016), pp. 39–79; 45–57.

20. Chastellux, *Travels*, I, pp. 212–13.

21. Alexander Scammell to Jonathan C. Chadbourn, "Camp Now or Never," September 26, 1777, in CL, James S. Schoff Revolutionary War Collection, Box 2.

22. John Burgoyne, *A State of the Expedition from Canada: As laid before the House of Commons, by Lieutenant-General Burgoyne* (J. Almon, London, 1780), p. 122.

23. Burgoyne, *State of the Expedition*, p. 16; Lloyd A. Brown and Howard H. Peckham (eds.), *Revolutionary War Journals of Henry Dearborn, 1775–1783* (Chicago, 1939), p. 107.

24. *Annual Register*, 1777, cited in Murdoch, *Rebellion in America*, p. 483.

25. Wilkinson to St. Clair, Camp at Bemis Heights, September 21, 1777, in William Henry Smith (ed.), *The St. Clair Papers: The life and public services of Arthur St. Clair* (Cincinnati, OH, 1882), I, p. 443; Wilkinson, *Memoirs*, I, p. 245.

26. Varick to Schuyler, "Camp near Stillwater," September 19, 1777, in NYPL, Philip Schuyler Papers, Reel 16.

27. "Diary of Joshua Pell, Junior: An officer of the British army in America, 1776–1777," *Magazine of American History with Notes and Queries*, II (February 1878), p. 109.

28. See Maria Campbell, *Revolutionary Services and Civil Life of General William Hull, Prepared from his Manuscripts by his daughter Mrs. Maria Campbell* (D. Appleton and Co., New York, 1848), pp. 92–5; Eric H. Schnitzer, "Cook's and Latimer's Connecticut militia battalions in the northern campaign of 1777," *Bulletin of the Fort Ticonderoga Museum*, XVII, 1 (2016), pp. 10–33; 24; Thacher, *Military Journal*, p. 98.

29. Varick to Schuyler, "Camp Still Water," September 22, 1777, "9 o'clock p.m.," in NYPL, Philip Schuyler Papers, Reel 16. For detailed discussions of Arnold's role, see Nickerson, *Turning Point*, pp. 473–7, and Wallace, *Traitorous Hero*, pp. 326–32. Both conclude that Arnold *was* present on the battlefield, and exercised active command.

30. See "Memoranda" of correspondence between Clinton and Burgoyne, in Violet Stuart Wortley (ed.), *A Prime Minister and His Son* (John Murray, London, 1925), p. 118; Clinton to Burgoyne, September 11, 1777, CP, Vol. 23/file 39.

31. "A list of transports that can carry flat boats [September 1777]," CP, Vol. 24/file 30. See also Sam Willis, *The Struggle for Sea Power: A naval history of the American Revolution* (W.W. Norton and Company, New York, 2015), pp. 124–5.

32. For Hotham's flotilla, see *NDAR*, X, p. 43.

33. Willcox, *American Rebellion*, p. 73; John Robinson to Washington, September 15, 1754, and Washington to Robinson, Williamsburg, October 23, 1754, in W.W. Abbot and Dorothy Twohig (eds.), *The Papers of George Washington, Colonial Series*, 10 vols. (University of Virginia Press, Charlottesville, 1983–1995), I, pp. 209–10, 219–20.

34. Stephen Brumwell, *George Washington: Gentleman warrior* (Quercus, London, 2012), pp. 90–1.

35. See Robinson's obituary in *Gentleman's Magazine*, 1792 (May), p. 479. Also, Major-General Charles Walker Robinson, *Life of Sir John Beverley Robinson Bart., CB, DCC, Chief Justice of Upper Canada* (William Blackwood & Sons, Edinburgh and London, 1904), pp. 3–4. Colonel Beverly Robinson was the author's great-uncle.

36. D. Syrett, "The methodology of British amphibious operations during the Seven Years War and American Wars," *Mariner's Mirror*, LV (1972), pp. 269–80; Stephen Brumwell, *Redcoats: The British soldier and war in the Americas, 1755–1763* (Cambridge University Press, New York, 2002), pp. 236–45.

37. Both messages enclosed with "Extract of a letter from Sir William Howe to Lord George Germain," Philadelphia, October 21, 1777, in *The Parliamentary Register; or History of the Proceedings and Debates of the House of Commons*, VII (1778) (London, 1802), pp. 245–6. Yet another message from Burgoyne, dated September 27, and carried by Captain Thomas Scott of the 24th Foot, reached Clinton on October 9 (see CP, Vol. 24/file 22). Although "Captain Campbell" is usually identified as Alexander Campbell of the 62nd Foot, this is an error: that officer was listed among those present when Burgoyne's army capitulated on October 17, while the "Captain Campbell" in question was unable to reach him with Clinton's reply. As Burgoyne emphasized, the only communication he received from Clinton during the campaign was the letter of September 11. See the discussion in "Officers of the 62nd Regiment of Foot during the period of the Northern Campaign of 1777," www.62ndRegiment.org/officers.htm, accessed February 15, 2018.

38. This account is based on: Sir Henry Clinton to Sir William Howe, Fort Montgomery, October 9, 1777, in CP, Vol. 24/file 51; Commodore William Hotham to Vice-Admiral Viscount Howe, Preston off Peekskill Creek, October 9, 1777, in *NDAR*, X, pp. 96–7; and George Clinton to George Washington, New Windsor, October 9, 1777, in *Public Papers of George Clinton, First Governor of New York*, 10 vols. (New York and Albany, 1899–1914), II, pp. 391–4.

39. See William B. Willcox, *Portrait of a General: Sir Henry Clinton in the War of Independence* (Alfred A. Knopf, New York, 1964); also Andrew Jackson O'Shaughnessy, *The Men Who Lost America: British leadership, the American Revolution, and the fate of empire* (Yale University Press, New Haven, CT, 2013), pp. 207–46.

40. For the two messages, see *Parliamentary Register*, 1778, pp. 246–7; on Taylor, see Major-General Putnam to Major-General Heath, Headquarters, Peekskill, July 25, 1777, in Worthington Chauncey Ford (ed.), *Correspondence and Journals of Samuel Blachley Webb*, 3 vols. (New York, 1893), I, p. 301.

41. See Confession of Daniel Taylor, New Windsor, October 9, 1777, and George Clinton to the New York Council of Safety, Headquarters, "[at] Mrs. Falls," October 11, 1777, in *Public Papers of George Clinton*, II, pp. 398, 413.

42. General Court Martial, "Heights of New Windsor," October 14, 1777, and "General orders," Headquarters, Marbletown, October 16, 1777, in *Public Papers of George Clinton*, II, pp. 443–4; also, Thacher, *Military Journal*, pp. 105–6. Sir Henry Clinton learned that his "silver bullet" letter had been intercepted after Brigadier Vaughan sent him a page from the *New-York Packet*, published at Fishkill on October 16, 1777, which printed a letter from George Clinton to Israel Putnam, dated New Windsor, October 11, 1777, detailing Taylor's capture and reprinting the note. See Vaughan to Clinton, CP, Vol. 25/files 13–14.

43. Thacher, *Military Journal*, p. 99. It's likely that Palmer was the same man as the "Edmund Palmer," described as a "spy and robber," executed by Putnam after a general court martial on August 8, 1777. See Ford, *Correspondence and Journals of Webb*, I, p. 227.

44. Wortley, *A Prime Minister and His Son*, p. 121; Willcox, *American Rebellion*, pp. 79–80.

45. Varick to Schuyler, "Camp Still Water," September 22, 1777, NYPL, Philip Schuyler Papers, Reel 16; Arnold to Gates, Camp Stillwater, September 22, 1777, in N-YHS, Horatio Gates Papers, Reel 5.

46. Gates to John Hancock, September 22, 1777, given in Wilkinson, *Memoirs*, I, pp. 244–5; see also, *JCC*, VIII, p. 756.

47. Arnold to Gates, Camp Stillwater, September 22, 1777, in N-YHS, Horatio Gates Papers, Reel 5.

48. Wilkinson, *Memoirs*, I, p. 254; Arnold to Gates, Camp Stillwater, September 22, 1777, N-YHS, Horatio Gates Papers, Reel 5.

49. Livingston to Schuyler, "Camp on Behmus' Heights," September 23, 1777, in NYPL, Schuyler Papers, Reel 16; Arnold to Gates, Camp Stillwater, September 23, 1777, in N-YHS, Horatio Gates Papers, Reel 5.

50. Livingston to Schuyler, "Camp on Behmus' Heights," September 23, 1777, and "Camp on Beemus' Heights," September 26, 1777, in NYPL, Philip Schuyler Papers, Reel 16; Schuyler to Richard Varick, Albany, September 25, 1777, in GLC, MSS 06332.

51. See Brown to Horatio Gates, "North end of Lake George landing," September 18, 1777, in *Remembrancer, 1777*, pp. 458–9; Thacher, *Military Journal*, p. 99.

52. Wilkinson, *Memoirs*, I, pp. 260–1, and Arnold to Gates, Camp at Stillwater, October 1, 1777, ibid., p. 259. Interestingly, Gates did not report his dispute with Arnold to Congress, or even explain the command restructuring in his general orders.

53. See Schnitzer, "Tactics of the battles of Saratoga," in Griswold and Linebaugh, *Saratoga Campaign*, pp. 59–68.

54. See "Letters [*sic*] change view of Benedict Arnold, Gen. Gates," in *The Daily Gazette* [Schenectady], March 26, 2016.
55. Wilkinson, *Memoirs*, I, p. 273. Besides offering a more credible explanation of Arnold's conduct, the contemporaneous Bacheller letter also resolves an obvious discrepancy arising from Wilkinson's *Memoirs*: if Arnold assumed battlefield command in open defiance of Gates, why was he never court-martialed or even reprimanded for such glaring insubordination? This point was made in the Schenectady *Daily Gazette*'s coverage of the letter by Saratoga Battlefield Park Ranger and historian Eric Schnitzer.
56. See the narrative prepared by Woodruff to support his pension application in 1832, in Dann, *Revolution Remembered*, pp. 102–3; also an account Woodruff wrote in 1827, when he revisited Saratoga on the fiftieth anniversary of Burgoyne's capitulation, in William L. Stone, *The Campaign of Lieutenant-General John Burgoyne* (Joel Munsell, Albany, NY, 1877), pp. 314–25.
57. See "Autobiography of Philip Van Cortlandt, brig-gen. in the Continental Army," *Magazine of American History*, II (1878), pp. 278–98; 286. Van Cortlandt, who was writing after Arnold's treason, maintained that his intervention broke the momentum of the attack, and so contributed to the failure of the assault on the Balcarres Redoubt.
58. See "Journal of Oliver Boardman of Middletown, 1777" (entry for Tuesday, October 7, 1777), in "Orderly book and journals kept by Connecticut men while taking part in the American Revolution," *Collections of the Connecticut Historical Society*, VII (1899), p. 228.
59. Henry Dearborn, "A narrative of the Saratoga campaign, Boston, December 20th, 1815," *Bulletin of the Fort Ticonderoga Museum*, I, 5 (January 1929), pp. 2–12; 9. Dearborn prepared his "narrative" at the request of James Wilkinson, who chose not to use it in his 1816 *Memoirs*.
60. "Diary of Ezra Tilden," GLC, MSS 01450-004, pp. 131–2.
61. Wilkinson, *Memoirs*, I, pp. 313–14 (and note).
62. *New-York Packet*, October 30, 1777; Thacher, *Military Journal*, p. 105.
63. See Clinton to Gates, Kingston, October 16, 1777, in *Public Papers of George Clinton*, II, p. 445; Major-General Vaughan to Lieutenant-General Clinton, Fort Vaughan [Clinton], October 27, 1777, in *NDAR*, X, p. 300.
64. "Journal of Boardman," pp. 231, 235.
65. See "An Officer," *History of the Civil War in America*, p. 317; Webb's "Journal" for October 19, 1777, in Ford, *Correspondence and Journals of Webb*, I, p. 232.
66. Willcox, *American Rebellion*, pp. 80–1.
67. Thacher, *Military Journal*, p. 112.
68. Ibid., p. 103; Dr. James Browne to Dr. Jonathan Potts, Albany, December 24, 1777, in "Biographical sketch of Dr. Jonathan Potts," *New England Historical and Genealogical Register*, XVIII (1864), pp. 21–36; 34.
69. Gates to John Hancock, October 12, 1777, cited in Nelson, *Horatio Gates*, p. 137; *JCC*, IX, pp. 861, 871 (November 4 and 6, 1777).
70. *JCC*, IX, p. 862; Greene to Brig.-Gen. McDougall, June 1778, in Showman, *Papers of Greene*, II, p. 260.
71. *General Evening Post*, London, December 2–4, December 4–6, December 11–13, and December 18–20, 1777.
72. Burgoyne to Clinton, Albany, October 25, 1777, CP, Vol. 25/file 36; Burgoyne, *State of the Expedition from Canada*, pp. 17, 44; Tilghman to General John Cadwalader, Valley Forge, January 18, 1778, in "Selections from the military papers of General John Cadwalader," *PMHB*, XXXII, 3 (1908), pp. 149–74; 169.
73. Mackesy, *War for America*, pp. 141, 147, 160.
74. Charles Neilson, *An Original, Compiled and Corrected Account of Burgoyne's Campaign* (J. Munsell, Albany, NY, 1844), p. 150.
75. "Genuine history of Gen. Arnold," *Political Magazine*, I (1780), p. 748.

Chapter Four

1. Laurens to Arnold, York, November 29, 1777, in *LDC*, VIII, pp. 343–4; *JCC*, IX, p. 981 (November 29, 1777); Arnold to Laurens, Albany, January 11, 1778, PCC, "Letters from general officers 1775–89," I, p. 112.
2. Washington to Arnold, and to Lincoln, Headquarters Valley Forge, January 20, 1778, *PWRW*, XIII, pp. 288–9, 294–5.
3. Arnold to Washington, Middletown, March 12, 1778, *PWRW*, XIV, pp. 153–4.
4. See E.E. Atwater, *History of the City of New Haven* (New York, 1887), p. 651; *Connecticut Journal*, May 6, 1778.
5. See this text, pp. 5–6; Brown and Peckham, *Journals of Dearborn*, p. 121.

6. "General orders," Headquarters, "Towamensing," October 15, 1777, *PWRW*, XI, pp. 512–13; Washington to Carter, October 27, 1777, *PWRW*, XII, p. 27.

7. Greene to Miss Susanna Livingston, "Camp near Philadelphia," November 11, 1777, in Showman, *Papers of Greene*, II, p. 195; Ira D. Gruber (ed.), *John Peebles' American War, 1776–1782* (Army Records Society, Stroud, 1998), p. 138 (September 26, 1777).

8. "An authentic account of that greatly lamented officer, Major John André . . . solely composed from materials furnished by the late major's most intimate friends, both in this country, and in America," *First Supplement to the Political Magazine* (1781), pp. 171–2; see also Winthrop Sargent, *The Life and Career of Major John André* (1861; revised ed., William Abbatt, New York, 1902); and Flexner, *Traitor and Spy*, pp. 20–9.

9. Lichtenberg to Schernhagen, Göttingen, November 30, 1780, in Richard D. Loewenberg (ed.), "A letter on Major John André in Germany," *American Historical Review*, XLIX, 2 (January 1944), pp. 260–1.

10. André to Miss Mary André, Quebec, March 5, 1775, in CL, James S. Schoff Revolutionary War Collection, Box 1.

11. Sargent/Abbatt, *Life of André*, pp. 92–3; see also J. Robert Maguire, "A self-portrait by Major John André," *Bulletin of the Fort Ticonderoga Museum*, XVI, 3 (2000), pp. 200–1; 243. Despite a focus on André's portraiture, this article contains much valuable information on his career in general.

12. "Authentic account of Major André," *First Supplement to the Political Magazine* (1781), p. 171.

13. "John André's Journal, Germantown, 28 September 1777 to Philadelphia Camp, 20 November 1777," in CL, James S. Schoff Revolutionary War Collection, Box 2.

14. "André's Journal," CL.

15. André to Louisa André, Philadelphia Camp, November 30, 1777, GLC, MSS 07272.

16. "A letter of Miss Rebecca Franks, 1778," in *PMHB*, XVI, 2 (July 1892), pp. 216–18; Nicholas B. Wainwright (ed.), "'A diary of trifling occurrences': Philadelphia, 1776–1778," *PMHB*, LXXXII, 4 (October 1958), pp. 411–65; 462.

17. Sophie Howard Ward, "Major André's story of the Mischianza," *Century Magazine*, XLVII (March 1894), pp. 684–91; 684–6.

18. André to Margaret "Peggy" Chew, New York, *c.* May 1779, in Van Doren, *Secret History*, pp. 440–1. See also Stephen Case and Mark Jacob, *Treacherous Beauty: Peggy Shippen, the woman behind Benedict Arnold's plot to betray America* (Lyons Press, Guilford, CT, 2012).

19. "Particulars of the Mischianza exhibited in America at the departure of Gen. Howe – Copy of a letter from an officer at Philadelphia to his correspondent in London, Philadelphia, 23 May 1778," *Gentleman's Magazine*, 1778 (August), pp. 353–7; see also Ward, "Major André's story of the Mischianza," pp. 684–91. This account, written and illustrated by André as a memento for Margaret "Peggy" Chew, confirms the absence of the Shippen sisters; it omits their names from the listing, leaving gaps.

20. Willcox, *Portrait of a General*, pp. 223–4.

21. Reginald E. Rabb, "The role of William Eden in the British Peace Commission of 1778," *The Historian*, XX, 2 (February 1958), pp. 153–78.

22. Nathan R. Einhorn, "The reception of the British peace offer of 1778," *Pennsylvania History*, XVI (1949), pp. 191–214.

23. Wainwright, "'Diary of trifling occurrences'," pp. 463–64; Gruber, *Peebles' American War*, pp. 174–5, 188.

24. Washington to Arnold, Headquarters, June 19, 1778, *PWRW*, XV, p. 472.

25. Wayne to Peters, Paramus, New Jersey, July 12, 1778, in Charles Janeway Stillé, *Major-General Anthony Wayne and the Pennsylvania Line in the Continental Army* (J.B. Lippincott, Philadelphia, 1893), p. 153.

26. On Reed's role in 1776, see Brumwell, *George Washington: Gentleman warrior*, pp. 259–60, 270–1.

27. William B. Reed, *The Life and Correspondence of Joseph Reed*, 2 vols. (Lindsay and Blackiston, Philadelphia, 1847), I, pp. 382–92; *JCC*, XI, pp. 770–4.

28. Reed, *Life and Correspondence of Reed*, I, p. 391.

29. Washington to Greene, September 1, 1778, *PWRW*, XVI, pp. 458–9.

30. Einhorn, "Reception of British peace offer," pp. 207–10.

31. *Major André's Journal: Operations of the British army under Lieutenant-Generals Sir William Howe and Sir William Clinton* (Tarrytown, New York, 1930), p. 98; Holger Hoock, *Scars of Independence: America's violent birth* (Crown, New York, 2017), pp. 253–72.

32. See Arnold to Washington, Philadelphia, July 19, 1778, and Washington to Arnold, Headquarters, White Plains, August 3, 1778, *PWRW*, XVI, pp. 104–5, 225; see Gérard to Vergennes, Philadelphia, July 16 and September 12, 1778, in John J. Meng (ed.), *Despatches and Instructions of Conrad Alexandre Gérard, 1778–1780* (Johns Hopkins Press, Baltimore, 1939), pp. 160, 283–4 (in French); see also *JCC*, XII, p. 885 (September 7, 1778).

33. "Extract of a letter from an American gentleman, dated Amsterdam, December 12, 1780," *Remembrancer, 1781* (Part 1), p. 100.
34. On "Continella," see Benjamin H. Irvin, "The streets of Philadelphia: Crowds, Congress and the political culture of revolution, 1774–1783," *PMHB*, CXXIX, 1 (January 2005), pp. 7–44; 28–9; *JCC*, XII, pp. 1,001, 1,018 (October 12 and 16, 1778).
35. See Sparks, *Life and Treason of Arnold*, pp. 126–8; Arnold, *Life of Arnold*, 216–21; Frothingham, *Life of Warren*, pp. 542–4; *JCC*, XVII, p. 581 (July 1, 1780).
36. Reed to Greene, Philadelphia, November 5, 1778, in Showman, *Papers of Greene*, III, pp. 42–5.
37. See Reed, *Life and Correspondence of Reed*, II, pp. 33–7.
38. Cadwalader to Greene, Philadelphia, December 5, 1778, Showman, *Papers of Greene*, III, p. 103.
39. Lewis Burd Walker, "Life of Margaret Shippen, wife of Benedict Arnold," *PMHB*, XXV, 1 (1901), pp. 20–46; 30–1.
40. Ibid., pp. 32–3, 36.
41. Van Doren, *Secret History*, pp. 169–70.
42. *General Court Martial for the Trial of General Arnold*, p. 32.
43. See "Matlack, Timothy," in Allen Johnson, Dumas Malone, et al. (eds.), *Dictionary of American Biography*, 22 vols. (Charles Scribner's Sons, New York, 1928–58), XII, pp. 409–10; Greene to Thomas Paine, January 9, 1777, in Showman, *Papers of Greene*, II, p. 3.
44. Matlack to Arnold, October 5, 1778, and Arnold's response of October 6; and Matlack's letter of October 10, with Arnold's answer of October 12, in *General Court Martial for the Trial of General Arnold*, pp. 25–31.
45. *Pennsylvania Packet*, November 14, 1778.
46. *Pennsylvania Packet*, November 12 and 17, 1778; Wallace, *Traitorous Hero*, pp. 166–7.
47. *General Court Martial for the Trial of General Arnold*, pp. 10–13.
48. See Arnold to Schuyler, Philadelphia, November 30, 1778, CL, James S. Schoff Revolutionary War Collection, Box 2; Van Doren, *Secret History*, pp. 182–3.
49. Morris to Clinton, Philadelphia, January 26, 1779, in *LDC*, XI, pp. 520–1; New York Delegates [John Jay, James Duane, William Floyd, and Francis Lewis] to Clinton, Philadelphia, February 3, 1779, in *LDC*, XII, pp. 17–18; also Arnold, *Life of Arnold*, p. 241.
50. *Remembrancer, 1778–1779*, pp. 349–51.
51. Walker, "Life of Margaret Shippen," pp. 36–8; Henry Knox to William Knox, Philadelphia, February 3, 1779, GLC, MSS 2437-00748.
52. Walker, "Life of Margaret Shippen," pp. 36–9.
53. *Remembrancer, 1778–1779*, pp. 351.
54. Tilghman to Burd, March 13, 1779, in Walker, "Life of Margaret Shippen," p. 39; Henry Knox to William Knox, Pluckemin, NJ, February 13, 1779, GLC, MSS 2437-00750.
55. See *General Court Martial for the Trial of General Arnold*, Introduction, pp. xv–xvi, xvii; *Pennsylvania Packet*, February 27 and March 4 and 6, 1779.
56. Paca to Bryan, March 4, and to the Pennsylvania Council, March 9, 1779, in *LDC*, XII, pp. 152–3, 178–80.
57. *JCC*, XIII, pp. 324–6.
58. Arnold to Jay, Philadelphia, March 17 and 18, 1779, in PCC, "Letters of general officers, 1775–89," I, pp. 165, 169–70; and Arnold to Washington, Philadelphia, March 19, 1779, *PWRW*, XIX, p. 527.
59. See Colonel Charles Pettit to Nathanael Greene, Philadelphia, March 29, 1779, in Showman, *Papers of Greene*, III, p. 374.
60. Arnold to Jay, Philadelphia, March 27, 1779, in PCC, "Letters from general officers, 1775–89," I, p. 173; *JCC*, XIII (3 April 1779), pp. 412–17.
61. Arnold to Jay, Philadelphia, April 16, 1779, in PCC, "Letters from general officers, 1775–89," I, pp. 177–8.
62. Pettit to Greene, Philadelphia, March 29, 1779, in Showman, *Papers of Greene*, III, p. 375; Wallace, *Traitorous Hero*, p. 174.
63. Chastellux, *Travels*, I, p. 312 (note 61). Grieve took such a prurient interest in matters relating to sex, whether involving humans or barnyard fowls, that the disapproving editor of an early one-volume edition of the *Travels* felt obliged to apologize for his poor taste. See Preface to "The American Edition" (New York, 1828), p. 4.
64. *PWRW*, XX, p. 112.
65. See Washington to Arnold, Headquarters, Middlebrook, April 20 and 28, and May 7, 1779, *PWRW*, XX, pp. 141, 250, 357.
66. Arnold to Washington, Philadelphia, May 5, 1779, ibid., pp. 327–9.
67. Washington to Arnold, Middlebrook, May 15, 1779, ibid., pp. 498–9.
68. Deane to Greene, Philadelphia, May 29, 1779, in Showman, *Papers of Greene*, IV, pp. 98–9.

Chapter Five

1. See "Authentic account of Major André," *First Supplement to the Political Magazine* (1781), pp. 171–2; William H.W. Sabine (ed.), *Historical Memoirs (from 26 August 1778 to 12 November 1783) of William Smith* (Arno Press, New York, 1971), p. 97 (entry for April 24, 1779); Willcox, *American Rebellion*, p. xxxvii.

2. See André to Clinton, "York Island," May 10, 1779, in Van Doren, *Secret History*, p. 440; for André's appointment as Clinton's "intelligence officer," see Roger Kaplan, "The hidden war: British intelligence operations during the American Revolution," *WMQ*, XXXXVII, 1 (January 1990), pp. 115–38; 123. Stansbury had settled in Philadelphia in 1767, "where his business enabled him to support in a genteel manner a wife, and numerous family." See "Memorial of Joseph Stansbury," AO 13/83A, fol. 560.

3. Declaration of Joseph Stansbury, London, March 4, 1784 (in support of Benedict Arnold's claim for compensation from the American Loyalist Claims Commission), AO, 13/96A, fol. 75.

4. See André to Clinton, "York Island," May 10, 1779, enclosing André to Stansbury, undated, but clearly of the same date, in Van Doren, *Secret History*, pp. 439–40.

5. On Clinton as the instigator of the treason, see, for example, "Some account of Benedict Arnold, brigadier-general in the British army," *European Magazine and London Review for 1783* (February), p. 85; for Grieve's comments, see Chastellux, *Travels*, I, p. 273; also, first English edition (1787), I, pp. 97–8 (note).

6. See André to Robinson, Headquarters, Denyses, October 6, 1779, in Benedict Arnold Papers (MSS AM 1446), Houghton Library, Harvard University; Lorenzo Sabine, *The American Loyalists, or Biographical Sketches of Adherents to the British Crown in the War of the Revolution* (Charles C. Little and James Brown, Boston, 1847), pp. 562–3; see also Van Doren, *Secret History*, p. 193.

7. For Hamilton's verdict, see "Letter from a gentleman in camp to his friend in Philadelphia," *Pennsylvania Evening Post*, October 14, 1780; among numerous references to Arnold's alleged love of gold, see *Connecticut Journal*, October 5, 1780, under "Fishkill, September 28," and "Extract of a letter from camp, Tappan, September 26," *Pennsylvania Packet*, September 30, 1780; Wallace, *Traitorous Hero*, p. 196; Nathaniel Philbrick, *Valiant Ambition: George Washington, Benedict Arnold, and the fate of the American Revolution* (Viking, New York, 2016), p. 241.

8. See "Declaration of Stansbury," March 4, 1784, and "The memorial of Benedict Arnold late of the Province of Pennsylvania in America, and now of the city of London esquire" [1784], in AO, 13/96A, fols. 75–6; for Arnold's deliberate haggling, see, for example, Charles Royster, " 'The nature of treason': Revolutionary virtue and American reactions to Benedict Arnold," *WMQ*, XXXVI, 2 (April 1979), pp. 163–93; 186.

9. See Arnold's address "To the inhabitants of America," New York, October 7, 1780, in Arnold, *Life of Arnold*, pp. 330–2; "Arnold's memorial," [1784], in AO 13/96A, fol. 76. James Kirby Martin has emphasized the "mounting bitterness" that gradually transformed Arnold "from an intensely enthusiastic patriot to a dangerous enemy of the Revolution" (*Benedict Arnold, Revolutionary Hero*, p. 5); see also his earlier article, "Benedict Arnold's treason as political protest," in *Parameters: The Journal of the US Army War College*, XI, 3 (1981), pp. 63–74.

10. Arnold to Johnstone, July 18, 1784, in *Magazine of American History*, X (1883), p. 314.

11. Smith, *Authentic Narrative*, p. 15.

12. Ibid.

13. Undated Clinton memorandum, CP, Vol. 241/file 6; Willcox, *American Rebellion*, pp. 214, 462 (draft of letter to Germain, New York, October 11, 1780).

14. Smith, *Authentic Narrative*, p. 16; Robertson to Amherst, New York, October 6, 1780, in Milton M. Klein and Ronald W. Howard (eds.), *The Twilight of British Rule in Revolutionary America: The New York letter book of General James Robertson, 1780–83* (New York State Historical Association, Cooperstown, NY, 1983), p. 156; Hamilton's "Letter from a gentleman at camp to his friend in Philadelphia," *Pennsylvania Evening Post*, October 14, 1780.

15. Arnold to Washington, "On board the *Vulture*," September 25, 1780, in Jared Sparks, *The Writings of George Washington*, 12 vols. (Ferdinand Andrews, Boston, 1833–39), VII, p. 533; Arnold's address "To the inhabitants of America," in Arnold, *Life of Arnold*, p. 331.

16. Arnold to Washington, Philadelphia, May 14, 1779, *PWRW*, XX, pp. 481–2; Clinton to Arnold, mid-June 1779, in Van Doren, *Secret History*, p. 448.

17. "Arnold's memorial," [1784], in AO 13/96A, fol. 76; Arnold to Clinton, Holles Street, London, July 23, 1792, and Clinton to Arnold, Orwell Park, August 2, 1792, PRO 30/8/108, fols. 203–5.

18. Willcox, *American Rebellion*, p. 215; Simcoe to Lord Portland ("Private"), Wolford Lodge, Honiton, October 17, 1797, in NA, HO [Home Office], 42/41/81, fol. 243; Simcoe, *Remarks*, pp. 50, 53.

19. Chastellux, *Travels*, I, p. 147 (December 5, 1780).

20. Thomson to John Jay, Philadelphia, October 12, 1780, in *LDC*, XVI, p. 196; on André's letter to Mrs. Arnold, which was found among her husband's papers after the treason was exposed, see also *Pennsylvania Packet*, September 30, 1780, and below, pp. 183–4.

21. Sparks, *Life and Treason of Arnold*, pp. 152–3, 162.

22. *General Court Martial for the Trial of Major-General Arnold*, Introduction, p. viii; Sargent/Abbatt, *Life of André*, p. 246; Albert Bushnell Hart, "New light on Arnold's treason from the Varick Papers," in introduction to *The Varick Court of Inquiry to Investigate the Implication of Colonel Varick (Arnold's Private Secretary) in the Arnold Treason* (Bibliophile Society, Boston, 1907), p. 44.

23. André to Margaret Chew, New York [*c*. May] 1779, in Van Doren, *Secret History*, pp. 440–1.

24. On Odell's role, see ibid., pp. 197–8.

25. "Memorial of Jonathan Odell, Master of Arts, and late Rector of Burlington and Mount Holly in New Jersey, London, 23 March 1784," in AO 13/19, fols. 256–7.

26. André to Clinton, York Island, May 10, 1779, in Van Doren, *Secret History*, p. 440.

27. Odell to André, New York, May 31, 1779 in ibid., pp. 442–3.

28. Arnold to André, May 23, 1779, in ibid., pp. 441–2.

29. Willcox, *American Rebellion*, pp. 124–6.

30. Sargent/Abbatt, *Life of André*, p. 244.

31. Willcox, *Portrait of a General*, p. 276; Gruber, *Peebles' American War*, pp. 266–8; Wortley, *A Prime Minister and his Son*, p. 148; Willcox, *American Rebellion*, p. 125.

32. André to Arnold, mid-June 1779, in Van Doren, *Secret History*, p. 448.

33. See André to Arnold, undated draft, *c*. mid-June 1779, in ibid., pp. 446–7.

34. *General Court Martial for the Trial of Major-General Arnold*, pp. 2–3.

35. Arnold to Washington, Philadelphia, July 13, 1779, *PWRW*, XXI, p. 462.

36. For Drummond, see CP, Vol. 274: "John André intelligence reports, 1779–80" (entry for June 24, 1779); Tenny to Dr. Peter Turner, Philadelphia, March 20, 1782, in "Dr. Peter Turner letterbook (9 September 1774–16 May 1789)," CL, James S. Schoff Revolutionary War Collection.

37. Stansbury to André, July 11, 1779, and Odell to André, July 18, 1779, in Van Doren, *Secret History*, pp. 449–51.

38. See extracts of letters from Collier to "Mr. Stephens," *Raisonable*, off New York, July 27, 1779, and Tryon to Clinton, New York, July 20, in *Remembrancer, 1779*, pp. 355, 362–5.

39. Washington to Wayne, New Windsor, July 10, 1779, *PWRW*, XXI, pp. 432–4.

40. Kaplan, "Hidden war," pp. 123–6.

41. Wallace, *Appeal to Arms*, pp. 196–8; Wayne to Washington, Stony Point, July 16 (2 a.m.), and July 17, 1779, *PWRW*, XXI, pp. 522, 541–5.

42. "André's Intelligence Book, 1779–80," CP, Vol. 274 (July 24, 1779).

43. See Armstrong Starkey, "Paoli to Stony Point: Military ethics and weaponry during the American Revolution," *Journal of Military History*, LVIII (January 1994), pp. 7–27; Congress's resolutions of July 26, 1779, *Remembrancer, 1779*, pp. 372–3.

44. Wortley, *A Prime Minister and His Son*, p. 149.

45. Odell to André, July 18, 1779, in Van Doren, *Secret History*, pp. 450–1.

46. André to Arnold, late July 1779, ibid., p. 453.

47. Stansbury to André (undated, but in response to André's letter to Arnold of late July 1779), ibid., pp. 453–4.

48. André to Mrs. Margaret Arnold, Headquarters, New York, August 16, 1779, and Mrs. Arnold to Captain André, Philadelphia, October 13, 1779, ibid., pp. 454–5.

49. Washington to Major-General Lord Stirling, August 21, 1779, and to Lafayette, September 12, 1779, in *WW*, XVI, pp. 145–6, 267–8; in Wortley, *A Prime Minister and his Son*, pp. 150–1.

50. Willcox, *Portrait of a General*, pp. 284–5.

51. Gruber, *Peebles' American War* (October 22, 1779), p. 301.

52. Rodney to Germain, "Sandwich," St. Lucia, December 22, 1780 ("Private"), in *Stopford-Sackville Manuscripts*, II, p. 193; also, William B. Willcox, "Rhode Island in British strategy, 1780–1781," *Journal of Modern History*, XVII, 4 (December 1945), pp. 304–31.

53. Paul David Nelson, *Francis Rawdon-Hastings, Marquess of Hastings: Soldier, peer of the realm, governor-general of India* (Fairleigh Dickinson University Press, Madison, 2005), pp. 66–8; Van Doren, *Secret History*, p. 233.

Chapter Six

1. "Williamsburg, 15 January," *Pennsylvania Gazette*, January 26, 1780.

2. "Intelligence of January 10, 1780," *Pennsylvania Packet*, January 27, 1780.

3. "Circular to governors of the middle states," Headquarters, Morristown, December 16, 1779, in *WW*, XVII, pp. 273–4.
4. Washington to the magistrates of New Jersey, Headquarters, Morristown, January 8, 1780, ibid., pp. 362–5.
5. "General orders," Morristown, January 3, 1780, ibid., pp. 343–7; Washington to the major-generals and officers commanding brigades, Headquarters, Morristown, January 27, 1780, ibid., p. 425. For "the gauntlet," see Caroline Cox, *A Proper Sense of Honor: Service and sacrifice in George Washington's army* (University of North Carolina Press, Chapel Hill, NC, 2004), pp. 86–7, 108, and Charles Patrick Neimeyer, *America Goes to War: A social history of the Continental Army* (New York University Press, New York, 1995), p. 140.
6. See *General Court Martial for the Trial of General Arnold*.
7. Ibid., pp. 103–7.
8. Ibid., pp. 103, 132.
9. Ibid., p. 133.
10. See Cadwalader's "Reply," in *A Reprint of the Reed and Cadwalader Pamphlets, with an Appendix* (J. Munsell, Albany, NY, 1863), pp. 9–10, 21.
11. Ibid., p. 36.
12. Huntington to Colonel Samuel Webb, Morristown, January 22, 1780, in Ford, *Correspondence and Journals of Webb*, II, p. 242; *JCC*, XVI, pp. 161–2; "General orders," April 6, 1780, in *WW*, XVIII, p. 225.
13. Council of Pennsylvania to Congress, February 3, 1780, in *General Court Martial for the Trial of General Arnold*, p. 168; Cadwalader's "Reply," p. 36.
14. Charles Stedman, *History of the Origin, Progress and Termination of the American War*, 2 vols. (London, 1794), II, p. 274.
15. "[Washington's] Instructions to Major Benjamin Tallmadge," [West Point], October 17, 1779, in *PWRW*, XXII, pp. 749–51.
16. Washington to Tallmadge, Middlebrook, New Jersey, March 21, 1779, in *PWRW*, XIX, pp. 561–3. Remarkably, the identities of the Culper Ring were only revealed last century, when Morton Pennypacker published his *General Washington's Spies on Long Island and in New York* (Long Island Historical Association, New York, 1939). While Pennypacker discovered and presented much extremely useful information, including the texts of original documents from the George Washington Papers in the Library of Congress, some of his conclusions, particularly regarding the significance of the Culper Ring's reports for the outcome of major military operations, are speculative, and unsupported by credible evidence. The belief that the Culpers were unsung heroes who "saved" the American Revolution has nonetheless been spread through best-selling books, and the popular AMC television series *Turn* (four seasons, 2013–17), loosely based on Alexander Rose's non-fictional *Washington's Spies: The story of America's first spy ring* (Bantam, New York, 2006).
17. Washington to the president of Congress, Headquarters, Morristown, January 18, 1780, in *WW*, XVII, p. 406; Gruber, *Peebles' American War* (December 16, 1779), pp. 315–16.
18. See Washington to Brigadier-General William Woodford, December 13, 1779, in *WW*, XVII, pp. 253–4; "Baltimore, 21 December 1779," *Pennsylvania Gazette*, January 5, 1780.
19. Washington to Irvine, Morristown, January 9, 1780, in *WW*, XVII, pp. 368–9.
20. Paul David Nelson, *William Alexander, Lord Stirling* (University of Alabama Press, Tuscaloosa, AL, 1987).
21. Washington to Stirling, Morristown, January 12, 1780, in *WW*, XVII, pp. 379–84.
22. Report under "January 16" in *New Jersey Journal*, January 18, 1780; Simcoe, *Journal of the Operations of the Queen's Rangers*, pp. 79–80; Stirling to Washington, January 16, 1780, in GWP (MSS 44693, Reel 063).
23. While Washington never nominated Greene in writing, it was widely believed that he was the commander-in-chief's favored successor. See, for example, Thacher, *Military Journal*, p. 209 (September 21, 1780); also Terry Golway, *Washington's General: Nathanael Greene and the triumph of the American Revolution* (Henry Holt, New York, 2006), p. 3.
24. Tarleton to unknown recipient, "Princes Town Decr. 17, 1776," in Richard Ketchum (ed.), "New war letters of Banastre Tarleton," in *Narratives of the Revolution in New York: A collection of articles from the New-York Historical Society* (New-York Historical Society, New York, 1975), pp. 120–37, 128; "Particulars of the Mischianza," *Gentleman's Magazine*, 1778 (August), p. 355.
25. See Washington to Brigadier-General Samuel Holden Parsons, Valley Forge, March 5 and 8, 1778, in Hall, *Life and Letters of Parsons*, pp. 158–9; Abbatt, *Memoirs of Heath*, pp. 247–8.
26. Simcoe, *Journal of the Operations of the Queen's Rangers*, pp. 87–9.
27. St. Clair to Washington, Springfield, New Jersey, February 11, 1780, in Smith, *St. Clair Papers*, I, pp. 499–500; Washington to St. Clair, Headquarters, Morristown, February 12, 1780, in *WW*, XVIII, pp. 6–7.

28. Washington to Heath, Morristown, February 2, 1780, in *WW*, XVII, pp. 478–9; Heath to Washington, Highlands, January 27, 1780, *The Heath Papers*, III, in *Collections of the Massachusetts Historical Society*, 7th Series, V (1905), p. 23.

29. Abbatt, *Memoirs of Heath*, p. 1; Chastellux, *Travels*, I, p. 92.

30. See David Hackett Fischer, *Paul Revere's Ride* (Oxford University Press, New York, 1994), pp. 246–53.

31. Washington to Heath, February 3, 1777, in *PWRW*, VIII, p. 229.

32. Heath to Washington, Headquarters, "Robinson's House," January 10, 1780, in *Heath Papers*, III, pp. 8–9.

33. See Heath to Washington, Headquarters, January 10, January 27, and February 2, 1780, ibid., pp. 8–9, 22, 27–9.

34. Heath to Clinton, Headquarters, Highlands, January 25, 1780, and also Heath to Washington, Highlands, January 26, 1780, ibid., pp. 15–16, 17–18.

35. Heath to Howe, Headquarters, Highlands, February 18, 1780, ibid., p. 34.

36. John K. Alexander, "The Fort Wilson incident of 1779: A case study of the revolutionary crowd," *WMQ*, XXXI, 4 (October 1974), pp. 589–612; Irvin, "Streets of Philadelphia," *PMHB* (2005), pp. 37–39; Wallace, *Traitorous Hero*, pp. 207–8.

37. Arnold to Washington, Philadelphia, March 6, 1780, in Jared Sparks, *Correspondence of the American Revolution; being letters of eminent men to George Washington*, 4 vols. (Little Brown, Boston, 1853), II, p. 409.

38. Washington to the Board of Admiralty, Headquarters, Morristown, March 15, 1780, in *WW*, XVIII, pp. 114–15.

39. Arnold to Washington, Philadelphia, March 20, 1780, in Sparks, *Correspondence of the American Revolution*, II, pp. 410–11, including note on Arnold to Deane, March 22, 1780; Washington to Arnold, Morristown, March 28, 1780, in *WW*, XVIII, p. 173.

40. The report of the Board of Congress is in *JCC*, XVI, pp. 393–6; see also the helpful discussions in Van Doren, *Secret History*, pp. 254–7, and Wallace, *Traitorous Hero*, pp. 210–12.

41. Barbé-Marbois's *Complot d'Arnold et de Sir Henry Clinton* (Paris, 1816) was translated as the "Conspiracy of Arnold, 1780" in *The American Register, or the Summary Review of History, Politics, and Literature*, II (1817), pp. 15–63; 25, 32–3. For the cautionary comments of editor and translator Robert Walsh, see the Introduction, p. xvi. The "interpolations" included a long letter purportedly "from an emissary of Sir Henry Clinton," making the first approach to Arnold and "supposed" to have been found among his papers after the exposure of the treason. Walsh was so skeptical of the letter's authenticity that he omitted it from his translation. By contrast, Winthrop Sargent believed it was genuine, and probably written by Colonel Beverly Robinson; he included a translation in his 1861 biography of André (Sargent/Abbatt, *Life of André*, pp. 502–5). Evidence subsequently revealed by Carl Van Doren's examination of Sir Henry Clinton's papers, which leaves no doubt that Arnold initiated the correspondence with the British general himself, shows that Walsh was fully justified in dismissing the letter as one of Barbé-Marbois's fabrications.

42. Barbé-Marbois, "Conspiracy of Arnold," pp. 27–9; *Pennsylvania Packet*, September 30, 1780; Van Doren, *Secret History*, pp. 253–4.

43. Kaplan, "Hidden war," *WMQ* (1990), p. 129.

44. See "Knyphausen's notes regarding Arnold," in Beckwith's hand, in Van Doren, *Secret History*, pp. 458–9.

45. Lafayette to Washington, "At the entrance of Boston Harbor," April 27, 1780, cited in Douglas Southall Freeman, *George Washington, a Biography*, Vol. 5: *Victory with the Help of France* (Charles Scribner's Sons, New York, 1952), p. 161; Lee Kennett, *The French Forces in America, 1780–83* (Greenwood Press, Westport, CT, 1977), pp. 3–19.

46. Willcox, *American Rebellion*, pp. 177, 439–40.

47. Arnold to Beckwith, Philadelphia, June 7, 1780, in Van Doren, *Secret History*, pp. 459–60; Washington to Arnold, Morristown, June 4, 1780, in *WW*, XVIII, p. 476 (and note); Arnold to Washington, June 7, 1780, *FO*, Washington/99-01-02-02021.

48. Arnold to Beckwith, June 7, 1780, in Van Doren, *Secret History*, p. 460; "General Arnold's services," [1792], PRO 30/8/108, fols. 194–5. This revealing document was written by Arnold in 1792 to support his appeal to Prime Minister William Pitt the Younger for financial assistance. Despite this motive it deserves careful consideration, as it includes unique details and insights. There is a copy, with some small—but telling—amendments, among Sir Henry Clinton's papers in the Clement's Library at the University of Michigan (CP, Vol. 215/file 64).

49. Barbé-Marbois, "Conspiracy of Arnold," p. 34; Arnold to Beckwith or André, Morristown, June 12, 1780, in Van Doren, *Secret History*, p. 460.

50. Schuyler to Arnold, Morristown, June 2, 1780, in *LDC*, XV, p. 240.

51. Washington to Joseph Reed, Headquarters, Passaic Falls, October 18, 1780, in *WW*, XX, pp. 213–14; Livingston to Washington, Trenton, June 22, 1780, in *LDC*, XV, pp. 363–4; Washington to Livingston, June 29, 1780, in *WW*, XIX, pp. 90–2; Arnold to Beckwith or André, June 15, 1780, in Van Doren, *Secret History*, p. 460.

52. See Arnold to Beckwith or André (extract), Fishkill, June 16, 1780, in Van Doren, *Secret History*, pp. 460–1; Howe to Washington, Orange Town, September 26, 1780, *FO*, Washington/99-01-02-03393.

53. On the protest of the Connecticut troops, see Carl Van Doren, *Mutiny in January* (Viking Press, New York, 1943), pp. 20–3; N-YHS, Sebastian Bauman Papers, 1775–1803 (Microfilm 658); Washington to Jones, May 31, 1780, in *WW*, XVIII, p. 453.

54. For the British raid on New Jersey, see Thomas Fleming, *The Forgotten Victory: The battle for New Jersey, 1780* (Reader's Digest Press, New York, 1973).

55. Greene to Washington, Springfield, June 24, 1780, Showman, *Papers of Greene*, VI, pp. 34–8; also C. Bray and Paul E. Bushnell (eds.), *Diary of a Common Soldier in the American Revolution, 1775–1783: An annotated edition of the military journal of Jeremiah Greenman* (Northern Illinois University Press, DeKalb, IL, 1978), p. 174; "Casualty list," in Roberts, *March to Quebec*, p. 38 (Captain Ward's Company).

56. Clinton to [William Eden], New York, August 18, 1780, in B.F. Stevens, *Facsimiles of Manuscripts in European Archives Relating to America, 1775–1783*, 25 vols. (London, 1889–98), VII, item 730.

57. For the planned attack on Rhode Island, see Willcox, *Portrait of a General*, pp. 324–30; Willcox, "Rhode Island in British strategy, 1780–81," *Journal of Modern History* (1945), pp. 308–9.

58. Howard C. Rice Jr. and Anne S.K. Brown (trans. and ed.), *The American Campaigns of Rochambeau's Army, 1780, 1781, 1782, 1783. Vol. 1: The Journals of Clermont-Crèvecoeur, Verger, and Berthier* (Princeton University Press, Princeton, NJ, and Brown University Press, Providence, RI, 1972), p. 17; Simcoe, *Journal of the Operations of the Queen's Rangers*, p. 101.

59. Dayton to Washington, July 21, 1780, via *FO*, Washington/99-01-02-02590; Hamilton to Lafayette, Preakness, July 21, 1780, in Harold C. Syrett (ed.), *The Papers of Alexander Hamilton*, 27 vols. (Columbia University Press, New York, 1961–1987), II, pp. 362–3.

60. Acomb, *Journal of von Closen*, p. 32; Rice and Brown, *American Campaigns of Rochambeau's Army*, I, p. 120.

61. Washington to Greene, July 14, 1780, in *WW*, XIX, p. 169; Heath to Washington, Newport, July 25, 1780, 9 p.m., *FO*, Washington/99-01-02-02567; Lafayette to Washington, Newport, July 27, 1780, *FO*, Washington/99-01-02-02674; Washington to Lund Washington, Headquarters in Bergen city, July 17, 1780, *FO*, Washington/99-01-02-02537.

62. Washington to Lafayette, "Robinson's in the Highlands," July 31, 1780, in *WW*, XIX, pp. 283–4; Willcox, *American Rebellion*, p. 202; Willcox, *Portrait of a General*, p. 331 (note).

63. Acomb, *Journal of von Closen*, p. 35; "Narrative of George Matthew of the Coldstream Guards," *Historical Magazine*, I (1857), pp. 102–6; 105.

64. Willcox, *American Rebellion*, pp. 207–8.

65. "General Arnold's services [1792]," PRO 30/8/108, fol. 194.

66. Clinton to William Pitt, *c.* November 17, 1792, CP, Vol. 215/file 48, 1–2 (memo).

67. Stansbury to Beckwith or André, July 7, 1780, in Van Doren, *Secret History*, p. 462.

68. See Arnold to André, July 11 and 12, 1780, in ibid., pp. 462–3.

69. André to Arnold (undated, but received by Arnold on July 13, 1780), and Arnold to André, July 15, 1780, in ibid., pp. 464–5.

70. *JCC*, XVII, p. 649.

71. "Extract from a diary kept by Mr. [Tobias] Lear at Mount Vernon, in 1786" (entry for October 23), in Rush, *Occasional Productions*, pp. 80–1; "General orders," Peekskill, August 1, 1780, in *WW*, XIX, p. 302.

72. Greene to Washington, Verplanck's Point, August 3, 1780, in Showman, *Papers of Greene*, VI, pp. 178–9.

73. "General orders (and after orders)," Peekskill, August 3, 1780, in *WW*, XIX, pp. 311–3; *Pennsylvania Gazette*, August 16, 1780 (under "Chatham, August 9"); Arnold to André, July 12, in Van Doren, *Secret History*, p. 463.

Chapter Seven

1. Smith, *Authentic Narrative*, p. 13; Thacher, *Military Journal*, p. 131; Arnold to Howe, "Robinson's House," August 5, 1780, GWP (MSS 44693, Reel 069); Matthew L. Davis (ed.), *Memoirs of Aaron Burr, with Miscellaneous Selections from His Correspondence*, 2 vols. (Harper, New York, 1837–38), I, pp. 219–20.

2. Washington to Arnold, August 3, 1780, in *WW*, XIX, pp. 309–11; for the "Neutral Ground," see Campbell, *Revolutionary Services of General Hull*, p. 147; Song Bok Kim, "The limits of politicization in the American Revolution: The experience of Westchester County, New York," *Journal of American History*, LXXX, 3 (December 1993), pp. 868–89.

3. Beckwith to André, Headquarters, Morris House, July 30, 1780, in Van Doren, *Secret History*, p. 467.

4. Stansbury to Odell, August 14, 1780, and "extracts" of two letters from Arnold to Margaret Arnold, sent by Stansbury to Odell, in ibid., pp. 467–8; see also Stansbury to André, July 7, 1779, and Beckwith to André, July 30, 1780, in ibid., pp. 449–50, 467.

5. *Memoirs, Correspondence and Manuscripts of General Lafayette*, 3 vols. (Saunders and Otley, New York, 1837), I, p. 254; Louis Gottschalk, *Lafayette and the Close of the American Revolution* (University of Chicago Press, Chicago, 1942), p. 131; Stansbury to Beckwith or André, July 7, 1780, in Van Doren, *Secret History*, p. 462; Arnold to Howe, "Robinson's House," August 5, 1780, GWP (MSS 44693, Reel 069).

6. Howe to Arnold, "near Orangetown," August 14, 1780, and Arnold to Howe, "Robinson's House," August 16, 1780, in GWP (MSS 44693, Reel 069).

7. For the context, see Arnold to Sheldon, "Robinson's House," September 7, 1780, in Sparks, *Washington's Writings*, VII (Appendix), p. 522; on Hunter, see John Bakeless, *Turncoats, Traitors and Heroes: Espionage in the American Revolution* (Lippincott, New York, 1959), pp. 241–3, and Kenneth A. Daigler, *Spies, Patriots, and Traitors: American intelligence in the Revolutionary War* (Georgetown University Press, Washington, DC, 2014), p. 173.

8. *Pennsylvania Gazette*, August 16, 1780; Abbatt, *Memoirs of Heath*, p. 264.

9. Washington to Brigadier-General John Cadwalader, Tappan, October 5, 1780, in *WW*, XX, pp. 121–4.

10. George Rudé, *The Crowd in History: A study of popular disturbances in France and England, 1730–1848* (1964; revised ed., Lawrence & Wishart, London, 1981), p. 59; Thomas Bartlett, "'A weapon of war yet untried': Irish Catholics and the armed forces of the Crown, 1760–1830," in T.G. Fraser and Keith Jeffery (eds.), *Men, Women and War* (Lilliput Press, Dublin, 1993), pp. 66–85. For the riots in general, see Frank McLynn, *Crime and Punishment in Eighteenth-Century England* (Routledge, Oxford, 1989), pp. 232–9.

11. *Gentleman's Magazine*, 1780 (June), p. 265.

12. *Gentleman's Magazine*, 1780 (July), p. 314.

13. For the king's proclamation, see *General Evening Post*, June 8–10, 1780.

14. Colonel Stuart to his father, John, earl of Bute, [June] 1780, and June 10, 1780, in Wortley, *A Prime Minister and his Son*, pp. 187, 190.

15. *Gentleman's Magazine*, 1780 (July), pp. 342–3; *Whitehall Evening Post*, July 11–13, 1780.

16. *Gentleman's Magazine*, 1780 (July), p. 347.

17. Lord Mountstuart to Charles Stuart, Hill Street, June 14, 1780, in Wortley, *A Prime Minister and His Son*, p. 193.

18. Hamilton to Elizabeth Schuyler, Teaneck, NJ, [-] August 1780, in Syrett, *Papers of Hamilton*, II, p. 398.

19. Washington to Rochambeau, Headquarters near Fort Lee, August 26, 1780, in *WW*, XIX, pp. 443–4.

20. See statement of Tobias Wrightman, in "Information of deserters and others not included in private intelligence" (unpaginated), Emmett Collection, NYPL. This ledger was maintained by Captain Beckwith as a supplement to the "Intelligence Book" started by Major André during the previous summer. While most of the entries are undated, many can be fixed by the context; Howe to Washington, August 26, 1780, *FO*, Washington/99-01-02-03061.

21. André to Arnold, c. July 24, 1780, enclosed in Odell to Stansbury, July 24, 1780, in Van Doren, *Secret History*, pp. 465–6.

22. "General orders, 1780," Orderly Book Collection, N-YHS.

23. Lamb to Arnold, West Point, August 12 and 18, 1780, in Leake, *Life of Lamb*, p. 251; Washington to Arnold, Headquarters, Bergen County, September 7, 1780, in *WW*, XX, p. 11; Arnold to Washington, "Robinson's House," September 12, 1780 in *FO*, Washington/99-01-02-03263.

24. Clinton to an unidentified correspondent, undated but early October 1780, in Van Doren, *Secret History*, p. 477; André to Chew, New York, June 18, 1780, in GLC, MSS 05533-01.

25. For a valuable study of Smith's role, see Richard J. Koke, *Accomplice in Treason: Joshua Hett Smith and the Arnold conspiracy* (New-York Historical Society, New York, 1973).

26. Varick to Arnold, Hackensack, New Jersey, August 7, 1780, in Hart, *Varick Court of Inquiry*, p. 84.

27. See testimony in ibid., pp. 134, 138, 183–4.

28. "General orders, 1780," N-YHS.

29. Arnold to André, August 30, 1780, in Van Doren, *Secret History*, p. 470.

30. Hart, *Varick Court of Inquiry*, pp. 124–5, 171–2.
31. Parsons to Washington, Danbury, April 6, 1782, *FO*, Washington/99-01-02-08096.
32. See Parsons to Washington, October 1780, *FO*, Washington/99-01-02-03773. This explanation followed a brief covering note, written from "Camp" on October 1, by which Parsons forwarded to Washington the "Gustavus" letter of August 30, 1780. See *FO*, Washington/99-01-02-03456; "Certificate of Mr. William Heron," October 26, 1780, in Hart, *Varick Court of Inquiry*, pp. 99–102.
33. Heron to Washington, New York, July 26, 1790, in Dorothy Twohig, Mark A. Mastromarino, et al. (eds.), *Papers of Washington, Presidential Series*, 18 vols. (University of Virginia Press, Charlottesville, 1987–2015), VI, pp. 125–9.
34. See "Intelligence" from "H" [William Heron], received by Oliver De Lancey, September 4, 1780, in CP, Vol. 121/file 31; "Mr. Heron's information at a conversation in New York, Monday, 4 September 1780," in Stevens, *Facsimiles*, VII, item 733; Sabine, *Historical Memoirs of Smith*, p. 329 (entries for September 4–5, 1780).
35. See "Intelligence" from William Heron to Oliver De Lancey, October 1, 1780 (original in cipher and disguised hand, sent to the "care of Revd John Sayre," New York; deciphered version in De Lancey's hand), in CP, Vol. 125/file 2.
36. See "The petition of Mary McCarthay" [*sic*] to Sir Guy Carleton, New York, August 23, 1783, PRO 30/55/78, no. 8798; "Information of deserters and others," NYPL.
37. Hart, *Varick Court of Inquiry*, pp. 124–5, 171–2; Arnold to Barber, Headquarters, "Robinson's House," September 4, 1780, in GWP (MSS 44693, Reel 170). Arnold's letter of September 3 has not yet been found.
38. Arnold to Greene, Headquarters, "Robinson's House," August 23, 1780, in Showman, *Papers of Greene*, VI, p. 230.
39. Parsons to Arnold, September 5, 1780, in Hall, *Life and Letters of Parsons*, p. 303.
40. "Information of deserters and others," NYPL; Cramond to André, Morris House, Manhattan, September 12, 1780, CP, Vol. 123/file 1.
41. See Shaw to Lamb, "Camp at Preakenis," July 12, 1780, in Leake, *Life of Lamb*, p. 243; and Shaw to Nathaniel Shaw, August 10, 1780, in Joseph Quincy (ed.), *The Journals of Major Samuel Shaw* (Boston, 1847), p. 76.
42. Arnold to Parsons, September 12, 1780, cited in Richard H. Kohn, "American generals of the revolution: Subordination and restraint," in Don Higginbotham (ed.), *Reconsiderations on the Revolutionary War: Selected essays* (Greenwood Press, Westport, CT, 1978), pp. 104–23; 116.
43. See Cornwallis to Germain, Camden, August 21, 1780, in CP, Vol. 118/file 20; and Barrette to Clinton, "Camp near Camden," August 26, 1780, in CP, Vol. 118/file 41.
44. Roger Lamb, *An Original and Authentic Journal of Occurrences During the Late American War* (Wilkinson & Courtney, Dublin, 1809), pp. 262, 305.
45. Gruber, *Peebles' American War*, pp. 404–5, 407–8 (entries for September 5, 7, and 20, 1780).
46. Arnold to Greene, Headquarters, "Robinson's House," September 12, 1780, Showman, *Papers of Greene*, VI, p. 281.
47. Arnold to Sheldon, "Robinson's House," September 7 and 10, 1780; "John Anderson" to Sheldon, New York, September 7, 1780; Sheldon to Arnold, Lower Salem, September 9, 1780, all in Sparks, *Washington's Writings*, VII (Appendix), pp. 522–4.
48. Arnold to André, September 10, 1780, in Van Doren, *Secret History*, pp. 471–2.
49. Arnold to Washington, Dobbs Ferry, September 11, 1780, via *FO*, Washington/99-01-02-03249.
50. Clinton to André, September 11, 1780, in Van Doren, *Secret History*, p. 472.
51. See Arnold's "Services," enclosed in Arnold to William Pitt, Holles Street, August 23, 1792, PRO 30/8/108, fol. 194. In the copy in Sir Henry Clinton's Papers, the phrasing of this passage is given more diplomatically as "... the neglect or mismanagement of some persons, in the army or navy, which prevented the appointment of a flag of truce meeting General Arnold on the North River ..." See CP, Vol. 215/file 64.
52. Arnold to Tallmadge, "Robinson's House," September 13, 1780, and Tallmadge to Arnold, Lower Salem, September 21, 1780, in GWP (MSS 44693, Reels 070-071).
53. Arnold to André, September 15, 1780, in Van Doren, *Secret History*, p. 472.
54. Washington to Rochambeau, Headquarters, Bergen County, September 8, and to Arnold, September 14, 1780, in *WW*, XX, pp. 16, 48; Arnold to André, September 15, in Van Doren, *Secret History*, p. 473.
55. Robinson to Putnam (two letters, the second intended for Arnold), "On board the *Vulture* off Teller's Point," September 17, 1780, in GWP (MSS 44693, Reel 071).
56. Henry B. Dawson (ed.), *Record of the Trial of Joshua Hett Smith, Esq., for Alleged Complicity in the Treason of Benedict Arnold, 1780* (Morrisania, New York, 1866), pp. 103–4.
57. Gottschalk, *Lafayette and the Close of the American Revolution*, p. 131.

58. Arnold to Robinson (two letters), Headquarters, "Robinson's House," September 18, 1780, in Van Doren, *Secret History*, p. 483.
59. See Robinson to Arnold, "*Vulture*, off Teller's Point," September 19, 1780, and "Gustavus" to "John Anderson," September 15, 1780, in Sparks, *Washington's Writings*, VII, pp. 527–8; Sabine, *Historical Memoirs of Smith*, pp. 339–40 (October 11, 1780). See also the careful analysis in Van Doren, *Secret History*, p. 318.
60. Willcox, *American Rebellion*, p. 214, and pp. 463–4 (draft of letter to Germain, New York, October 11, 1780). For Rodney, see O'Shaughnessy, *The Men Who Lost America*, pp. 289–319.
61. "Instructions for spies," September 10 [?], 1780, in *WW*, XX, pp. 26–7; Willcox, *American Rebellion*, p. 214; Madison to Joseph Jones, September 19, 1780, in *LDC*, XVI, pp. 95–6; Tallmadge to Arnold, Lower Salem, September 21, 1780, GWP (MSS 44693, Reel 071); Tallmadge to Washington, Greenfield, September 19, 1780, enclosing intelligence from "Samuel Culper," September 15, 1780, *FO*, Washington/99-01-02-03344.
62. Clinton to Germain, New York, October 11, 1780, in Willcox, *American Rebellion*, p. 464; also Clinton to Rodney, New York, September 18, 1780, CP, Vol. 123/file 38; Sabine, *Historical Memoirs of Smith*, p. 335 (September 28, 1780).
63. See Willcox, *American Rebellion*, p. 214 (note). This listing mentions the 34th Foot, but the 84th is clearly meant; also, "Narrative of George Matthew," *Historical Magazine*, I (1857), pp. 102–6; 105; "John André's letter book, 1778–80," entry of August 29, 1780, in CP, Vol. 275; for the inspecting officer's comments on individual units, see "Return of the corps under the command of Major General Leslie, as embarked at New York 6 October 1780," in CP, Vol. 125/file 18.
64. See André to Simcoe, September 12, 1780, sold at auction in 1928 and cited in Van Doren, *Secret History*, p. 320.
65. Simcoe, *Journal of Operations of the Queen's Rangers*, p. 102.
66. Sabine, *Historical Memoirs of Smith*, p. 333 (September 17, 1780).
67. "Clinton's narrative," in Van Doren, *Secret History*, p. 484.
68. Sargent/Abbatt, *Life of André*, p. 387; André to his mother, New York, September 1, 1780, cited in Flexner, *Traitor and Spy*, p. 324.
69. André to Arnold, mid-June 1779, in Van Doren, *Secret History*, p. 448; André's account of his expectations, as recalled by Benjamin Tallmadge in 1834, and sent to Jared Sparks for use in his *Life and Treason of Arnold*, pp. 256–7; see also "Arnold the traitor and André the sufferer: Correspondence between Josiah Quincy, Jared Sparks, and Benjamin Tallmadge," *Magazine of American History*, III (1879), pp. 747–56; 755–6.
70. See *Letters and Memoirs relating to the War of American Independence . . . by Madame de Riedesel* (G.C. Carvill, New York, 1827), pp. 241–4.
71. "The Cow Chase" is given in full in Sargent/Abbatt, *Life of André*, pp. 277–8. André's congratulatory letter to Colonel Cuyler is reproduced in ibid., p. 273. For Wayne's attack on the Bull's Ferry blockhouse, see Clinton to Germain, Long Island, August 20, 1780, *Remembrancer, 1780* (Part 2), p. 261, and Paul David Nelson, *Anthony Wayne: Soldier of the early republic* (Indiana University Press, Bloomington, IN, 1985), pp. 108–11.

Chapter Eight

1. André to Clinton (two letters), on board the *Vulture*, September 21, 1780, in Van Doren, *Secret History*, pp. 484–5.
2. Dawson, *Record of Trial of Smith*, p. 116.
3. Smith, *Authentic Narrative*, pp. 20–37; Hart, *Varick Court of Inquiry*, pp. 123–4 (evidence of Franks).
4. Robinson to Arnold, September 21, 1780, quoted in Robinson to Clinton, "*Vulture* off Sinsink," September 24, 1780, and Sutherland to Clinton, "*Vulture* off Spiken Devil," October 5, 1780, in Van Doren, *Secret History*, pp. 474, 494.
5. Dawson, *Record of Trial of Smith*, pp. 98–9.
6. Arnold to Robinson, September 21, 1780, in Van Doren, *Secret History*, p. 485.
7. Sutherland to Clinton, October 5, 1780, ibid., p. 494; "Paper drawn up by Major André," in Sparks, *Washington's Writings*, VII, p. 536.
8. See Robinson to Clinton, "*Vulture* off Sinsink," September 24, 1780, "Clinton's narrative," and Arnold to Washington, New York, October 1, 1780, in Van Doren, *Secret History*, pp. 474, 485, 491. Madame Riedesel maintained that the "duty" of meeting Arnold "really belonged" to Robinson. But as the colonel was "old, and too well known," André had volunteered to go ashore in his place, "to save him from the dangers to which he thought he would, on that account, be more exposed than himself." See *Letters and Memoirs by Madame de Riedesel*, pp. 244–5.

9. Smith, *Authentic Narrative*, p. 20; Sutherland to Clinton, "*Vulture* off Spiken Devil," October 5, 1780, in Van Doren, *Secret History*, pp. 493–4.

10. Smith, *Authentic Narrative*, pp. 20–1; Arnold to Clinton, New York, October 18, 1780, in Van Doren, *Secret History*, pp. 480–1; also, Arnold to Clinton, Holles Street, London, July 23, 1792, in PRO 30/8/108, fol. 205.

11. Robertson to Amherst, New York, October 6, 1780, in Klein and Howard, *New York Letter Book of General Robertson*, p. 156; Benjamin Tallmadge's account of his conversation with André on September 28, 1780, written in 1834, and given in Sparks, *Life and Treason of Arnold*, pp. 256–7.

12. "Narrative of George Matthew," *Historical Magazine*, I (1857), p. 106; Lafayette to La Luzerne, West Point, September 26, 1780, in Charlemagne Tower Jr. (ed.), *The Marquis de La Fayette in the American Revolution*, 2 vols. (J.P. Lippincott Company, Philadelphia, 1895), II, p. 167; Houston to Livingston, Philadelphia, September 27, 1780, in *LDC*, XVI, p. 115.

13. For Washington's anticipated arrival on September 24, see "Paper of intelligence transmitted by Andrew Elliot, New York, 4 October 1780," in Stevens, *Facsimiles*, VII, item 739. On the reported timing of the proposed attack, see, for example, Bray and Bushnell, *Military Journal of Jeremiah Greenman*, p. 182 ("the evening of the 25th"); Anthony Wayne to "a member of Congress," September 27, 1780, in Henry Dawson (ed.), *Papers Concerning the Capture and Detention of Major John André* (Yonkers, New York, 1866) ("the 26th was the day fixed on for this exploit"); "Extract of a letter from a gentleman at Camp, Tappan, 28 September 1780," *Pennsylvania Packet*, October 3, 1780 ("the night of the 25th instant"); Madison to Joseph Jones, September 19, 1780, in *LDC*, XVI, pp. 95–6.

14. William Stevens to Betsy Stevens, Camp Orange Town, October 1, 1780, in CP, Vol. 125/file 5; this letter must have been intercepted by the British on its way to Betsy, of Dedham, near Boston; Stiles to Benjamin Franklin, Newport, RI, October 10, 1780, in Leonard W. Labaree, Barbara B. Oberg, et al. (eds.), *The Papers of Benjamin Franklin*, 41 vols. (Yale University Press, New Haven, CT, 1957–2014), XXXIII, pp. 407–8; Sabine, *Historical Memoirs of Smith, 1778–1783*, p. 335 (September 28, 1780).

15. "Extract of a letter from a gentleman at Camp, Tappan, 28 September 1780," *Pennsylvania Packet*, October 3, 1780; for Arnold's "life guard," see pension application of Alpheus Parkhurst of the "Massachusetts States Troops," in Dann, *Revolution Remembered*, p. 57.

16. Draft of letter from Clinton to Germain, New York, October 11, 1780, in Willcox, *American Rebellion*, p. 464.

17. Dawson, *Record of Trial of Smith*, pp. 8–9.

18. "Paper drawn up by Major André," in Sparks, *Washington's Writings*, VII, p. 536.

19. See Robinson to Clinton, "*Vulture* off Sinsink," September 24, 1780, in Van Doren, *Secret History*, p. 475; Lamb to Livingston, West Point, September 20, 1780, Leake, *Life of Lamb*, p. 258; Dawson, *Record of Trial of Smith*, p. 72; Logs of Captain Andrew Sutherland and Master William Stubbs of the *Vulture* (September 22, 1780), in Sargent/Abbatt, *Life of André*, pp. 328–9 (notes); see also Koke, *Accomplice in Treason*, pp. 73, 87. Although Chastellux said Livingston informed him that he employed just one 4-pounder (Chastellux, *Travels*, I, p. 98), the fact that both shot *and* shell were used indicates a howitzer, too. There was clearly more than a single gun. Other contemporary sources mention "two cannon and one hoytres [howitzer]," and "two field pieces" (see Brown and Peckham, *Journals of Henry Dearborn*, p. 204; Bray and Bushnell, *Military Journal of Greenman*, p. 181).

20. Dawson, *Papers Concerning André*, pp. 51, 61.

21. "Paper drawn up by Major André," in Sparks, *Washington's Writings*, VII, p. 536.

22. Smith, *Authentic Narrative*, p. 23; recollection of Joshua King, formerly lieutenant in Sheldon's Dragoons, Ridgefield, June 9, 1817, in Dawson, *Papers Concerning André*, p. 47.

23. Dawson, *Record of Trial of Smith*, pp. 17–18.

24. Ibid., pp. 42–5; Smith, *Authentic Narrative*, p. 27.

25. Letter of Joshua King, June 9, 1817, in Dawson, *Papers Concerning André*, p. 48. See also William Abbatt, *The Crisis of the Revolution: Being the story of Arnold and André* (New York, 1899), pp. 21–2.

26. "Paper drawn up by Major André," in Sparks, *Washington's Writings*, VII, p. 536.

27. Shaw to Reverend Eliot, "Robinson's House," September 27, 1780, in Quincy, *Journals of Shaw*, p. 77.

28. See Paulding's testimony at the trial of Joshua Smith, October 4, 1780, in Dawson, *Record of Trial of Smith*, pp. 52–6; and "Recollection of General Van Cortlandt," in Dawson, *Papers Concerning André*, p. 164.

29. Jameson to Arnold, North Castle, September 23, 1780, in Van Doren, *Secret History*, pp. 485–6.

30. Jameson to Washington, North Castle, September 23, 1780, FO, Washington/99-01-02-03360. The historian Charles Stedman reported that while still maintaining the identity of Anderson, André "requested that a messenger might be sent to General Arnold to acquaint him of his detention." See Stedman, *History of the American War*, II, p. 277.

31. Benjamin Tallmadge, *Memoir of Col. Benjamin Tallmadge, Prepared by Himself, at the Request of his Children* (New York, 1858), pp. 35–6 (emphasis in original); Jameson to Washington, North Castle, September 27, 1780, in Dawson, *Papers Concerning André*, p. 82.

32. Jameson to Allen, North Castle, September 23, 1780, in Van Doren, *Secret History*, p. 486. As this note and the letter to Arnold form part of "Clinton's narrative," enclosed with his report to Germain of October 11, 1780, the originals must have been pocketed by Arnold.

33. Tallmadge, *Memoir*, p. 36.

34. André to Washington, Salem, September 24, 1780, in Sparks, *Washington's Writings*, VII, pp. 531–2; Tallmadge, *Memoir*, p. 36.

35. For this sequence of events, see especially Sparks, *Life and Treason of Arnold*, p. 246.

36. Hart, *Varick Court of Inquiry*, pp. 228, 149–51, 173–5 (testimonies of Franks, Lamb, and Varick).

37. Varick to Reverend Dirk Romeyn, "Robinson's House," September 24 ("6 and a quarter o'clock"), GLC, MSS 03265; Washington's recollection in October 1786, as recorded by Tobias Lear, in Rush, *Occasional Productions*, p. 82.

38. See "Extract of a letter from a gentleman [James McHenry] at camp, to his friend in this city, dated Highlands, Robinson's House, Sept. 26, 1780," *Pennsylvania Packet*, October 3, 1780.

39. Shaw to Rev. Mr. Eliot, Headquarters at "Robinson's House," September 27, 1780, in Quincy, *Journals of Shaw*, pp. 78–9.

40. "Paper of intelligence transmitted by Andrew Elliot, New York. Narrative of the capture and execution of Major John André, 4–5 October 1780," in Stevens, *Facsimiles*, VII, item 739.

41. See the concise but well-informed narrative of events under the heading "Poughkeepsie, October 2," in the *Connecticut Journal*, October 12, 1780; Chastellux, *Travels*, I, p. 98 (November 22, 1780).

42. Dann, *Revolution Remembered*, p. 58; Rush, *Occasional Productions*, pp. 82–3.

43. Quincy, *Journals of Shaw*, p. 79; Lafayette to the Chevalier de La Luzerne, "Robinson's House, across from West Point," September 26, 1780, in Stanley F. Idzerda (ed.), *Lafayette in the Age of the American Revolution: Selected letters and papers, 1776–1790*, 5 vols. (Cornell University Press, Ithaca, NY, 1977), III, p. 179.

44. "Anecdote of the soldiers of Arnold," in *Collections of the Massachusetts Historical Society*, 2nd Series, IV (1816), pp. 51–2. This information was contributed by Dr. William Eustis, who heard the details from Lurvey and the other bargemen; for Lurvey, see also Heath to Washington, West Point, February 7, 1781, FO, Washington/99-01-02-04785.

45. See General Arnold's "Services," PRO 30/8/108, fols. 194–5; Washington to Lieutenant-Colonel John Laurens, Headquarters, Passaic Falls, October 13, 1780, in *WW*, XX, p. 173; Hamilton to Col. John Laurens, Preakness, NJ, October 11, 1780, in Syrett, *Papers of Hamilton*, II, p. 464; Col. Richard Butler to Congressman John Montgomery, West Point, October 8, 1780, in Hart, *Varick Court of Inquiry*, p. 210; Stevens, *Facsimiles*, VII, item 739.

46. Robinson to Clinton, "*Vulture* off Sinsink," September 24, 1780, in Van Doren, *Secret History*, p. 475; Elliot's intelligence report, in Stevens, *Facsimiles*, VII, item 739; Arnold to Washington, and Robinson to Washington, "*Vulture* off Sing Sing," September 25, 1780, in Sparks, *Washington's Writings*, VII, pp. 533–4.

47. Arnold to Washington, "On board the *Vulture*," September 25, 1780, in Sparks, *Washington's Writings*, VII, p. 533.

48. See Hamilton to Laurens, October 11, 1780, in Syrett, *Papers of Hamilton*, II, pp. 464–5; Lafayette to La Luzerne, West Point, September 25 [actually 26], 1780, in Tower, *La Fayette in the American Revolution*, II, p. 167.

49. Varick to his sister, "Robinson's House," "Sunday Morning," October 1, 1780, in Hart, *Varick Court of Inquiry*, pp. 189–93 (emphasis in original).

50. Hamilton to Elizabeth Schuyler, "Robinson's House," Highlands, New York, September 25[–26], 1780, in Syrett, *Papers of Hamilton*, II, pp. 441–2.

51. Lafayette to La Luzerne, September 26, 1780, in Tower, *La Fayette in the American Revolution*, II, pp. 167–8.

52. Margaret Arnold to Varick, "Robinson's House," September 26, 1780, in N-YHS, Benedict Arnold Collection, 1772–80 (MSS 2958.286), Folder 1.

53. Davis, *Memoirs of Aaron Burr*, I, pp. 219–20. Burr died in 1836. For the repudiation of his *Memoirs*, see Lewis Burd Walker, "Life of Margaret Shippen, wife of Benedict Arnold," *PMHB*, XXV, 2 (1901) pp. 145–90; 152–6, 178–90; on Varick, see T. Jones, *History of New York during the Revolutionary War*, 2 vols. (New-York Historical Society, New York, 1879), I, pp. 745–6.

54. Stevens, *Facsimiles*, VII, 739; Clinton to Washington, and Arnold to Clinton, New York, September 26, 1780, in Sparks, *Washington's Writings*, VII, pp. 534–5.

55. Sabine, *Historical Memoirs of Smith*, pp. 334–5 (September 26 and 28, 1780).

56. See Washington to Wade, September 25, 1780, and to George Clinton and Samuel Huntington, September 26 (all from the Robinson House), in *WW*, XX, pp. 85–95.

57. Hamilton to Washington and Greene, Verplanck's Point, September 25, 1780, in Syrett, *Papers of Hamilton*, II, pp. 438–41.

58. "Recollections" of William North, New London, September 18, 1823, in GLC, MSS 02541-02; Bray and Bushnell, *Military Journal of Jeremiah Greenman*, p. 182.

59. "General Greene's After Orders, 25 September 1780," in Showman, *Papers of Greene*, VI, p. 312; Wayne to Washington, "Smith's White House" [Haverstraw], 6 a.m., September 27, 1780, and Wayne to Dr. H.A. Sheel, Haverstraw, near Stony Point, October 2 [September 27?], 1780, in Stillé, *Anthony Wayne and the Pennsylvania Line*, pp. 234–7.

60. Knox to Bauman, "Robinson's House," 9 p.m., September 23, 1780, N-YHS, Sebastian Bauman Papers (Microfilm 658); Howe to Washington, Orange Town, September 26, 1780, *FO*, Washington/99-01-02-03393.

61. Washington to Laurens, Headquarters, Passaic Falls, October 13, 1780, in *WW*, XX, p. 173; also Washington to Heath, "Robinson's House," September 26, 1780, in ibid., pp. 88–9. For Washington's long-standing conviction that "Providence" or "destiny" controlled human affairs, see Paul K. Longmore, *The Invention of George Washington* (University Press of Virginia, Charlottesville, 1999), p. 169.

62. Washington to Jameson, "Robinson's House," September 25, 1780, in *WW*, XX, pp. 86–7; "Information of deserters and others," NYPL.

63. Simcoe, "at Mr. Weir's," to Major William Crosbie, at headquarters, undated [but late September], 1780, in CP, Vol. 124/file 45; Simcoe, *Journal of the Operations of the Queen's Rangers*, Appendix (unpaginated).

64. "Proceedings of a board of general officers," September 29, 1780, in Dawson, *Papers Concerning André*, pp. 19–30; Washington to Clinton, Headquarters, September 30, 1780, in *WW*, XX, pp. 103–4.

65. "Autobiography of Colonel Aaron Ogden, of Elizabethtown," in *Proceedings of the New Jersey Historical Society*, 2nd Series, XII (1892), pp. 13–31; 23–4; "Information of deserters and others," NYPL.

66. Clinton to Washington, New York, September 30, 1780, in Van Doren, *Secret History*, p. 488. In his first draft, written at "9 o'clock at night," Clinton had not doubted that Washington would "be cautious of putting to death an officer of the British Army under my command," being "perfectly convinced of the real humanity which governs your conduct on all occasions." See PRO 30/55/25, no. 3029. The "shorter and more peremptory" letter actually sent was framed by Lieutenant-General Robertson (Sabine, *Historical Memoirs of Smith*, pp. 336–7 (September 30, 1780).

67. André to Clinton, Tappan, September 29, 1780, in Van Doren, *Secret History*, pp. 475–6.

68. Tallmadge to Samuel Webb, Headquarters, Tappan, September 30, 1780, in Ford, *Correspondence and Journals of Webb*, II, p. 293; Hamilton to Laurens, October 11, 1780, in Syrett, *Papers of Hamilton*, II, p. 467.

69. "Intelligence" from William Heron to Oliver De Lancey, October 1, 1780, in CP, Vol. 125/file 2.

70. "General orders," Headquarters, Orange Town, Sunday, October 1, 1780, in *WW*, XX, p. 110; André to Washington, Tappan, October 1, 1780, in Sparks, *Washington's Writings*, VII, p. 543.

71. *General Evening Post* (London), July 11–13, 1780; see also Peter Linebaugh, "The Tyburn Riot against the surgeons," in Douglas Hay et al. (eds.), *Albion's Fatal Tree: Crime and society in eighteenth-century England* (Allen Lane, London, 1975), pp. 65–117; 66–67.

72. Dawson, *Papers Relating to André*, p. 41; Hamilton to Miss Schuyler, Tappan, October 2, 1780, in Syrett, *Papers of Hamilton*, II, p. 448.

73. Robertson to Clinton, off Dobbs Ferry, October 1, 1780, in Van Doren, *Secret History*, pp. 488–9.

74. Ibid., pp. 366–7, 476, with a reproduction opposite p. 376.

75. Hamilton to Miss Schuyler, October 2, 1780, in Syrett, *Papers of Hamilton*, II, pp. 445–6; "Paper of intelligence transmitted to Mr. Elliot," in Stevens, *Facsimiles*, VII, item 739; Simcoe, *Journal of the Operations of the Queen's Rangers*, Appendix (unpaginated). When the editor of Washington's *Writings*, John C. Fitzpatrick—who was well acquainted with Hamilton's handwriting from the many letters and reports he had drafted on his commander's behalf—was invited to inspect the letter in 1938, he was "completely satisfied that the original was written by Hamilton and endorsed by Sir Henry." The verdict of Fitzpatrick, dated April 18, 1938, is with the original letter in CP, Vol. 124/file 34.

76. Arnold to Washington (two letters), New York, October 1, 1780, in Sparks, *Washington's Writings*, VII, pp. 540–1.

77. Greene to Robertson, Camp, Tappan, October 2, 1780, in Sparks, *Washington's Writings*, VII, pp. 541; "General orders," Headquarters, Orange Town, Sunday, October 1, 1780, in *WW*, XX, p. 111.

78. See Maguire, "A self-portrait by André," *Bulletin of the Fort Ticonderoga Museum* (2000), p. 235.

79. Tallmadge to Heath, Pine's Bridge, October 10, 1780, in *Heath Papers*, III, p. 112; Van Dyke in Dawson, *Papers Relating to André*, pp. 186–9; Dann, *Revolution Remembered*, p. 61. Jacobs received his pension in 1832.

80. Thacher, *Military Journal*, pp. 222–3; "Letter from Benjamin Russell, to Dr. James Thacher" and "Narrative of Major André's execution, by a soldier belonging to Colonel Baldwin's Regiment," in Dawson, *Papers Relating to André*, pp. 184–9, 190–4; Tallmadge to Col. Wadsworth, Haverstraw, October 4, 1780, cited in Ford, *Correspondence and Journals of Webb*, II, pp. 293–4 (note).

81. "Diary of Theodore Woodbridge," Library of Congress, MSS 16,795, cited in Maguire, "Self-portrait by Major André," p. 241; Townsend (Culper junior) to Tallmadge (Bolton), October 20, 1780, in Pennypacker, *George Washington's Spies*, p. 186; Sabine, *Historical Memoirs of Smith*, p. 339 (October 5, 1780).

82. Simcoe, *Journal of the Operations of the Queen's Rangers*, pp. 103–4; A.R. Newsome (ed.), "A British orderly book, 1780–81," *North Carolina Historical Review*, IX, 1 (January 1932), pp. 57–78; 76.

Chapter Nine

1. Huntington to Oliver Ellsworth, Philadelphia, October [2?], 1780, in *LDC*, XVI, pp. 129–30; see also *Pennsylvania Packet*, October 3, 1780.

2. "Journal of Samuel Rowland Fisher, of Philadelphia, 1779–1781," *PMHB*, XXXXI, 3 (1917), pp. 274–333; 314.

3. *Pennsylvania Packet*, October 3, 1780.

4. "Journal of Samuel Fisher," p. 311.

5. Lillian B. Miller (with Sidney Hart and Toby A. Appel) (eds.), *The Selected Papers of Charles Willson Peale and his Family: Volume 1: Charles Willson Peale: Artist in revolutionary America, 1735–1791* (Yale University Press, New Haven, CT, 1983), pp. 352–5; Irvin, "Streets of Philadelphia," *PMHB*, (2005), pp. 32–42. On Peale, see also Holger Hoock, *Empires of the Imagination: Politics, war, and the arts in the British world, 1750–1850* (Profile Books, London, 2010), pp. 104–9.

6. E.P. Thompson, *Customs in Common* (Penguin Books, London, 1993), Chapter 8, "Rough Music."

7. Shaw to Rev. Mr. Eliot, Tappan, October 1, 1780, in Quincy, *Journals of Shaw*, pp. 80–1.

8. John Hanson to Philip Thomas, Philadelphia, October 2, 1780, in *LDC*, XVI, pp. 124–6; Governor William Livingston of New Jersey to Washington, Trenton, October 7, 1780, *FO*, Washington/99-01-02-03508; Washington to John Laurens and to Joseph Reed, Passaic Falls, October 13 and 18, 1780, in *WW*, XX, pp. 173, 213; Bauman to Henry Knox, September 26, 1780, Bauman Papers, N-YHS: for the public thanksgiving, to be held on December 7, see for example, *Norwich Packet*, November 14, 1780.

9. "Fishkill, September 28," *New-York Packet and American Advertiser*, September 28, 1780, and "Extract of a letter from Camp, Tappan, 26 September," *Pennsylvania Packet*, September 30, 1780.

10. *New-York Packet*, October 12, 1780, subsequently published in *Pennsylvania Gazette*, October 18, 1780, and *Norwich Packet*, October 24, 1780. For a detailed discussion of the authorship of this essay, and the possibility that it is a previously overlooked work by Hamilton, see Stephen Brumwell, "Alexander Hamilton, Benedict Arnold, and a 'forgotten' Publius," in Todd Andrlik and Don N. Hagist (eds.), *Journal of the American Revolution Annual Volume 2017* (Westholme Publishing, Yardley, PA, 2017), pp. 373–83.

11. "Daniel Newton's diary," N-YHS, Miscellaneous Microfilm 55; *Pennsylvania Packet*, October 3, 1780.

12. Lafayette to La Luzerne, West Point, September 26, 1780, in Tower, *La Fayette in the American Revolution*, II, pp. 166–7; Greene to Elihue Greene, Tappan, October 2, 1780, Showman, *Papers of Greene*, VI, p. 327; Oswald to Lamb, Philadelphia, December 11, 1780, in Leake, *Life of Lamb*, pp. 266–7.

13. *New Jersey Journal*, November 21, 1781; *Connecticut Courant*, December 12, 1780, under "Hartford, 12 December."

14. Townsend to Tallmadge, cited in Pennypacker, *Washington's Spies*; Jones, *History of New York during the Revolution*, I, pp. 164, 341.

15. Robertson to Amherst, New York, October 6, 1780, in Klein and Howard, *New York Letter Book of General Robertson*, pp. 155–7.

16. Sir George Rodney to Germain, *Sandwich*, St. Lucia, "Private," December 22, 1780, *Stopford-Sackville Manuscripts*, II, pp. 192–3.

17. *Lloyd's Evening Post and British Chronicle*, December 11–13, 1780.

18. Arnold to Clinton, New York, October 18, 1780, in Van Doren, *Secret History*, pp. 480–1; Ewald, *Diary of the American War*, pp. 250, 295–6.

19. Damer to Germain, New York, October 13, 1780, *Stopford-Sackville Manuscripts*, II, p. 184.
20. Arnold's address "To the inhabitants of America" is in Arnold, *Life of Arnold*, pp. 330–2; see also the discussion in Van Doren, *Secret History*, pp. 373–5.
21. Arnold to Germain, New York, October 28, 1780, in CP, Vol. 127/file 8; the "Present state . . ." is dated October 7 (CP, Vol. 127/file 9).
22. For the proclamation, see Arnold, *Life of Arnold*, pp. 332–4.
23. Arnold to Tallmadge, October 25, 1780, and Tallmadge to Washington, Wethersfield, January 28, 1781, given in Pennypacker, *Washington's Spies*, pp. 196–7; recollections of Tallmadge to Jared Sparks, February 17, 1834, *Magazine of American History*, III (1879), p. 754.
24. Shaw to Rev. Mr. Eliot, Tappan, October 1, 1780, in Quincy, *Journals of Shaw*, p. 81; *New-York Packet*, October 12, 1780; see also Edmund Pendleton to James Madison [Edmundsbury, VA], October 17, 1780, GLC, MSS 00099-050.
25. *British Mercury & Evening Advertiser*, November 28, 1780; Van Doren, *Secret History*, p. 394; Wallace, *Traitorous Hero*, p. 268; Martin, *Benedict Arnold, Revolutionary Hero*, p. 6; Philbrick, *Valiant Ambition*, pp. xv, 321–2.
26. Royster, *Revolutionary People at War*, p. 287.
27. Deposition of John Porter, CP, Vol. 127/file 35; "Information of deserters and others," NYPL.
28. Gilbert to his parents, Orange Town, October 6, and Totoway, October 15, 1780, in CL, "Benjamin Gilbert Letter Book"; for the reduction of the army, see *JCC*, XVIII, pp. 893–7.
29. *Morning Herald and Daily Advertiser*, December 4, 1780. The "Address of the general officers of New England" was dated October 7, and Hamilton's letter October 12, 1780.
30. *Lloyd's Evening Post and British Chronicle*, November 13–15, 1780; *Morning Herald and Daily Advertiser*, December 5, 1780; *London Courant and Westminster Chronicle*, November 15, 1780.
31. For Champe, see "Information of deserters and others," October 23, 1780, in NYPL; the Washington–Lee correspondence is gathered in Sparks, *Washington's Writings*, VII, pp. 545–9.
32. Henry Lee, *Memoirs of the War in the Southern Department of the United States*, 2 vols. (New York, 1869), II, pp. 159–87. Although the basics of the plan can be corroborated, as Carl Van Doren cautions, Lee's "spirited narrative" veers "close to historical fiction" (*Secret History*, p. 393).
33. Willcox, *American Rebellion*, pp. 235–6; For Clinton's orders to Arnold, Simcoe, and Dundas, dated December 14, 1780, see PRO 30/55/27, nos. 3,204 and 3,205; also Wallace, *Traitorous Hero*, p. 272.
34. "General Arnold's services [1792]," PRO 30/8/108, fol. 195; Willcox, *American Rebellion*, pp. 236–7; Clinton to Pitt, November 14, 1792, CP Vol. 215/file 47; Frederick Mackenzie, *Diary of Frederick Mackenzie, giving a daily narrative of his military service*, 2 vols. (Harvard University Press, Cambridge, MA, 1930), II, p. 466.
35. Shaw to Rev. Eliot, New Windsor, January 6, 1781, in Quincy, *Journals of Shaw*, pp. 84–5; Wayne to Washington, Princeton, January 8, 1781, *FO*, Washington/99-01-02-04474; "Intelligence from 'Mr. McFarlan'," January 20, 1781, in Thomas Addis Emmett, "Sir Henry Clinton's original secret record of private daily intelligence," *Magazine of American History*, X (1883), pp. 327–42; 336; see also Van Doren, *Mutiny in January*, and Royster, *Revolutionary People at War*, pp. 303–8.
36. "Intelligence from 'Gould'," January 20, 1781, *Magazine of American History*, X (1883), p. 331; Washington to the president of Congress, January 23, 1781, in *WW*, XXI, p. 136; Gilbert to his father, Daniel Gilbert, after January 31, 1781, in CL, "Benjamin Gilbert Letter Book."
37. Gottschalk, *Lafayette and the Close of the American Revolution*, pp. 189–208.
38. Jefferson to J.P.G. Muhlenberg, Richmond, January 31, 1781, in Julian P. Boyd, Charles T. Cullen, et al. (eds.), *The Papers of Thomas Jefferson*, 41 vols. (Princeton University Press, Princeton, NJ, 1950–2014), IV, pp. 487–8; "Intelligence, 15 and 17 March 1781," in Thomas Addis Emmett, "Sir Henry Clinton's secret record of private daily intelligence," *Magazine of American History*, XI (1884), pp. 53–70; 54; Oswald to Lamb, Philadelphia, December 11, 1780, in Leake, *Life of Lamb*, pp. 266–7; Washington to Lafayette, February 20, 1781, in *WW*, XXI, p. 255.
39. Ewald, *Diary of the American War*, pp. 260–1.
40. "An anecdote," *Providence Gazette and Country Journal*, August 11, 1781; Thorsten Sellin, "The Philadelphia gibbet iron," *Journal of Criminal Law and Criminology*, XXXXVI, 1 (1955), pp. 11–25; Ewald, *Diary of the American War*, p. 295.
41. Gilbert to Lt. Jack Saul, Bottom Bridge, VA, May 5, 1781, in CL, "Benjamin Gilbert Letter Book"; Jones, *New York during the Revolutionary War*, II, pp. 177–9.
42. Washington to John Laurens, New Windsor, April 9, 1781, in *WW*, XXI, pp. 438–9.
43. See "Memorandum taken of a conversation with Heron," April 25, 1781, *Magazine of American History*, XI (1884), pp. 64–5.
44. George W. Kyte, "A projected British attack upon Philadelphia in 1781," *PMHB*, LXXVI, 4 (October 1952), pp. 379–93; for the Phillips–Arnold plan, dated Portsmouth, April 18, 1781, see Willcox, *American Rebellion*, pp. 510–11.

45. "The memorial of William Rankin Esquire," in AO 13/71B. This is undated, but an attached schedule of claims is dated New York, September 3, 1783.

46. See Cornwallis to Clinton, Byrd's Plantation, North of James River, May 26, 1781, in PRO 30/55/30, no. 3,532, p. 3. The best analysis of the campaign's strategy is William B. Willcox, "The British road to Yorktown: A study in divided command," *American Historical Review*, LII (1946), pp. 1–35.

47. Willcox, *American Rebellion*, p. 331; Wallace, *Traitorous Hero*, pp. 278–83.

48. See Arnold's report to Clinton, off Plumb Island, Long Island Sound, September 8, 1780, in Willcox, *American Rebellion*, pp. 565–7. For a comprehensive discussion of the evidence, see Walter L. Powell, *Murder or Mayhem? Benedict Arnold's New London, Connecticut Raid, 1781* (Thomas Publications, Gettysburg, PA, 2000); also, Eric D. Lehman, *Homegrown Terror: Benedict Arnold and the burning of New London* (Wesleyan University Press, Middletown, CT, 2014), pp. 140–61.

49. Sabine, *Historical Memoirs of Smith*, p. 469 (December 10, 1781).

50. See, for example, "Genuine history of Gen. Arnold," *Political Magazine*, I (1780), and "Some interesting particulars relating to General Arnold," *British Mercury and Evening Advertiser*, November 28, 1780; Walpole to Sir Horace Mann, Berkeley Square, November 20, 1780, and February 7, 1782, in W.S. Lewis (ed.), *Horace Walpole's Correspondence*, 39 vols. (Yale University Press, New Haven, CT, 1934–37), XXV, pp. 98, 241; Sargent/Abbatt, *Life of André*, p. 510; John Bull to Clinton, March 5, 1782, cited in Willcox, *Portrait of a General*, p. 460 (note 3); Franklin to Robert R. Livingston, Passy, March 4, 1782, in Labaree, et al. *Papers of Franklin*, XXXVI, p. 463.

51. "Thoughts on the American War, by an American," [1782], in Arnold, *Life of Arnold*, Appendix, pp. 419–27.

52. See Arnold to William Pitt the Younger, London, May 28, 1792, PRO 30/8/108, fol. 230; also, Arnold to Sir Guy Carleton, London, November 3, 1782, PRO 30/55/53, no. 6,081, p. 3.

53. For Rankin, see AO 13/71 B, fols. 169–75; for Smith, Koke, *Accomplice in Treason*, pp. 297–304; and for Robinson, AO 13/32 (Box 2), fol. 430, and Sir Henry Clinton's memorial on his behalf in AO 13/116, fol. 513. On the loyalist diaspora, see Maya Jasanoff, *Liberty's Exiles: American loyalists in the revolutionary world* (Alfred A. Knopf, New York, 2011).

54. See "Arnold's memorial," [1784], AO 13/96A, fols. 76–80. This includes (at fols. 78–80) "A true account of the real and personal property and debts of Brigadier General B. Arnold."

55. Arnold to the Honorable Commissioners of American Claims, London, April 26, 1785, AO 13/96A, fol. 83.

56. For Peggy Arnold's pension, see Arnold, *Life of Arnold*, p. 363. The original is in NA, T [Treasury] 64/291; Clinton's comment is in his note of a conversation with Pitt on November 14, 1792, in CP, Vol. 215/file 47; see also Arnold to Pitt, Holles Street, November 15, 1792, and to George Rose, July 29, 1792, in PRO 30/8/108, fols. 197 and 209.

57. For Arnold's years in New Brunswick, see Wallace, *Traitorous Hero*, pp. 290–6; for Lamb's defense of Arnold, see "Family tradition," cited in Leake, *Life of Lamb*, p. 262.

58. Arnold to Johnstone, July 18, 1784, and Johnstone to Arnold, Kensington Gore, London, July 21, 1784, in *Magazine of American History*, X (1883), pp. 314–16.

59. Arnold to William Pitt, London, May 28 and December 15, 1792, and to George Rose, Holles Street, July 29, 1792, in PRO 30/8/108, fols. 210, 214, 230–1.

60. Arnold to Clinton, Holles Street, July 23, 1792, and to Pitt, London, May 28, 1792, in PRO 30/8/108, fols. 206 and 230; see also Arnold to Clinton, London, May 22, 1787, in CP, Vol. 207/file 24; for detailed coverage of the duel, see Arnold, *Life of Arnold*, pp. 375–84.

61. Duc de Broglie, *Memoirs of the Prince de Talleyrand*, 5 vols. (New York, 1891), I, pp. 174–5; Arnold to William Pitt, London, September 8, 1792, in PRO 30/8/108, fol. 200.

62. Reverend Cooper Willyams, *An Account of the Campaign in the West Indies in the Year 1794* (T. Bensley, London, 1796), p. 127, note; Sir John Fortescue, *A History of the British Army*, IV (Part 1) (Macmillan, London, 1906), p. 376; *Gentleman's Magazine*, 1794, Part 2 (August), pp. 685–6; "Additions and corrections to former obituaries," in *Gentleman's Magazine*, 1801, Part 2 (July), p. 671; Arnold, *Life of Arnold*, pp. 385–9; Simcoe to Lord Portland, "Private," Woolford Lodge, Honiton, October 17, 1797, in NA, HO 42/41/81, fol. 243.

63. Arnold, *Life of Arnold*, p. 395.

FURTHER READING

While this reassessment of Benedict Arnold and his treason is grounded on an examination of original sources—both published and in manuscript—it also draws on a wide range of secondary studies. The literature of the American Revolution is extensive and ever increasing; to keep the endnotes within realistic bounds, only materials actually cited, along with especially relevant works, have been referenced in them. This short selection of recommended further reading is therefore intended to highlight some of the many other publications that provide invaluable background and context for Arnold's life and times.

For a thoughtful and comprehensive overview of the entire era, Alan Taylor's *American Revolutions: A Continental history, 1750–1804* (Norton and Company, New York, 2016) offers a thematic approach reflecting the latest scholarship. It can be complemented by John Ferling's more narrative-driven account, *A Leap in the Dark: The struggle to create the American republic* (Oxford University Press, New York, 2003). Benedict Arnold was a product of the wider Anglo-American Atlantic world; themes pertinent to his experiences within that environment, particularly trade, warfare, and identity, receive scholarly treatment in P.J. Marshall (ed.), *The Oxford History of the British Empire: Volume II: The Eighteenth Century* (Oxford University Press, Oxford, 1998).

The military struggle for American independence has generated many books, including studies of most campaigns and battles. For accounts of the conflict as a whole, written respectively by recognized British and American authorities, see Piers Mackesy, *The War for America, 1775–1783* (Harvard University Press, Cambridge, MA, 1964; new edition, University of Nebraska Press, Lincoln, NE, 1993), and Don Higginbotham, *The War of American Independence: Military attitudes, policies, and practice, 1763–1789* (Macmillan, New York, 1971). Professor Higginbotham also edited *Reconsiderations on the Revolutionary War: Selected essays* (Greenwood Press, Westport, CT, 1978); read in conjunction with another very useful selection of contributions by leading historians, Ronald Hoffmann and Peter J. Albert (eds.), *Arms and Independence: The military character of the American Revolution* (University Press of Virginia, Charlottesville, VA, 1984), it engages with issues that together help to explain the trajectory of Arnold's career as a soldier.

For the military organization in which Arnold made his reputation, see: Charles Royster, *A Revolutionary People at War: The Continental Army and American character, 1775–1783* (University of North Carolina Press, Chapel Hill, NC, 1979); James K. Martin and Mark E. Lender, *A Respectable Army: The military origins of the republic, 1763–1789*, 3rd edition (Wiley-Blackwell, Hoboken, NJ, 2015); and Charles Patrick Neimeyer, *America Goes to War: A social history of the Continental Army* (New York University Press, New York, 1995).

Like Benedict Arnold, most of the Revolutionary War's leading personalities have attracted biographers. Given his enduring reputation as the "father" of his country, George Washington has naturally been the subject of numerous books; despite an outpouring of titles in recent decades, the most insightful and reliable account of his Revolutionary War career, and the challenges that he faced during eight grindingly frustrating years, is contained in the relevant volumes (4: *Leader of the Revolution*, and 5: *Victory with the Help of France*) of Douglas Southall Freeman's classic *George Washington, a Biography* (Charles Scribner's Sons, New York, 1951–52). Washington's chief opponent from 1778 onward has attracted comparatively little attention, although in his *Portrait of a General: Sir Henry Clinton in the War of Independence* (Alfred A. Knopf, New York, 1964), William B. Willcox delivered another work of lasting value. Short but insightful assessments of Washington, Clinton, and other commanders can be found in George A. Billias (ed.), *George Washington's Generals and Opponents: Their exploits and leadership* (originally published in two volumes, 1964–69 by William Morrow & Company, New York; paperback edition, Da Capo, Cambridge, MA, 1994). Both military and political figures are reassessed in Andrew Jackson O'Shaughnessy, *The Men Who Lost America: British leadership, the American Revolution, and the fate of empire* (Yale University Press, New Haven, CT, and London, 2013), a thought-provoking book that invites a companion study of the winning side.

For the political infighting behind the Patriots' military struggle, and the partisan atmosphere that proved so toxic for Arnold, two books are particularly instructive: H. James Henderson, *Party Politics in the Continental Congress* (McGraw-Hill, New York, 1974); and Jack N. Rakove, *The Beginnings of National Politics: An interpretive history of the Continental Congress* (Random House, New York, 1979). The wider diplomatic picture is well covered in Jonathan R. Dull, *A Diplomatic History of the American Revolution* (Yale University Press, New Haven, CT, 1985), and H.M. Scott, *British Foreign Policy in the Age of the American Revolution* (Oxford University Press, Oxford, 1990).

The following titles explore other relevant topics: on Loyalism, Paul H. Smith, *Loyalists and Redcoats: A study in British revolutionary policy* (University of North Carolina Press, Chapel Hill, NC, 1964); for the events of 1775 to 1783 as an uncompromisingly brutal "civil war," Holger Hoock, *Scars of Independence: America's violent birth* (Crown, New York, 2017); and on the techniques of espionage, John A. Nagy, *Invisible Ink: Spycraft of the American Revolution* (Westholme, Yardley, PA, 2009). Finally, although it appeared too late to be considered in the text of *Turncoat*, Larrie D. Ferreiro's *Brothers at Arms: American independence and the men of France and Spain who saved it* (Knopf, New York, 2016) presents a realistic analysis of the foreign aid that transformed the prospects of the American Patriots, and by Benedict Arnold's own account, influenced his decision to reject their cause.

ACKNOWLEDGMENTS

*T*urncoat was written during an ongoing revolution in historical research. Owing to the proliferation of online digitized material, many books and journals that until recently had to be consulted in major libraries, or ordered through the interlibrary loan system, have become readily available to anyone with internet access. Paradoxically, it's now often easier to locate a publication from 1780 than a scholarly monograph written just twenty years ago. This transformation is not restricted to the printed word: some major archival collections, like the George Washington Papers and the Papers of the Continental Congress, can also be explored online.

While certainly momentous, this information technology revolution is not yet complete: at the time of writing, most manuscripts are still undigitized, and likely to remain so for many years. In the meantime, they must be examined in time-honoured fashion, by visiting an archive, perusing catalogues, ordering-up boxes and volumes of documents, and then methodically sifting through them in hopes of striking lucky.

Not only are there limits to what is available online, but deciphering the handwriting of digitized documents can be a frustrating business: not every eighteenth-century correspondent wrote elegant copperplate, while fading, blotting, and the bleeding-through of ink from reverse pages makes many manuscript letters virtually illegible on screen. Because of such problems, modern scholarly editions of correspondence are particularly valuable.

Researchers of America's Revolutionary era can refer to printed collections that are also available via the excellent Founders Online website, administered by the National Archives, Washington, D.C., in conjunction with the University of Virginia Press. For *Turncoat*, the *Papers of George Washington, Revolutionary War Series* was a vital resource. To date, its printed coverage has not yet reached the climactic phase of Benedict Arnold's conspiracy, but thanks to the Founders Online Early Access program (a far-sighted initiative that makes documents available ahead of publication), I was able to consider important material that might otherwise have been missed.

Spanning several years, this investigation embraced both the new and the traditional approaches to research. Although it undoubtedly profited from the extraordinary growth in online sources, it's nonetheless significant that the most revealing evidence was found in the *old* way; and for all its convenience, no amount of internet trawling can match the excitement of viewing and handling original letters written by individuals who inhabit the narrative—there's a sense of connection that's missing when staring at a computer screen.

Given the continuing importance of archival work in the internet age, I'm especially thankful to the institutions that have generously supported my research. The award of a Jacob M. Price Visiting Research Fellowship from the William L. Clements Library gave access to its treasure-trove of sources, and a fellowship from the Gilder Lehrman Institute of American History not only allowed me to exploit its rich collections in Manhattan, but also the holdings of the New-York Historical Society and New York Public Library. For backing my applications for funding I'm extremely grateful to professors Andrew Jackson O'Shaughnessy, Colin G. Calloway and Stephen Conway.

As an "independent historian" working outside academia, I've always valued the chance to chat with others who share my interests: while working on *Turncoat*, I've particularly enjoyed conversations with Brian Leigh Dunnigan, associate director at the Clements Library; David Preston of the Citadel, Charleston; Doug Bradburn, the founding director of the Fred W. Smith Library at George Washington's Mount Vernon; and Matthew Keagle, curator of collections at Fort Ticonderoga. Sincere thanks are also due to my good friend Walt Powell, who not only shared his deep knowledge of Arnold's life and times, but also his extensive personal library. My old comrades from the School of History at the University of Leeds,

Craig Gibson and Pete Edwards, volunteered valuable feedback on early chapters. Three anonymous readers commented on the entire manuscript; their constructive criticism was extremely helpful in refining the text.

Throughout this project I have appreciated the professionalism of all at Yale University Press, London. I'm indebted to Heather McCallum, publisher and managing director, for her unswerving conviction that a new look at Arnold and his treason was justified; to Marika Lysandrou, for all her patience, and for close and insightful criticism of the evolving manuscript; and to Rachael Lonsdale, for the enthusiasm and efficiency she brought to overseeing the book's production and design. The final draft was much improved by Clive Liddiard's exemplary copy-editing, while Samantha Cross and her team transformed my rough sketches into clear and elegant maps.

Writing is typically a solitary business, requiring a self-discipline that doesn't always come easily. Time lost to illness meant that delivering *Turncoat* took even more concentrated effort than usual: for offering unstinting support that allowed me to maximize my work time, I'm grateful as ever to my wife Laura Durnford. I'm also very conscious—and deeply appreciative—of the understanding shown by our children during those spells when I was too fixated upon Revolutionary America: at least now Ivan will no longer have to respond to the name of "Arnold," and Milly finally has an answer to her recurring question: "Dad, when *will* your book be finished?" I'm likewise very appreciative of the encouragement that I have always received from both my own and Laura's parents, and from our wider family and scattered friends.

It's also a pleasure to acknowledge another way in which this venture benefited from the digital revolution—through the continuing resurrection of vintage music on YouTube. Here, special thanks are due to the dedicated "Vibracobra23" for locating and remastering sessions originally recorded decades ago for John Peel's late-evening show on BBC Radio 1. I first heard many of these between 1979 and 1982, issuing from the old radio that was invariably playing in the back bar of Webb's Hotel in Liskeard, Cornwall. Resembling the set of an Agatha Christie murder mystery, this was an incongruous backdrop for such an eclectic cocktail of "alternative" music, but a welcome haven in which to enjoy a pint or two with my fellow reporter Mike Taylor of the *Western Morning News*—refreshment that was sorely needed after we'd endured the protracted deliberations of the local council.

Hearing those bands once again, still sounding so fresh after all these years, was a welcome tonic that helped me to keep writing and meet my deadline.

* * *

While finishing *Turncoat*, I was saddened to learn of the untimely death of Professor Bill Speck. In September 1990, after I arrived at the University of Leeds as a mature student, and was immediately left wondering whether I'd made a rash decision in giving up my job to study history, Bill was a reassuring presence who treated me as an adult and swiftly became my unofficial mentor. Besides offering friendship and encouragement, Bill was unstinting with practical advice and guidance: this was instrumental in setting me upon the path of published author. Besides pioneering an interdisciplinary approach that reflected his interests in politics and literature, Bill was among the first historians to view Britain and her North American colonies as part of a broader "British Atlantic Empire" —a perspective that Benedict Arnold and his contemporaries would surely have recognized. I would therefore like to dedicate this book to Bill, in fond and respectful memory of a good friend and a fine scholar.

INDEX